# THE BEST

# AMERICAN

# MAGAZINE

# WRITING

# 2018

# THE BEST AMERICAN MAGAZINE WRITING

# 2018

Edited by
Sid Holt for the
American Society
of Magazine
Editors

Columbia University Press    New York

Columbia University Press
*Publishers Since 1893*
New York    Chichester, West Sussex
cup.columbia.edu
Copyright © 2019 the American Society of Magazine Editors
All rights reserved

Library of Congress Cataloging-in-Publication Data
ISSN 1541-0978
ISBN 978-0231-18999-6 (pbk.)

Columbia University Press books are printed on permanent and durable acid-free paper.
Printed in the United States of America

Cover design: Nancy Rouemy

# Contents

**xi**   *Introduction*
        *Alison Overholt, vice president and editor in chief,* ESPN the
        Magazine, espnW, *and the ESPYs*

**xv**   *Acknowledgments*
        *Sid Holt, chief executive,*
        *American Society of Magazine Editors*

**3**    Abuses of Power *and* Weighing the Costs of
        Speaking Out About Harvey Weinstein *and*
        Harvey Weinstein's Army of Spies
                                    Ronan Farrow
                                    *The New Yorker*
                                    WINNER—Public Interest

*57* Why the Harvey Weinstein Sexual-Harassment Allegations Didn't Come Out Until Now *and* Your Reckoning. And Mine. *and* This Moment Isn't (Just) About Sex. It's Really About Work

Rebecca Traister

*New York*

WINNER—Columns and Commentary

*93* The Horizon of Desire *and* We're All Mad Here: Weinstein, Women, and the Language of Lunacy *and* The Unforgiving Minute

Laurie Penny

*Longreads*

FINALIST—Columns and Commentary

*121* The Last Person You'd Expect to Die in Childbirth

Nina Martin and Renee Montagne

*ProPublica* with NPR

FINALIST—Public Interest

*151* The Uncounted

Azmat Khan and Anand Gopal

*New York Times Magazine*

WINNER—Reporting

**187**   How the U.S. Triggered a Massacre in Mexico
Ginger Thompson
*National Geographic* and
*ProPublica*
Finalist—Reporting

**221**   What Ever Happened to the Russian Revolution?
Ian Frazier
*Smithsonian*
Finalist—Essays and Criticism

**271**   The Uninhabitable Earth
David Wallace-Wells
*New York*
Finalist—Essays and Criticism

**295**   My President Was Black
Ta-Nehisi Coates
*The Atlantic*
Finalist—Feature Writing

**347**   Standing Down *and* Roger Goodell Has a
Jerry Jones Problem
Seth Wickersham and Don
Van Natta Jr.
*ESPN the Magazine*
Finalist—Reporting

**379**   How the Oscar Flub Demonstrates the Limits of
Black Graciousness *and* How Oprah Got Her
Acting Groove Back *and* Maria Sharapova's
Rivalry With Serena Williams Is in Her Head

Bim Adewunmi

*BuzzFeed News*

FINALIST—Columns and
Commentary

**399**   The Williams Movement *and* Power Play *and*
How Is This Still a Debate?

Howard Bryant

*ESPN the Magazine*

FINALIST—Columns and
Commentary

**409**   Lola's Story

Alex Tizon

*The Atlantic*

WINNER—Essays and Criticism

**435**   Love in the Time of Robots

Alex Mar

*Wired* with *Epic Magazine*

FINALIST—Feature Writing

*473*  Cat Person

Kristen Roupenian
*The New Yorker*
Finalist—ASME Award
for Fiction

*495*  *Permissions*
*499*  *List of Contributors*

Alison Overholt

# Introduction

W hen we think of magazines, either as readers or
as creators (for those of us who are in the business
of making them), we realize that so much of magazine making is about the packaging of stories into a specific
physical form—that inextricable intertwining of the written
word with the photography, the glossy layouts, and the covers
that combines to present a particular kind of tactile storytelling
experience.

Yet there's a reason that other, definitively not printed media
characterize the work they do as "magazine"-like: the television
"news magazine" programs that communicate the significance
of their video feature packages by attaching that label or the digital long-form sites that articulate their value by describing them
as "magazine quality." So it would seem that the most distin-
guishing aspect of magazines isn't necessarily their printed form
or even the inventive and wildly creative visual packaging those
printed products take. What distinguishes magazines is the
quality of the stories they present.

Magazine writing is beautifully crafted. Its storytelling and
commentary are deep and immersive, built on both dogged reporting and the painstaking review and critique provided by an editorial process that prizes intellectual rigor and the opportunity to
challenge assumptions. It emerges on the other side with a point of

view—one that doesn't require you necessarily to agree with the writer's every conclusion but that asks you to consider and form your own questions.

Take, for example, Ronan Farrow's "Abuses of Power," the culmination of a ten-month investigation into accounts of sexual assault and harassment by the disgraced Hollywood executive Harvey Weinstein—the investigation a product of years of reporting leads developed and followed up, until the moment that the story was possible to corroborate. Between that piece and the two follow-ups by Farrow, all part of this collection (not to mention the tremendous reporting also done by Jodi Kantor and Megan Twohey of the *New York Times* in their series of stories), the entertainment world began to reckon with a darkness that had stained the industry for decades. The outcome was the broader cultural conversation and movement that we now know as #MeToo. Such an achievement doesn't happen without the investment and the commitment of resources afforded by the supporting institution—in Farrow's case, *The New Yorker.*

Similarly, Nina Martin and Renee Montagne's deep dive into the dangers of maternal care in their *ProPublica*-NPR piece, "The Last Person You'd Expect to Die in Childbirth," required months of not just combing through medical studies and analyses but also identifying and reporting on the experiences of some 450 women who, since 2011, had died during or soon after childbirth. "The death of a new mother is not like any other sudden death," Martin writes. "It blasts a hole in the universe." And it is not an overstatement to say that this piece blasted a hole in the understanding many Americans—particularly women and mothers, both current and expecting—had of the care they might expect or may already have received during the delivery of their own children.

And these are just two of the incredible stories you will read in this anthology.

The subjects of this year's stories are, more often than not, dark or challenging. These are challenging and polarized times, after all. But part of their gift is that even as the world mostly speeds past then, disappears with an ephemeral scroll or swipe, even as we too often over-rely on the minute-by-minute hot take to parse current events, these pieces ask us to press pause and think, hard, about why the world we live in is the way it is. And what we might do to participate differently.

That's why I love this collection that you now hold in your hand, this annual effort to boil magazine storytelling down to just the writing—that sparest and, ultimately, most essential aspect. Each piece affords us the same precious gift that was bestowed upon the reporters and writers who created them: the gift of time.

Time to consider. Time to challenge and be challenged. Time to ask questions, and then more questions, and then more questions still. Time to think.

From all of us who took the time to create for you, please read and enjoy every last word.

# Acknowledgments

Since 2000, the American Society of Magazine Editors has gathered together some of the finest journalism of the previous year in *Best American Magazine Writing*. Each of the stories in this edition was chosen by the judges of the National Magazine Awards for Print and Digital Media as a finalist or winner in one of five categories: Reporting, Feature Writing, Essays and Criticism, Columns and Commentary, and Public Interest (the only outlier is Kristen Roupenian's "Cat Person," one of three short stories entered by *The New Yorker* in the competition for the 2018 ASME Award for Fiction).

Why these five categories? In 2018, ASME awarded National Magazine Awards in twenty categories, ranging from Design and Photography to Social Media and Digital Innovation. Each of the finalists and winners in these latter categories is well worth the attention of every magazine reader, but as the names of these categories suggest, it would be impossible to present them here. Nonetheless, they are reminders that magazines today, whether published in print or online, are more than paper and ink.

When the National Magazine Awards were established in the early 1960s, there was of course only paper and ink. The winners of those early awards—publications such as *Look* and *Life*, stories such as Truman Capote's "In Cold Blood" and Grace Paley's "Enormous Changes at the Last Moment"—are now part of the proud history of American magazines. But history was not what the members of ASME had in mind when they first partnered with the Columbia Journalism School to found the National Magazine Awards. ASME's intention was to win for magazines the same kind of recognition the Pulitzer Prizes had brought to newspapers.

Five decades later the once-sharp distinction between magazine journalism and much of what you read in newspapers has largely blurred. Alison Overholt's introduction to this edition of *Best American Magazine Writing* explains what happened. As competition for the attention of the reader grew—driven first by television, now by smartphones—print and electronic media of every kind adopted magazine storytelling as their own.

The results of the 2018 National Magazine Awards and Pulitzer Prizes prove the point. Two of this year's National Magazine Award winners—Ronan Farrow's reporting for *The New Yorker* on Harvey Weinstein's long history of sexual abuse and Rachel Kaadzi Ghansah's story for *GQ* "A Most American Terrorist: The Making of Dylann Roof"—also won Pulitzer Prizes. The work of another Pulitzer Prize winner, *New York*'s Jerry Saltz, received a National Magazine Award in 2015.

When the first National Magazine Award was presented to *Look* in 1966, there was only one award and a handful of judges (all men, all besuited). Today ASME sponsors not only the National Magazine Awards and the ASME Award for Fiction but also the ASME Best Cover Contest and the ASME Next Awards for Journalists Under Thirty. And there are dozens of judges, editors, and educators, men and women, representing every kind of magazine—from large-circulation consumer magazines headquartered in New York, San Francisco, Des Moines, and Birmingham to city and regional magazines scattered across the country.

One more history lesson: In 1970, the first four winners of the National Magazine Award—*Life*, *Newsweek*, and *American Machinist* along with *Look*—purchased Alexander Calder's stabile *Elephant* from the artist and presented it to ASME to be used, with

Calder's permission, as the symbol of the awards. Since then every National Magazine Award winner has received a copper "Ellie," modeled on the original. Which is why the National Magazine Awards are called the Ellies, at least by ASME members.

This year 281 publications submitted 1,368 Ellie entries. There were, to be precise, 269 judges, who, after hours of preliminary reading and two days of debate at Columbia University, chose five to seven finalists in each category. Fifty-eight media organizations were nominated overall. Twenty-one titles received multiple nominations, led by *New York* with ten and *The New Yorker* with eight. *New York* and *The New Yorker* also won the most awards—three each—followed by *GQ* with two. For more information about the judges, the finalists, and the winners, please visit the ASME website at http://www.magazine .org/asme/.

Hundreds of magazine journalists make the Ellies possible: the editors in chief who choose to enter the awards; the assistant, associate, and senior editors who decipher the annual call for entries and then organize sometimes dozens of submissions; the judges, many of whom take time out over the year-end holidays to read entries, then fly to New York in January to spend those two days of debate in often cramped, overheated classrooms, reading still more entries; the reporters, photographers, story editors, and art directors whose work only occasionally receives the kind of recognition it deserves, even at the Ellies. Gratitude is due to each of them.

The sixteen members of the ASME board of directors are responsible for overseeing the administration, judging, and presentation of the Ellie Awards. You can find their names on the mastheads of your favorite print and digital magazines—and on the ASME website. Most of all, I want to thank Christopher Keyes, the editor in chief of *Outside*, who as president of the board is largely responsible for the success of the Ellies. In addition, I must acknowledge the work of Nina Fortuna, the director of ASME, who every year sets aside the demands of friends, family, and Maltese to make the Ellies happen.

I also want to thank CNN's Don Lemon for hosting the awards presentation this year—and for bringing his mother, Katherine Clark, to cheer on every finalist and winner.

ASME has cosponsored the National Magazine Awards with the Columbia Journalism School for more than half a century. The members of ASME wish to thank Steve Coll, the Pulitzer Prize–winning reporter who now serves as the dean of the journalism school, for his continuing support of the Ellies. Thanks also to Abi Wright, the executive director of professional prizes at Columbia, for her help in organizing the Ellies judging and for her invaluable service as a member of the National Magazine Awards Board.

David McCormick of McCormick Literary has long represented ASME as its agent. The members of ASME are truly appreciative of his work on our behalf. The editors of *Best American Magazine Writing* at the Columbia University Press are Philip Leventhal and Michael Haskell. Philip's enthusiasm not only for the work represented in this book but also for every Ellie winner is an annual source of inspiration. And without Michael's skill and determination, I am afraid this book would never make it to the printer—at least on time.

In closing, I want to thank Alison Overholt, the editor in chief of *ESPN the Magazine*, for stealing time from the World Cup to write the introduction of *BAMW 2018*. And finally, I want to offer ASME's thanks to the writers who graciously consented to the publication of their work in *Best American Magazine Writing*. You can find their names in the table of contents and at the beginning of every story in this book. All they get from ASME is a certificate of recognition. From readers, they get more—time, attention and loyalty.

# THE BEST
# AMERICAN
# MAGAZINE
# WRITING
# 2018

## The New Yorker

*A powerful movie producer and influential fundraiser for the Democratic Party, Harvey Weinstein was also widely rumored to be a sexual predator. In fact, his behavior was, as Ronan Farrow writes in "Abuses of Power," "an open secret." Weinstein was finally called to account in this series of print and online stories from* The New Yorker. *"Farrow's reporting helped spark the national discussion about gender and power," said the judges who awarded the National Magazine Award for Public Interest to this work. "Farrow listened as Weinstein's accusers told their stories and then explained the machinery Weinstein used to silence his victims."* The New Yorker *also won the Pulitzer Prize for Public Service for Farrow's reporting, an award the magazine shared with the* New York Times.

Ronan Farrow

# Abuses of Power *and* Weighing the Costs of Speaking Out About Harvey Weinstein *and* Harvey Weinstein's Army of Spies

## Abuses of Power

Since the establishment of the first studios, a century ago, there have been few movie executives as dominant, or as domineering, as Harvey Weinstein. He cofounded the production-and-distribution companies Miramax and the Weinstein Company, helping to reinvent the model for independent films with movies including *Sex, Lies, and Videotape, The Crying Game, Pulp Fiction, The English Patient, Shakespeare in Love,* and *The King's Speech.* Beyond Hollywood, he has exercised his influence as a prolific fund raiser for Democratic Party candidates, including Barack Obama and Hillary Clinton. Weinstein combined a keen eye for promising scripts, directors, and actors with a bullying, even threatening, style of doing business, inspiring both fear and gratitude. His movies have earned more than three hundred Oscar nominations, and, at the annual awards ceremonies, he has been thanked more than almost anyone else in movie history, ranking just after Steven Spielberg and right before God.

For more than twenty years, Weinstein, who is now sixty-five, has also been trailed by rumors of sexual harassment and assault. His behavior has been an open secret to many in Hollywood and beyond, but previous attempts by many publications, including *The New Yorker*, to investigate and publish the story over the years fell short of the demands of journalistic evidence. Too few people were willing to speak, much less allow a reporter to use their names, and Weinstein and his associates used nondisclosure agreements, payoffs, and legal threats to suppress their accounts. Asia Argento, an Italian film actress and director, said that she did not speak out until now—Weinstein, she told me, forcibly performed oral sex on her—because she feared that Weinstein would "crush" her. "I know he has crushed a lot of people before," Argento said. "That's why this story—in my case, it's twenty years old, some of them are older—has never come out."

On October 5, the *New York Times*, in a powerful report by Jodi Kantor and Megan Twohey, revealed multiple allegations of sexual harassment against Weinstein, an article that led to the resignation of four members of the Weinstein Company's all-male board, and to Weinstein's firing.

The story, however, is complex, and there is more to know and to understand. In the course of a ten-month investigation, I was told by thirteen women that, between the 1990s and 2015, Weinstein sexually harassed or assaulted them. Their allegations corroborate and overlap with the *Times*'s revelations and also include far more serious claims.

Three of the women—among them Argento and a former aspiring actress named Lucia Evans—told me that Weinstein had raped them, forcibly performing or receiving oral sex or forcing vaginal sex. Four women said that they had experienced unwanted touching that could be classified as an assault. In an audio recording captured during a New York Police Department sting operation in 2015, Weinstein admits to groping a Filipina Italian model named Ambra Battilana Gutierrez, describing it as behavior he is "used to." Four of the women I interviewed cited encounters in which Weinstein exposed himself or masturbated in front of them.

Sixteen former and current executives and assistants at Weinstein's companies told me that they witnessed or had knowledge of unwanted sexual advances and touching at events associated with Weinstein's films and in the workplace. They and others described a pattern of professional meetings that were little more than thin pretexts for sexual advances on young actresses and models. All sixteen said that the behavior was widely known within both Miramax and the Weinstein Company. Messages sent by Irwin Reiter, a senior company executive, to Emily Nestor, one of the women who alleged that she was harassed, described the "mistreatment of women" as a serial problem that the Weinstein Company had been struggling with in recent years. Other employees described what was, in essence, a culture of complicity at Weinstein's places of business, with numerous people throughout his companies fully aware of his behavior but either abetting it or looking the other way. Some employees said that they were enlisted in a subterfuge to make the victims feel safe. A female executive with the company described how Weinstein's assistants and others served as a "honeypot"—they would initially join a meeting along with a woman Weinstein was interested in, but then Weinstein would dismiss them, leaving him alone with the woman. (On October 10, the Weinstein Company's board issued a statement, writing that "these allegations come as an utter surprise to the Board. Any suggestion that the Board had knowledge of this conduct is false.")

Virtually all of the people I spoke with told me that they were frightened of retaliation. "If Harvey were to discover my identity, I'm worried that he could ruin my life," one former employee told me. Many said that they had seen Weinstein's associates confront and intimidate those who crossed him and feared that they would be similarly targeted. Four actresses, including Mira Sorvino and Rosanna Arquette, told me they suspected that, after they rejected Weinstein's advances or complained about them to company representatives, Weinstein had them removed from projects or dissuaded people from hiring them. Multiple sources said that Weinstein frequently bragged about planting items in media outlets about those who spoke against him; these sources feared similar retribution. Several pointed to Gutierrez's case: after she went to the police, negative items discussing her sexual history and impugning her credibility began rapidly appearing in New York gossip pages. (In the taped conversation, part of which *The New Yorker* posted online, Weinstein asks Gutierrez to join him for "five minutes," and warns, "Don't ruin your friendship with me for five minutes.")

Several former employees told me that they were speaking about Weinstein's alleged behavior now because they hoped to protect women in the future. "This wasn't a one-off. This wasn't a period of time," an executive who worked for Weinstein for many years told me. "This was ongoing predatory behavior toward women—whether they consented or not."

It's likely that the women who spoke to me have recently felt increasingly emboldened to talk about their experiences because of the way the world has changed regarding issues of sex and power. Their disclosures follow in the wake of stories alleging sexual misconduct by public figures, including Donald Trump, Bill O'Reilly, Roger Ailes, and Bill Cosby. In October 2016, a month before the election, a tape emerged of Trump telling a celebrity-news reporter, "And when you're a star, they let you do it. You can do anything. . . . Grab 'em by the pussy. You can do anything." This past April, O'Reilly, a host at Fox News, was forced to resign after Fox was discovered to have paid five women millions of dollars in exchange for silence about their accusations of sexual harassment. Ailes, the former head of Fox News, resigned in

July 2016 after he was accused of sexual harassment. Cosby went on trial this summer, charged with drugging and sexually assaulting a woman. The trial ended with a hung jury.

In the *Times* piece, Weinstein made an initial effort at damage control by partly acknowledging what he had done, saying, "I appreciate the way I've behaved with colleagues in the past has caused a lot of pain, and I sincerely apologize for it." In an interview with the *New York Post*, he said, "I've got to deal with my personality, I've got to work on my temper, I have got to dig deep. I know a lot of people would like me to go into a facility, and I may well just do that—I will go anywhere I can learn more about myself." He went on, "In the past I used to compliment people, and some took it as me being sexual, I won't do that again." In his written statement to the *Times*, Weinstein claimed that he would "channel that anger" into a fight against the leadership of the National Rifle Association. He also said that it was not "coincidental" that he was organizing a foundation for women directors at the University of Southern California. "It will be named after my mom and I won't disappoint her." (USC has since rejected his funding pledge.)

Sallie Hofmeister, a spokesperson for Weinstein, issued a new statement in response to the allegations detailed here. It reads in full: "Any allegations of non-consensual sex are unequivocally denied by Mr. Weinstein. Mr. Weinstein has further confirmed that there were never any acts of retaliation against any women for refusing his advances. Mr. Weinstein obviously can't speak to anonymous allegations, but with respect to any women who have made allegations on the record, Mr. Weinstein believes that all of these relationships were consensual. Mr. Weinstein has begun counseling, has listened to the community and is pursuing a better path. Mr. Weinstein is hoping that, if he makes enough progress, he will be given a second chance."

While Weinstein and his representatives have said that the incidents were consensual, and were not widespread or severe, the women I spoke to tell a very different story.

## 2.

Lucia Stoller, now Lucia Evans, was approached by Weinstein at Cipriani Upstairs, a club in New York, in 2004, the summer before her senior year at Middlebury College. Evans, who is now a marketing consultant, wanted to be an actress, and although she had heard rumors about Weinstein she let him have her number. Weinstein began calling her late at night or having an assistant call her, asking to meet. She declined, but said that she would do readings during the day for a casting executive. Before long, an assistant called to set up a daytime meeting at the Miramax office in Tribeca, first with Weinstein and then with a casting executive, who was a woman. "I was, like, Oh, a woman, great, I feel safe," Evans said.

When Evans arrived for the meeting, the building was full of people. She was led to an office with exercise equipment in it and takeout boxes on the floor. Weinstein was there, alone. Evans said that she found him frightening. "The type of control he exerted—it was very real," she told me. "Even just his presence was intimidating."

In the meeting, Evans recalled, "he immediately was simultaneously flattering me and demeaning me and making me feel bad about myself." Weinstein told her that she'd "be great in *Project Runway*"—the show, which Weinstein helped produce, premiered later that year—but only if she lost weight. He also told her about two scripts, a horror movie and a teen love story, and said one of his associates would discuss them with her.

"At that point, after that, is when he assaulted me," Evans said. "He forced me to perform oral sex on him." As she objected, Weinstein took his penis out of his pants and pulled her head down onto it. "I said, over and over, 'I don't want to do this, stop, don't,'" she recalled. "I tried to get away, but maybe I didn't try hard enough. I didn't want to kick him or fight him." In the end, she said, "he's a big guy. He overpowered me." She added, "I just sort of gave up. That's the most horrible part of it, and that's why he's been able to do this for so long to so many women: people give up, and then they feel like it's their fault."

Weinstein appeared to find the encounter unremarkable. "It was like it was just another day for him," Evans said. "It was no emotion." Afterward, he acted as if nothing had happened. She wondered how Weinstein's staff could not know what was going on.

Following the encounter, she met with the female casting executive, who sent her the scripts and also came to one of her acting-class readings a few weeks later. (Evans does not believe that the executive was aware of Weinstein's behavior.) Weinstein, Evans said, began calling her again late at night. She told me that the entire sequence of events had a routine quality. "It feels like a very streamlined process," she said. "Female casting director, Harvey wants to meet. Everything was designed to make me feel comfortable before it happened. And then the shame in what happened was also designed to keep me quiet."

Evans said that, after the incident, "I just put it in a part of my brain and closed the door." She continued to blame herself for not fighting harder. "It was always my fault for not stopping him," she said. "I had an eating problem for years. I was disgusted with myself. It's funny, all these unrelated things I did to hurt myself because of this one thing." Evans told friends some of what had happened, but felt largely unable to talk about it. "I ruined several really good relationships because of this. My schoolwork definitely suffered, and my roommates told me to go to a therapist because they thought I was going to kill myself."

In the years that followed, Evans encountered Weinstein occasionally. Once, while she was walking her dog in Greenwich Village, she saw him getting into a car. "I very clearly saw him. I made eye contact," she said. "I remember getting chills down my spine just looking at him. I was so horrified. I have nightmares about him to this day."

3.

Asia Argento, who was born in Rome, played the role of a glamorous thief named Beatrice in the crime drama *B. Monkey*, which was released in the United States in 1999. The distributor was Miramax. In a series of long and often emotional interviews, Argento told me that Weinstein assaulted her while they were working together.

At the time, Argento was twenty-one and had twice won the Italian equivalent of the Oscar. Argento said that, in 1997, one of Weinstein's producers invited her to what she understood to be a party thrown by Miramax at the Hôtel du Cap-Eden-Roc, on the French Riviera. Argento felt professionally obliged to attend. When the producer led her upstairs that evening, she said, there was no party, only a hotel room, empty but for Weinstein: "I'm, like, 'Where is the fucking party?'" She recalled the producer telling her, "Oh, we got here too early," before he left her alone with Weinstein. (The producer denies bringing Argento to the room that night.) At first, Weinstein was solicitous, praising her work. Then he left the room. When he returned, he was wearing a bathrobe and holding a bottle of lotion. "He asks me to give a massage. I was, like, 'Look, man, I am no fucking fool,'" Argento told me. "But, looking back, I am a fucking fool. And I am still trying to come to grips with what happened."

Argento said that, after she reluctantly agreed to give Weinstein a massage, he pulled her skirt up, forced her legs apart, and performed oral sex on her as she repeatedly told him to stop. Weinstein "terrified me, and he was so big," she said. "It wouldn't stop. It was a nightmare."

At some point, she stopped saying no and feigned enjoyment, because she thought it was the only way the assault would end. "I was not willing," she told me. "I said, 'No, no, no.' . . . It's twisted. A big fat man wanting to eat you. It's a scary fairy tale." Argento, who insisted that she wanted to tell her story in all its complexity, said that she didn't physically fight him off, something that has prompted years of guilt.

"The thing with being a victim is I felt responsible," she said. "Because, if I were a strong woman, I would have kicked him in the balls and run away. But I didn't. And so I felt responsible." She described the incident as a "horrible trauma." Decades later, she said, oral sex is still ruined for her. "I've been damaged," she told me. "Just talking to you about it, my whole body is shaking."

Argento recalled sitting on the bed after the incident, her clothes "in shambles," her makeup smeared. She said that she told Weinstein, "I am not a whore," and that he began laughing. He said he would put the phrase on a T-shirt. Afterward, Argento said, "He kept contacting me." For a few months, Weinstein seemed obsessed, offering her expensive gifts.

What complicates the story, Argento readily allowed, is that she eventually yielded to Weinstein's further advances and even grew close to him. Weinstein dined with her, and introduced her to his mother. Argento told me, "He made it sound like he was my friend and he really appreciated me." She said that she had consensual sexual relations with him multiple times over the course of the next five years, though she described the encounters as one-sided and "onanistic." The first occasion, several months after the alleged assault, came before the release of *B. Monkey*. "I felt I had to," she said. "Because I had the movie coming out and I didn't want to anger him." She believed that Weinstein would ruin her career if she didn't comply. Years later, when she was a single mother dealing with childcare, Weinstein offered to pay for a nanny. She said that she felt "obliged" to submit to his sexual advances.

Argento told me that she knew this contact would be used to attack the credibility of her allegation. In part, she said, the initial assault made her feel overpowered each time she encountered Weinstein, even years later. "Just his body, his presence, his face, bring me back to the little girl that I was when I was twenty-one," she told me. "When I see him, it makes me feel little and stupid and weak." She broke down as she struggled to explain. "After the rape, he won," she said.

In 2000, Argento released *Scarlet Diva*, a movie that she wrote and directed. In the film, a heavyset producer corners Anna, the character played by Argento, in a hotel room, asks her for a massage, and tries to assault her. After the movie came out, women began approaching Argento, saying that they recognized Weinstein's behavior in the portrayal. "People would ask *me* about *him* because of the scene in the movie," she said. Some recounted similar details to her: meetings and professional events moved to hotel rooms, bathrobes and massage requests, and, in one other case, forced oral sex.

Weinstein, according to Argento, saw the film after it was released in the United States and apparently recognized himself. "Ha, ha, very funny," Argento remembered him saying to her. But he also said that he was "sorry for whatever happened." The movie's most significant departure from the real-life incident, Argento told me, was how the hotel-room scene ended. "In the movie I wrote," she said, "I ran away."

Other women were too afraid to allow me to use their names, but their stories are uncannily similar to these allegations. One, a woman who worked with Weinstein, explained her reluctance to be identified. "He drags your name through the mud, and he'll come after you hard with his legal team."

Like others I spoke to, this woman said that Weinstein brought her to a hotel room under a professional pretext, changed into a bathrobe, and, she said, "forced himself on me sexually." She told him no, repeatedly and clearly. Afterward, she experienced "horror, disbelief, and shame," and considered going to the police. "I thought it would be a 'he said, she said,' and I thought about how impressive his legal team is, and I thought about how much I would lose, and I decided to just move forward," she said. The woman continued to have professional contact with Weinstein after the alleged rape, and acknowledged that subsequent communications between them might suggest a normal working relationship. "I was in a vulnerable position and I needed my job," she told me. "It just increases the shame and the guilt."

## 4.

Mira Sorvino, who starred in several of Weinstein's films, told me that he sexually harassed her and tried to pressure her into a physical relationship while they were working together. She said that, at the Toronto International Film Festival in September 1995, she found herself in a hotel room with Weinstein, who produced the movie she was there to promote, *Mighty Aphrodite*, for which she later won an Academy Award. "He started massaging my shoulders, which made me very uncomfortable, and then tried to get more physical, sort of chasing me around," she recalled. She scrambled for ways to ward him off, telling him that it was against her religion to date married men. (At the time, Weinstein was married to Eve Chilton, a former assistant.) Then she left the room.

A few weeks later, in New York City, her phone rang after midnight. It was Weinstein, saying that he had new marketing ideas for the film and asking to get together. Sorvino offered to meet him at an all-night diner, but he said he was coming over to her apartment and hung up. "I freaked out," she told me. She called a friend and asked him to come over and pose as her boyfriend. The friend hadn't arrived by the time Weinstein rang her doorbell. "Harvey had managed to bypass my doorman," she said. "I opened the door terrified, brandishing my twenty-pound Chihuahua mix in front of me, as though that would do any good." When she told Weinstein that her new boyfriend was on his way, he became dejected and left.

Sorvino said that she struggled for years with whether to come forward with her story, partly because she was aware that it was mild compared with the experiences of other women, including Sophie Dix, an actress she spoke to at the time. (Dix told me that she had locked herself in a hotel bathroom to escape Weinstein and that he had masturbated in front of her. She said it was "a classic case" of "someone not understanding the word 'no.' . . . I must have said no a thousand times.") The fact that Weinstein was so instrumental in Sorvino's success also made her hesitate: "I have great respect for Harvey as an artist and owe him and his brother a debt of gratitude for the early success in my career, including the Oscar." She had professional contact with Weinstein for years after the incident and remains a close friend of his brother and business partner, Bob Weinstein. (She never told Bob about his brother's behavior.)

Sorvino said that she felt afraid and intimidated, and that the incidents had a significant impact on her. When she told a female employee at Miramax about the harassment, the woman's reaction "was shock and horror that I had mentioned it." Sorvino appeared in a few more of Weinstein's films afterward but felt that saying no to Weinstein and reporting the harassment had ultimately hurt her career. She said, "There may have been other factors, but I definitely felt iced out and that my rejection of Harvey had something to do with it."

## 5.

In March 2015, Ambra Battilana Gutierrez, who was once a finalist in the Miss Italy contest, met Harvey Weinstein at a reception for *New York Spring Spectacular*, a show that he was producing at Radio City Music Hall. Weinstein introduced himself to Gutierrez, who was twenty-two, remarking repeatedly that she looked like the actress Mila Kunis.

Following the event, Gutierrez's modeling agency e-mailed her to say that Weinstein wanted to set up a business meeting as soon as possible. Gutierrez arrived at Weinstein's office in Tribeca early the next evening with her modeling portfolio. In the office, she sat with Weinstein on a couch to review the portfolio, and he began staring at her breasts, asking if they were real. Gutierrez later told officers of the New York Police Department's Special Victims Division that Weinstein then lunged at her, groping her breasts and attempting to put a hand up her skirt while she protested. He finally backed off and told her that his assistant would give her tickets to *Finding Neverland*, a Broadway musical that he was producing. He said he would meet her at the show that evening.

Instead of going to the show, Gutierrez went to the nearest police station and reported the assault. Weinstein telephoned her later that evening, annoyed that she had failed to appear at the show. She picked up the call while sitting with investigators from the Special Victims Division, who listened in and devised a plan: Gutierrez would agree to see the show the following day and then meet with Weinstein. She would wear a wire and attempt to extract a confession or an incriminating statement.

The next day, Gutierrez met Weinstein at the bar of the Tribeca Grand Hotel. A team of undercover officers helped guide her through the interaction. On the recording, which I have heard in full, Weinstein lists actresses whose careers he has helped and offers Gutierrez the services of a dialect coach. Then he presses her to join him in his hotel room while he showers. Gutierrez says no repeatedly; Weinstein persists, and after a while she accedes to his demand to go upstairs. But, standing in the hallway outside his room, she refuses to go farther. In an increasingly tense exchange, he presses her to enter. Gutierrez says, "I don't want to," "I want to leave," and "I want to go downstairs." She asks him directly why he groped her breasts the day before.

"Oh, please, I'm sorry, just come on in," Weinstein says. "I'm used to that. Come on. Please."

"You're used to that?" Gutierrez asks, sounding incredulous.

"Yes," Weinstein says. He adds, "I won't do it again."

After almost two minutes of back-and-forth in the hallway, Weinstein finally agrees to let her leave.

According to a law-enforcement source, Weinstein, if charged, would most likely have faced a count of sexual abuse in the third degree, a misdemeanor punishable by a maximum of three months in jail. But, as the police investigation proceeded and the allegation was widely reported, details about Gutierrez's past began to appear in the tabloids. In 2010, as a young contestant in the Miss Italy beauty pageant, Gutierrez had attended one of Prime Minister Silvio Berlusconi's infamous "Bunga Bunga" parties. She claimed that she had been unaware of the nature of the party before arriving, and she eventually became a witness in a bribery case against Berlusconi, which is still ongoing. Gossip outlets also reported that Gutierrez, as a teenager, had made an allegation of sexual assault against an older Italian businessman but later declined to cooperate with prosecutors.

Two sources close to the police investigation of Weinstein said that they had no reason to doubt Gutierrez's account of the incident. One of them, a police source, said that the department had collected more than enough evidence to prosecute Weinstein. But the other said that Gutierrez's statements about her past complicated the case for the office of the Manhattan district attorney, Cyrus Vance Jr. After two weeks of investigation, the DA's office decided not to file charges. The office declined to comment on this story but pointed me to its statement at the time: "This case was taken seriously from the outset, with a thorough investigation conducted by our Sex Crimes Unit. After analyzing the available evidence, including multiple interviews with both parties, a criminal charge is not supported."

"We had the evidence," the police source involved in the operation told me. "It's a case that made me angrier than I thought possible, and I have been on the force a long time."

Gutierrez, when contacted for this story, said that she was unable to discuss the incident. Someone close to the matter told me that, after the DA's office decided not to press charges, Gutierrez, facing Weinstein's legal team, and in return for a payment, signed a highly restrictive nondisclosure agreement with Weinstein, including an affidavit stating that the acts he admits to in the recording never happened.

Weinstein's use of such settlements was reported by the *Times* and confirmed to me by numerous people. A former employee with firsthand knowledge of two settlement negotiations that took place in London in the 1990s recalled, "It felt like David versus Goliath . . . the guy with all the money and the power flexing his muscle and quashing the allegations and getting rid of them."

## 6.

The *Times* story disclosed a complaint to the Weinstein Company's office of human resources, filed on behalf of a temporary front-desk assistant named Emily Nestor in December 2014. Her own account of Weinstein's conduct is being made public here for the first time. Nestor was twenty-five when she started the job and, after finishing law school and starting business school, was considering a career in the movie industry. On her first day in the position, Nestor said, two employees told her that she was Weinstein's "type" physically. When Weinstein arrived at the office, he made comments about her appearance, referring to her as "the pretty girl." He asked how old she was and then sent all of his assistants out of the room and made her write down her telephone number.

Weinstein told her to meet him for drinks that night. Nestor invented an excuse. When he insisted, she suggested an early-morning coffee the next day, assuming that he wouldn't accept. He did, and told her to meet him at the Peninsula hotel in Beverly Hills, where he was staying. Nestor said that she had talked with friends in the entertainment industry and employees in the company who had warned her about Weinstein's reputation. "I dressed very frumpy," she said.

Nestor told me that the meeting was "the most excruciating and uncomfortable hour of my life." After Weinstein offered her career help, she said, he began to boast about his sexual liaisons with other women, including famous actresses. "He said, 'You know, we could have a lot of fun,'" Nestor recalled. "'I could put you in my London office, and you could work there and you could be my girlfriend.'" She declined. He asked to hold her hand; she said no. In Nestor's account of the exchange, Weinstein said, "Oh, the girls always say no. You know, 'No, no.' And then they have a beer or two and then they're throwing themselves at me." In a tone that Nestor described as "very weirdly proud," Weinstein added "that he'd never had to do anything like Bill Cosby." She assumed that he meant he'd never drugged a woman. "It's just a bizarre thing to be so proud of," she said. "That you've never had to resort to doing that. It was just so far removed from reality and normal rules of consent."

"Textbook sexual harassment" was how Nestor described Weinstein's behavior to me. "It's a pretty clear case of sexual harassment when your superior, the CEO, asks one of their inferiors, a temp, to have sex with them, essentially in exchange for mentorship." She recalled refusing his advances at least a dozen times. "'No' did not mean 'no' to him," she said. "I was very aware of how inappropriate it was. But I felt trapped."

Throughout the breakfast, she said, Weinstein interrupted their conversation to yell into his cell phone, enraged over a spat that Amy Adams, a star in the Weinstein movie *Big Eyes*, was having in the press. Afterward, Weinstein told Nestor to keep an eye on the news cycle, which he promised would be spun in his favor. Later in the day, there were indeed negative news items about his opponents, and Weinstein stopped by Nestor's desk to be sure that she'd seen them.

By that point, Nestor recalled, "I was very afraid of him. And I knew how well connected he was. And how if I pissed him off then I could never have a career in that industry." Still, she told a friend about the incident, and he alerted the company's office of human resources, which contacted her. (The friend did not respond to a request for comment.) Nestor had a conversation with company officials about the matter but didn't pursue it further: the officials said that Weinstein would be informed of anything she told them, a practice not uncommon in businesses the size of the Weinstein Company. Several former Weinstein employees told me that the company's human-resources department was utterly ineffective; one female executive described it as "a place where you went to when you didn't want anything to get done. That was common knowledge across the board. Because everything funneled back to Harvey." She described the department's typical response to allegations of misconduct as "This is his company. If you don't like it, you can leave."

Nestor told me that some people at the company did seem concerned. Irwin Reiter, a senior executive who had worked for Weinstein for almost three decades, sent her a series of messages via LinkedIn. "We view this very seriously and I personally am very sorry your first day was like this," Reiter wrote. "Also if there are further unwanted advances, please let us know." Last year, just before the presidential election, he reached out again, writing, "All this Trump stuff made me think of you." He described Nestor's experience as part of Weinstein's serial misconduct. "I've fought him about mistreatment of women 3 weeks before the incident with you. I even wrote him an email that got me labelled by him as sex police," he wrote. "The fight I had with him about you was epic. I told him if you were my daughter he would have not made out so well." (Reiter declined to comment for this article, but his lawyer, Debra Katz, confirmed the authenticity of the messages and said that Reiter had made diligent efforts to raise these

issues, to no avail. Katz also noted that Reiter "is eager to cooperate fully with any outside investigation.")

Though no assault occurred, and Nestor left after completing
her temporary placement, she was profoundly affected by the
experience. "I was definitely traumatized for a while, in terms of
feeling so harassed and frightened," she said. "It made me feel
incredibly discouraged that this could be something that happens
on a regular basis. I actually decided not to go into entertainment
because of this incident."

## 7.

Emma de Caunes, a French actress, met Weinstein in 2010, at a
party at the Cannes Film Festival. A few months later, he asked
her to a lunch meeting at the Hôtel Ritz, in Paris. In the meeting,
Weinstein told de Caunes that he was going to be producing a
movie with a prominent director, that he planned to shoot it in
France, and that it had a strong female role. It was an adaptation
of a book, he said, but he claimed he couldn't remember the title.
"But I'll give it to you," Weinstein said, according to de Caunes.
"I have it in my room."

De Caunes replied that she had to leave since she was already
running late for a TV show she was hosting—Eminem was
appearing on the show that afternoon, and she hadn't written her
questions yet. Weinstein pleaded with her to retrieve the book
with him, and finally she agreed. As they got to his room, she
received a telephone call from one of her colleagues, and Weinstein disappeared into a bathroom, leaving the door open. She
assumed that he was washing his hands.

"When I hung up the phone, I heard the shower go on in the
bathroom," she said. "I was, like, What the fuck, is he taking a
shower?" Weinstein came out, naked and with an erection. "What
are you doing?" she asked. Weinstein demanded that she lie

on the bed and told her that many other women had done so before her.

"I was very petrified," de Caunes said. "But I didn't want to show him that I was petrified, because I could feel that the more I was freaking out, the more he was excited." She added, "It was like a hunter with a wild animal. The fear turns him on." De Caunes told Weinstein that she was leaving, and he panicked. "We haven't done anything!" she remembered him saying. "It's like being in a Walt Disney movie!"

De Caunes told me, "I looked at him and I said—it took all my courage, but I said, 'I've always hated Walt Disney movies.' And then I left. I slammed the door." She was shaking on the stairs going down to the lobby. A director she was working with on the TV show confirmed that she arrived at the studio distraught and that she recounted what had happened. Weinstein called relentlessly over the next few hours, offering de Caunes gifts and repeating his assertion that nothing had happened.

De Caunes, who was in her early thirties at the time, was already an established actress, but she wondered what would happen to younger and more vulnerable women in the same situation. Over the years, she said, she's heard similar accounts from friends. "I know that everybody—I mean *everybody*—in Hollywood knows that it's happening," de Caunes said. "He's not even really hiding. I mean, the way he does it, so many people are involved and see what's happening. But everyone's too scared to say anything."

## 8.

One evening in the early nineties, the actress Rosanna Arquette was supposed to meet Weinstein for dinner at the Beverly Hills Hotel to pick up the script for a new film. At the hotel, Arquette was told to meet Weinstein upstairs, in his room.

Arquette recalled that, when she arrived at the room, Weinstein opened the door wearing a white bathrobe. He said that his neck was sore and that he needed a massage. She told him that she could recommend a good masseuse. "Then he grabbed my hand," she said. He put it on his neck. When she yanked her hand away, Weinstein grabbed it again and pulled it toward his penis, which was visible and erect. "My heart was really racing. I was in a fight-or-flight moment," she said. She told Weinstein, "I will never do that."

Weinstein told her that she was making a huge mistake by rejecting him and named an actress and a model who he claimed had given in to his sexual overtures and whose careers he said he had advanced as a result. Arquette said she responded, "I'll never be that girl," and left.

Arquette said that after she rejected Weinstein her career suffered. In one case, she believes, she lost a role because of it. "He made things very difficult for me for years," she told me. She did appear in one subsequent Weinstein film—*Pulp Fiction*. Arquette believes that she only got that role because of its small size and Weinstein's deference to the filmmaker, Quentin Tarantino. (Disputes later arose over her entitlement to payment out of the film's proceeds.) Arquette said that her silence was the result of Weinstein's power and reputation for vindictiveness. "He's going to be working very hard to track people down and silence people," she explained. "To hurt people. That's what he does."

There are other examples of Weinstein's using the same modus operandi. Jessica Barth, an actress who met him at a Golden Globes party in January 2011, told me that he invited her to a business meeting at the Peninsula. When she arrived, he asked her over the phone to go up to his room. Weinstein assured her it was "no big deal"—because of his high profile, he simply wanted privacy to "talk career stuff." In the room, she found that Weinstein had ordered champagne and sushi.

Barth said that, in the conversation that followed, Weinstein alternated between offering to cast her in a film and demanding a naked massage in bed. "So, what would happen if, say, we're having some champagne and I take my clothes off and you give me a massage?" she recalled him asking. "And I'm, like, 'That's not going to happen.'"

When she moved toward the door to leave, Weinstein lashed out, saying that she needed to lose weight "to compete with Mila Kunis," and then, apparently in an effort to mollify her, promising a meeting with one of his female executives. "He gave me her number, and I walked out and I started bawling," Barth told me. (Immediately after the incident, she spoke with two people; they confirmed to me that she had described her experience to them at the time.) Barth said that the promised meeting at Weinstein's office seemed to be purely a formality. "I just knew it was bullshit," she said. (The executive she met with did not respond to requests for comment.)

## 9.

Weinstein's behavior deeply affected the day-to-day operations of his companies. Current and former employees described a pattern of meetings and strained complicity that closely matches the accounts of the many women I interviewed. The employees spoke on condition of anonymity because, they said, they feared for their careers in Hollywood and because of provisos in their work contracts.

"There was a large volume of these types of meetings that Harvey would have with aspiring actresses and models," one female executive told me. "He would have them late at night, usually at hotel bars or in hotel rooms. And, in order to make these women feel more comfortable, he would ask a female executive or assistant to start those meetings with him." She was repeatedly asked to join such meetings, she said, but she refused.

The executive said that she was especially disturbed by the involvement of other employees. "It almost felt like the executive or assistant was made to be a honeypot to lure these women in, to make them feel safe," she said. "Then he would dismiss the executive or the assistant, and then these women were alone with him. And that did not feel like it was appropriate behavior or safe behavior."

One former employee told me that she was frequently asked to join for the beginning of meetings that, she said, had in many cases already been moved from day to night and from hotel lobbies to hotel rooms. She said that Weinstein's conduct in the meetings was brazen. During a meeting with a model, the former employee said, he turned to her and demanded, "Tell her how good of a boyfriend I am." She said that when she refused to join one such meeting, Weinstein became enraged. Often, she was asked to keep track of the women, who, in keeping with a practice established by Weinstein's assistants, were all filed under the same label in her phone: FOH, which stood for "Friend of Harvey." She added that the pattern of meetings was nearly uninterrupted in her years of working for Weinstein. "I have to say, the behavior did stop for a little bit after the groping thing," she told me, referring to Gutierrez's allegation to the police. "But he couldn't help himself. A few months later, he was back at it."

Two staffers who facilitated these meetings said that they felt morally compromised by them. One male former staffer noted that many of the women seemed "not aware of the nature of those meetings" and "were definitely scared." He told me that most of the encounters that he saw seemed consensual, but others gave him pause. He was especially troubled by his memory of one young woman: "You just feel terrible because you could tell this girl, very young, not from our country, was now in a room waiting for him to come up there in the middle of the day, and we were not to bother them." He said that he was never asked to facilitate these meetings for men.

None of the former executives or assistants I spoke to quit because of the misconduct, but many expressed guilt and regret over not having said or done more. They talked about what they believed to be a culture of silence about sexual assault inside Miramax and the Weinstein Company and across the entertainment industry more broadly.

## 10.

Weinstein and his legal and public-relations teams have conducted a decades-long campaign to suppress these stories. In recent months, that campaign escalated. Weinstein and his associates began calling many of the women in this article. Weinstein asked Argento to meet with a private investigator and give testimony on his behalf. One actress who initially spoke to me on the record later asked that her allegation be removed from this piece. "I'm so sorry," she wrote. "The legal angle is coming at me and I have no recourse." Weinstein and his legal team have threatened to sue multiple media outlets, including the *New York Times*.

Several of the former executives and assistants in this story said that they had received calls from Weinstein in which he attempted to determine if they had talked to me or warned them not to. These employees continued to participate in the article partly because they felt that there was a growing culture of accountability, embodied in the relatively recent disclosures about high-profile men such as Cosby and Ailes. "I think a lot of us had thought—and hoped—over the years that it would come out sooner," the former executive who was aware of the two legal settlements in London told me. "But I think now is the right time, in this current climate, for the truth."

The female executive who declined inappropriate meetings told me that her lawyer advised her that she could be liable for hundreds of thousands of dollars in damages for violating the nondisclosure agreement attached to her employment contract. "I believe this is more important than keeping a confidentiality agreement," she said. "The more of us that can confirm or validate for these women if this did happen, I think it's really important for their justice to do that." She continued, "I wish I could have done more. I wish I could have stopped it. And this is my way of doing that now."

"He's been systematically doing this for a very long time," the former employee who had been made to act as a "honeypot" told me. She said that she often thinks of something Weinstein whispered—to himself, as far as she could tell—after one of his many shouting sprees at the office. It so unnerved her that she pulled out her phone and tapped it into a memo, word for word: "There are things I've done that nobody knows."

# Weighing the Costs of Speaking Out About Harvey Weinstein

In March, Annabella Sciorra, who received an Emmy nomination for her role in *The Sopranos*, agreed to talk with me for a story I was reporting about Harvey Weinstein. Speaking by phone, I explained that two sources had told me that she had a serious allegation regarding the producer. Sciorra, however, told me that Weinstein had never done anything inappropriate. Perhaps she just wasn't his type, she said, with an air of what seemed to be studied nonchalance. But, two weeks ago, after *The New Yorker* published the story, in which thirteen women accused Weinstein of sexual assault and harassment, Sciorra called me. The truth, she said, was that she had been struggling to speak about Weinstein for more than twenty years. She was still living in fear of him and slept with a baseball bat by her bed. Weinstein, she told me, had violently raped her in the early 1990s and, over the next several years, sexually harassed her repeatedly.

"I was so scared. I was looking out the window of my living room, and I faced the water of the East River," she said, recalling our initial conversation. "I really wanted to tell you. I was like, 'This is the moment you've been waiting for your whole life....'" she said. "I really, really panicked," she added. "I was shaking. And I just wanted to get off the phone."

All told, more than fifty women have now leveled accusations against Weinstein, in accounts published by the *New York Times*, *The New Yorker*, and other outlets. But many other victims have continued to be reluctant to talk to me about their experiences, declining interview requests or initially agreeing to talk and then wavering. As more women have come forward, the costs of doing so have certainly shifted. But many still say that they face overwhelming pressures to stay silent, ranging from the specter of career damage to fears about the life-altering consequences of being marked as sexual-assault victims. "Now when I go to a restaurant or to an event, people are going to know that this happened to me," Sciorra said. "They're gonna look at me and they're gonna know. I'm an intensely private person, and this is the most unprivate thing you can do."

The actress Daryl Hannah told me this week about two incidents that occurred, during the early aughts, in which Weinstein pounded on her hotel-room door until she, in one case, escaped out a back entrance. When it happened again the following day, she barricaded herself in her room using furniture. Another time, Weinstein asked her if he could touch her breasts. She believes that, after she refused, Weinstein retaliated against her professionally. "I am a private person, with a rule of speaking to the press only for professional reasons," she told me. Hannah said that she had decided to speak publicly about her experiences for the first time, more than a decade after they occurred, because "I feel a moral obligation to support the women who have suffered much more egregious transgressions." She, like many women who have come forward, still had doubts about the trade-offs she would have to make for speaking openly. "It's one of those things your body has to adjust to. You get dragged into the gutter of nastiness and pettiness and shame and all of these things, and it sometimes seems healthier and wiser to just move on with your life and not allow yourself to be revictimized."

A woman who appeared anonymously in my previous article, alleging that Weinstein raped her while she worked for him, and who has chosen to remain nameless, told me that she has yet to tell even people close to her about the full extent of her allegation. "I want to be braver. I really do," she told me. "I want to be able to put my name to this and talk through what happened, but I am surrounded by people who, the first thing they'll do is read this article, and I'll be working three desks from them, and they'll know details of my life I haven't even told my family." For many women, this was the most difficult decision of their lives. Sciorra, too, still has doubts. "Even now, as I tell you, and have had all these women around saying it's OK," Sciorra told me, "I'm petrified again."

Sallie Hofmeister, a spokesperson for Weinstein, issued a statement in response to the allegations by Sciorra and Hannah. "Mr. Weinstein unequivocally denies any allegations of nonconsensual sex," she said.

·　　·　　·

Sciorra first met Weinstein in the early nineties, when she was an emerging star after appearing in films such as *The Hand That Rocks the Cradle*. Her agent introduced them at an industry party in Los Angeles. Weinstein was friendly, she said, and gave her a ride home; they talked about their shared love of film. Several months later, when her friend Warren Leight was trying to get a romantic-comedy screenplay he'd written made, Sciorra called

Weinstein about it. Weinstein said that he wanted to make the film, which was called *The Night We Never Met*, and to start filming with Sciorra in a leading role. He wanted her to start work immediately after she finished two back-to-back shoots she already had planned for that summer. "I said, 'Harvey, I cannot do this right now. I need some time,'" she recalled. "That's the first time he threatened to sue me." (Sources close to Weinstein deny that he threatened to sue Sciorra.)

After Sciorra finished making *The Night We Never Met*, she said that she became ensconced in "this circle of Miramax," referring to Weinstein's studio, which was then gaining an increasingly dominant role in the industry. There were so many screenings and events and dinners, Sciorra said, that it was hard to imagine life outside of the Weinstein ecosystem. At one dinner, in New York, she recalled, "Harvey was there, and I got up to leave. And Harvey said, 'Oh, I'll drop you off.' Harvey had dropped me off before, so I didn't really expect anything out of the ordinary—I expected just to be dropped off." In the car, Weinstein said goodbye to Sciorra, and she went upstairs to her apartment. She was alone and getting ready for bed a few minutes later when she heard a knock on the door. "It wasn't that late," she said. "Like, it wasn't the middle of the night, so I opened the door a crack to see who it was. And he pushed the door open." She paused to collect herself. Weinstein, she continued, "walked in like it was his apartment, like he owned the place, and started unbuttoning his shirt. So it was very clear where he thought this was going to go. And I was in a nightgown. I didn't have much on." He circled the apartment; to Sciorra, it appeared that he was checking whether anyone else was there.

Sciorra told me that listening to a recording from 2015 that *The New Yorker* released earlier this month, in which Weinstein is heard demanding that a model enter his hotel room, "really triggered me." Sciorra remembered Weinstein employing the same tactics as he cornered her, backing her into her bedroom. "Come here, come on, cut it out, what are you doing, come here," she remembered him saying. She tried to be assertive. "This is not happening," she told him. "You've got to go. You have to leave. Get out of my apartment."

Then Weinstein grabbed her, she said. "He shoved me onto the bed, and he got on top of me." Sciorra struggled. "I kicked and I yelled," she said, but Weinstein locked her arms over her head with one hand and forced sexual intercourse on her. "When he was done, he ejaculated on my leg, and on my nightgown." It was a family heirloom, handed down from relatives in Italy and embroidered in white cotton. "He said, 'I have impeccable timing,' and then he said, 'This is for you.'" Sciorra paused. "And then he attempted to perform oral sex on me. And I struggled, but I had very little strength left in me." Sciorra said that her body started to shake violently. "I think, in a way, that's what made him leave, because it looked like I was having a seizure or something."

In the weeks and months that followed the alleged attack, Sciorra didn't tell anyone about it. "Like most of these women, I was so ashamed of what happened," she said. "And I fought. I *fought*. But still I was like, Why did I open that door? Who opens the door at that time of night? I was definitely embarrassed by it. I felt disgusting. I felt like I had fucked up." She grew depressed and lost weight. Her father, unaware of the attack but concerned for her well-being, urged her to seek help, and she did see a therapist, but, she said, "I don't even think I told the therapist. It's pathetic."

Sciorra never spoke to the police. Neither did the anonymous woman who alleged rape in the earlier *New Yorker* article, although two others did. The anonymous woman said that, although "I regret not being maybe stronger in the moment," her fears that charging Weinstein publicly might change her life permanently were too great. "It's hard to know. . . . It's like choosing a different life path."

Some of the obstacles that Sciorra and other women believed they faced were related to Weinstein's power in the film industry. Sciorra said that she felt the impact on her livelihood almost immediately. "From 1992, I didn't work again until 1995," she said. "I just kept getting this pushback of 'We heard you were difficult; we heard this or that.' I think that that was the Harvey machine." The actress Rosie Perez, a friend who was among the first to discuss Sciorra's allegations with her, told me, "She was riding high, and then she started acting weird and getting reclusive. It made no sense. Why did this woman, who was so talented, and riding so high, doing hit after hit, then all of a sudden fall off the map? It hurts me as a fellow actress to see her career not flourish the way it should have."

Several years later, Sciorra did begin working again. Weinstein again pursued her with unwanted sexual advances, she said. In 1995, she was in London shooting *The Innocent Sleep*, which Weinstein did not produce. According to Sciorra, Weinstein began leaving her messages, demanding that she call him or that they meet at his hotel. "I don't know how he found me," she said. "I'd come home from work and there'd be a message that Harvey Weinstein had called. This went on and on." He sent cars to her hotel to bring her to him, which she ignored. One night, he showed up at her room and began pounding on the door, she said. "For nights after, I couldn't sleep. I piled furniture in front of the door, like in the movies." Finally, she pleaded with Matthew Vaughn, then a twenty-two-year-old producer on the film, and more recently a prominent director, to move her secretly to a different hotel. (Vaughn said that he recalled booking her a room elsewhere.)

Two years later, Sciorra appeared in the crime drama *Cop Land* as Liz Randone, the wife of a corrupt police officer. She said that she auditioned for the part without realizing at first that it was a Miramax film, and she learned that Weinstein's company was involved only when she began contract negotiations. (A person close to Weinstein contested this, saying that the script had the studio's name on it.) In May 1997, shortly before the film's release, she went to the Cannes Film Festival. When she checked into the Hôtel du Cap-Eden-Roc, in Antibes, France, a Miramax associate told her that Weinstein's room would be next to hers. "My heart just sank," Sciorra recalled. Early one morning, while she was still asleep, there was a knock on the door. Groggy, and thinking she must have forgotten about an early hair-and-makeup call, she opened the door. "There's Harvey in his under-wear, holding a bottle of baby oil in one hand and a tape, a movie, in the other," she recalled. "And it was horrific, because I'd been there before." Sciorra said that she ran from Weinstein. "He was closing in really quickly, and I pressed all the call buttons for valet service and room service. I kept pressing all of them until someone showed up." Weinstein retreated, she said, when hotel staff arrived.

Over time, Sciorra opened up to a small number of people. Perez said that she heard from an acquaintance about Weinstein's behavior at the hotel in London and questioned Sciorra about what happened. Sciorra told Perez about the attack in her apart-ment, and Perez, who was sexually assaulted by a relative during her childhood, began crying. "I said, 'Oh, Annabella, you've gotta go to the police.' She said, 'I can't go to the police. He's destroy-ing my career.'"

·　　·　　·

Unlike Sciorra, Daryl Hannah, who is known for her roles in *Splash*, *Wall Street*, and many other films, told colleagues about what had happened to her. "I did tell people about it," she told me. "And it didn't matter." Hannah first met Weinstein at the Cannes Film Festival, in the early aughts, before she appeared in *Kill Bill: Volume 1*, which Weinstein produced. She was returning to her room at the Hôtel du Cap-Eden-Roc, the same hotel where

Sciorra said Weinstein harassed her. She saw Weinstein, who was at a reception in the hotel bar nearby. He called her over and told her that he loved her work. Then he asked for her room number so that he could call her to schedule a meeting.

"That seemed pretty normal to me, you know, how people talk in business, and I didn't know his reputation or anything," Hannah said. She was in her room, already in her pajamas and getting ready for bed, when the phone calls started. "It felt like it was too late to have a meeting. I didn't want to answer." Though she didn't pick up, she guessed that it was Weinstein. "And then, shortly thereafter, the knocking on the door began," she told me. "It was sort of incessant, and then it started turning into pounding on my door," she said. She was certain that it was Weinstein—as she recalls, she saw him through the peephole in the door. The pounding became so frightening that Hannah, who was staying on the ground floor, left her room via an exterior door. She spent the night in her makeup artist's room. The following evening, Hannah was in her room with the makeup artist, packing her things ahead of their departure the next morning, when the pounding on the door began again. "The knocking started again and again. And I was like, 'Oh, shit,'" Hannah recalled. "We actually pushed a dresser in front of the door and just kind of huddled in the room." The next morning, as they left, Weinstein was standing outside the hotel, and appeared, she felt, to be waiting for her. She left quickly and went to the airport.

Several years later, while she was promoting *Kill Bill: Volume 2*, Hannah was in Rome for the film's Italian première. She and the rest of the cast were scheduled to depart the following morning on a private plane belonging to Miramax. The premiere was followed by a reception, after which Hannah was in her suite at the Hotel de Russie with another hair-and-makeup artist, Steeve Daviault. The two had changed into their pajamas and were sitting on Hannah's bed with an order of room-service spaghetti, watching a Sophia Loren movie, when Weinstein entered the bedroom. "He had a key," Hannah recalled. "He came through the living room and into the bedroom. He just burst in like a raging bull. And I know with every fiber of my being that if my male makeup artist was not in that room, things would not have gone well. It was scary." Daviault remembered the incident vividly. "I was there to keep her safe," he told me.

When Hannah asked Weinstein what he was doing, he became flustered and angry, she said. Weinstein demanded that she get dressed and attend a party downstairs. Hannah pointed out that no one had ever mentioned a party. Weinstein stormed out, and she quickly took off her glasses and pajamas, donned a dress, and headed downstairs. When she arrived at the reception room Weinstein had mentioned, it was "completely empty," Hannah recalled. "And it wasn't even like there had been a party there. I didn't see drinks around." As she turned to leave, Weinstein was standing by the elevator. Hannah asked him what was happening and Weinstein replied, "Are your tits real?" Then he asked if he could feel them. "I said, 'No, you can't!' And then he said, 'At least flash me, then.' And I said, 'Fuck off, Harvey.'" She took the elevator back to her room and went to sleep.

"I experienced instant repercussions," she told me. The next morning, the Miramax private plane left without Hannah on it. Her flights for a trip to Cannes for the film's French premiere were canceled, as were her hotel room in Cannes and her hair-and-makeup artist for the festival. "I called everybody," she recalled, including her manager, a producer on the film, and its director, Quentin Tarantino, who has since told the *Times* that he knew enough, from his years collaborating with Weinstein, to have done more to stop him and regrets his failure to do so. "I called all the powers that be and told them what had happened," Hannah said. "And that I thought that was the repercussion, you know, the backlash from my experience."

"And it didn't matter," Hannah said. "I think that it doesn't matter if you're a well-known actress, it doesn't matter if you're twenty or if you're forty, it doesn't matter if you report or if you don't, because we are not believed. We are more than not believed—we are berated and criticized and blamed."

Other women told me that Hannah's fear of retaliation was well founded. The actress Ellen Barkin told me that, though she was never a victim of Weinstein's sexual advances, he frequently verbally abused her, calling her a "cunt" and "cunt bitch" during the filming of *Into the West*, which he produced. "The repercussions are real," she said. "I was terrified Harvey was going to make it impossible to go back to work, with those tentacles of his." She continued, "This fear of losing your career is not losing your ticket to a borrowed dress and earrings someone paid you to wear. It's losing your ability to support yourself, to support your family, and this is fucking real whether you are the biggest movie star or the lowest-pay-grade assistant."

•        •        •

Many of the women with allegations about Weinstein told me that the forces that kept them quiet continue to this day. Beginning in the early months of this year, Weinstein and his associates began calling women to determine who had spoken to the press. Three women who received those calls said that they were pressed for details about their communications with reporters. The calls nearly silenced them. In addition, Sciorra and several other individuals connected to the story received calls from a man they believed was working for Weinstein and posing as a journalist, who offered few details about himself and did not name any publication he was working for. "He said he was doing a piece about how movies have changed in the last thirty years, and I was like, 'You fucker.'"

Sciorra and others said that Weinstein has a reputation for using the press to smear and intimidate people he sees as threats. "I've known now for a long time how powerful Harvey became, and how he owned a lot of journalists and gossip columnists," Sciorra told me. Three sources with knowledge of the activities of Miramax Books corroborated some of Sciorra's suspicions, saying that Weinstein would offer book deals to gossip columnists. The implication, the sources felt, was that he was trying to influence them. Weinstein's reputation for manipulating the media created an atmosphere of paranoia. During one of our conversations, Sciorra said to me, "As I was talking to you, I got scared that it wasn't really you."

The power of the tabloid press to help silence women has been underscored in recent weeks. While there has been an enormous outpouring of support for those who have spoken out against Weinstein, there has also been a backlash. Asia Argento, an Italian actress who alleged, in the earlier *New Yorker* story, that Weinstein forcibly performed oral sex on her and also described, in all its nuance, their ensuing relationship, which included consensual sex, told me that, when she decided to speak, she was knowingly sacrificing her reputation. "This will completely destroy me," she predicted.

Since her story was made public, she has fled her native Italy, following public shaming there. The journalist Renato Farina wrote an article about her in the conservative daily *Libero*, titled "First they give it away, then they whine and pretend to repent." In a radio interview, the paper's editor, Vittorio Feltri, said that Argento should be thankful that Weinstein had forced oral sex on her. Some women joined the chorus, including the commentator Selvaggia Lucarelli. She suggested that it was not "legitimate" to raise an allegation twenty years after the fact.

"I knew, when I spoke up, that things would be difficult. That there would be some who would doubt me, mock me, even malign me. I knew this," Argento told me this week. "But I was unprepared for the naked contempt, the unapologetically hateful public shaming and vilification I received in my own country. Much of it from women. Women!. . . It hurt me. Badly."

Sciorra said that the attacks on Argento and other accusers reinforced her fears about speaking out, but they also finally made her believe that she had no choice but to do so. "The way they're treating Asia, and the way they're treating a lot of women, is so infuriating," she said. The attempts to downplay the significance of Argento's allegations made her realize the importance of her own story. "OK, you want rape?" she said, addressing those commentators who questioned whether Argento's experience qualified. "Here's fucking rape."

Virtually all the women I talked to who were struggling with whether to speak publicly said that advice from friends, loved ones, and colleagues was a deciding factor. Sciorra was one of several who told me that those they had consulted urged them to stay quiet. "I spoke with two people in the business who I've known for a while, and they were very clearly against me saying anything," she told me. "And they were people I always really trusted and I respect. And they felt that no good could come out of it. Immediately, the response was 'Stay as far away from this as possible.'"

Rosie Perez said that she urged Sciorra to speak by describing her own experience of going public about her assault. "I told her, 'I used to tread water for years. It's fucking exhausting, and maybe speaking out, that's your lifeboat. Grab on and get out,'" Perez recalled. "I said, 'Honey, the water never goes away. But, after I went public, it became a puddle, and I built a bridge over it, and one day you're gonna get there, too.'"

# Harvey Weinstein's Army of Spies

In the fall of 2016, Harvey Weinstein set out to suppress allegations that he had sexually harassed or assaulted numerous women. He began to hire private security agencies to collect information on the women and the journalists trying to expose the allegations. According to dozens of pages of documents, and seven people directly involved in the effort, the firms that Weinstein hired included Kroll, which is one of the world's largest corporate-intelligence companies, and Black Cube, an enterprise run largely by former officers of Mossad and other Israeli intelligence agencies. Black Cube, which has branches in Tel Aviv, London, and Paris, offers its clients the skills of operatives "highly experienced and trained in Israel's elite military and governmental intelligence units," according to its literature.

Two private investigators from Black Cube, using false identities, met with the actress Rose McGowan, who eventually publicly accused Weinstein of rape, to extract information from her. One of the investigators pretended to be a women's-rights advocate and secretly recorded at least four meetings with McGowan. The same operative, using a different false identity and implying that she had an allegation against Weinstein, met twice with a journalist to find out which women were talking to the press. In other cases, journalists directed by Weinstein or the private investigators interviewed women and reported back the details.

The explicit goal of the investigations, laid out in one contract with Black Cube, signed in July, was to stop the publication of the abuse allegations against Weinstein that eventually emerged in the *New York Times* and *The New Yorker*. Over the course of a year, Weinstein had the agencies "target," or collect information on, dozens of individuals, and compile psychological profiles that sometimes focused on their personal or sexual histories. Weinstein monitored the progress of the investigations personally. He also enlisted former employees from his film enterprises to join in the effort, collecting names and placing calls that, according to some sources who received them, felt intimidating.

In some cases, the investigative effort was run through Weinstein's lawyers, including David Boies, a celebrated attorney who represented Al Gore in the 2000 presidential-election dispute and argued for marriage equality before the U.S. Supreme Court. Boies personally signed the contract directing Black Cube to attempt to uncover information that would stop the publication of a *Times* story about Weinstein's abuses while his firm was also representing the *Times*, including in a libel case.

Boies confirmed that his firm contracted with and paid two of the agencies and that investigators from one of them sent him reports, which were then passed on to Weinstein. He said that he did not select the firms or direct the investigators' work. He also denied that the work regarding the *Times* story represented a conflict of interest. Boies said that his firm's involvement with the investigators was a mistake. "We should not have been contracting with and paying investigators that we did not select and direct," he told me. "At the time, it seemed a reasonable accommodation for a client, but it was not thought through, and that was my mistake. It was a mistake at the time."

Techniques like the ones used by the agencies on Weinstein's behalf are almost always kept secret, and, because such relationships are often run through law firms, the investigations are theoretically protected by attorney-client privilege, which could prevent them from being disclosed in court. The documents and sources reveal the tools and tactics available to powerful individuals to suppress negative stories and, in some cases, forestall criminal investigations.

In a statement, Weinstein's spokesperson, Sallie Hofmeister, said, "It is a fiction to suggest that any individuals were targeted or suppressed at any time."

.        .        .

In May 2017, McGowan received an e-mail from a literary agency introducing her to a woman who identified herself as Diana Filip, the deputy head of sustainable and responsible investments at Reuben Capital Partners, a London-based wealth-management firm. Filip told McGowan that she was launching an initiative to combat discrimination against women in the workplace and asked McGowan, a vocal women's-rights advocate, to speak at a gala kickoff event later that year. Filip offered McGowan a fee of sixty thousand dollars. "I understand that we have a lot in common," Filip wrote to McGowan before their first meeting, in May, at the Peninsula Hotel in Beverly Hills. Filip had a UK cell-phone number, and she spoke with what McGowan took to be a German accent. Over the following months, the two women met at least three more times at hotel bars in Los Angeles and New York and other locations. "I took her to the Venice boardwalk and we had ice cream while we strolled," McGowan told me, adding that Filip was "very kind." The two talked at length about issues relating to women's empowerment. Filip also repeatedly told McGowan that she wanted to make a significant investment in McGowan's production company.

Filip was persistent. In one e-mail, she suggested meeting in Los Angeles and then, when McGowan said she would be in New York, Filip said she could meet there just as easily. She also began pressing McGowan for information. In a conversation in July, McGowan revealed to Filip that she had spoken to me as part of my reporting on Weinstein. A week later, I received an e-mail from Filip asking for a meeting and suggesting that I join her campaign to end professional discrimination against women. "I am very impressed with your work as a male advocate for gender equality, and believe that you would make an invaluable addition to our activities," she wrote, using her wealth-management firm's e-mail address. Unsure of who she was, I did not respond.

Filip continued to meet with McGowan. In one meeting in September, Filip was joined by another Black Cube operative, who used the name Paul and claimed to be a colleague at Reuben Capital Partners. The goal, according to two sources with knowledge of the effort, was to pass McGowan to another operative to extract more information. On October 10, the day *The New*

*Yorker* published my story about Weinstein, Filip reached out to McGowan in an e-mail. "Hi Love," she wrote. "How are you feeling? . . . Just wanted to tell you how brave I think you are." She signed off with an "xx." Filip e-mailed McGowan as recently as October 23.

In fact, "Diana Filip" was an alias for a former officer in the Israeli Defense Forces who originally hailed from Eastern Europe and was working for Black Cube, according to three individuals with knowledge of the situation. When I sent McGowan photos of the Black Cube agent, she recognized her instantly. "Oh my God," she wrote back. "Reuben Capital. Diana Filip. No fucking way."

Ben Wallace, a reporter at *New York* who was pursuing a story on Weinstein, said that the same woman met with him twice last fall. She identified herself only as Anna and suggested that she had an allegation against Weinstein. When I presented Wallace with the same photographs of Black Cube's undercover operative, Wallace recalled her vividly. "That's her," he said. Like McGowan, Wallace said that the woman had what he assumed to be a German accent, as well as a UK cell-phone number. Wallace told me that Anna first contacted him on October 28, 2016, when he had been working on the Weinstein story for about a month and a half. Anna declined to disclose who had given her Wallace's information. Over the course of the two meetings, Wallace grew increasingly suspicious of her motives. Anna seemed to be pushing him for information, he recalled, "about the status and scope of my inquiry, and about who I might be talking to, without giving me any meaningful help or information." During their second meeting, Anna requested that they sit close together, leading Wallace to suspect that she might be recording the exchange. When she recounted her experiences with Weinstein, Wallace said, "it seemed like soap-opera acting." Wallace wasn't the only journalist the woman contacted. In addition to her e-mails to me, Filip also e-mailed Jodi Kantor, of the *Times*, according to sources involved in the effort.

The UK cell-phone numbers that Filip provided to Wallace and McGowan have been disconnected. Calls to Reuben Capital Partners' number in London went unanswered. As recently as Friday, the firm had a bare-bones website, with stock photos and generic text passages about asset management and an initiative called Women in Focus. The site, which has now been taken down, listed an address near Piccadilly Circus, operated by a company specializing in shared office space. That company said that it had never heard of Reuben Capital Partners. Two sources with knowledge of Weinstein's work with Black Cube said that the firm creates fictional companies to provide cover for its operatives and that Filip's firm was one of them.

Black Cube declined to comment on the specifics of any work it did for Weinstein. The agency said in a statement, "It is Black Cube's policy to never discuss its clients with any third party, and to never confirm or deny any speculation made with regard to the company's work. Black Cube supports the work of many leading law firms around the world, especially in the US, gathering evidence for complex legal processes, involving commercial disputes, among them uncovering negative campaigns. . . . It should be highlighted that Black Cube applies high moral standards to its work, and operates in full compliance with the law of any jurisdiction in which it operates—strictly following the guidance and legal opinions provided by leading law firms from around the world." The contract with the firm also specified that all of its work would be obtained "by legal means and in compliance with all applicable laws and regulations."

.　　.　　.

Last fall, Weinstein began mentioning Black Cube by name in conversations with his associates and attorneys. The agency had made a name for itself digging up information for companies in Israel, Europe, and the United States that led to successful legal judgments against business rivals. But the firm has also faced legal questions about its employees' use of fake identities and other tactics. Last year, two of its investigators were arrested in Romania on hacking charges. In the end, the company reached an agreement with the Romanian authorities, under which the operatives admitted to hacking and were released. Two sources familiar with the agency defended its decision to work for Weinstein, saying that they originally believed that the assignment focused on his business rivals. But even the earliest lists of names that Weinstein provided to Black Cube included actresses and journalists.

On October 28, 2016, Boies's law firm, Boies Schiller Flexner, wired to Black Cube the first hundred thousand dollars, toward what would ultimately be a six-hundred-thousand-dollar invoice. (The documents do not make clear how much of the invoice was paid.) The law firm and Black Cube signed a contract that month and several others later. One, dated July 11, 2017, and bearing Boies's signature, states that the project's "primary objectives" are to "provide intelligence which will help the Client's efforts to completely stop the publication of a new negative article in a leading NY newspaper" and to "obtain additional content of a book which currently being written and includes harmful negative information on and about the Client," who is identified as Weinstein in multiple documents. (In one e-mail, a Black Cube executive asks lawyers retained by the agency to refer to Weinstein as "the end client" or "Mr. X," noting that referring to him by name "will make him extremely angry.") The article mentioned in the contract was, according to three sources, the story that ultimately ran in the *Times* on October 5. The book was *Brave*, a memoir by McGowan, scheduled for publication by HarperCollins in January. The documents show that, in the end, the agency delivered to Weinstein more than a hundred pages of transcripts and descriptions of the book, based on tens of hours of recorded conversations between McGowan and the female private investigator.

Weinstein's spokesperson, Hofmeister, called "the assertion that Mr. Weinstein secured any portion of a book . . . false and among the many inaccuracies and wild conspiracy theories promoted in this article."

The July agreement included several "success fees" if Black Cube met its goals. The firm would receive an additional three hundred thousand dollars if the agency "provides intelligence which will directly contribute to the efforts to completely stop the Article from being published at all in any shape or form." Black Cube would also be paid fifty thousand dollars if it secured "the other half" of McGowan's book "in readable book and legally admissible format."

The contracts also show some of the techniques that Black Cube employs. The agency promised "a dedicated team of expert intelligence officers that will operate in the USA and any other necessary country," including a project manager, intelligence analysts, linguists, and "Avatar Operators" specifically hired to create fake identities on social media, as well as "operations experts with extensive experience in social engineering." The agency also said that it would provide "a full time agent by the name of 'Anna' (hereinafter 'the Agent'), who will be based in New York and Los Angeles as per the Client's instructions and who will be available full time to assist the Client and his attorneys for the next four months." Four sources with knowledge of Weinstein's work with Black Cube confirmed that this was the same woman who met with McGowan and Wallace.

Black Cube also agreed to hire "an investigative journalist, as per the Client request," who would be required to conduct ten interviews a month for four months and be paid forty thousand dollars. Black Cube agreed to "promptly report to the Client the results of such interviews by the Journalist."

In January, 2017, a freelance journalist called McGowan and had a lengthy conversation with her that he recorded without telling her; he subsequently communicated with Black Cube about the interviews, though he denied he was reporting back to them in a formal capacity. He contacted at least two other women with allegations against Weinstein, including the actress Annabella Sciorra, who later went public in *The New Yorker* with a rape allegation against Weinstein. Sciorra, whom he called in August, said that she found the conversation suspicious and got off the phone as quickly as possible. "It struck me as B.S.," she told me. "And it scared me that Harvey was testing to see if I would talk." The freelancer also placed calls to Wallace, the *New York* reporter, and to me.

Two sources close to the effort and several documents show that the same freelancer received contact information for actresses, journalists, and business rivals of Weinstein from Black Cube, and that the agency ultimately passed summaries of those interviews to Weinstein's lawyers. When contacted about his role, the freelancer, who spoke on condition of anonymity, said that he had been working on his own story about Weinstein, using contact information fed to him by Black Cube. The freelancer said that he reached out to other reporters, one of whom used material from his interviews, in the hopes of helping to expose Weinstein. He denied that he was paid by Black Cube or Weinstein.

Weinstein also enlisted other journalists to uncover information that he could use to undermine women with allegations. A December, 2016, e-mail exchange between Weinstein and Dylan Howard, the chief content officer of American Media Inc., which publishes the *National Enquirer*, shows that Howard shared with Weinstein material obtained by one of his reporters, as part of an effort to help Weinstein disprove McGowan's allegation of rape. In one e-mail, Howard sent Weinstein a list of contacts. "Let's discuss next steps on each," he wrote. After Weinstein thanked him, Howard described a call that one of his reporters made to Elizabeth Avellan, the ex-wife of the director Robert Rodriguez, whom Rodriguez left to have a relationship with McGowan.

Avellan told me that she remembered the interview. Howard's reporter "kept calling and calling and calling," she said, and also contacted others close to her. Avellan finally called back, because "I was afraid people might start calling my kids." In a long phone call, the reporter pressed her for unflattering statements about McGowan. She insisted that the call be off the record, and the reporter agreed. The reporter recorded the call, and subsequently passed the audio to Howard.

In subsequent e-mails to Weinstein, Howard said, "I have something AMAZING . . . eventually she laid into Rose pretty hard." Weinstein replied, "This is the killer. Especially if my fingerprints r not on this." Howard then reassured Weinstein, "They are not. And the conversation . . . is RECORDED." The next day, Howard added, in another e-mail, "Audio file to follow." (Howard denied sending the audio to Weinstein.) Avellan told me that she would not have agreed to coöperate in efforts to discredit McGowan. "I don't want to shame people," she said. "I wasn't interested. Women should stand together."

In a statement, Howard said that, in addition to his role as the chief content officer at American Media Inc., the *National Enquirer's* publisher, he oversaw a television-production agreement with Weinstein, which has since been terminated. He said that, at the time of the e-mails, "absent a corporate decision to terminate the agreement with The Weinstein Company, I had an obligation to protect AMI's interests by seeking out—but not publishing—truthful information about people who Mr. Weinstein insisted were making false claims against him. To the extent I provided 'off the record' information to Mr. Weinstein about one of his accusers—at a time when Mr. Weinstein was denying any harassment of any woman—it was information which I would never have allowed AMI to publish on the internet or in its magazines." Although at least one of Howard's reporters made calls related to Weinstein's investigations, Howard insisted that he strictly divided his work with Weinstein from his work as a journalist. "I always separated those two roles carefully and completely—and resisted Mr. Weinstein's repeated efforts to have AMI titles publish favorable stories about him or negative articles about his accusers," Howard said. An A.M.I. representative noted that, at the time, Weinstein insisted that the encounter was consensual, and that the allegations were untrue.

Hofmeister, Weinstein's spokesperson, added, "In regard to Mr. Howard, he has served as the point person for American Media's long-standing business relationship with The Weinstein Company. Earlier this year, Mr. Weinstein gave Mr. Howard a news tip that Mr. Howard agreed might make a good story. Mr. Howard pursued the tip and followed up with Mr. Weinstein as a courtesy, but declined to publish any story."

.        .        .

Weinstein's relationship with Kroll, one of the other agencies he contracted with, dates back years. After Ambra Battilana Gutierrez, an Italian model, accused Weinstein of sexually assaulting her, in 2015, she reached a settlement with Weinstein that required her to surrender all her personal devices to Kroll, so that they could be wiped of evidence of a conversation in which Weinstein admitted to groping her. A recording of that exchange, captured during a police sting operation, was released by *The New Yorker* last month.

During the more recent effort to shut down emerging stories, Kroll again played a central role. E-mails show that Dan Karson, the chairman of Kroll Americas' Investigations and Disputes practice, contacted Weinstein at his personal e-mail address with information about women with allegations. In one October, 2016, e-mail, Karson sent Weinstein eleven photographs of McGowan and Weinstein together at different events in the years after he allegedly assaulted her. Three hours later, Weinstein forwarded Karson's e-mail to Boies and Weinstein's criminal-defense attorney, Blair Berk, and told them to "scroll thru the extra ones." The next morning, Berk replied that one photo, which showed McGowan warmly talking with Weinstein, "is the money shot."

Berk defended her actions. "Any criminal-defense lawyer worth her salt would investigate unproven allegations to determine if they are credible," she said. "And it would be dereliction of duty not to conduct a public-records search for photographs of the accuser embracing the accused taken after the time of the alleged assault."

Another firm, the Los Angeles-based *PSOPS*, and its lead private investigator, Jack Palladino, as well as another one of its investigators, Sara Ness, produced detailed profiles of various individuals in the saga, sometimes of a personal nature, which included information that could be used to undermine their credibility. One report on McGowan that Ness sent to Weinstein last December ran for more than a hundred pages and featured McGowan's address and other personal information, along with sections labelled "Lies/Exaggerations/Contradictions," "Hypocrisy," and "Potential Negative Character Wits," an apparent abbreviation of "witnesses." One subhead read "Past Lovers." The section included details of acrimonious breakups, mentioning Avellan, and discussed Facebook posts expressing negative sentiments about McGowan. (Palladino and Ness did not respond to multiple requests for comment.)

Other firms were also involved in assembling such profiles, including ones that focussed on factors that, in theory, might make women likely to speak out against sexual abuse. One of the other firm's profiles was of Rosanna Arquette, an actress who later, in *The New Yorker*, accused Weinstein of sexual harassment. The file mentions Arquette's friendship with McGowan, social-media posts about sexual abuse, and the fact that a family member had gone public with an allegation that she had been molested as a child.

All of the security firms that Weinstein hired were also involved in trying to ferret out reporters' sources and probe their backgrounds. Wallace, the reporter for *New York*, said that he was suspicious when he received the call from the Black Cube operative using the pseudonym Anna, because Weinstein had already requested a meeting with Wallace; Adam Moss, the editor-in-chief of *New York*; David Boies; and a representative from Kroll. The intention, Wallace assumed, was to "come in with dossiers slagging various women and me." Moss declined the meeting.

In a series of e-mails sent in the weeks before Wallace received the call from Anna, Dan Karson, of Kroll, sent Weinstein preliminary background information on Wallace and Moss. "No adverse information about Adam Moss so far (no libel/defamation cases, no court records or judgments/liens/UCC, etc.)," Karson wrote in one e-mail. Two months later, Palladino, the *PSOPS* investigator, sent Weinstein a detailed profile of Moss. It stated, "Our research did not yield any promising avenues for the personal impeachment of Moss."

Similar e-mail exchanges occurred regarding Wallace. Kroll sent Weinstein a list of public criticisms of Wallace's previous reporting and a detailed description of a U.K. libel suit filed in response to a book he wrote, in 2008, about the rare-wine market. *PSOPS* also profiled Wallace's ex-wife, noting that she "might prove relevant to considerations of our response strategy when Wallace's article on our client is finally published."

In January, 2017, Wallace, Moss, and other editors at *New York* decided to shelve the story. Wallace had assembled a detailed list of women with allegations, but he lacked on-the-record statements from any victims. Wallace said that the decision not to run a story was made for legitimate journalistic reasons. Nevertheless, he said, "There was much more static and distraction than I've encountered on any other story."

Other reporters were investigated as well. In April, 2017, Ness, of *PSOPS*, sent Weinstein an assessment of my own interactions with "persons of interest"—a list largely consisting of women with allegations, or those connected to them. Later, *PSOPS* submitted a detailed report focussing jointly on me and Jodi Kantor, of the *Times*. Some of the observations in the report are mundane. "Kantor is NOT following Ronan Farrow," it notes, referring to relationships on Twitter. At other times, the report reflects a detailed effort to uncover sources. One individual I interviewed, and another whom Kantor spoke to in her separate endeavor, were listed as having reported the details of the conversations back to Weinstein.

For years, Weinstein had used private security agencies to investigate reporters. In the early aughts, as the journalist David Carr, who died in 2015, worked on a report on Weinstein for *New York*, Weinstein assigned Kroll to dig up unflattering information about him, according to a source close to the matter. Carr's widow, Jill Rooney Carr, told me that her husband believed that he was being surveilled, though he didn't know by whom. "He thought he was being followed," she recalled. In one document, Weinstein's investigators wrote that Carr had learned of McGowan's allegation in the course of his reporting. Carr "wrote a number of critical/unflattering articles about HW over the years," the document says, "none of which touched on the topic of women (due to fear of HW's retaliation, according to HW)."

·　　·　　·

Weinstein's relationships with the private investigators were often routed through law firms that represented him. This is designed to place investigative materials under the aegis of attorney-client privilege, which can prevent the disclosure of communications, even in court.

David Boies, who was involved in the relationships with Black Cube and *PSOPS*, was initially reluctant to speak with *The New Yorker*, out of concern that he might be "misinterpreted either as trying to deny or minimize mistakes that were made, or as agreeing with criticisms that I don't agree are valid."

But Boies did feel the need to respond to what he considered "fair and important" questions about his hiring of investigators. He said that he did not consider the contractual provisions directing Black Cube to stop the publication of the *Times* story to be a conflict of interest, because his firm was also representing the newspaper in a libel suit. From the beginning, he said, he advised Weinstein "that the story could not be stopped by threats or influence and that the only way the story could be stopped was by convincing the *Times* that there was no rape." Boies told me he never pressured any news outlet. "If evidence could be uncovered to convince the *Times* the charges should not be published, I did not believe, and do not believe, that that would be averse to the *Times*' interest."

He conceded, however, that any efforts to profile and undermine reporters, at the *Times* and elsewhere, were problematic. "In general, I don't think it's appropriate to try to pressure reporters," he said. "If that did happen here, it would not have been appropriate."

Although the agencies paid by his firm focussed on many women with allegations, Boies said that he had only been aware of their work related to McGowan, whose allegations Weinstein denied. "Given what was known at the time, I thought it was entirely appropriate to investigate precisely what he was accused of doing, and to investigate whether there were facts that would rebut those accusations," he said.

Of his representation of Weinstein in general, he said, "I don't believe former lawyers should criticize former clients." But he expressed regrets. "Although he vigorously denies using physical force, Mr. Weinstein has himself recognized that his contact with women was indefensible and incredibly hurtful," Boies told me. "In retrospect, I knew enough in 2015 that I believe I should have been on notice of a problem, and done something about it. I don't know what, if anything, happened after 2015, but to the extent it did, I think I have some responsibility. I also think that if people had taken action earlier it would have been better for Mr. Weinstein."

•        •        •

Weinstein also drafted individuals around him into his efforts—willingly and not. In December, 2016, Weinstein asked the actress Asia Argento, who ultimately went public in *The New Yorker* with her allegation of rape against Weinstein, to meet in Italy with his private investigators to give testimony on his behalf. Argento, who felt pressure to say yes, declined after her partner, the chef and television personality Anthony Bourdain, advised her to avoid the meeting. Another actress, who declined to be named in this story, said that Weinstein asked her to meet with reporters to extract information about other sources.

Weinstein also enlisted two former employees, Denise Doyle Chambers and Pamela Lubell, in what turned out to be an effort to identify and call people who might speak to the press about their own, or others', allegations. Weinstein secretly shared the lists they compiled with Black Cube.

Hofmeister, speaking on Weinstein's behalf, said, "Any 'lists' that were prepared included names of former employees and others who were relevant to the research and preparation of a book about Miramax. Former employees conducting interviews for the book reported receiving unwanted contacts from the media."

Doyle Chambers declined an interview request. But Lubell, a producer who worked for Weinstein at Miramax decades ago, told me that she was manipulated into participating. In July, 2017, Lubell visited Weinstein's offices to pitch him on an app that she was developing. In the middle of the meeting, Weinstein asked Lubell if they could have a private conversation in his office. Lubell told me that a lawyer working with Weinstein was already there, along with Doyle Chambers. Weinstein asked if Lubell and Doyle Chambers could write a "fun book on the old times, the heyday, of Miramax." "Pam," she recalled him saying, "write down all the employees that you know, and can you get in touch with them?"

A few weeks later, in August, after they had made the list, Weinstein "called us back into the office," Lubell recalled. "And he said, 'You know what, we're going to put a hold on the book.'" He asked Doyle Chambers and Lubell to "call some of your friends from the list and see if they got calls from the press." In early September, Weinstein summoned Lubell and Doyle Chambers to his office and asked them to start making calls to people connected to several actresses. "It got kind of intense," Lubell recalled. "We didn't know these people, and all of a sudden this was something very different from what we signed up for." Several of the targeted women said that they felt the calls they received from Lubell and Doyle Chambers, and from Weinstein himself, were frightening.

Lubell told me that hours before the first *Times* story broke, on October 5th, Weinstein summoned her, Doyle Chambers, and others on his team, including the attorney Lisa Bloom, who has since resigned, to his office. "He was in a panic," Lubell recalled. "He starts screaming, 'Get so-and-so on the phone.'" After the story was published, the team scrambled to respond to it. Bloom and others pored over pictures that, like the ones featured in the Kroll e-mails, showed ongoing contact between Weinstein and women who made allegations. "He was screaming at us, 'Send these to the board members,'" Lubell recalled. She e-mailed the photographs to the board ahead of the crisis meeting at which Weinstein's position at his company began unravelling.

Since the allegations against Weinstein became public, Lubell hasn't slept well. She told me that, although she knew that Weinstein "was a bully and a cheater," she "never thought he was a predator." Lubell has wondered if she should have known more, sooner.

After a year of concerted effort, Weinstein's campaign to track and silence his accusers crumbled. Several of the women targeted, however, said that Weinstein's use of private security agencies deepened the challenge of speaking out. "It scared me," Sciorra said, "because I knew what it meant to be threatened by Harvey. I was in fear of him finding me." McGowan said that the agencies and law firms enabled Weinstein's behavior. As she was targeted, she felt a growing sense of paranoia. "It was like the movie 'Gaslight,'" she told me. "Everyone lied to me all the time." For the past year, she said, "I've lived inside a mirrored fun house."

## New York

*On October 5, 2017, the* New York Times *published "Harvey Weinstein Paid Off Sexual Harassment Accusers for Decades," by Jodi Kantor and Megan Twohey. Five days later* The New Yorker *published "Abuses of Power," by Ronan Farrow. Writing for New York Media's web vertical* The Cut *soon after, Rebecca Traister explained what happened next—anger, rage, sometimes confusion—as more stories about more men appeared. Yet, Traister wrote, "it's possible that we're missing the bigger picture altogether: this is not, at its heart, about sex at all—or at least not wholly. What it's really about is work, and women's equality in the workplace." Said the Ellie judges: "In a year when issues of gender and sexuality dominated the national conversation, no one shaped that discussion more than Traister."*

Rebecca Traister

# Why the Harvey Weinstein Sexual-Harassment Allegations Didn't Come Out Until Now *and* Your Reckoning. And Mine. *and* This Moment Isn't (Just) About Sex. It's Really About Work

## Why the Harvey Weinstein Sexual-Harassment Allegations Didn't Come Out Until Now

I have been having conversations about Harvey Weinstein's history of sexual harassment for more than seventeen years.

The conversations started when I was a young editorial assistant at *Talk*, the magazine he financed, in 1999; back then it was with young people, friends—women and men—who worked for him, at Miramax, and told tales of hotel rooms, nudity, suggestion, and coercion and then of whispered payoffs, former assistants who seemingly dropped off the face of the Earth. Reading the story published on Thursday in the *New York Times* about claims against Weinstein, I was pole-axed by the familiarity of the recollection of Karen Katz, a friend and colleague of one of the young Miramax employees who was propositioned by Weinstein, who said, "We were so young at the time . . . We did not understand how wrong it was or how Laura should deal with it."

In my midtwenties, I became a reporter and fact checker at the New York *Observer*, and part of my beat was covering the film business in New York. The night before the 2000 election, I was working on a story—perhaps my first seriously reported story—about *O*, the violent reimagining of *Othello* that Miramax's Dimension division was then sitting on, perhaps out of deference to the cringey clean-media message of the Al Gore–Joe Lieberman campaign, which Weinstein was publicly supporting; already there was talk of Weinstein's ambitions in Democratic politics. After Weinstein failed to respond to my calls for comment, I was sent, on Election Eve 2000, to cover a book party he was hosting, along with my colleague Andrew Goldman. Weinstein didn't like my question about *O*, there was an altercation; though the recording has alas been lost to time, I recall that he called me a cunt and declared that he was glad he was the "fucking sheriff of this fucking lawless piece-of-shit town." When my colleague Andrew (who was also then my boyfriend) intervened, first calming him down and then trying to extract an apology, Weinstein went nuclear, pushing Andrew down a set of steps inside the Tribeca Grand—knocking him over with such force that his tape recorder hit a woman, who suffered long-term injury—and dragging Andrew, in a headlock, onto Sixth Avenue.

Such was the power of Harvey Weinstein in 2000 that despite the dozens of camera flashes that went off on that sidewalk that night, capturing the sight of an enormously famous film executive trying to pound in the head of a young newspaper reporter, I have never once seen a photo. Back then, Harvey could spin—or suppress—anything; there were so many journalists on his payroll, working as consultants on movie projects, or as screenwriters or for his magazine.

After that incident, which was reported as a case of an aggressive reporter barging into a party she wasn't invited to and asking impertinent questions, I began to hear from lots of other people, now other reporters, who were working, often for years, to nail down the story of Harvey's sexual abuses, and thought that I, as someone who'd been a firsthand witness to his verbal and physical ones, could help.

I couldn't, except by passing on whatever I'd heard, helping to make sense of timelines and rumored accounts. I never really thought of trying to write the story myself. Back then, I didn't write about feminism; there *wasn't* a lot of journalism about feminism. All the stories people were trying to write about Harvey were film stories: profiles, exposés of his loutish behavior perhaps, examinations of the outsize ways he exercised his considerable influence, the manner in which his reputation so closely mirrored that of his monstrous but legendary forebears—the Louis B. Mayers of old Hollywood.

His behavior toward women was obviously understood to be a bad thing—this was a decade after Anita Hill's accusations against Clarence Thomas had helped the country to understand that sexual harassment was not just a quirk of the modern workplace but a professional and economic crime committed against women as a class. But the story felt fuzzier, harder to tell about

Harvey: the notion of the "casting couch" still had an almost romantic reverberation, and those who had encountered Weinstein often spoke of the conviction that they would never be believed.

But another reason that I never considered trying to report the story myself, even, truly, in the years after I did start writing about gender and power as my beat, was because it felt impossible. Sisyphean. I remembered what it was like to have the full force of Harvey Weinstein—back then a mountainous man—screaming vulgarities at me, his spit hitting my face. I had watched him haul my friend into the street and try to hurt him. That kind of force, that kind of power? I could not have won against that.

And indeed, no one could, for a really, really long time. The best reporters out there tried, for years, perhaps most memorably David Carr, for this magazine. But Weinstein didn't just exert physical power. He also employed legal and professional and economic power. He supposedly had every employee sign elaborate, binding nondisclosure agreements. He gave jobs to people who might otherwise work to bring him down and gave gobs of money to other powerful people, who knows how much, but perhaps just enough to keep them from listening to ugly rumors that might circulate among young people, among less powerful people. For decades, the reporters who tried to tell the story of Harvey Weinstein butted up against the same wall of sheer force and immovable power that was leveraged against those ambitious actors, the vulnerable assistants, the executives whose careers, salaries, and reputations were in his hands.

The accounts in the remarkable *New York Times* piece offer evidence of the ways in which power imbalance is so key to sexual assault, and in the case of Weinstein, to the ability to keep it from coming to light for so very long. The stories of hotel-room meetings, requests for massages, professional interactions undertaken naked—they all speak of the abusive thrill gained not from sex but from the imposition of your will on someone who has no ability to resist or defend themselves from you, an exertion of power on the powerless.

Something has changed. Sources have gone on the record. It's worth it to wonder why. Perhaps because of shifts in how we understand these kinds of abuses. Recent years have seen scores of women, finding strength and some kind of power in numbers, come forward and tell their stories about Bill Cosby, Roger Ailes, Bill O'Reilly, Donald Trump. In all of those cases, as in this case, the history of allegations has been an almost wholly open secret, sometimes even having been reported in major outlets, and yet somehow ignored, allowed to pass, unconsidered.

But now our consciousness has been raised. And while repercussions have been mixed—Cosby is set to go to trial again in April; Ailes and O'Reilly lost powerful jobs but walked away with millions; Donald Trump was elected president—it is in part the fact that we have had a public conversation that has helped those for whom telling their stories seemed impossible for so long suddenly feel that speaking out might be within their reach.

That is surely one part of the story. But I don't think it's the whole story. I think there is more. I saw Harvey Weinstein earlier this year, at a Planned Parenthood celebration. I was struck by the fact that he was there—as the *Times* details, he has remained a donor to and supporter of liberal organizations, women's-rights organizations, and Democrats, including Hillary Clinton and Barack Obama, whose daughter recently worked as his intern. But I was also struck by his physical diminishment; he seemed small and frail, and, when I caught sight of him in May, he appeared to be walking with a cane. He has also lost power in the movie industry, is no longer the titan of independent film, the indie mogul who could make or break an actor's Oscar chances.

He clearly hasn't stopped working to protect himself. The attorney Lisa Bloom, whose business has recently been the representation of women lodging harassment and assault claims against powerful men, is a member of his legal team. I cannot imagine it coincidental that this spring he bought the rights to make her book about Trayvon Martin into a miniseries. (His legal team also includes David Boies and Charles Harder, the lawyer who successfully sued Gawker on behalf of Hulk Hogan. Anita Dunn, who worked in the Obama White House, reportedly gave Weinstein pro bono PR advice in recent weeks; Weinstein has also, supposedly, reached out to the Clintons' crisis PR honcho Lanny Davis.) It seems important that this story was reported nonetheless, and I suspect coming weeks will include more stories about Weinstein that have been bottled up for decades.

But it's hard not to consider the circumstances, the years, the risks, and the work put in by so many to convince so many others to be able to come forward, and the fact that perhaps only a weakening of Weinstein's grip permitted his expensive self-crafted armor to finally be pierced.

# Your Reckoning. And Mine.

The anger window is open. For decades, centuries, it was closed: Something bad happened to you, you shoved it down, you maybe told someone but probably didn't get much satisfaction—emotional or practical—from the confession. Maybe you even got blowback. No one really cared, and certainly no one was going to do anything about it.

But for the past six weeks, since reports of one movie producer's serial predation blew a Harvey-size hole in the news cycle, there is suddenly space, air, for women to talk. To yell, in fact. To make dangerous lists and call reporters and text with their friends about everything that's been suppressed.

This is not feminism as we've known it in its contemporary rebirth—packaged into think pieces or nonprofits or Eve Ensler plays or Beyoncé VMA performances. That stuff has its place and is necessary in its own way. This is different. This is seventies-style, organic, mass, radical rage, exploding in unpredictable directions. It is loud, thanks to the human megaphone that is social media and the "whisper networks" that are now less about speaking sotto voce than about frantically typed texts and all-caps group chats.

Really powerful white men are losing jobs—that *never* happens. Women (and some men) are breaking their silence and telling painful and intimate stories to reporters, who in turn are putting them on the front pages of major newspapers.

It's wild and not entirely fun. Because the stories are awful, yes. And because the conditions that created this perfect storm of female rage—the suffocating ubiquity of harassment and abuse; the election of a multiply accused predator who now controls the courts and the agencies that are supposed to protect us from criminal and discriminatory acts—are so grim.

But it's also harrowing because it's confusing; because the wrath may be fierce, but it is not uncomplicated. In the shock of the house lights having been suddenly brought up—of being forced to stare at the ugly scaffolding on which so much of our professional lives has been built—we've had scant chance to parse what exactly is inflaming us and who. It's our tormentors, obviously, but sometimes also our friends, our mentors, *ourselves*.

Since the reports of Weinstein's malevolence began to gush, I've received somewhere between five and twenty e-mails every day from women wanting to tell me their experiences: of being groped or leered at or rubbed up against in their workplaces. They tell me about all kinds of men—actors and publishers; judges and philanthropists; store managers and social-justice advocates; my own colleagues, past and present—who've hurt them or someone they know. It happened yesterday or two years ago or twenty. Few can speak on the record, but they all want to recount how the events changed their lives, shaped their careers; some wish to confess their guilt for not reporting the behavior and thus endangering those who came after them. There are also women who *do* want to go on the record, women who've summoned armies of brave colleagues ready to finally out their repellent bosses. To many of them I must say that their guy isn't well known enough, that the stories are now so plentiful that offenders must meet a certain bar of notoriety or power or villainy before they're considered newsworthy.

This is part of what makes me, and them, angry: this replication of hierarchies—hierarchies of harm and privilege—even now. "It's a 'seeing the matrix' moment," says one woman whom I didn't know personally before last week, some of whose deepest secrets and sharpest fears and most animating furies I'm now privy to. "It's an absolutely bizarre thing to go through, and it's fucking exhausting and horrible, and I hate it. And I'm glad. I'm so glad we're doing it. And I'm in hell."

Part of the challenge, for me, has been in my exchanges with men—the friends and colleagues self-aware enough to be uneasy, to know they're on a list somewhere or imagine that they might be. They text and call, not quite saying why, but leaving no doubt: They once cheated with a colleague; they once made a pass they suspect was wrong; they aren't sure if they got consent that one time. Are they condemned? What is the nature and severity of their crime? The anxiety of this—how to speak to guys who seek feminist absolution but whom I suspect to be compromised—is real. Some of my friends have no patience for men's sudden penchant for introspection, but I'm a sucker; I feel for them. When they reach out, my impulse is to comfort. But reason—and a determination not to placate, not now—drives me to be direct, colder than usual: Yes, this is a problem. In fact, it's your problem. Seek to address it.

·　　　·　　　·

Then there are the men who are looking at the world with fresh eyes, who are startled by the unseemly parade of sexual molesters and manipulators—the cascading allegations against Louis C.K., the conservative former judge and Alabama Senate candidate Roy Moore, and so many more. These men have begun to understand my journalistic beat for the first time: They didn't know it was *this* bad. They didn't see how systemic, architectural, it was— how they were part of it even if they didn't paw anyone, didn't *rape* anyone. This faction includes my husband, a criminal-defense attorney who's definitely not ignorant of the pervasiveness of sexual assault yet reads the endless stream of reports with furrowed brow. "Who does this?" he asks. "Who *does* this?" Then one night, with genuine feeling: "How can you even want to have sex with me at this point?"

At elementary-school drop-off, a friend who's a theater director tells me he's been sorting through his own memories. "There's this one woman, and I did ask her out, but only after she'd auditioned and hadn't gotten the part. I wrote her, like I write to all actors who I don't cast, to explain why. And then in that e-mail, I asked if she wanted to go to a Holocaust puppet show with me. She said yes, and we went out a few times. This was probably 2004. Do you think that was bad?"

I laugh, put my hand on his arm, and tell him no, it doesn't sound bad, but in fact I don't know: Maybe it *was* bad or maybe it was human and they really liked each other. We are turning over incidents that don't fall into the categories that have been established—a spectrum that runs from Weinstein-level brutality to non-rapey but creepy massages to lurid-but-risible pickup lines—and wondering whether or how any of it relates to actual desire for another person.

Still, I'm half-frustrated by men who can't differentiate between harmless flirtation and harassment, because I believe that most women can. The other half of me is glad that these guys are doing this accounting, reflecting on the instances in which they wielded power. Maybe some didn't realize at the time that they were putting the objects of their attention at a disadvantage, but I must acknowledge that some, even my friends, surely did.

Women, of course, are doing our own accounting, attempting to classify moments from our pasts to gauge how they fit into the larger picture. *Sure, he DM-ed me late at night asking me what my sexual fantasies were, but he didn't masturbate against my leg and then threaten to kill me, as James Toback allegedly did; he didn't hire ex–Mossad agents to dig up dirt about my exes and my sex life, like Weinstein did.* Okay, but why can't we stop thinking about it? Why does it feel so closely related?

Which, again, isn't to suggest that we don't know the differences. We are not dumb. We knew, when we looked at the Shitty Media Men list circulated in October—an anonymously compiled Google document of unattributed and varied claims about some seventy-eight men in our business—that there were legal distinctions, and moral ones. There are the cheating dogs who proposition us, the artless boy-men who make fumbling passes over work lunches, the bosses who touch us against our will, the men who retaliate professionally if we dare reject them.

And yet the rage that many of us are feeling doesn't necessarily correspond with the severity of the trespass: Lots of us are on some level as incensed about the guy who looked down our shirt at a company retreat as we are about Weinstein, even if we can acknowledge that there's something nuts about that, a weird overreaction. Part of it is the decades we've spent being pressured to *under*react, our objections to the small stuff (and also to the big stuff!) bantered away, ignored, or attributed to our own lily-livered inability to cut it in the real world. Resentments accrete, mature into rage.

"I stuffed all my harassment memories in an emotional trash compactor because there are just so many," says my friend Amina Sow. "Now the trash compactor is broken, and everything is coming up." Sow said that among the things she's recalled over the past few weeks are an old boss in Washington "who definitely jerked off in the office and would make sure to let me see the porn on his computer. He has a bigger job now. And the man who pinned me to the wall in the copy room and told me I should be grateful he's paying attention to me because I'm a fat pig. I reported both those incidents, by the way, and nothing happened."

And that's before we get to the real mind-fuck: the recognition of how we've participated in this system.

Starting when she was twenty-eight, Deanna Zandt, an artist and activist, had a secret, consensual relationship with a boss in his midfifties who was a widely known sexual harasser of her coworkers. "It sounds so fucking stupid now," says forty-two-year-old Zandt, unspooling the mix of fear, self-doubt, and self-interest that kept her in the relationship. "I didn't know how to get away from him, because if he were just a complete douche-bag, I wouldn't be with someone like that. But he was also very charming and publicly very feminist, and he introduced me to people and did all these other things that were supportive." At the same time, "he was this known abuser, and I even defended him: 'Oh, he's just an old stoner hippie; he doesn't mean anything by it.' So I participated—and I saw other women get targeted by him."

Because I used to work at *The New Republic*, though not with Leon Wieseltier, who recently lost his post at a new magazine after the exposure of his decades as a harasser, I've heard from many friends and former colleagues who are pained about the situation. "He was, really, my champion," one woman told me. "All these things about him are true, but it is simultaneously true that if you were on his good side, you felt special—protected, cared for, like he believed in you and wanted you to succeed." In a profession where far too few women find that kind of support from powerful men, Wieseltier's mentorship felt like a prize.

But many of even his most conflicted former admirers admit that the stories about him—reportedly thanking women for wearing short skirts, kissing colleagues against their will, threatening to tell the rest of the company he was fucking a subordinate if she displeased him—have convinced them that sacking Wieseltier was the correct choice. They're sad for him, for his family, but he should not be in charge of women. It has left some of them reexamining how they excused his conduct, worked around it: how they were, in the parlance of Michelle Cottle, who wrote with nuance about Wieseltier, "game girls," and thus reaped the professional rewards. "I got so much from him intellectually and emotionally, but I wonder if part of it was because I was game," says one woman, "and what's the cost of that?"

Other women who played along with their bosses expressed a degree of shame, as well as pride. "Men have their fraternities and golf games to get ahead. Why shouldn't I have used the advantage of my sexuality to my benefit? God, what else was I supposed to do?" says one woman in her early fifties. Her attitude suggests something of a generational divide. On one side are women who came of age before Anita Hill's groundbreaking testimony against Clarence Thomas, who were perhaps raised to assume they'd encounter harassment and resolved to tough it out. To this contingent, younger women's complaints can sound hand-wringingly excessive: What did those girls expect? What they expected was the world they'd been assured had arrived: a postfeminist one, in which they were something close to equal, in which their career paths were no longer supposed to be determined by big, swinging dicks—real ones.

Then there are those who were never directly targeted, perhaps for reasons relating to aesthetic preferences or perhaps because they resisted. Several women have spoken to me with curiosity and concern about these colleagues, more than a few left to wither on the professional vine: What ever happened to them? Were their careers, their ambitions, irreparably damaged?

One woman, discussing a print journalist who harassed her in her early twenties, tells of an inverse dynamic: "Other female writers *weren't* getting harassed, as far as we knew, which meant that they were the serious writers. We were silly little girls, not deserving of being thought of as real journalists if we were singled out for this treatment." The slow-drip degradation, she says, led her to quit the profession. "He didn't grope me, and he didn't succeed in fucking me. But the way it made me feel—these insidious sexual advances you barely understand at that age, plus the constant professional undermining—it felt like you were never going to win, like you had no value."

The reason that handsy colleagues exist on the same plane as violent predators is that the harm done to women doesn't end with the original offense. It's also how we're evaluated based on our reactions to it. Do we smile or remain stone-faced, reciprocate or retreat, ignore or complain? What becomes of us hangs on what we choose.

Considering all of these angles, it's easy to conclude that this moment actually isn't radical enough because it's limited to sexual grievances. One sixty-year-old friend, who is single and in a precarious professional situation, says, "I'm burning with rage watching some assholes pose as good guys just because they never put their hands on a colleague's thigh, when I know for a fact they've run capable women out of workplaces in deeply gendered ways. I'm very frustrated, because I'm not in a position right now to spill some beans."

.        .        .

When I thought about my #metoo moments, I first recalled the restaurant manager who instructed me to keep my blouse unbuttoned as I served pizzas with fried eggs on top, about the manager at Bruegger's Bagels who'd rub his dick against my ass as he passed me setting out the cream cheeses in the morning. I've never had a job in which there wasn't a resident harasser, but in my postcollege life, I believed I'd stayed out of his crosshairs.

Perhaps, in the story I've told myself, it was because I was never wowed by powerful men, sensing on some visceral level that they were mostly full of shit. I gravitated toward female mentors instead. But even given my wariness of Important Men, as a young woman I could never truly believe that members of the opposite sex could be as cartoonishly grotesque as they sometimes were.

I once heard that a choking person reflexively leaves the room, embarrassed for others to see her gasping for breath. I have no idea if that's true, but it's how I've dealt with harassment. One time on the subway, the man next to me wound his hand under my thigh and between my legs, as I sat there debating whether or not to stand up or scream because *I didn't want to embarrass him on a full train.* That's why, when an important writer took me to coffee, offering to help me find a new job, and asked if I'd ever fantasized about fucking a married man, I simply laughed maniacally, as if he'd just made a *joke* about a sixty-five-year-old man who suggests to a twenty-five-year-old woman that she fuck him during a professional coffee.

At one of my early and formative workplaces, there was a textbook harasser: a high-on-the-food-chain, late-night direct-messager, a guy who stuck his hand down the dress of a colleague at a Christmas party, who propositioned and sometimes slept with female subordinates, who could be vindictive if turned down, and who'd undertake elaborate, misogynistic pranks, including sending provocative e-mails under another staffer's name. One of the preyed-upon women was older than I: talented, glamorous, and definitely not game. She recently recalled to me how she'd initially believed that she could ride it out but instead was undone by her bewilderment and humiliation at being played for a fool, for a *girl.* She quit after about a year at the company. I remember watching her treatment, appalled, almost disbelieving that something this outrageous could happen; yet I also remember not wanting to get too close to her, as if her status as quarry was catching. I also remember hearing company honchos say that they were well aware that we had a "walking lawsuit" in our midst. Even then, it struck me that the concern was for the potential tarring of the institution, not for the women who were suffering within it.

That harasser didn't sexually pursue me, but he did endeavor to undermine me. When I began dating a slightly older colleague, my direct supervisor (a married man on whom I had a fierce and never-requited crush, in part because it was safe; he was a model mentor) pulled me aside and confided that some other people at the office—i.e., the Harasser—were spreading rumors about how all of my work ideas were being fed to me by my boyfriend. In short, I was trying to sleep my way to the top.

Just a few years ago, I was working at another job. A new boss had been installed and wanted to hire the Harasser from my old workplace; I told him I would not work in the same office as that man. I was on maternity leave; he promised that the hire was only temporary, that the Harasser would be gone by the time I returned. And he was. But soon after I got back, the office's youngest women began to come to me confessing that in the few months the Harasser had been in place, he'd creeped them out and sent them off-color, middle-of-the-night DMs. I had made my stand on my own behalf—I would not work with that man!—but had failed to protect my less powerful colleagues.

So, no, I was never serially sexually harassed. But the stink got on me anyway. I was implicated. We all are, our professional contributions weighed on scales of fuckability and willingness to go along, to be good sports, to not be humorless scolds or office gorgons; our achievements chalked up to male affiliation—the boyfriend who supposedly supplies you with ideas or the manager who took you under his wing because he wanted to get inside your pants. We can rebuff the harasser; we can choose not to fuck the boss. But in a world where men hold inordinate power, we're still in bed with the guy.

There is another realm of anger here, arising from our knowledge that even the long-delayed chance to tell these repugnant
truths is built on several kinds of privilege. As others have
observed, it matters that the most public complaints so far have
come from relatively affluent white women in elite professions,
women who've worked closely enough with powerful white men
to be available for harassment. Racism and class discrimination
determine whose stories get picked up and which women are
readily believed.

That reality fogs some of the satisfaction we feel in watching
monstrous men lose their influence; we know that it's a drop in a
bottomless bucket. "Maybe we can get another two horrible people to have to step down or say they're sorry," one Democratic lawmaker told me, "but that helps only 20 people, and it's 20 million
who need things to change. Plus, you're a farmworker? A lady who
cleans offices? You're a prostitute or an immigrant? You're not
going to tell your story."

My sister-in-law has taught sexual-harassment prevention at
a national retail chain for nine years, and she notes that not only
do media and entertainment figures "have a bigger rooftop to
shout from," but many are freelancers, independent professionals with multiple employment options. The question she gets more
than any other, she says, is: "'What's going to happen to me if
I speak up? Because at my last job, nothing happened and I got
kind of punished.' Even if I tell them this place is different and
they should feel safe in lodging complaints, I don't think they
believe me."

Heather McLaughlin, a sociology professor at Oklahoma State
University, recently described in an interview with *Marketplace*
radio her study showing that about half of women in their late
twenties who've experienced harassment start looking for a new
job within two years of the incident. For those who've endured
more serious harassment, the figure is around 80 percent—and
many opt to leave their chosen professions altogether: to start

over, often in less male-dominated fields, which of course tend to be lower-paying. Ina Howard-Parker, a former book publicist who told me she was harassed at several progressive publishing houses, did just that. "I ended up deciding I'd rather work at Trader Joe's, where at least there's an HR department and rules of engagement at work." She now renovates houses in rural Pennsylvania.

Perhaps most galling, the current conflagration has laid bare a pattern of hiring, rewarding, and protecting men even after their transgressions have become known. That is the history, even the recent history, of America. As John Oliver has noted, the actor Casey Affleck—accused by two women of sexual harassment during filming (charges he denies)—will be giving out the Best Actress statue at the next Oscars. Bill Cosby received lifetime-achievement awards even after many of his alleged sexual assaults were made public. Reports suggest that members of the SEIU had formally complained about Fight for 15 architect and top labor organizer Scott Courtney for ages, but only now has he been ousted, along with a coterie of coworkers who covered for him.

In late October, as I wrote columns and tweeted about this wave of stories, I discovered that a male colleague had been hired here at *New York* despite documented claims of sexual harassment in a prior job. I'm angry not just because *New York* saw fit to bring him on. It's also the impossibility of the situation now: Should the guy (who doesn't supervise anyone) be let go, even though no one at *New York* has complained about him? Mostly I'm mad that he was chosen, at all, over at least two talented women who also were in the running.

The progressive journalist Matt Taibbi recently published a lengthy apology/explanation in which he despaired that the public reappraisal of the work that established him (in particular, a book about Russia that he now says is satirical and includes accounts of pushing women under the table for blow jobs, of telling them to lighten up when they object to such high jinks) is coinciding with the publication of his book about the death of Eric Garner. It's the kind of important book that he's been working toward writing for thirty years, he laments. Reading this, I couldn't help but think of all the women who've wanted to be writers for thirty years, who've yearned to make the world a better place by telling stories of injustice, but who haven't had the opportunity in part because so much journalistic space is occupied by men like Taibbi: dudes who in some measure gained their professional footholds by objectifying women—and not just in big, bad Russia. Take the piece Taibbi wrote in 2009 about athletes' wives. "The problem with the Smoking-Hot Skank as a permanent life choice," he opined, "is that she eventually gets bored and starts calling up reporters to share her Important Political Opinions." Taibbi may feel demoralized because the hilarious misogynistic stylings of his youth are now interfering with his grown-up career, but lots of women never even got their careers off the ground because the men in their fields saw them as Smoking-Hot Skanks whose claim to having a thought in their heads was no more than a punch line.

Men have not succeeded in spite of their noxious behavior or disregard for women; in many instances, they've succeeded because of it. They've been patted on the back and winked along—their retro-machismo hailed as funny or edgy—at the same places that are now dramatically jettisoning them. "The incredible hypocrisy of the boards, employers, institutions, publicists, brothers, friends who have been protecting powerful men/harassers/rapists for years and are now suddenly dropping them," says one of my colleagues at *New York*, livid and depressed. "What changed? Certainly not their beliefs about the behavior, right? Only their self-interest. On the one hand, I'm so happy they're finally being called out and facing consequences, but there's something so craven and superficially moralizing about the piling on by the selfsame people who were the snickerers and protectors."

Another woman, who works in politics, grimly observes, "Sure, good liberal thinkers will go to their sexual-harassment seminars and do all the things they should be doing. But ultimately, this is a cover-your-ass moment, not a change-the-rules moment."

As cries of alarm for the ladies pour from the mouths of men we know through experience or plausible rumor to be culprits themselves, it's easy to feel jaded and apprehensive: One day, my friends and I learn that a man who's been bemoaning the prevalence of harassment also stuck his hand up a colleague's skirt when he was her boss. "It feels like Allison Williams with the keys in *Get Out*," says my friend Irin Carmon. "Trust no one."

And yet, we are still the protectors on some level. Despite the talk of witch hunts and the satisfaction of finally seeing a few men penalized *in any way whatsoever* for their wrongdoing, most women I know feel torn about both the vague prospect and the observed reality of these men losing their jobs. We think of their feelings and their families, fret that the disclosure of their misdeeds might cost them future employment or even provoke them to harm themselves. But this is something else we're now being compelled to notice: how we're still conditioned to worry for the men, but somehow to not afford the same compassion for women—their families, their feelings, their future prospects—even in a reckoning that is supposed to be about them, about us.

The truth is, the risk of exposure that makes us feel anxious about the well-being of our male friends and colleagues—the risk of being named and never recovering—is one of the only things that could ever force change. Because without real, genuine penalties on the line, without generations of men fearing that if they abuse their power, if they treat women like shit, they'll be out of jobs, shamed, their families devastated—without that actual, electric, dangerous possibility: Nothing. Will. Change. Companies will simply start investing more in sexual-harassment insurance (a real thing!) and make payouts a line item in the budget, and we'll go back to talking about how men are just men.

Women I've spoken to already predict, drily, that even the men suffering the harshest consequences will be rehabilitated soon enough: that eighteen months from now, some ambitious *New York Times* editor will assign Leon Wieseltier an essay on identity politics, pitching it as counterintuitive, knowing it will get zillions of clicks; someone a decade from now will ask an eighty-two-year-old James Toback to direct an artsy realist movie about sexual assault, and it will be admired by some prominent person as trenchant and gutsy.

That's because this world is stacked in favor of men, yes, in a way that is so widely understood as to be boring, invisible, just life. But more deeply, this will happen because we can see in men—even in the bad ones—talent. We manage to look past their flaws and sexual violations to what value they bring to the world. It is the direct opposite, in many ways, of how we view women, whose successes can still be blithely attributed to the fact that the boss wanted to fuck them.

I struggled a lot internally about whether to name the Harasser at my former job. I decided not to, largely because I understand something about how things have turned out. In a rare outcome, I—along with some of the women he pestered—now have more power than he does. He is, as far as I know, short on work, not in charge of any young women. And so I decided, in consultation with former colleagues, not to identify him.

But here's a crucial reason he behaved so brazenly and badly for so long: He did not consider that the women he was torturing, much less the young woman who was mutely and nervously watching his performance (that would be me), might one day have greater power than he did. He didn't consider this because in a basic way, he did not think of us as his equals.

That makes me angry, too.

Letting all this out is undeniably exciting. Its power, to some extent, comes from the fact that it is almost terrifyingly out of control. Anything is possible, good or bad. And yes, there is satisfaction that for a month or so, it's like we've been living in the last ten minutes of an M. Night Shyamalan movie where the big twist is that women have been telling the truth all along.

Yet you can feel the backlash brewing. All it will take is one particularly lame allegation—and given the increasing depravity of the charges, the milder stuff looks lamer and lamer, no matter how awful the experience—to turn the tide from deep umbrage on behalf of women to pity for the poor, bullied men. Or one false accusation could do it. One man unfairly fired over a misinterpreted bump in the elevator could transform all of us women into the marauding aggressors, the men our hapless victims.

MSNBC's Mike Barnicle, himself once having been returned to power after a plagiarism scandal, has mourned publicly for the injury done to his friend and former colleague Mark Halperin, who got canned after being accused of pushing his penis against younger female subordinates: "He deserves to have what he did deplored," Barnicle declared. "But does he deserve to die? How many times can you kill a guy?"

A powerful white man losing a job is a death, and don't be surprised if women wind up punished for the spate of killings.

Many men will absorb the lessons of late 2017 to be not about the threat they've posed to women but about the threat that women pose to them. So there will be more—perhaps unconscious— hesitancy about hiring women, less eagerness to invite them to lunch or send them on work trips with men; men will be warier of mentoring women.

The only real solution may be one that is hardest to envision: equality. As Kristen Gwynne, who has worked for and with multiple harassers, says, "What bothers me is that this moment, as good as it is, prompts the question: What are women getting out of it? I lost time. It affected my self-esteem and my ability to produce work. So even if the people who did target me were punished, I still feel like I deserve some sort of compensation. I don't want them to release a public apology—I want them to send me a check. I wish we could storm the offices of these men, kick them out, and change the locks. We should demand something different of men that's not just them going to rehab. Put women in power."

At the risk of sounding Pollyannaish, I felt a glimmer of hope on that front after the recent election. For the first time in twelve long, hard months, it seemed that women might be on the verge of substantially increasing their political numbers. As the results rolled in, a story line emerged: Women's anger—at Trump and their own powerlessness—had been turned into electoral participation. A trans woman had prevailed over a white male lawmaker who authored a bathroom bill; a white man who insulted the Women's March back in January lost at the polls to a woman of color who was incensed at his show of disrespect. This wasn't just about retribution; it was about *replacement*.

I got a text from an old friend, a woman who'd worked on the Clinton campaign, who'd been there next to me on that shell-shocked night a year earlier. She said she was crying watching the latest results come in. "Maybe *we're* the backlash," she wrote.

# This Moment Isn't (Just) About Sex. It's Really About Work

It would be easy—a hard kind of easy—to understand the painful news happening all around us to be about sexual assault. After all, for weeks now, each day has brought fresh, lurid tales. And if our typically prurient American interests have led us to focus on the carnal nitty-gritty, the degree of sexual harm sustained, the vital questions of consent, that's fair enough; there has been, we are really absorbing for the first time, a hell of a lot of sexual damage done.

But in the midst of our great national calculus, in which we are determining what punishments fit which sexual crimes, it's possible that we're missing the bigger picture altogether: that this is not, at its heart, about sex at all—or at least not wholly. What it's really about is work and women's equality in the workplace and, more broadly, about the rot at the core of our power structures that makes it harder for women to do work because the whole thing is tipped toward men.

Sexual assault is one symptom of that imbalance, but it is not the only one. The can-opener here—the sharp point that pierced the aluminum that had sealed all this glop in—was indeed a story about a man, Harvey Weinstein, who committed professional harm that was also terrible sexual violence. And yes, many of the stories that have poured forth since—from James Toback's unsolicited ejaculations, to the playwright Israel Horovitz's alleged forced encounters with much younger women—have turned on nonconsensual contact, violent physical and sexual threat, the stuff of sex crimes. But even those tales—the ones about rape and assault—have been told by accusers who first interacted with these men in hopes of finding professional opportunity, who were looking not for flirtation or dates but for work. And they have reported—they have taken care to clearly lay out—the impact of the sexual violence not just on their emotional well-being, not just on their bodies, but on their careers, on their place in the public sphere.

Masha Gessen has written for *The New Yorker* with perspicacity in past weeks about how this moment risks becoming a sex panic, that one of the perils at hand—as we try to parse how butt groping or unsolicited kissing can exist on the same scale as violent rape—is a reversion to attitudes about women as sexually infantilized victims. Her concerns are valid, pressing. Yet I fear that the category collapse that makes Gessen anxious is being misunderstood in part because we are making a crucial category error. Because the thing that unites these varied revelations isn't necessarily sexual harm but *professional* harm and power abuse. These infractions and abuses are related, sometimes they are combined. But their impact, the reasons that they are sharing conversational and journalistic space during this reckoning, need to be clarified. We must regularly remind everyone paying attention that sexual harassment is a crime not simply on the grounds that it is a sexual violation but because it is a form of discrimination.

The term "sexual harassment" was used for the first time in public in 1975 by feminist scholar Lin Farley, when she testified at a hearing on women in the workplace before the New York City Human Rights Commission. Farley, who was teaching a class on women and work at Cornell University, coined the term after hearing about Carmita Wood. Wood was an administrative assistant at Cornell and quit her job after years of having been rubbed up against, groped, and kissed against her will by her boss. In 1977, an appeals court upheld decisions defining sexual harassment as sex discrimination, barred by Title VII of the Civil Rights Act. The Supreme Court upheld this view in 1986, when it ruled in favor of Mechelle Vinson, the assistant bank manager who was assaulted and raped by her boss in the bank's vaults and basements more than fifty times. Justice William Rehnquist wrote in the unanimous decision, "Without question, when a supervisor sexually harasses a subordinate because of the subordinate's sex, the supervisor discriminates on the basis of sex."

In other words, sexual harassment *may* entail behaviors that on their own would be criminal—assault or rape—but the legal definition of its harm is about the systemic disadvantaging of a gender in the public and professional sphere. And those structural disadvantages do not begin or end with the actual physical incursions—the groping, kissing, the rubbing up against. In fact, the gender inequity that creates the need for civil-rights protections is what has permitted so many of these trespasses to have occurred so frequently and for so long; gender inequity is what explains why women are *vulnerable* to harassment before they are even harassed; it explains why it's difficult for them to come forward with stories after they have been harassed, why they are often ignored when they do; it clarifies why so many women work with or maintain relationships with harassers and why their reactions to those harassers become key to how they themselves will be evaluated, professionally. Gender inequity is cyclical, all-encompassing.

We got to where we are because men, specifically white men, have been afforded a disproportionate share of power. That leaves women dependent on those men—for economic security, for work, for approval, for any share of power they might aspire to. Many of the women who have told their stories have explained that they did not do so before because they feared for their jobs. When women *did* complain, many were told that putting up with these behaviors was just part of working for the powerful men in question—"That's just Charlie being Charlie"; "That's just Harvey being Harvey." Remaining in the good graces of these men, because they were the bosses, the hosts, the rainmakers, the legislators, was the only way to preserve employment, and not just their own: Whole offices, often populated by female subordinates, are dependent on the steady power of the male bosses. When a prominent alleged abuser loses his job, he's not the only one whose salary stops; it often means that his employees, many of them women, also lose their paychecks, which are smaller to begin with. When men hold the most politically powerful posts, people who are less powerful than they are depend on them for advocacy and representation; complaints that imperil these leaders immediately imperil entire political parties and ideological agendas on both the left and right.

What's more, to cross powerful men is to jeopardize not just an individual job in an individual office; it's to risk far broader professional harm within whole professions where men hold sway, to cut yourself off from future opportunity. Lauren Greene, an ambitious congressional staffer who accused her former boss, the Republican congressman Blake Farenthold, of sexual harassment after he reportedly told another aide of his wet dreams about Greene and commented on her nipples, says that her complaints against her boss left her blackballed from politics, the profession she wanted to succeed in. She now works part time as an assistant to a home builder in North Carolina, babysitting on the side to make extra money.

These are the economics of sexual harassment but also, simply, of sexism.

It's worth considering why those Harvey allegations caught the public's attention where little else had. As hard as it is to stir concern over women's sexual autonomy, we *do* have a long history of wanting to protect (some) women's virtue. It is also true that we still rile ourselves up more about a woman's sexual violability than we do about her professional autonomy or rights to public and economic equality. Or at least we rile ourselves up if the woman in question is white and well-off: Two decades of settlements and accusations against the singer R. Kelly, who is alleged to have serially assaulted young black women, have fallen on deaf ears. (It is also worth noting that the professions that remain still unexamined in this reckoning are those populated by poorer women, disproportionately by women of color.)

One of the reasons that the story about former New York public-radio personality John Hockenberry was so arresting was because it made clear that there was a web of ill treatment, a connection between his comparatively mild but still discomfiting come-ons to colleagues and his ugly treatment of his cohosts. To one of them, Farai Chideya, he reportedly said, "You shouldn't stay here just as a 'diversity hire'"; another, Celeste Headlee, complained of how he'd interrupt and sabotage her on air. This man literally broadcast, on air, his disdain for the women—notably women of color—who were his professional peers. Headlee said she was told that her poor performance was to blame for Hockenberry's bullying behavior; she, like the two women who preceded her, eventually lost her post as cohost, while Hockenberry retained his position. All of that was public record. But none of it would have made it to print last week had there not *also* been an accusation of sexual impropriety.

We need to understand that the sexual harm is not always at the heart of a gendered power imbalance and is not always about the sexualized act itself. The case of *New York Times* reporter Glenn Thrush, who is accused of making unwanted advances outside of his workplace, against colleagues he did not directly supervise, would seem to give fodder to those worried about a sex panic: It raises the concern that bad passes, made between adults at a bar, might get condemned as sexual harassment in a way that assumes the women in question to be incapable of full sexual participation. But the damaging part of the story written in *Vox* about Thrush, by Laura McGann, one of his former colleagues at *Politico*, was, to my eye, not about the unwanted kissing, though that did sound bad. The worse part was McGann's recollection of how Thrush had later characterized their encounter to colleagues, making it sound as though she had pursued him and he had rejected her, as opposed to her view, which was the opposite. (Thrush denies that he disparaged McGann to colleagues.)

The damage wasn't exactly *sexual* in nature, at least not sexual in the physical sense; it was in how the woman in question might be viewed by her colleagues, based on the account of a man who was allegedly mispresenting the encounter. In this story, even Thrush's allegedly retouched tale isn't crime or sexual trespass; it's gossip. And surely women in offices are as likely to participate in hookup gossip as their male colleagues. But here's where double standards come into play: When men's sexual appetites are regarded as healthy, a sign of confidence and appeal, and women's sexual appetites are understood very often as trashy or desperate, all gossip is not equal. A man telling a story about how a female colleague came on to him and he put a stop to it has the potential to do damage to the woman's professional standing—rendering her as needy, undesirable, and showing professional bad judgment—while bolstering the man's, by framing him as responsible, mature, professional, and ultimately desirable to the opposite sex.

None of this is to say that Thrush should face consequences commensurate with, say Charlie Rose or Harvey Weinstein. In fact, the focus on the repercussions to prominent men—the professional and reputational damage done to them—takes the revelations of this moment further away from the reputational and professional prices paid by generations of women. While understanding that the threat of actual repercussion is crucial to getting men to stop behaving this way, I also find myself almost wishing that we could have a moratorium on firings and resignations, in exchange for the full stories, from every woman, about the ways in which she feels she has been harassed and discriminated against, and not only sexually.

Buried in one of the reports on Matt Lauer is a detail from a woman who recalls him speaking about how unattractive her cold sore was. Farai Chideya has recalled how John Hockenberry urged her to lose weight while she was his cohost. These are not *sexual* traumas. But they show how women are evaluated aesthetically by men whose evaluations matter more than women's work, in contexts that have nothing to do with aesthetics.

My frustrations hit an early high point when I read the apology from Louis C.K. in the wake of a story about how he masturbated in front of women. Several of them told the *New York Times* that after they had spoken openly about their experiences with him, they had heard that his powerful manager was furious with them. They decided to take themselves out of the running for any projects involving that manager. "The power I had over these women is that they admired me," Louis C.K. said in his statement. "I learned yesterday the extent to which I left these women who admired me feeling badly about themselves and cautious around other men who would never have put them in that position." *No, you dope*, I yelled in my head. *The power you had over those women was professional. What you should have learned how your actions damaged their careers.* The harm done to women simply doesn't begin or end in the hotel room with the famous comic masturbating in front of them. It shades everything about what women choose to do—or not do—afterward; it has an impact on those who weren't even in the room.

What makes women vulnerable is not their carnal violability but rather the way that their worth has been understood as fundamentally erotic, ornamental; that they have not been taken seriously as equals; that they have been treated as some ancillary reward that comes with the kinds of power men are taught to reach for and are valued for achieving. How to make clear that the trauma of the smaller trespasses—the boob grabs and unwanted kisses or come-ons from bosses—is not necessarily even *about* the sexualized act in question; so many of us learned to maneuver around hands-y men without sustaining lasting emotional damage when we were fourteen. Rather, it's about the cruel reminder that these are still the terms on which we are valued by our colleagues, our bosses, sometimes our competitors, the men we tricked ourselves into thinking might see us as smart, formidable colleagues or rivals, not as the kinds of objects they can just grab and grope and degrade without consequence. It's not that we're horrified like some Victorian damsel; it's that we're horrified like a woman in 2017 who briefly believed she was equal to her male peers but has just been reminded that she is not, who has suddenly had her comparative powerlessness revealed to her. "I was hunting for a job," said one of the women who accused Charlie Rose of assault. "And he was hunting for me."

A woman who is harassed, or who is in a workplace where other women are, might feel vividly the full weight of the system that's not set up with her in mind and see with clarity how much more difficult her professional path will be at every turn, how success might not be on her terms but on terms set by powerful men. She might feel shame or embarrassment that worms its way into her head, affects her confidence. She will likely spend time and energy focusing on how to maneuver around the harasser, time and energy that might otherwise be spent on her own advancement. Some women decide to play along; maybe their careers will benefit from it or maybe they will suffer, but they may long wonder whether their success or failure was determined not by their own talents or even by a lucky break but rather by how they responded to a man. This is especially difficult for very young women, those with fewer economic or social resources, who lack professional networks and professional stability; it's these women who are most likely to be targeted. The whole thing might begin to feel overwhelmingly difficult, hopeless, perhaps not worth the fight. It can mean a sapping of ambition.

At the end of the *New York Times* report on Horovitz, accused by nine women of having sexually assaulted them, some of whom when they were in their teens and he was their professional mentor or employer, the reporter Jessica Bennett noted that one of Horovitz's accusers, despite being a promising playwright, has struggled with depression and writer's block while others left the theater altogether. "He took this thing that was such a beautiful thing," one of the accusers told Bennett of Horovitz's effect on the aspirations of the young women he is alleged to have molested, "and he just ruined it." Here's another example: In response to a story about Alex Kozinski, now a judge and formerly chief judge of the Ninth Circuit Court of Appeals, who allegedly showed female clerks pornography in his office, civil-rights attorney Alexandra Brodsky tweeted, "In law school, everyone knew, and women didn't apply to clerk for

Judge Kosinski [*sic*] despite his prestige and connections to the Supreme Court."

All this while networks—sometimes, literal *television* networks—of male power work to build, protect, and further reinforce male power. Recall how the Fox News chief, Roger Ailes, protected Bill O'Reilly, keeping him in a multi-million-dollar berth for years after public claims of harassment surfaced; O'Reilly in turn defended Ailes when Ailes was accused of serial harassment of the women on his network; the president, Donald Trump, whose roles as birther and politician were built in part by the Fox News team, in turn defended both O'Reilly and Ailes, even as their network was providing Trump his own robust defense against harassment charges. Meanwhile, the female accusers of all these men received no such support, no such defense; instead they were called liars from public, political, and media pulpits as they were chased out of the news business, hushed up with settlement money and nondisclosure agreements, insulted by the man who is now our president as being too ugly to grope. That same man was given a free pass from Lauer at the presidential forum in which the anchor grilled Hillary Clinton about her e-mails and interrupted her repeatedly but failed to challenge Trump at all, even on outright untruths.

Little of this cycle itself directly entails sexual incursion. But it is central to understanding the story unfolding around us. Women's access to work and to power within their workplaces is curtailed, often via the very same mechanisms that promote, protect, and forgive men, the systems that give them double, triple chances to advance and to abuse those around them, over and over again.

A few weeks ago, the CNN reporter Dylan Byers was harshly criticized for a (quickly deleted) tweet, in which he bemoaned the fact that in the purge of accused harassers and predators "never has so much talent left the industry all at once." But the point is that the pool of men in whom we've been able to discern talent to begin with is pre-poisoned by sexism. These men are known to us in part because they, and the system in which they've risen, have cleared the field of female competition. So of course theirs are the voices and faces that reach us every morning via our televisions and radios, they are the ones we understand to be talented. Of course they're the ones we rely on to explain the world; to be the politicians we trust—that we must depend on—to legislate on our behalf. That means that when they fall, we feel for them, even as we recoil from them, because their power has allowed them to be made known to us, admired by us. Meanwhile, the women they're alleged to have harassed remain mostly nameless, faceless, having had so many fewer opportunities to become icons. We don't consider all the women who—driven out, banished, self-exiled, or marginalized—might have been *more* talented or brilliant or comforting to us, on our airwaves or in our governing bodies, but whom we have never even gotten the chance to know.

Then of course there's how we feel about the women who *did* manage to ascend within these structures. When stories about the webs that protected Harvey Weinstein or Charlie Rose get published, the women—often women who are themselves anomalies within male-dominated institutions and cultures—get the most attention: Hillary Clinton's (rather than Bill's) friendship with Harvey Weinstein is craven, while Nancy Pelosi's words about John Conyers are parsed more closely than anything uttered (or not uttered) by any one of his male colleagues. Rose's producer Yvette Vega, who didn't address the complaints of women who'd been harassed is seen as a more sinister villain than her dick-flashing boss.

None of this is an exculpation of those women or of any of us who have, frankly, lived in the world ruled by men and tried to make our way in it. When individual women, no matter how powerful, climb to their perches through a system that was not built by or for them, then their grip on power has never wholly been their own. It's always existed in relation to the men they must work with, protect, acquiesce to, apologize for, or depend on for support.

When a group of female Democratic senators, kicked off by Kirsten Gillibrand and followed quickly by dozens of her colleagues, urged Al Franken to resign, they made a wildly risky choice: Open challenge and rebuke to a beloved and powerful man has rarely endeared women to us. But it's easy to imagine, as allegations against Franken trickled out, day by day, that it was Franken's female colleagues who felt the heat. According to one Democratic aide, the frustrated conversations between some Democratic women in the Senate had gone on for a week, held sometimes, literally, in the Senate's women's restrooms: What should they do?

Those women surely knew that if they did not speak out against Franken, they would be tarred as self-interested hypocrites; they probably also understood that if they *did* speak out against him, they would be viewed as self-interested executioners. That they chose the latter path speaks volumes about the unprecedented shifts in possibility this moment seems, at least right now, to be heralding. (Startling polling released by Perry Undem the day before Franken announced he was stepping down showed that 86 percent of those surveyed said they believed that men harass women out of "desire for power and control over women," more than because they want to date them.)

But it should also tell us about the shitty position women are so often put in: as the designated guardians, entrusted—whether as colleagues or wives—with policing men's bad behaviors, they will get dinged for complicity if they don't police it vigilantly enough, and risk being cast as castrating villainesses if they issue sentence. The women senators' call for the end of Franken's tenure may, in the end, make them feminist heroines, or it may backfire terribly, confirming them as leaders of a ravening mob and lighting the fuse for the looming backlash. But let's not ignore the fact that on the same day that many were side-eyeing Hillary Clinton's friendly dinners with Harvey Weinstein, in the same weeks in which many commentators have cast critical eyes back on the feminists who defended Bill Clinton, the *New York Times* Metro section's Twitter account promptly asked of Kirsten Gillibrand, a woman who *did* rebuke a man in her own party: "Is courage or opportunism at play?"

None of this is simple; none of it is easy; it's increasingly difficult to parse and to live through. That's precisely *because* what we're picking apart is not some single thread; it's the knotted weave of inequity that is the very stuff of which our professional and political and social assumptions and institutions are made. Having this conversation as if it's about sex, and not about equality, involves trauma and pain in its own ways: memories of the visceral fear, physical pain, emotional suffering of nonconsensual contact that so many of us have experienced, to one degree or another.

But even with all that pain, a focus on sex also lets us off the hook, permitting us to look away from broader horrors, whole complex systems of disempowerment and economic, professional vulnerability. Understanding the moment, and women's reaction to it, as only about sex crimes does contribute to a comfortably regressive understanding of women as perpetually passive victims of men's animal sexuality run amok. And while I share Masha Gessen's fear that this moment will end with a recommitment to patrolling women's virtue and undermining their sexual agency, I am just as worried about what we will *not* do—the thing that is harder and more uncomfortable and ultimately inconceivable: addressing and beginning to dismantle men's unjustly disproportionate claim to every kind of power in the public and professional world.

## Longreads

FINALIST—COLUMNS
AND COMMENTARY

*"It turns out that this isn't about individual monsters. It never was. This is about structural violence, about a culture that decided long ago that women's agency and dignity were worth sacrificing to protect the reputation of powerful men and the institutions that enabled their entitlement."*
*So wrote Laurie Penny in November 2017 as the cultural reckoning that began with the work of a handful of reporters spread across the Atlantic. Born in London, educated at Oxford, Penny is the author of six books, including, most recently,* Bitch Doctrine: Essays for Dissenting Adults. *Praised by the Ellie judges for "their fierceness, eloquence, and moral clarity," these columns were published with reader support by* Longreads, *an online-only publication "dedicated to helping people find and share the best storytelling in the world."*

Laurie Penny

# The Horizon of Desire *and* We're All Mad Here: Weinstein, Women, and the Language of Lunacy *and* The Unforgiving Minute

## The Horizon of Desire

"Man fucks woman. Man: subject. Woman: object."
—*The Fall*, Episode 3, "Insolence and Wine"

The first thing you need to understand about consent is that consent is not, strictly speaking, a thing. Not in the same way that teleportation isn't a thing. Consent is not a thing because it is not an item, nor a possession. Consent is not an object you can hold in your hand. It is not a gift that can be given and then rudely requisitioned. Consent is a state of being. Giving someone your consent—sexually, politically, socially—is a little like giving them your attention. It's a continuous process. It's an interaction between two human creatures. I believe that a great many men and boys don't understand this. I believe that lack of understanding is causing unspeakable trauma for women, men, and everyone else who is sick of how much human sexuality still hurts.

We need to talk about what consent really means, and why it matters more, not less, at a time when women's fundamental rights to bodily autonomy are under attack across the planet, and the Hog-Emperor of Rape Culture is squatting in the White House making your neighborhood pervert look placid. We still get consent all wrong, and we have to try to get it a bit less wrong, for all our sakes.

To explain all this, I'm going to have to tell you some stories. They're true stories, and some of them are rude stories, and I'm telling you now because the rest of this ride might get uncomfortable and I want you to have something to look forward to.

·　　·　　·

So, I've got this friend with a shady past. He's a clever and conscientious person who grew up in the patriarchy, and he knows that he's done things which may not have been criminal but have hurt people, and by people he means women. My friend has hurt women, and he doesn't know what to do about that now, and from time to time we talk about it. That's how it happened that, a few weeks ago, halfway through an effervescent confession in a coffee shop, the following words came out of his mouth: "Technically, I don't think I've raped anyone."

*Technically.* Technically, my friend doesn't think he is a rapist. That *technically* haunted me for days. Not because I don't believe it, but because I do. It's not the first time I've heard it, or something like it, from otherwise well-meaning male friends who are frantically reassessing their sexual history in the light of the awkward fact that shame is no longer enough to stop women from naming abusers. It's so far from the first time I've heard it, in fact, that I ought to add a caveat, for a few select readers: If you haven't given me permission to share your story, this isn't you I'm talking about.

"Technically, I haven't raped anyone." What did he mean, technically? My friend went on to describe how, over years of drinking and shagging around before he got sober, he considers it a matter of luck rather than pride that he has never, to his knowledge, committed serious sexual assault. The fact is that, like any number of men growing up in the last decade, his concept of consent could have been written in crayon. Sex was something you persuaded women to let you do to them, and if they weren't passed out, saying no, or actively trying to throw you off, you were probably fine.

All the way home from the coffee shop, I thought about consent and why the very concept is so fearful to anyone invested in not looking under the carpet of modern morality. I thought about the number of situations I've encountered where no, technically, nobody committed a crime, and yes, technically, what happened was consensual. Maybe someone pushed a boundary to its breaking point. Maybe someone simply lay there and let something be done to them because they didn't feel able, for whatever reason, to say no.

That *technically*, of course, is not just something one hears from men. You hear that same *technically*, in a different key, from girls and grown women who don't want to think of the things that happened to them that way, even though the fact that those things happened to them, with or without their say-so, is the whole problem. We learn, just as men do, that our instincts about what we feel and experience are not to be trusted. We learn that our desire is dangerous and so we tamp it down until we no longer recognize the difference between wanting and being wanted. We learn that our sexuality is contemptible and so we crush it; we become alienated from our own bodies. I've told myself before that technically, this or that person committed no crime, so technically, I've got no reason to feel used like a human spittoon, and technically I did invite him back to my house, so technically, I should have expected nothing less, and technically, there's no reason to be angry and upset, because really, what is female sexuality but a set of technicalities to be overcome?

The problem is that *technically* isn't good enough. "At least I didn't actively assault anyone" is not a gold standard for sexual morality, and it never was. Of course, we have to start somewhere, and "try not to rape anyone" is as good a place as any, but it can't end there. Our standards for decent sexual and social behavior should not be defined purely by what is likely to get us publicly shamed or put in prison because we are not toddlers, and we can do better.

This is what consent culture means. It means expecting more—demanding more. It means treating one another as complex human beings with agency and desire, not just once, but continually. It means adjusting our ideas of dating and sexuality beyond the process of prying a grudging "yes" out of another human being. Ideally you want them to say it again, and again, and mean it every time. Not just because it's hotter that way, although it absolutely is; consent doesn't have to be sexy to be centrally important. But because when you get down to it, sexuality should not be about arguing over what you can get away with and still call consensual.

When you put it that way, it sounds simple. Easy to understand. But there are a great many simple ideas that we are taught not to understand and a great many more that we choose not to understand when our self-image as decent human beings is at stake, and that's where a lot of men and boys I know are at right now. Bewildered. Uncomfortable. Wrestling with the specter of their own wrongdoing. Frightened, most of all, about how the ground rules for being a worthwhile person are changing so fast.

●          ●          ●

So let's talk about getting away with it. Let's talk about what happens in a society where women's bodies are contested commodities for men to fight over. Let's talk about rape culture.

The naming and shaming of rape culture has been one of the most important feminist interventions of recent years and one of the most controversial and misunderstood. "Rape culture" does not imply a society in which rape is routine, although it remains unconscionably common. Rape culture describes the process whereby rape and sexual assault are normalized and excused, the process whereby women's sexual agency is continuously denied and women and girls are expected to be afraid of rape and to guard against it, the process whereby men are assumed to have the erotic self-control of a gibbon with a sweetie jar of Viagra, creatures who ought to be applauded for not flinging turds everywhere rather than encouraged to apply critical thinking.

(I have never understood why more men aren't offended by this assumption, why more of them aren't arguing that possession of a penis does not automatically cripple a person's moral capacity, but then again, that might mean that behaving with basic decency wouldn't get you a gold star every time. Who wouldn't want to live in a world where all it takes to be considered an upstanding guy is lack of actively violent misogyny? Oh, that's right—women.)

You do not have to be a victim of rape to be affected by rape culture. You do not have to be a convicted rapist to perpetuate rape culture. You don't have to be an active, committed misogynist to benefit from rape culture. I sincerely believe that a staggering proportion of straight and bisexual men are working with some ingrained assumptions about sex and sexuality that they have not fully analyzed. Assumptions about the way women are, what they do, and what they have the capacity to want. Assumptions like: men want sex, and women are sex. Men take, and women need to be persuaded to give. Men fuck women; women allow themselves to be fucked. Women are responsible for drawing up those boundaries, and if men overstep them, that's not their fault: boys will be boys.

What is confusing to a great many men, including otherwise accomplished, successful, and sensitive men, is that women can and should be trusted to make their own choice at all. Right now, one of the fundamental operating principles of rape culture, rarely articulated but routinely defended, is this: men's right to sexual intercourse is as important or more important than women's basic bodily autonomy. Therefore, while it's women's job to police the boundaries of sexuality, to control themselves where men are not required to, they cannot and should not be trusted with any choice that might affect men's ability to stick it wherever they like and still think of themselves as decent people, even retrospectively. Women's agency, choices, and desires may matter, but they matter much less, and they always will.

The thing is, if you accept the idea a woman has the absolute right to sexual choice, you must also wrestle with the prospect that she might not make the choice you want. If she's really free to say no, even if she's said yes before, even if she's naked in your bed, even if you've been married for twenty years, well then—you might not get to fuck her. And that's the hill that far too many dudes mistake for the moral high ground as they prepare to die on it.

Quite a few people, most of them men, are truly confused as to why the ladies are so upset that they keep getting hit on by potential investors and having to chase creeps out of their apartments when they thought they were having a business meeting. After all, few of the allegations in question involve violent penetration by a stranger. That's what rape looks like in films, where the villain may be identified by his suspicious facial hair and the creepy theme music that follows him around and is nothing like you or your friends because you're all the heroes of your own story, and heroes don't rape.

In the real world, as the sex-pest scandals roll over America's earthquake zones, almost nobody is being directly threatened with jail for sex crimes. The complaints are about the everyday sleaze and scumbaggery that have been tolerated for decades in male-dominated industries: grabbing, lewd comments, bosses hassling you for sex, the ubiquitous, unspoken understanding that women are first and foremost objects of desire, not individuals with desires—sexual, professional—of their own.

We are surrounded by so many images of sexuality that it's easy to think of ourselves as liberated. But liberation, by definition, involves everyone. Instead, the messages that bombard us from marketing and pop culture to mainstream pornography insist that acceptable desire goes only in one direction: from men to women. It's a homogenous, dehumanizing vision of straight sex, a simple story where only men have agency, and women are passive points on a spectrum of fuckability. This is sexual license, not liberation. Today's sexual freedom is rather like today's market freedom, in that what it practically entails is freedom for people with power to dictate terms and freedom for everyone else to shut up and smile. We have come to accept, as in so many areas of life, a vision of freedom whereby the illusion of choice is a modesty slip for unspeakable everyday violence.

·　　·　　·

Consent culture, first named by activist and sex-critical feminist Kitty Stryker, is the alternative to all this. Resisting a culture of rape and abuse must involve more than insisting on the individual right to say no—although that's both a decent starting place and a difficult concept for some people to wrap their RedTube-rotted brains around. There's a reason for that. The reason that the notion of real, continuous, enthusiastic sexual consent is so outrageous is that the concept of female sexual agency—let alone active desire—is still a fearful one. Our culture still has very little room for the idea that women and queer people, given the chance, want and enjoy sex just as much as men do.

Well before they are old enough to start thinking about having it, girls are still trained to imagine sex as something that will be done to them rather than something they might like to do for its own sake. We grow up with warnings that sexuality in general and heterosexuality in particular is a fearful, violent thing; sex is something we must avoid rather than something we have. If we're able to recognize that we want it of our own accord, we learn that we are deviant, dirty, and wicked. The legion of one handed-typers on misogynist subreddits, wondering why on earth it's so hard for them to get laid, wondering why women don't make approaches, why we use sex as a social bargaining strategy, would do well to remember that straight women didn't come up with those rules. Most of us are proficient at suffocating our own desires because withholding sexuality is the only social power we are permitted—even if that permission is given grudgingly and unreliably by a culture that calls us sluts and bitches and whores when we don't say no but can't be relied on to believe us when we do. This, too, is rape culture. Rape culture is not about demonizing men. It is about controlling female sexuality. It is anti-sex and anti-pleasure. It teaches us to deny our own desire as an adaptive strategy for surviving a sexist world.

# We're All Mad Here: Weinstein, Women, and the Language of Lunacy

We're through the looking glass now. As women all over the world come forward to talk about their experiences of sexual violence, all our old certainties about what was and was not normal are peeling away like dead skin.

It's not just Hollywood, and it's not just Silicon Valley. It's not just the White House or Fox News.

It's everywhere.

It's happening in the art world and in mainstream political parties. It's happening in the London radical left and in the Bay Area burner community. It's happening in academia and in the media and in the legal profession. I recently heard that it was happening in the goddamn Lindy Hop dance scene, which I didn't even know was a thing. Men with influence and status who have spent years or decades treating their community like an all-you-can-grope sexual-harassment buffet are suddenly being presented with the bill. Names are being named. A lot of women have realized that they were never crazy, that even if they were crazy they were also right all along, and—how shall I put this?—they (we) are pissed.

"It's like finding out aliens exist," said a friend of mine last night. He was two gins in and trying to process why he never spoke up, over a twenty-year period, about a mutual friend who is facing public allegations of sexual violence. "Back in the day we'd all heard stories about it, but . . . well, the people telling them were all a bit crazy. You know, messed up. So nobody believed them."

I took a sip of tea to calm down, and suggested that perhaps the reason these people were messed up—if they were messed up—was because they had been, you know, sexually assaulted. I reminded him that some of us had always known. I knew. But then, what did I know? I'm just some crazy girl.

·　　　·　　　·

The process we are going through in our friendship group and in our culture as a whole is something akin to first contact. Abusers, like little green men in flying saucers, have a habit of revealing their true selves to people nobody's going to find credible—to women who are vulnerable or women who are marginalized or who are just, you know, women. But abusers don't come from any planet but this. We grew up with them. We've worked with them. Admired them. Loved them. Trusted them. And now we have to deal with the fact that our reality is not what it seemed.

So who's the crazy one now? To be the victim of sexual assault is to fall down a rabbit hole into a reality shaped by collective delusion: specifically, the delusion that powerful or popular or ordinary-seeming men who do good work in the world cannot also be abusers or predators. To suggest otherwise is to appear insane. You question yourself. Even before anyone calls you a liar—which they will—you're wondering if you've overreacted. Surely he couldn't be like that. Not him. Anyway, it would be insanity to go against someone with so much clout. The girls who do that are sick in the head. At least, that was what we used to think.

Something important has changed. Suddenly women are speaking up and speaking out in numbers too big to shove aside. The public narrative around abuse and sexual entitlement and the common consensus around who is to be believed are changing so fast you can see the seams between one paradigm and the next, the hasty stitching where one version of reality becomes another. Now, instead of victims and survivors of rape and assault being written off as mentally ill, it's the abusers who need help.

"I'm hanging on in there," said Harvey Weinstein, in the wake of revelations about a pattern of abuse that has upended the entertainment industry, tipping all its secrets out. "I'm not doing OK, but I'm trying. I've got to get help. You know what—we all make mistakes."

Days earlier, Weinstein e-mailed other Hollywood higher-ups frantic not to be fired, asking for their assistance convincing the Weinstein Company board to keep him, begging to be sent to therapy as an alternative. The same pleas for mercy on the grounds of mental illness have been issued on behalf of powerful predators in the tech industry. Here's 500 Startups' statement on the actions of its founder, Dave McClure: "He recognizes he has made mistakes and has been going through counseling to work on addressing changes in his previous unacceptable behavior."

The social definition of sanity is the capacity to accept the consensus of how the world ought to work, including between men and women. Anyone who questions or challenges that consensus is by definition unhinged. It is only when the abuse becomes impossible to deny, when patterns emerge, when photographs and videos are available and are enough to lead to conviction—then we start hearing the pleas for mercy. *It was just twenty minutes of action. He's got such a bright future. Think of his mother. Think of his wife. He couldn't help himself.*

These excuses are never just about the abuser and his reputation. They are desperate attempts to bargain with a rapidly changing reality. They are justifications for continuing, collectively, to deny systemic abuse. Suddenly, it's Weinstein, not the women calling him a rapist and a pig, who gets to be the one with "demons." He needs to see a therapist, not a judge. He's a very unhappy and very sick man. And so is Bill Cosby. And so is Woody Allen. And so was Cyril Smith. And so is that guy in your industry everyone respects so much, the one with the big smile and all those crazy ex-girlfriends.

What's the word for what happens when a lot of people are very sick all at the same time? It's an epidemic. I'm not sure what started this one, but there's a lot of bullshit in the water.

·　　·　　·

The language of mental illness is also a shorthand for the articulation of truths that are outside the realm of political consensus. Anyone who challenges that consensus is deemed mad by default, including women who dare to suggest that predators in positions of power might have to be accountable for their actions.

There's a long, grim history behind the idea that women lie about systemic sexual abuse because they're mentally unwell. Freud was one of the first to look for a psychiatric explanation for the number of women patients he saw who told him they had been molested or raped. To report that such things were going on in polite society would have outraged Freud's well-heeled and intellectual social circles. So in the course of his later writings, the father of modern psychoanalysis found alternative explanations: perhaps some of these girls were unconsciously obsessed with the erotic idea of the father figure, as opposed to an actual father figure who might have committed actual abuse. Or perhaps they were just hysterical. Either way, no reason to ruffle whiskers in the gentlemen's club by giving too much credence to unhappy young women.

A century later, in absolutely every situation like this that I have ever encountered, the same rhetoric applies. Women are overemotional. They cannot be trusted because they are crazy, which is a word patriarchy uses to describe a woman who doesn't know when to shut her pretty mouth. They are not to be believed because they are unwell, which is a word patriarchy uses to describe women who are angry.

Well, of course they're angry. Of course they are hurt. They have been traumatized, first by the abuse and then by their community's response. They are not able to express righteous rage without consequence because they are not men. If you had been assaulted, forcibly penetrated, treated like so much human meat; if you had sought justice or even just comfort and found instead rank upon rank of friends and colleagues closing together to call you a liar and a hysteric, telling you you'd better shut up—how would you feel? You'd be angry, but you'd better not show it. Angry women are not to be trusted, which suits abusers and their enablers just fine.

This is what we're talking about when we talk about rape culture—not just the actions of lone sociopaths but the social architecture that lets them get away with it, a routine of silencing, gaslighting, and selective ignorance that keeps the world at large from having to face realities they'd rather rationalize away. If everyone around you gets together to dismiss the inconvenient truth of your experience, it's tempting to believe them, especially if you are very young.

Ten years ago, when I was raped and spoke out about it, I was told I was toxic, difficult, a compulsive liar. I was told that so consistently that eventually I came to accept it, and I moved away to heal in private while the man who had hurt me went on to hurt other people. In the intervening decade, every time women I know have spoken out about sexual abuse, they have been dismissed as mentally ill. And yes, some of them were mentally ill—at least one in four human beings will experience mental health problems in their lifetime, after all, and violence and trauma are contributing factors. More to the point, predators seek out victims who look vulnerable. Women and girls with raw sparking wires who nobody will believe because they're already crazy.

The thing that is happening now is exactly the thing that the sanity and safety of unnamed thousands of women was once sacrificed to avoid: a giant flaming fuss. It is amazing what people will do to avoid a fuss. They will ostracize victims, gaslight survivors, and provide cover for predators; they will hire lawyers and hand out hundreds of thousands of dollars under the table and, if pressed, rearrange entire social paradigms to make it seem like anyone asking for basic justice is a screeching hysteric.

In decades gone by, women who made a scene, who made the mistake of confronting abusers or even just closing the door on them, were carted off to rot in the sort of hospitals that featured fewer rehabilitation spas and more hosing down with ice water to get you to stop screaming. Now it's the abusers who are seeking asylum. Asking to be treated as sufferers of illness, rather than criminals.

The language of lunacy is the last resort when society at large cannot deny the evidence of structural violence. We hear the same thing in the wake of a mass shooting or a white-supremacist terror attack. *He was always such a nice boy. Something broke. We couldn't have seen him coming. He was depressed and frustrated.* We can't pretend it didn't happen, so instead we pretend that there's no pattern here, just individual maladaption. A chemical imbalance in the brain, not a systemic injustice baked into our culture. Harvey Weinstein is not a rapist, he's a "very sick guy"—at least according to Woody Allen (who may or may not have special insight, being famously interested in both psychoanalysis and recreational sexual harassment).

Woody Allen feels at least as sorry for Weinstein as he does for the forty-plus women and girls who, at the time of writing, have come forward to claim they were assaulted or raped by the movie mogul. We're now supposed to feel pity for rapists because they're messed up. Well, join the queue. All of us are messed up, and having low self-esteem and a dark obsession with sexually intimidating the women around you aren't excuses for abuse. At best, they are explanations; at worst, they are attempts to derail the discussion just as we've started talking about women's feelings as if they matter. In fact, according to researchers like Lundy Bancroft, who has spent decades working with abusive men, abusers are no more or less likely to be mentally ill than anyone else. "Abusiveness has little to do with psychological problems and everything to do with values and beliefs," says Bancroft. "Abusers have a distorted sense of right and wrong. Their value system is unhealthy, not their psychology."

At the end of the day, we're now encouraged to ask, aren't these men the real victims—victims of their own demons? Come off it. We've all got demons and baggage and all of the other euphemisms we use to talk about the existential omnishambles of modern life. The moment I meet someone who has arrived at something like adulthood psychologically unscathed by the

nightmare fun-house of white-supremacist capitalist patriarchy, I assume they're hiding something or on enough tranquil-
izers to fell a small elephant or both. We've all got broken hearts
and complicated childhoods, and survivors have spent too long
being quietly directed to seek therapy rather than justice.

The abusers who are now being excused as mentally ill are not
monsters or aberrations. They were acting entirely within the
unhealthy value system of a society which esteems the reputation
and status of men above the safety of women. Many abusers, on
some level, do not know that what they are doing is wrong. They
believe that they are basically decent. Most men who prey on
women have had that belief confirmed over the course of years
or decades of abuse. They believe they're basically decent, and a
whole lot of other people believe they're basically decent, too.
They're nice guys who just have a problem with women or booze
or their mothers or all three.

·　　　·　　　·

Pleas for mercy on the grounds of emotional distress are surprisingly effective when it's men doing the pleading. Right now, all
around me, I see women working to support men, as well as each
other, through this difficult time. It's not just because we're nice
and it's not just because we're suckers, although it's probably a little bit of both.

It's because we know how much this is going to hurt.

We should. We've carried it all for so long in private. We know
how deep the damage goes, how much there is still unsaid. Even
as we come together to demand an end to sexual violence, we
worry that men are too weak to cope with the consequences of
what they've done and allowed to be done to us.

I have for the past three months been nursing intermittent jags
of panic at the knowledge of what was about to be revealed (and
has now been revealed) about a person I once cared for deeply

and, because I am a soft-hearted fool, still care about very much. A person who, it turns out, has hurt more women than any of us guessed when we started joining the puncture wounds in our pasts to make a picture. Panic because none of us want him to hurt himself. Panic because we worry that he might. We want him to be safe, even though none of us have been. Isn't that just delicious? As more stories of private pain come out, it is still the men we're supposed to worry about.

The threat of extreme self-harm is a classic last-resort tactic for abusers who suspect that they're losing control, that their partner is about to leave them or tell someone or both. It's effective because it's almost always plausible, and who wants to be the person who put their own freedom and safety ahead of another person's life? Not a great many women, certainly, given the bone-deep knowledge drilled into us from birth that we were put on this earth to protect men from, among other things, the consequences of their actions. We've been raised to believe that men's emotions are our responsibility. Even the men who hurt us.

As the list of names grows longer, the plea for mercy on the grounds of mental illness is being deployed in exactly the same way. These guys are suffering, too. If you carry on calling for them to come clean and change their behavior, well, that might just push them over the edge. And you wouldn't want that, would you? You're a nice girl, aren't you?

I've been told several times by controlling partners that if I left them, they might break down or even kill themselves. Each time, I stayed longer than I should have because I loved them and wanted them alive, and every time, when it finally became unbearable, they were absolutely fine. Not one of them made an attempt to carry out their threat. That doesn't mean they didn't mean it at the time. But the demand that even as we attempt to free ourselves from structural or specific violence, women prioritize the well-being of men over and above our own is a tried-and-true way of keeping a rein on females who might just be about to stand up for ourselves. We are expected to show a level of concern for our abusers that it would never occur to them to show to us—if they'd been at all concerned about our well-being in the first place, we wouldn't be where we are. And where we are is extremely dark and very difficult, and it'll get darker and more difficult before we're done.

.        .        .

I'm worried about a lot of people right now. I'm worried about the several men I know who have hurt women in the past and who are now facing the consequences. I'm worried about the men who are analyzing their own behavior in horror, who stood aside and let it happen, and who are suddenly realizing their own complicity—and struggling to cope with the guilt, the shame of that knowledge. That's allowed. Empathy is not being rationed here, and we can worry about whoever we like—as long as we worry about the survivors first. We were not liars or hysterical. We were telling the truth. And if the men are a mess today because they finally have to reckon with that truth, we must not let that stop us from building a world where love and sexuality and gender hurt less, a world where this does not have to happen again as it has happened, in silence, for so many generations.

Reframing serial abuse as a mental-health disorder stashes it conveniently on the high shelf marked "not a political issue." The trouble is that sickness does not obviate social responsibility. It never has. Sickness might give a person the overwhelming urge to act in repulsive ways but sickness does not cover for them during business meetings or pay off their lawyers or make sure they get women dropped from films: it takes a village to protect a rapist.

I am perfectly willing to accept that toxic masculinity leaves a lot of broken men in its maw. That culture conspires to prevent men and boys from being able to handle their sexuality, their aggression, and their fear of rejection and loss of status in any adult way; that it is unbearable at times to exist inside a male body without constant validation. But very few men—very few people, period—grow up with wholly healthy attitudes towards their own gender. Not everyone with fucked-up ideas about women goes on to do fucked-up things to women. Toxic masculinity, as Bancroft observes, is a social illness before it is a psychological one.

So what about the rest of us? People say that they are shocked, and perhaps they are. But shock is very different from surprise. When was the last time you were really, truly surprised to hear a story like this? The truth is that a great many of those surrounding Weinstein did know. Just as the friends and associates of most sexual predators probably know—not everything, but enough to guess, if they cared to. The reason they didn't say or do anything is simple and painful. The reason is that nobody had enough of a problem with what was going on to make a fuss. They thought that what was going on was morally acceptable. Polite society or whatever passed for it in their industry told them that this was all normal and par for the course, even if your heart told you otherwise. Polite society hates a fuss. Polite society can be a very dangerous place for a young girl to walk alone, and on this issue, most of us have been. Until now.

It is easier to cope with the idea of sick men than it is to face the reality of a sick society; we've waited far too long to deal with our symptoms because we didn't want to hear the diagnosis. The prognosis is good, but the treatment is brutal. The people finally facing the consequences of having treated women and girls like faceless pieces of property may well be extremely unhappy about it. That's understandable. I'm sure it's not a lot of fun to be Harvey Weinstein right now, but sadly for the producer and those like him, the world is changing, and for once, cosseting the feelings of powerful men is not and cannot be our number-one priority. For once, the safety and sanity of survivors is not about to be sacrificed so that a few more unreconstructed bastards can sleep at night.

# The Unforgiving Minute

I'm sick of being asked to suffer so a man can grow.
                                        —Alexandra Petri

Everyone. Fucking. Knew.
                                        —Scott Rosenberg

This is actually happening.

The so-called revelations about endemic male sexual aggression in Hollywood, in the media, in politics, in the tech world, and in communities large and small have not stopped, despite every conceivable effort to dismiss, discredit, shame, and belittle the survivors coming forward to demand a different world. The most uncomfortable revelation is the fact that none of this, really, was that revelatory.

A great many people knew. Maybe they didn't know all of it, but they knew enough to feel tainted by a complicity that hobbled their compassion.

It turns out that this isn't about individual monsters. It never was. This is about structural violence, about a culture that decided long ago that women's agency and dignity were worth sacrificing to protect the reputation of powerful men and the institutions that enabled their entitlement. Everyone, including the "good guys," knew it was happening. We just didn't think it was all that wrong. At least, not wrong enough to make a fuss about, because the people groping their callous, violent way through life knew they'd get away with it, and most of the men around them were permitted the luxury of ignorance.

Except that now that seems to be changing. Now, Old Dinosaurs are wondering how to negotiate with an oncoming asteroid. Current or former Stupid Young Men are in a state of panic about their imminent introduction to the concept of "consequences," leading to the question: What, precisely, is the age when men are expected to take responsibility for their behavior?

The answer, with any luck, is "The Digital One."

Very few men seem sure what to do in this situation. I have been asked, repeatedly, what men and boys ought to be doing now. How should we behave differently? How guilty should we be feeling? What do women actually want?

Good. You're finally asking. I suspect that if more of you had asked that question earlier, if you'd asked it often, and if you'd paid attention to the answers, we wouldn't have to have this conversation—which nobody wants to be having—right now. It's a shame, honestly, that it had to come to this. But here we are, and here we're going to stay while powerful scumbags all over the world take a break from public life to spend more time with the police and while people who've nursed private hurts for years start putting the puzzle pieces together until they recognize the shape of injustice.

I'm sorry; you're new here. The notion that women's agency and dignity might be more important than men's right to act like grabby children whenever they want may feel like uncharted territory, but some of us have lived here all along. You don't know your way around, and the whole place seems full of hidden terrors, and you're tired and scared, and being here makes you feel ignorant and powerless. You haven't learned the language—they didn't offer it at your school—and you wish you knew how to ask basic questions, like *where is the nearest station*, and *how much is that sandwich*, and *do you know the name of a good defense lawyer?* You wish you knew how to translate simple ideas, like: *I'm hungry*, and *I'm lonely*, and *my entire life I've let my fear of women's rejection control my behavior and that fear seemed so overwhelming that it didn't matter who got hurt as long as I didn't have to feel it and everyone else seemed to agree and now I don't know who to be or how to act*, or *I think there's a train leaving soon and I might need to be on it*.

Lately I've been spending a good deal of time at the help desk, pointing men in the direction of possible answers. I mind this sort of work less than most because it actually happens to be my job. I write about this for a living. I listen and I take notes. The messages wink on my phone in freakish chromagreen, like Gatsby's lights across the harbor: men reaching out to a world of women they have never really known, across a gulf they don't know if they're brave enough to bridge.

My friend's husband wants to know if he did the right thing in standing up to a superior at work who said he was going to stop hiring "hot women" because he'd only want to assault them.

My photographer friend wants to know why he didn't listen properly to the rumors about predators in his industry and if he can make up for that now.

My environmental activist friend is worried that the stupid things he did as a teenager will obviate the work he's doing today.

Nobody wants to be having this conversation, but we need to have it. Avoidance of this conversation has shaped our culture; cultures are defined not only by the stories they tell but also by the ones they don't. It's the negative space that gives definition to the picture we have of how men and women ought to live together—and that picture, of course, is the work of a series of old masters.

We have built entire lives, families, and communities around the absence of this conversation. And yet here we are, having it anyway. So let's deal with some common queries, the very first of which is: how do we handle what we know now about how women have been treated for so long?

·　　·　　·

This is a question in two parts. It's a question about how men should now relate to women in particular and to their own sexuality in general. It is also a question about how we all cope with the consequences. How do we deal with suspecting what we suspect, with knowing what we know about our own past behavior? The very first thing we must do is to continue to know it—to actively know it, rather than filing it away in the spam folder of our collective consciousness. We must stay here, in this difficult place. We must look at what we have done and allowed to be done to others, without flinching or making excuses.

Last week, as a fresh set of allegations threatened to topple the British government, a radio host asked me if flirting is now banned. No. It isn't. To the mainly female people who are on the receiving end, the difference between flirting and harassment— between sex and rape—are extremely clear. To some of the mainly male people who do these things, there appears to be no difference, and when you start to explain the difference they run, in short succession, out of excuses and out of the room.

The fact that a great many men I have spoken to genuinely seem to think that the main issue here is how and whether they're going to be able to get laid in the future is . . . I'm going to swallow a scream, and say that it's "interesting." Shockingly, this conversation is not about you and your boner. But since the difference between sex and sexual violence apparently needs explaining, put both hands on the table for a second and listen.

(Nobody here thinks that the entire arena of sexuality is necessarily dangerous and violent for women. Actually, no, that's not true: plenty of people think that. Mostly male people who have spent generations imagining sex and violent conquest as one and the same, fetishizing the two together until the popular erotic imagination left little clear air between passion and assault. Some of us have been on the wrong end of that trajectory for so damn long that we've given up trying to find a way to be intimate with men that doesn't cause us pain or risk our lives, and I imagine that those people, the vast majority of whom are women, do think of the male sex itself as inherently treacherous, unsalvageable, and irredeemably violent.)

Sex, however, is not the problem. Sexism is the problem, as is the fact that a great many men seem unable to tell the difference. It is maddening, the way those of us who complain about abuse are accused of trying to shut down sex and sexuality, as if we'd ever been allowed to be active sexual participants, as if abuse and the fear of abuse hadn't made pleasurable sex all but impossible for so many of us.

Sex is not the problem, but for some people sexism itself has become eroticized, and that, yes, is a problem. "It's not flirtation that any of us take issue with," said my best friend, late one night after another round of exhausting emotional work trying to shore up the shuddering self-image of the men we know so they don't collapse on top of us. "It's entitlement. Projection. Objectification. We know when we're being dehumanized. Good flirting is the kind where they see us. They won't know how to flirt the right way until they start unlearning how to look at us."

John Berger famously said that "men look at women, and women watch themselves being looked at." I'm sick of being looked at. I want to be seen. There are none so emotionally blind as those who look at a person standing right in front of them and see a mirror, not a window.

Many of the men I have talked to about this have begun of their own volition to speak about "no longer objectifying women." To wonder whether they should just stop looking at pretty women at all, if the act of desiring another person is itself violent. It's very sad that that confusion has arisen; it should be possible to want someone without dehumanizing them. But we have apparently created a world where it is incredibly difficult for a man to desire a woman and treat her as a human being at the same time.

So no, we are not trying to outlaw sexuality. We are trying to liberate it. You ask how the species is going to survive if we have to constantly check for consent before we get to the means of reproduction, but I promise you that the species has more pressing problems than that.

•     •     •

The biggest missing piece of this picture is women's desire. If femme and female citizens were allowed to actually articulate our own desires then we could skip a few lessons and move straight to the advanced level of learning-to-treat-women-as-people, the one where we talk about managing our feelings like grown-ups.

Some men I speak to are worried, now, that "having to ask" will mean more rejection. I would draw attention to the fact that even as women everywhere are confessing to crimes others have committed against them, describing lifetimes of humiliation and hurt, still the second or third thought on some men's minds is anxiety about whether this will affect their chances of getting laid.

I understand that you are terrified of rejection. Join the club. Rejection is the worst. So awful that an entire architecture of quiet violence, shame, and blame has been built up to help men avoid it. If women's desire is absent from this conversation—if women are not thought of as desiring beings, if female desire is so terrifying we can barely speak of it without nervous laughter—then yes, we are going to remain confused about the difference between seduction and assault. That confusion is not human nature. Human nature is a lazy excuse for not doing the work of change here, and I'm sick of hearing it.

Men who believe they cannot change are already being shown up every day by the growing number of their fellow male humans who have changed, who are changing. We can rewrite the sexual script of humanity. We've done it before.

Unfortunately, we are in one of those rare and curious moments where we have to do something unfair and hurtful in order to answer decades of pain and injustice. We didn't want to have to make an example of anyone. We tried to ask nicely for our humanity and dignity. We tried to put it gently. Nobody gave a shit. Now that there are consequences, now that there is finally, for once, some sort of price to pay for treating women like interchangeable pieces of flesh and calling it romance, you're paying attention.

This is what happens when women actively place their own needs first. The whole damn world freaks out. I don't blame you for freaking out right now. I'm freaking out. I didn't expect this to happen so fast.

You were led to believe that when it came to sex—and it somehow always came to sex—women weren't people in quite the same way as you. You were taught that sex was a commodity you could acquire by bargaining, badgering, pestering, or force. You were never told that was wrong to do these things. Well, you were told, but not often, or not by anyone who *mattered*.

That all feels unfair to you, though it was far less fair—and a lot more dangerous—to us.

It also feels unfair that some men who have hurt women will be made examples of in their communities and workplaces while others who have done the same will escape, for now. It feels unfair that the cost of mistakes you made in your youth may well be professional respect, job security, money, and power. But it has been a lot less fair for a lot longer for people who were hurt and humiliated, disrespected and degraded, and who were expected to choose between shameful silence and blowing up their careers or communities by speaking out.

For so long, women have been confessing to crimes men have committed and being punished accordingly. That, I think you'll agree, is truly unfair.

·　　·　　·

You are wondering if forgiveness is possible. If amnesty is on the horizon. If you fish your crimes out of the past and lay them dripping to dry in front of us will we accept you, forgive you, let you back into the loving female place you've been told is the only respite you're allowed from the awfulness of the world?

The answer will eventually be yes. Well, my answer will eventually be yes. I can't speak for everyone, ever, and particularly not in this case, as I'm pathologically forgiving and have often been told by people who care about my well-being that my life would be better if I didn't let the men in it get away with quite so much bullshit because I expect no better. Still, my answer will always eventually be yes, yes, you are forgiven. But I'm just one person, and I'm not always a wise one, and even I can tell you that this is a bad fucking time to ask for forgiveness. Give it a while.

There will be time for apologies. We have the rest of our lives to do this differently. There will be time to reach out to those you may have wronged and say that you were a younger and different person, you are sorry, you didn't know, you tried not to know, you know now. There will be time to make it right, but it will take precisely that. It will take time.

What women like me want in the long term is for you to stop this shit and treat us like people. We want you to accept that you have done bad things, so that in the future you can do better. We want a flavor of equality that none of us have tasted before. We want to share it with you. We want a world where love and violence are not so easily confused. We want a species of sexuality that isn't a game where we're the prey to be hung bleeding on your bedroom wall.

Right now, we also want to rage. We are not done describing all the ways this shit isn't okay and hasn't been okay for longer than you can believe. We want you to make space for our pain and anger before you start telling us how you've suffered, too, no, really you have. We are angry, and we are disappointed.

Because you made everything precious in our lives conditional on not making a fuss.

Because you behaved as if your right never to have to deal with anyone else's emotions or learn the shape of your own was more important than our very humanity.

Because you made us carry the weight of all the hurt that had ever been done to you, and then you praised us for being so strong.

Because we tried for so long to believe the best of you, because it felt like we had no other option.

I promise you will survive our rage. We have lived in fear of yours for so long.

Stay here, in this difficult place. Stay here actively. Breathe through the discomfort and pay attention to what it's telling you. Listen to women. Believe women. There will be a lot to learn, and a lot more to unlearn.

Sure, we can draw up a list of rules, and in the short term it might even help. Don't make someone's job conditional on allowing you to grab and hassle her when you're drunk. Don't fuck people who are unconscious. Don't assume that any woman who's made the barest effort with her hair and makeup has thereby given anyone within ass-patting distance an invitation. I can go on. I wish I didn't have to.

You've just arrived in this strange new country where women are human beings whose lives and feelings matter and while you find your way around, yes, it's useful to memorize a few key phrases. *May I kiss you? Ok, that's fine. Do you like this? Do you want me? Here's what I want; what do you want?* You can sound out the shapes of these sentences, but teaching you is a lot of effort, and frankly in the long run it'd be much less work for everyone involved if you'd just learn the language yourselves. Just think of the interesting conversations we could have in a rhetoric of mutual humanity.

Think on that, and be brave. Have the goddamn courage to admit that you got it wrong so that you can start getting it right. There's a train leaving soon. It makes a few stops on the way to a less monstrous future, and I advise you to be on it.

## *ProPublica* with NPR

FINALIST—PUBLIC
INTEREST

*Lauren Bloomstein was a neonatal
nurse; her husband, Larry, was an
orthopedic surgeon. She gave birth
in the hospital where she worked.
She died in the same hospital
twenty hours later. This is her
story. But it also the story of the
nearly 900 women who die every
year in the United States from
causes related to pregnancy or
childbirth. Copublished by two
nonprofit news organizations,*
ProPublica *and NPR, "The Last
Person You'd Expect to Die in
Childbirth" was the first article in
a three-part series, which included
a heartbreaking photo gallery,
"Lost Mothers," and a second
major story, "Nothing Protects
Black Women from Dying in
Pregnancy and Childbirth." The
Ellie judges described "The Last
Person You'd Expect to Die in
Childbirth" as "electrifying" and
praised the series for "its life-
saving impact."*

Nina Martin and
Renee Montagne

# The Last Person You'd Expect to Die in Childbirth

As a neonatal-intensive-care nurse, Lauren Bloomstein had been taking care of other people's babies for years. Finally, at thirty-three, she was expecting one of her own. The prospect of becoming a mother made her giddy, her husband, Larry, recalled recently—"the happiest and most alive I'd ever seen her." When Lauren was thirteen, her own mother had died of a massive heart attack. Lauren had lived with her older brother for a while, then with a neighbor in Hazlet, New Jersey, who was like a surrogate mom, but in important ways she'd grown up mostly alone. The chance to create her own family, to be the mother she didn't have, touched a place deep inside her. "All she wanted to do was be loved," said Frankie Hedges, who took Lauren in as a teenager and thought of her as her daughter. "I think everybody loved her, but nobody loved her the way she wanted to be loved."

Other than some nausea in her first trimester, the pregnancy went smoothly. Lauren was "tired in the beginning, achy in the end," said Jackie Ennis, her best friend since high school, who talked to her at least once a day. "She gained what she's supposed to. She looked great, she felt good, she worked as much as she could"—at least three twelve-hour shifts a week until late into her ninth month. Larry, a doctor, helped monitor her blood pressure at home, and all was normal.

On her days off she got organized, picking out strollers and car seats, stocking up on diapers and onesies. After one last prebaby vacation to the Caribbean, she and Larry went hunting for their forever home, settling on a brick colonial with black shutters and a big yard in Moorestown, not far from his new job as an orthopedic trauma surgeon in Camden. Lauren wanted the baby's gender to be a surprise, so when she set up the nursery she left the walls unpainted—she figured she'd have plenty of time to choose colors later. Despite all she knew about what could go wrong, she seemed untroubled by the normal expectant-mom anxieties. Her only real worry was going into labor prematurely. "You have to stay in there at least until thirty-two weeks," she would tell her belly. "I see how the babies do before thirty-two. Just don't come out too soon."

When she reached thirty-nine weeks and six days—Friday, September 30, 2011—Larry and Lauren drove to Monmouth Medical Center in Long Branch, the hospital where the two of them had met in 2004 and where she'd spent virtually her entire career. If anyone would watch out for her and her baby, Lauren figured, it would be the doctors and nurses she worked with on a daily basis. She was especially fond of her obstetrician-gynecologist, who had trained as a resident at Monmouth at the same time as Larry. Lauren wasn't having contractions, but she and the OB-GYN agreed to schedule an induction of labor—he was on call that weekend and would be sure to handle the delivery himself.

Inductions often go slowly, and Lauren's labor stretched well into the next day. Ennis talked to her on the phone several times: "She said she was feeling okay, she was just really uncomfortable." At one point, Lauren was overcome by a sudden, sharp pain in her back near her kidneys or liver, but the nurses bumped up her epidural and the stabbing stopped.

Inductions have been associated with higher cesarean-section rates, but Lauren progressed well enough to deliver vaginally. On

Saturday, October 1, at six-forty-nine p.m., twenty-three hours after she checked into the hospital, Hailey Anne Bloomstein was born, weighing five pounds, twelve ounces. Larry and Lauren's family had been camped out in the waiting room; now they swarmed into the delivery area to ooh and aah, marveling at how Lauren seemed to glow.

Larry floated around on his own cloud of euphoria, phone camera in hand. In one thirty-five-second video, Lauren holds their daughter on her chest, stroking her cheek with a practiced touch. Hailey is bundled in hospital-issued pastels and flannel, unusually alert for a newborn; she studies her mother's face as if trying to make sense of a mystery that will never be solved. The delivery room staff bustles in the background in the low-key way of people who believe everything has gone exactly as it's supposed to.

Then Lauren looks directly at the camera, her eyes brimming. Twenty hours later, she was dead.

·   ·   ·

The ability to protect the health of mothers and babies in childbirth is a basic measure of a society's development. Yet every year in the U.S., 700 to 900 women die from pregnancy- or childbirth-related causes, and some 65,000 nearly die—by many measures, the worst record in the developed world.

American women are more than three times as likely as Canadian women to die in the maternal period (defined by the Centers for Disease Control as the start of pregnancy to one year after delivery or termination), six times as likely to die as Scandinavians. In every other wealthy country, and many less affluent ones, maternal mortality rates have been falling; in Great Britain, the journal *Lancet* recently noted, the rate has declined so dramatically that "a man is more likely to die while his partner is pregnant than she is." But in the United States, maternal deaths increased from 2000 to 2014. In a recent analysis by the CDC Foundation, nearly 60 percent of such deaths were preventable.

While maternal mortality is significantly more common among African Americans, low-income women, and in rural areas, pregnancy and childbirth complications kill women of every race and ethnicity, education, and income level, in every part of the United States. *ProPublica* and NPR spent the last several months scouring social media and other sources, ultimately identifying more than 450 expectant and new mothers who have died since 2011. The list includes teachers, insurance brokers, homeless women, journalists, a spokeswoman for Yellowstone National Park, a cofounder of the YouTube channel WhatsUp-Moms, and more than a dozen doctors and nurses like Lauren Bloomstein. They died from cardiomyopathy and other heart problems, massive hemorrhage, blood clots, infections, and pregnancy-induced hypertension (preeclampsia), as well as rarer causes. Many died days or weeks after leaving the hospital. Maternal mortality is commonplace enough that three new mothers who died, including Lauren, were cared for by the same OB-GYN.

The reasons for higher maternal mortality in the United States are manifold. New mothers are older than they used to be, with more complex medical histories. Half of pregnancies in the United States are unplanned, so many women don't address chronic health issues beforehand. Greater prevalence of C-sections leads to more life-threatening complications. The fragmented health system makes it harder for new mothers, especially those without good insurance, to get the care they need. Confusion about how to recognize worrisome symptoms and treat obstetric emergencies makes caregivers more prone to error.

Yet the worsening U.S. maternal mortality numbers contrast sharply with the impressive progress in saving babies' lives. Infant mortality has fallen to its lowest point in history, the CDC reports, reflecting fifty years of efforts by the public-health community to prevent birth defects, reduce preterm birth, and improve outcomes for very premature infants. The number of babies who die annually in the United States—about 23,000 in 2014—still greatly exceeds the number of expectant and new mothers who die, but the ratio is narrowing.

The divergent trends for mothers and babies highlight a theme that has emerged repeatedly in *ProPublica*'s and NPR's reporting. In recent decades, under the assumption that it had conquered maternal mortality, the American medical system has focused more on fetal and infant safety and survival than on the mother's health and well-being.

"We worry a lot about vulnerable little babies," said Barbara Levy, vice president for health policy/advocacy at the American Congress of Obstetricians and Gynecologists (ACOG) and a member of the Council on Patient Safety in Women's Health Care. Meanwhile, "we don't pay enough attention to those things that can be catastrophic for women."

At the federally funded Maternal-Fetal Medicine Units Network, the preeminent obstetric research collaborative in the United States, only four of the thirty-four initiatives listed in its online database primarily target mothers, versus twenty-four aimed at improving outcomes for infants (the remainder address both). Under the Title V federal-state program supporting maternal and child health, states devoted about 6 percent of block grants in 2016 to programs for mothers, compared to 78 percent for infants and special-needs children. The notion that babies deserve more care than mothers is similarly enshrined in the Medicaid program, which pays for about 45 percent of births. In many states, the program covers moms for sixty days postpartum, their infants for a full year. The bill to replace the Affordable Care Act, adopted by the U.S. House of Representatives earlier this month, could gut Medicaid for mothers and babies alike.

At the provider level, advances in technology have widened the gap between maternal and fetal and infant care. "People became really enchanted with the ability to do ultrasound, and then high-resolution ultrasound, to do invasive procedures, to stick needles in the amniotic cavity," said William Callaghan, chief of the CDC's Maternal and Infant Health Branch.

The growing specialty of maternal-fetal medicine drifted so far toward care of the fetus that as recently as 2012, young doctors who wanted to work in the field didn't have to spend time learning to care for birthing mothers. "The training was quite variable across the U.S.," said Mary D'Alton, chair of OB-GYN at Columbia University Medical Center and author of papers on disparities in care for mothers and infants. "There were some fellows that could finish their maternal-fetal medicine training without ever being in a labor and delivery unit."

In the last decade or so, at least twenty hospitals have established multidisciplinary fetal care centers for babies at high risk for a variety of problems. So far, only one hospital in the U.S.—NewYork-Presbyterian/Columbia—has a similar program for high-risk moms-to-be.

In regular maternity wards, too, babies are monitored more closely than mothers during and after birth, maternal health advocates told *ProPublica* and NPR. Newborns in the slightest danger are whisked off to neonatal-intensive-care units like the one Lauren Bloomstein worked at, staffed by highly trained specialists ready for the worst, while their mothers are tended by nurses and doctors who expect things to be fine and are often unprepared when they aren't.

When women are discharged, they routinely receive information about how to breastfeed and what to do if their newborn is sick but not necessarily how to tell if they need medical attention themselves. "It was only when I had my own child that I realized, 'Oh my goodness. That was completely insufficient information,'" said Elizabeth Howell, professor of obstetrics and gynecology at the Icahn School of Medicine at Mount Sinai Hospital in New York City. "The way that we've been trained, we do not give women enough information for them to manage their health postpartum. The focus had always been on babies and not on mothers."

In 2009, the Joint Commission, which accredits 21,000 health-care facilities in the United States, adopted a series of perinatal "core measures"—national standards that have been shown to reduce complications and improve patient outcomes. Four of the measures are aimed at making sure the baby is healthy. One— bringing down the C-section rate—addresses maternal health.

Meanwhile, life-saving practices that have become widely accepted in other affluent countries—and in a few states, notably California—have yet to take hold in many American hospitals. Take the example of preeclampsia, a type of high blood pressure that only occurs in pregnancy or the postpartum period and can lead to seizures and strokes. Around the world, it kills an estimated five women an hour. But in developed countries, it is highly treatable. The key is to act quickly.

By standardizing its approach, Britain has reduced preeclampsia deaths to one in a million—a total of two deaths from 2012 to 2014. In the United States, on the other hand, preeclampsia still accounts for about 8 percent of maternal deaths—fifty to seventy women a year. Including Lauren Bloomstein.

·         ·         ·

When Lauren McCarthy Bloomstein was a teenager in the 1990s, a neighbor who worked for a New York publishing firm approached her about modeling for a series of books based on Louisa May Alcott's classic *Little Women*. Since her mother's death, Lauren had become solitary and shy; she loved to read, but she decided she wasn't interested. "Are you kidding? Go do it!" Frankie Hedges insisted. "That would be fabulous!" Lauren relented, and the publisher cast her as the eldest March sister, Meg. She appeared on the covers of four books, looking very much the proper nineteenth-century young lady with her long brown hair parted neatly down the middle and a string of pearls around her neck. The determined expression on her face, though, was pure Lauren. "She didn't want sympathy, she didn't want pity," Jackie Ennis said. "She wasn't one to talk much about her feelings [about] her mom. She looked at it as this is what she was dealt and she's gonna do everything in her power to become a productive person."

In high school, Lauren decided her path lay in nursing, and she chose a two-year program at Brookdale Community College. She worked at a doctor's office to earn money for tuition and lived in the garage apartment that Hedges and her husband had converted especially for her, often helping out with their young twin sons. Lauren "wasn't a real mushy person," Hedges said. "She wasn't the type to say things like 'I love you.'" But she clearly relished being part of a family again. "You can't believe how happy she is," Ennis once told Hedges. "We'll be out and she'll say, 'Oh, I have to go home for dinner!'"

After graduating in 2002, Lauren landed at Monmouth Medical Center, a sprawling red-brick complex a few minutes from the ocean that is part of the RWJBarnabas Health system and a teaching affiliate of Philadelphia's Drexel University College of Medicine. Her first job was in the medical surgical unit, where her clinical skills and work ethic soon won accolades. "I cannot remember too many healthcare employees that I respect as much as Lauren," Diane Stanaway, then Monmouth's clinical director of nursing, wrote in a 2005 commendation. "What a dynamite young lady and nurse!" When a top hospital executive needed surgery, Larry recalled, he paid Lauren the ultimate compliment, picking her as one of two private-duty nurses to help oversee his care.

Larry Bloomstein, who joined the unit as an orthopedic surgical resident in 2004, was dazzled, too. He liked her independent streak—"She didn't feel the need to rely on anyone else for anything"—and her levelheadedness. Even performing CPR on a dying patient, Lauren "had a calmness about her," Larry said. He thought her tough upbringing "gave her a sense of confidence. She didn't seem to worry about small things." Lauren, meanwhile, told Ennis, "I met this guy. He's a doctor, and he's very kind." Their first date was a Bruce Springsteen concert; five years later they married on Long Beach Island, on the Jersey shore.

One of Lauren's favorite books was *The Catcher in the Rye*— "she related to the Holden Caulfield character rescuing kids," Larry said. When a spot opened at Monmouth's elite neonatal intensive care unit in 2006, she jumped at it.

The hospital has the fifth-busiest maternity department in the state, delivering 5,449 babies in 2016. Monmouth earned an "A" grade from Leapfrog, a nonprofit that promotes safety in health care, and met full safety standards in critical areas of maternity care, such as rates of C-sections and early elective deliveries, a hospital spokeswoman said. Its NICU, a Level III facility for high-risk newborns, is the oldest in New Jersey.

"With NICU nursing, it's one of those things either you get it or you don't," said Katy DiBernardo, a twenty-year veteran of the unit. "The babies are little, and a lot of people aren't used to seeing a teeny tiny baby." The NICU staff included nurses, neonatologists, a respiratory therapist, and residents. Lauren, DiBernardo said, "just clicked."

One of the things Lauren liked best about her work was the bonds she formed with babies' families. Nurses followed the same newborns throughout their stay, sometimes for weeks or months. She was a touchstone for parents—very good at "calming people down who have a lot of anxiety," Larry said—and often stayed in contact long after the babies went home, meeting the moms for coffee and even babysitting on occasion.

She also cherished the deep friendships that a place like the NICU forged. The neonatal floor was like a world unto itself, Lauren Byron, another longtime nurse there, explained: "There's a lot of stress and pressure, and you are in life-and-death situations.

You develop a very close relationship with some people." The environment tended to attract very strong personalities. Lauren's nickname in the Bloomstein family football pool was "The Feisty One," so she fit right in. But she could stand her ground without alienating anyone. "She was one of those people that everyone liked," Byron said.

.        .        .

Another person everyone liked was OB-GYN John Vaclavik. He had come to Monmouth as a resident in 2004, around the same time as Larry, after earning his bachelor's from Loyola College in Baltimore and his medical degree at St. George's University on the island of Grenada. Medicine was the family profession: Two uncles and two brothers also became doctors and his wife was a perinatal social worker at the hospital. Lauren and her colleagues thought he was "very personable" and "a great guy," Larry said.

"She was good friends with my wife and she felt comfortable with me," Vaclavik would recall in a 2015 court deposition.

After his residency, Vaclavik joined Ocean Obstetric & Gynecologic Associates, a thriving practice that counted numerous medical professionals among its clients. Vaclavik was a "laborist"—part of a movement that aimed to reduce the number of C-sections, which tend to have more difficult recoveries and more complications than vaginal births. In a state with a C-section rate of 37 percent, Monmouth's rate in 2016 was just 21 percent.

The neonatal nurses had plenty of opportunity to observe Vaclavik and other OB-GYNs in action—someone from NICU was called to attend every delivery that showed signs of being complicated or unusual as well as every C-section. "We always laughed, 'They'll call us for a hangnail,'" DiBernardo said. Lauren was so impressed by Vaclavik that she not only chose him as her own doctor, she recommended him to her best friend. "She kept saying, 'You have to go to this guy. He's a good doctor. Good doctor,'" Ennis said.

In other ways, though, the NICU staff and the labor-and-delivery staff were very separate. The neonatal nurses were focused on their own fragile patients—the satisfaction that came from helping them grow strong enough to go home, the grief when that didn't happen. Once Ennis asked Lauren, "How do you deal with babies that don't make it? That's got to be so bad." Lauren replied, "Yeah, but we save more than we lose."

Loss was less common in labor and delivery, and when a new mother suffered life-threatening complications, the news did not always reach the NICU floor. Thus, when a twenty-nine-year-old special-education teacher named Tara Hansen contracted a grisly infection a few days after giving birth to her first child in March 2011, the tragedy didn't register with Lauren, who was then three months pregnant herself.

Hansen lived in nearby Freehold, New Jersey, with her husband, Ryan, her high school sweetheart. Her pregnancy, like Lauren's, had been textbook perfect, and she delivered a healthy nine-pound son. But Hansen suffered tearing near her vagina during childbirth. She developed signs of infection but was discharged anyway, a lawsuit by her husband later alleged.

Hansen was soon readmitted to Monmouth with what the lawsuit called "excruciating, severe pain beyond the capacity of a human being to endure." The diagnosis was necrotizing fasciitis, commonly known as flesh-eating bacteria; two days later Hansen was dead. One of Vaclavik's colleagues delivered Hansen's baby; Vaclavik himself authorized her discharge. According to court documents, he said nurses failed to inform him about Hansen's symptoms and that if he'd known her vital signs weren't stable, he wouldn't have released her. The hospital and nurses eventually settled for $1.5 million. The suit against Vaclavik and his colleagues is pending.

Vaclavik did not respond to several interview requests from *ProPublica* and NPR, including an e-mailed list of questions. "Due to the fact this matter is in litigation," his attorney responded, "Dr. Vaclavik respectfully declines to comment."

Citing patient privacy, Monmouth spokeswoman Elizabeth Brennan also declined to discuss specific cases. "We are saddened by the grief these families have experienced from their loss," she said in a statement.

·          ·          ·

Larry Bloomstein's first inkling that something was seriously wrong with Lauren came about ninety minutes after she gave birth. He had accompanied Hailey up to the nursery to be weighed and measured and given the usual barrage of tests for newborns. Lauren hadn't eaten since breakfast, but he returned to find her dinner tray untouched. "I don't feel good," she told him. She pointed to a spot above her abdomen and just below her sternum, close to where she'd felt the stabbing sensation during labor. "I've got pain that's coming back."

Larry had been at Lauren's side much of the previous twenty-four hours. Conscious that his role was husband rather than doctor, he had tried not to overstep. Now, though, he pressed Vaclavik: What was the matter with his wife? "He was like, 'I see this a lot. We do a lot of belly surgery. This is definitely reflux,'" Larry recalled. According to Lauren's records, the OB-GYN ordered an antacid called Bicitra and an opioid painkiller called Dilaudid. Lauren vomited them up.

Lauren's pain was soon ten on a scale of ten, she told Larry and the nurses; so excruciating, the nurses noted, "Patient [is] unable to stay still." Just as ominously, her blood pressure was spiking. An hour after Hailey's birth, the reading was 160/95; an hour after that, 169/108. At her final prenatal appointment, her reading had been just 118/69. Obstetrics wasn't Larry's specialty, but he knew enough to ask the nurse: Could this be preeclampsia?

Preeclampsia, or pregnancy-related hypertension, is a little-understood condition that affects 3 percent to 5 percent of expectant or new mothers in the United States, up to 200,000 women a year. It can strike anyone out of the blue, though the risk is higher for African Americans; women with preexisting conditions such as obesity, diabetes, or kidney disease; and mothers over the age of forty. It is most common during the second half of pregnancy but can develop in the days or weeks after childbirth and can become very dangerous very quickly. Because a traditional treatment for preeclampsia is to deliver as soon as possible, the babies are often premature and end up in NICUs like the one where Lauren worked.

As Larry suspected, Lauren's blood pressure readings were well past the danger point. What he didn't know was that they'd been abnormally high since she entered the hospital— 147/99, according to her admissions paperwork. During labor, she had twenty-one systolic readings at or above 140 and thirteen diastolic readings at or above 90, her records indicated; for a stretch of almost eight hours, her blood pressure wasn't monitored at all, the New Jersey Department of Health later found. Over that same period, their baby's vital signs were being constantly watched, Larry said.

In his deposition, Vaclavik described the 147/99 reading as "elevated" compared to her usual readings but not abnormal. He "would use 180 over 110 as a cutoff" to suspect preeclampsia, he said. Still, he acknowledged, Lauren's blood pressure "might have been recommended to be monitored more closely, in retrospect."

Leading medical organizations in the United States and the UK take a different view. They advise that increases to 140/90 for pregnant women with no previous history of high blood pressure signify preeclampsia. When systolic readings hit 160, treatment with anti-hypertensive drugs and magnesium sulfate to prevent seizures "should be initiated ASAP," according to guidelines from the Alliance for Innovation on Maternal Health. When other symptoms, such as upper abdominal (epigastric) pain, are present, the situation is considered even more urgent.

This basic approach isn't new: "Core Curriculum for Maternal-Newborn Nursing," a widely used textbook, outlined it in 1997. Yet failure to diagnose preeclampsia, or to differentiate it from chronic high blood pressure, is all too common.

California researchers who studied preeclampsia deaths over several years found one striking theme: "Despite triggers that clearly indicated a serious deterioration in the patient's condition, health care providers failed to recognize and respond to these signs in a timely manner, leading to delays in diagnosis and treatment." Preeclampsia symptoms—swelling and rapid weight gain, gastric discomfort and vomiting, headache and anxiety—are often mistaken for the normal irritations that crop up during pregnancy or after giving birth. "We don't have a yes-no test for it," said Eleni Tsigas, executive director of the Preeclampsia Foundation. "A lot of physicians don't necessarily see a lot of it." Outdated notions—for example, that delivering the baby cures the condition—unfamiliarity with best practices, and lack of crisis preparation can further hinder the response.

The fact that Lauren gave birth over the weekend may also have worked against her. Hospitals may be staffed differently on weekends, adding to the challenges of managing a crisis. A new Baylor College of Medicine analysis of 45 million pregnancies in the United States from 2004 to 2014 found mothers who deliver on Saturday or Sunday have nearly 50 percent higher mortality rates as well as more blood transfusions and more perineal tearing. The "weekend effect" has also been associated with higher fatality rates from heart attacks, strokes, and head trauma.

According to Lauren's records, Vaclavik did order a preeclampsia lab test around eight-forty p.m., but a nurse noted a half-hour later: "No abnormal labs present." (According to Larry, the results were borderline.) Larry began pushing to call in a specialist. Vaclavik attributed Lauren's pain to esophagitis, or inflammation of the esophagus, which had afflicted her before, he said in his deposition. Around ten p.m., according to Lauren's medical records, he phoned the on-call gastroenterologist, who ordered an X-ray and additional tests, more Dilaudid and different antacids—Maalox and Protonix. Nothing helped.

Meanwhile, Larry decided to reach out to his own colleagues in the trauma unit at Cooper University Hospital in Camden. In his training, perhaps the most important lesson he'd learned was to ask for help: "If there's a problem, I will immediately get another physician involved." By chance, the doctor on call happened to be a fairly new mother. As Larry described Lauren's symptoms, she interrupted him. "You can stop talking. I know what this is." She said Lauren had HELLP syndrome, an acronym for the most severe variation of preeclampsia, characterized by hemolysis, or the breakdown of red blood cells; elevated liver enzymes; and low platelet count, a clotting deficiency that can lead to excessive bleeding and hemorrhagic stroke.

Larry's colleague urged him to stop wasting time, he recalled. Lauren's very high blood pressure, the vomiting, and the terrible pain radiating from her kidneys and liver were symptoms of rapid deterioration. "Your wife's in a lot of danger," the trauma doctor said. (She didn't respond to *ProPublica*'s and NPR's requests for comment.)

·      ·      ·

Earlier this year, an analysis by the CDC Foundation of maternal mortality data from four states identified more than twenty "critical factors" that contributed to pregnancy-related deaths. Among the ones involving providers: lack of standardized policies, inadequate clinical skills, failure to consult specialists, and poor coordination of care. The average maternal death had 3.7 critical factors.

"It's never just one thing," said Roberta Gold, a member of the Council on Patient Safety in Women's Health Care, whose daughter and unborn grandson died from a pregnancy-related blood clot in 2010. "It's always a cascading combination of things. It's a slow-motion train wreck."

The last sixteen hours of Lauren's life were consistent with that grim pattern. Distressed by what the trauma doctor had told him, Larry immediately went to Lauren's caregivers. But they insisted the tests didn't show preeclampsia, he said. Not long after, Larry's colleague called back to check on Lauren's condition. "I don't believe those labs," he recalls her telling him. "They can't be right. I'm positive of my diagnosis. Do them again.'"

Meanwhile, Lauren's agony had become almost unendurable. The blood pressure cuff on her arm was adding to her discomfort, so around ten-thirty p.m. her nurse decided to remove it—on the theory, Larry said, "We know her blood pressure is high. There's no point to retaking it." According to Lauren's records, her blood pressure went unmonitored for another hour and forty-four minutes.

Larry had given up on getting a specialist to come to the hospital so late on a Saturday night, but he persuaded Vaclavik to call in a general surgical resident. Around eleven-fifty-five p.m., according to the nurses' notes, Lauren begged, "Do anything to stop this pain." Vaclavik prescribed morphine, to little effect.

Just after midnight, her blood pressure about to peak at 197/117, Lauren began complaining of a headache. As Larry studied his wife's face, he realized something had changed. "She suddenly looks really calm and comfortable, like she's trying to go to sleep." She gave Larry a little smile, but only the right side of her mouth moved.

In an instant, Larry's alarm turned to panic. He ordered Lauren, "Lift your hands for me." Only her right arm fluttered. He peeled off her blankets and scraped the soles of her feet with his fingernail, testing her so-called Babinski reflex; in an adult whose brain is working normally, the big toe automatically jerks downward. Lauren's right toe curled as it was supposed to. But her left toe stuck straight out, unmoving. As Larry was examining her, Lauren suddenly seemed to realize what was happening to her. "She looked at me and said, 'I'm afraid,' and, 'I love you.' And I'm pretty sure in that moment she put the pieces together. That she had a conscious awareness of . . . that she was not going to make it."

A CT scan soon confirmed the worst: The escalating blood pressure had triggered bleeding in her brain. So-called hemorrhagic strokes tend to be deadlier than those caused by blood clots. Surgery can sometimes save the patient's life, but only if it is performed quickly.

Larry was a realist; he knew that even the best-case scenario was devastating. Chances were that Lauren would be paralyzed or partially paralyzed. She'd never be the mother she had dreamed of being. She'd never be a nurse again. But at least there was a chance she would live. When the neurologist arrived, Larry asked, "Is there hope here?" As he recalls it, the neurologist responded, "That's why I'm here. There's hope."

Larry began gathering Lauren's loved ones—his parents; her brother; Frankie Hedges and her husband, Billy; Jackie Ennis. On the phone, he tried to play down the gravity of the situation, but everyone understood. When Larry's mother arrived, the hospital entrance was locked, and Larry and Vaclavik came to meet her. "The obstetrician just said, 'She's going to be all right,'" Linda Bloomstein said. "And Larry was standing behind him, and I saw the tears coming down, and he was shaking his head, 'No.'"

Around two a.m., the neurosurgeon finally confirmed what the trauma doctor had said four hours before: Lauren had HELLP syndrome. Then he delivered more bad news: Her blood platelets— essential to stopping the hemorrhage—were dangerously low. But, according to Larry, the hospital didn't have sufficient platelets on site, so her surgery would have to be delayed. Larry was dumbfounded. How could a regional medical center that delivered babies and performed all types of surgery not have platelets on hand for an emergency? Vaclavik called the Red Cross and other facilities, pleading with them to send any they had. "In my understanding, there was a complete shortage of platelets in the state of New Jersey," he said in the deposition. Hours passed before the needed platelets arrived.

The neuro team did another CT scan around six a.m. Larry couldn't bring himself to look at it, "but from what they've told me, it was horrifically worse." While Lauren was in surgery, friends began dropping by, hoping to see her and the baby, not realizing what had happened since her cheerful texts the night before. Around twelve-thirty p.m., the neurosurgeon emerged and confirmed that brain activity had stopped. Lauren was on life support, with no chance of recovery.

All this time, Hailey had been in the newborn nursery, being tended by Lauren's stunned colleagues. They brought her down to Lauren's room and Larry placed her gently into her mother's arms. After a few minutes, the nurses whisked the baby back up to the third floor to protect her from germs. A respiratory therapist carefully removed the breathing tube from Lauren's mouth. At 3:08 p.m., surrounded by her loved ones, she died.

.     .     .

In the United States, unlike some other developed countries, maternal deaths are treated as a private tragedy rather than as a public-health catastrophe. A death in childbirth may be mourned on Facebook or memorialized on GoFundMe, but it is rarely reported in the news. Most obituaries, Lauren's included, don't mention how a mother died.

Lauren's passing was more public than most, eliciting an outpouring of grief. Hundreds of people attended her wake and funeral—doctors and nurses from the hospital, friends from around the country, families Lauren had taken care of. Vaclavik was there, utterly devastated, Larry's family said. The head of Monmouth's OB-GYN department paid his respects and, according to Larry, promised in a private conversation at the wake to conduct a full investigation.

In the days after Lauren's death, Larry couldn't dwell on the implications of what had happened. He had to find a burial plot, choose a casket, write a eulogy. He was too shattered to return to the Mooresville house, so he took Hailey to his parents' place, a one-bedroom apartment they were renting while they renovated their home, and slept with the baby in the living room for the first month.

After the funeral, he turned all his attention to his daughter. He knew nothing about newborns, always imagining Lauren would teach him—"What could be better than having your own NICU nurse to take care of your baby?" he had thought. He relied on his mother and sister and Lauren's friends to guide him. He took time off from his job at Cooper, figuring three months would be enough. But as his return date approached, he knew he wasn't ready. "I don't think I can see a patient that's on a ventilator right now," he realized. "Or even just a hospital bed." He didn't want to leave Hailey. So he quit.

He sold the house, though he couldn't bring himself to attend the closing—"I couldn't stand handing those keys over to someone else." He took Hailey a couple of times to stay with his sister and her family in Texas, where he didn't have to answer the constant questions. But traveling with his baby daughter was painful in its own way. People didn't know what to make of him. "It's strange for people to see a father alone." Wherever he went, he felt disconnected from almost everything around him. "You're walking around this world and all these people are around you, and they're going on with their lives and I just felt very, very isolated and very alone with that."

Back in New Jersey, Larry found a job closer to his parents' place, performed one operation, and tried to quit. His new employers, though, persuaded him to stay. To avoid reliving the funeral, he returned to Texas for the first anniversary of Hailey's birth and Lauren's death in late September 2012. In one of his suitcases, he packed a giant cupcake mold Lauren had bought when they first married—she thought it would make a perfect first-birthday cake for the kids she yearned for. He baked the cake himself—chocolate, Lauren's favorite, covered with sprinkles.

.        .        .

Other people in Lauren's and Larry's circle had been asking questions about her care since the night she died. "That was the first thing I literally said when I walked [into the hospital]—I said, 'How did this happen?'" Jackie Ennis recalled. In the next week or two, she probed Larry again: "'Did they do everything they could for her?' He said, 'No, there were warning signs for hours before.'" Ennis was too upset to dig any deeper.

As Larry's numbness wore off, his orthopedist friends began pushing him as well. Larry was hesitant; despite the missteps he had witnessed, part of him wanted to believe that Lauren's death had been unavoidable. "And my friends were like, 'We can't accept that. . . . With our technology, every single time a woman dies [in childbirth], it's a medical error.'"

Lauren's death, Larry finally admitted to himself, could not be dismissed as either inevitable or a fluke. He had seen how Lauren's OB-GYN and nurses had failed to recognize a textbook case of one of the most common complications of pregnancy—not once but repeatedly over two days. To Larry, the fact that someone with Lauren's advantages could die so needlessly was symptomatic of a bigger problem. By some measures, New Jersey had one of the highest maternal mortality rates in the United States. He wanted authorities to get to the root of it—to push the people and institutions that were at fault to change.

That's the approach in the United Kingdom, where maternal deaths are regarded as systems failures. A national committee of experts scrutinizes every death of a woman from pregnancy or childbirth complications, collecting medical records and assessments from caregivers, conducting rigorous analyses of the data, and publishing reports that help set policy for hospitals throughout the country. Coroners also sometimes hold public inquests, forcing hospitals and their staffs to answer for their mistakes. The UK process is largely responsible for the stunning reduction in preeclampsia deaths in Britain, the committee noted its 2016 report—"a clear success story" that it hoped to repeat "across other medical and mental health causes of maternal death."

The United States has no comparable federal effort. Instead, maternal-mortality reviews are left up to states. As of this spring, twenty-six states (and one city, Philadelphia) had a well-established process in place; another five states had committees that were less than a year old. In almost every case, resources are tight, the reviews take years and the findings get little attention. A bipartisan bill in Congress, the Preventing Maternal Deaths Act of 2017, would authorize funding for states to establish review panels or improve their processes.

New Jersey's review team, the second-oldest in the United States, includes OB-GYNs, nurses, mental-health specialists, medical examiners, even a nutritionist. Using vital records and other reports, they identify every woman in New Jersey who died within a year of pregnancy or childbirth, from any cause, then review medical and other records to determine whether the death was "pregnancy-related" or not. Every few years, the committee publishes a report, focusing on things like the race and age of the mothers who died, the causes of death, and other demographic and health data. In the past, the findings have been used to promote policies to reduce postpartum depression.

But the New Jersey committee doesn't interview the relatives of the deceased, nor does it assess whether a death was preventable. Moreover, like every other state that conducts such reviews, New Jersey "de-identifies" the records—strips them of any information that might point to an individual hospital or a particular woman. Otherwise, the medical community and lawmakers would refuse to go along. The goal is to "improve care for patients in general," said Joseph Apuzzio, a professor of obstetrics and gynecology at Rutgers–New Jersey Medical School who heads the committee. This requires a process that is "nonjudgmental" and "not punitive," he said. "That's the best way to get a free discussion of all of the health care providers who are in the room."

Yet the result of de-identification, as Larry soon realized, is that the review is of little use in assigning responsibility for individual deaths, or evaluating whether some hospitals, doctors, or nurses are more prone to error than others. To Larry, this seemed like a critical oversight—or perhaps, willful denial. In a preventable death or other medical error, he said, sometimes the who and the where are as important as the why. "Unless someone points the finger specifically," he said, "I think the actual cause [of the problem] is lost."

·　　·　　·

Someone eventually steered Larry toward the New Jersey Department of Health's licensing and inspection division, which oversees hospital and nursing-home safety. He filed a complaint against Monmouth Medical Center in 2012.

The DOH examined Lauren's records, interviewed her caregivers, and scrutinized Monmouth's policies and practices. In December 2012 it issued a report that backed up everything Larry had seen firsthand. "There is no record in the medical record that the Registered Nurse notified [the OB-GYN] of the elevated blood pressures of patient prior to delivery," investigators found. And: "There is no evidence in the medical record of further evaluation and surveillance of patient from [the OB-GYN] prior to delivery." And: "There was no evidence in the medical record that the elevated blood pressures were addressed by [the OB-GYN] until after the Code Stroke was called."

The report faulted the hospital. "The facility is not in compliance" with New Jersey hospital licensing standards, it concluded. "The facility failed to ensure that recommended obstetrics guidelines are adhered to by staff."

To address these criticisms, Monmouth Medical Center had implemented a plan of correction, also contained in the report. The plan called for a mandatory educational program for all labor-and-delivery nurses about preeclampsia and HELLP syndrome; staff training in Advance Life Support Obstetrics and Critical Care Obstetrics; and more training on the use of evidence-based methods to assess patients and improve communications between caregivers.

Some of the changes were strikingly basic: "Staff nurses were educated regarding the necessity of reviewing, when available, or obtaining the patients [*sic*] prenatal records. Education identified that they must make a comparison of the prenatal blood pressure against the initial admission blood pressure." And: "Repeat vital signs will be obtained every 4 hours at a minimum."

An important part of the plan of correction involved Vaclavik, though neither he nor the nurses were identified by name. The head of Monmouth's OB-GYN department provided "professional remediation for the identified physician," the Department of Health report said. In addition, there was "monitoring of 100% of records for physician of record per month x 3 months." The monitoring focused on "compliance of timely physician intervention for elevated blood pressures/pain assessment and management."

The department chairman, Robert Graebe, found Vaclavik's charts to be 100 percent compliant, Vaclavik said in the deposition. Graebe was asked in a March 2017 deposition if Vaclavik was in good standing at the hospital at the time of Lauren's treatment. "Was and is," Graebe replied.

In a separate note, the Department of Health told Larry that it forwarded his complaint to the Board of Medical Examiners and the New Jersey Board of Nursing. Neither agency has taken disciplinary action, according to their websites.

[UPDATE: In a letter dated June 22, 2017, the State Board of Medical Examiners notified Larry that it had found no basis under its existing governing laws to discipline Vaclavik. Despite a full inquiry, the board was "unable to find undisputed facts to establish . . . sufficient proof to sustain a formal disciplinary action," executive director William V. Roeder wrote.]

Larry's copy of the DOH report arrived in the mail. He was gratified by the findings but dismayed that they weren't publicly posted. That meant hardly anyone would see them.

A few months after the DOH weighed in, he sued Monmouth, Vaclavik, and five nurses in Monmouth County Superior Court in Freehold, New Jersey. For a medical-malpractice lawsuit to go forward in New Jersey, an expert must certify that it has merit. Larry's passed muster with an OB-GYN. But beyond the taking of depositions, there's been little action in the case.

•     •     •

A s the maternal death rate has mounted around the United States, a small cadre of reformers has mobilized. Some of the earliest and most important work has come in California, where more babies are born than in any other state—500,000 a year, one-eighth of the U.S. total.

Modeled on the UK process, the California Maternal Quality Care Collaborative is informed by the experiences of founder Elliott Main, a professor of obstetrics and gynecology at Stanford and the University of California–San Francisco, who for many years ran the OB-GYN department at a San Francisco hospital. "One of my saddest moments as an obstetrician was a woman with severe preeclampsia that we thought we had done everything correct, who still had a major stroke and we could not save her," he said recently. That loss has weighed on him for 20 years. "When you've had a maternal death, you remember it for the rest of your life. All the details."

Launched a decade ago, CMQCC aims to reduce not only mortality but also life-threatening complications and racial disparities in obstetric care. It began by analyzing maternal deaths in the state over several years; in almost every case, it discovered, there was "at least some chance to alter the outcome." The most preventable deaths were from hemorrhage (70 percent) and preeclampsia (60 percent).

Main and his colleagues then began creating a series of "toolkits" to help doctors and nurses improve their handling of emergencies. The first one, targeting obstetric bleeding, recommended things like "hemorrhage carts" for storing medications and supplies, crisis protocols for massive transfusions, and regular training and drills. Instead of the common practice of "eye-balling" blood loss, which often leads to underestimating the seriousness of a hemorrhage and delaying treatment, nurses learned to collect and weigh postpartum blood to get precise measurements. Hospitals that adopted the toolkit saw a 21 percent decrease in near deaths from maternal bleeding in the first year; hospitals that didn't use the protocol had a 1.2 percent reduction. By 2013, according to Main, maternal deaths in California fell to around 7 per 100,000 births, similar to the numbers in Canada, France, and the Netherlands—a dramatic counter to the trends in other parts of the United States.

"Prevention isn't a magic pill," Main said. "It's actually teamwork [and having] a structured, organized, standardized approach" to care.

CMQCC's preeclampsia toolkit, launched in 2014, emphasized the kind of practices that might have saved Lauren Bloomstein: careful monitoring of blood pressure and early and aggressive treatment with magnesium sulfate and anti-hypertensive medications. Data on its effectiveness hasn't been published.

The collaborative's work has inspired ACOG and advocates in a few states to create their own initiatives. Much of the funding has come from a ten-year, $500 million maternal-health initiative by Merck, the pharmaceutical giant. Originally intended to focus on less-developed countries, Merck for Mothers decided it couldn't ignore the growing problem in the United States. The U.S. maternal-mortality rate is "unacceptable," said executive director Mary-Ann Etiebet. Making pregnancy and childbirth safer "will not only save women's lives but will improve and strengthen our health systems . . . for all."

But the really hard work is only beginning. According to the Institute of Medicine, it takes an average of seventeen years for a new medical protocol to be widely adopted. Even in California, half of the 250 hospitals that deliver babies still aren't using the toolkits, said Main, who largely blames inertia.

In New York state, some hospitals have questioned the need for what they call "cookbook medicine," said Columbia's Mary D'Alton. Her response: "Variability is the enemy of safety. Rather than have ten different approaches to obstetric hemorrhage or treatment of hypertension, choose one or two and make it consistent. . . . When we do things in a standardized way, we have better outcomes."

One big hurdle: training. Another: money. Smaller providers, in particular, may not see the point. "It's very hard to get a hospital to provide resources to change something that they don't see as a problem," ACOG's Barbara Levy said. "If they haven't had a maternal death because they only deliver 500 babies a year, how many years is it going to be before they see a severe problem? It may be ten years."

In New Jersey, providers don't need as much convincing, thanks to a recent project to reduce postpartum blood loss led by the Association of Women's Health, Obstetric, and Neonatal Nurses. A number of hospitals saw improvements; at one, the average length of a hemorrhage-related ICU stay plunged from 8 days to 1.5 days. But only thirty-one of the state's fifty-two birthing hospitals participated in the effort, in part—perhaps—because nurses led it, said Robyn D'Oria, executive director of the Central Jersey Family Health Consortium and a member of the state's maternal mortality committee. "I remember having a conversation with [someone from] a hospital that I would describe as progressive and she said to me, 'I cannot get past some of the physicians not wanting to buy into this.'"

So New Jersey hospitals are about to try again, this time adopting mini-toolkits created by the ACOG-led Alliance for Innovation on Maternal Health for hemorrhage and preeclampsia. "We're at the very beginning" of a rollout that is likely to take at least two years, D'Oria said. Among those helping to create momentum has been Ryan Hansen, the husband of the teacher who died at Monmouth Medical Center a few months before Lauren Bloomstein.

Still, as hospitals begin to revamp, mothers in the state continue to perish. One was Ashley Heaney Butler. A Rutgers University graduate, she lived in Bayville, where she decorated the walls of her house with anchors, reflecting her passion for the ocean. She worked for the state Division of Vocational Rehabilitation Services as a counselor, and served as president of the New Jersey Rehabilitation Association. Her husband Joseph was a firefighter. She gave birth at Monmouth last September to a healthy boy and died a couple of weeks later at the age of thirty-one, never leaving the hospital. It turned out that she had developed an infection late in her pregnancy, possibly related to a prior gastric bypass surgery. She was under the care of several doctors, including Vaclavik.

·        ·        ·

The death of a new mother is not like any other sudden death. It blasts a hole in the universe. "When you take that one death and what that does, not only to the husband, but to the family and to the community, the impact that it has in the hospital, on the staff, on everybody that's cared for her, on all the people who knew them, it has ripple effects for generations to come," Robyn D'Oria said.

Jackie Ennis felt Lauren's loss as an absence of phone calls. She and Lauren had been closer than many sisters, talking several times a day. Sometimes Lauren called just to say she was really tired and would talk later; she'd even called Ennis from Hawaii on her honeymoon. The night Lauren died, Ennis knew something was wrong because she hadn't heard from her best friend. "It took me a really long time not to get the phone calls," she said. "I still have trouble with that."

During Lauren's pregnancy, Frankie Hedges had thought of herself as Hailey's other grandmother. She and Lauren had made a lot of plans. Lauren's death meant the loss of their shared dreams for an entire extended family. "I just feel she didn't get what she deserved," Hedges said.

Vaclavik's obstetric practice is "larger" than in 2011, and he continues to have admitting privileges at Monmouth and two other hospitals, he said in his deposition. "I will never forget" Lauren's death, he said. ". . . I probably suffer some post-traumatic stress from this."

Hailey is five years old, with Lauren's brown hair and clear green eyes. She feels her mother's presence everywhere, thanks to Larry and his new wife, Carolyn, whom he married in 2014.

They met when she was a surgical tech at one of the hospitals he worked at after Lauren died. Photos and drawings of Lauren occupy the mantle of their home in Holmdel, the bookcase in the dining room, and the walls of the upstairs hallway. Larry and Carolyn and their other family members talk about Lauren freely, and even Larry's younger daughter, two-year-old Aria, calls her "Mommy Lauren." On birthdays and holidays, Larry takes the girls to the cemetery. He designed the gravestone—his handprint and Lauren's reaching away from each other, newborn Hailey's linking them forever. Larry has done his best to keep Lauren's extended family together—Ennis and Hedges and their families are included in every important celebration.

Larry still has the video of Lauren and Hailey on his phone. "By far the hardest thing for me to accept is [what happened] from Lauren's perspective," he said one recent evening, hitting the play button and seeing her alive once more. "I can't, I literally can't accept it. The amount of pain she must have experienced in that exact moment when she finally had this little girl. . . . I can accept the amount of pain I have been dealt," he went on, watching Lauren stroke Hailey's cheek. "But [her pain] is the one thing I just can't accept. I can't understand, I can't fathom it."

## New York Times Magazine

A middle-aged man looking at new cars on YouTube, his wife asleep upstairs, their daughter still awake in her room at midnight: at one he shuts down his computer and goes to bed. When Basim Razzo awakes, his wife and daughter are dead, and he is severely wounded, all victims of an airstrike conducted in error by the American-led coalition fighting the Islamic State. "The Uncounted" follows Razzo's pursuit of justice—acknowledgment by the United States of its mistake—while documenting the overall impact on civilians of the air campaign in Iraq. "Meticulously reported and movingly told, this investigation found that far more civilians were killed by airstrikes than the U.S. military would acknowledge," reads the award citation for "The Uncounted." "The judges deem this a stunning and important work of journalism."

Azmat Khan and
Anand Gopal

# The Uncounted

L ate on the evening of September 20, 2015, Basim Razzo
sat in the study of his home on the eastern side of Mosul,
his face lit up by a computer screen. His wife, Mayada,
was already upstairs in bed, but Basim could lose hours clicking
through car reviews on YouTube: the BMW Alpina B7, the Audi
Q7. Almost every night went like this. Basim had long harbored
a taste for fast rides, but around ISIS-occupied Mosul, the auto
showrooms sat dark, and the family car in his garage—a 1991
BMW—had barely been used in a year. There simply was nowhere
to go.

The Razzos lived in the Woods, a bucolic neighborhood on the
banks of the Tigris, where marble and stucco villas sprawled amid
forests of eucalyptus, chinar, and pine. Cafes and restaurants
lined the riverbanks, but ever since the city fell to ISIS the previous year, Basim and Mayada had preferred to entertain at home.
They would set up chairs poolside and put kebabs on the grill, and
Mayada would serve pizza or Chinese fried rice, all in an effort
to maintain life as they'd always known it. Their son, Yahya, had
abandoned his studies at Mosul University and fled for Erbil, and
they had not seen him since; those who left when ISIS took over
could reenter the caliphate, but once there, they could not
leave—an impasse that stranded people wherever they found
themselves. Birthdays, weddings, and graduations came and

went, the celebrations stockpiled for that impossibly distant moment: liberation.

Next door to Basim's home stood the nearly identical home belonging to his brother, Mohannad, and his wife, Azza. They were almost certainly asleep at that hour, but Basim guessed that their eighteen-year-old son, Najib, was still up. A few months earlier, he was arrested by the ISIS religious police for wearing jeans and a T-shirt with English writing. They gave him ten lashes and, as a further measure of humiliation, clipped his hair into a buzz cut. Now he spent most of his time indoors, usually on Facebook. "Someday it'll all be over," Najib had posted just a few days earlier. "Until that day, I'll hold on with all my strength."

Sometimes, after his parents locked up for the night, Najib would fish the key out of the cupboard and steal over to his uncle's house. Basim had the uncanny ability to make his nephew forget the darkness of their situation. He had a glass-half-full exuberance, grounded in the belief that every human life—every setback and success, every heartbreak and triumph—is written by the fortieth day in the womb. Basim was not a particularly religious man, but that small article of faith underpinned what seemed to him an ineluctable truth, even in wartime Iraq: Everything happens for a reason. It was an assurance he offered everyone; Yahya had lost a year's worth of education, but in exile he had met, and proposed to, the love of his life. "You see?" Basim would tell Mayada. "You see? That's fate."

Basim had felt this way for as long as he could remember. A fifty-six-year-old account manager at Huawei, the Chinese multinational telecommunications company, he studied engineering in the 1980s at Western Michigan University. He and Mayada lived in Portage, Mich., in a tiny one-bedroom apartment that Mayada also used as the headquarters for her work as an Avon representative; she started small, offering makeup and skin cream to neighbors, but soon expanded sales to Kalamazoo and Comstock. Within a year, she'd saved up enough to buy Basim a $700

Minolta camera. Basim came to rely on her ability to impose order on the strange and the mundane, to master effortlessly everything from Yahya's chemistry homework to the alien repartee of faculty picnics and Rotary clubs. It was fate. They had been married now for thirty-three years.

Around midnight, Basim heard a thump from the second floor. He peeked out of his office and saw a sliver of light under the door to the bedroom of his daughter, Tuqa. He called out for her to go to bed. At twenty-one, Tuqa would often stay up late, and though Basim knew that he wasn't a good example himself and that the current conditions afforded little reason to be up early, he believed in the calming power of an early-to-bed, early-to-rise routine. He waited at the foot of the stairs, called out again, and the sliver went dark.

It was one a.m. when Basim finally shut down the computer and headed upstairs to bed. He settled in next to Mayada, who was fast asleep.

Some time later, he snapped awake. His shirt was drenched, and there was a strange taste—blood?—on his tongue. The air was thick and acrid. He looked up. He was in the bedroom, but the roof was nearly gone. He could see the night sky, the stars over Mosul. Basim reached out and found his legs pressed just inches from his face by what remained of his bed. He began to panic. He turned to his left, and there was a heap of rubble. "Mayada!" he screamed. "Mayada!" It was then that he noticed the silence. "Mayada!" he shouted. "Tuqa!" The bedroom walls were missing, leaving only the bare supports. He could see the dark outlines of treetops. He began to hear the faraway, unmistakable sound of a woman's voice. He cried out, and the voice shouted back, "Where are you?" It was Azza, his sister-in-law, somewhere outside.

"Mayada's gone!" he shouted.

"No, no, I'll find her!"

"No, no, no, she's gone," he cried back. "They're all gone!"

.        .        .

Later that same day, the American-led coalition fighting the Islamic State in Iraq and Syria uploaded a video to its YouTube channel. The clip, titled "Coalition Airstrike Destroys Daesh VBIED Facility Near Mosul, Iraq 20 Sept 2015," shows spectral black-and-white night-vision footage of two sprawling compounds, filmed by an aircraft slowly rotating above. There is no sound. Within seconds, the structures disappear in bursts of black smoke. The target, according to the caption, was a car-bomb factory, a hub in a network of "multiple facilities spread across Mosul used to produce VBIEDs for ISIL's terrorist activities," posing "a direct threat to both civilians and Iraqi security forces." Later, when he found the video, Basim could watch only the first few frames. He knew immediately that the buildings were his and his brother's houses.

The clip is one of hundreds the coalition has released since the American-led war against the Islamic State began in August 2014. Also posted to Defense Department websites, they are presented as evidence of a military campaign unlike any other— precise, transparent, and unyielding. In the effort to expel ISIS from Iraq and Syria, the coalition has conducted more than 27,500 strikes to date, deploying everything from Vietnam-era B-52 bombers to modern Predator drones. That overwhelming air power has made it possible for local ground troops to overcome heavy resistance and retake cities throughout the region. "U.S. and coalition forces work very hard to be precise in airstrikes," Maj. Shane Huff, a spokesman for the Central Command, told us, and as a result "are conducting one of the most precise air campaigns in military history."

American military planners go to great lengths to distinguish today's precision strikes from the air raids of earlier wars, which were carried out with little or no regard for civilian casualties. They describe a target-selection process grounded in meticulously gathered intelligence, technological wizardry, carefully designed bureaucratic hurdles, and extraordinary restraint. Intelligence analysts pass along proposed targets to "targeteers," who study 3-D computer models as they calibrate the angle of attack. A team of lawyers evaluates the plan, and—if all goes well—the process concludes with a strike so precise that it can, in some cases, destroy a room full of enemy fighters and leave the rest of the house intact.

The coalition usually announces an airstrike within a few days of its completion. It also publishes a monthly report assessing allegations of civilian casualties. Those it deems credible are generally explained as unavoidable accidents—a civilian vehicle drives into the target area moments after a bomb is dropped, for example. The coalition reports that since August 2014, it has killed tens of thousands of ISIS fighters and, according to our tally of its monthly summaries, 466 civilians in Iraq.

Yet until we raised his case, Basim's family was not among those counted. Mayada, Tuqa, Mohannad, and Najib were four of an unknown number of Iraqi civilians whose deaths the coalition has placed in the "ISIS" column. Estimates from Airwars and other nongovernmental organizations suggest that the civilian death toll is much higher, but the coalition disputes such figures, arguing that they are based not on specific intelligence but local news reports and testimony gathered from afar. When the coalition notes a mission irregularity or receives an allegation, it conducts its own inquiry and publishes a sentence-long analysis of its findings. But no one knows how many Iraqis have simply gone uncounted.

Our own reporting, conducted over eighteen months, shows that the air war has been significantly less precise than the coalition claims. Between April 2016 and June 2017, we visited the sites of nearly 150 airstrikes across northern Iraq, not long after ISIS was evicted from them. We toured the wreckage; we interviewed hundreds of witnesses, survivors, family members, intelligence informants, and local officials; we photographed bomb fragments, scoured local news sources, identified ISIS targets in the vicinity, and mapped the destruction through satellite imagery. We also visited the American air base in Qatar where the coalition directs the air campaign. There, we were given access to the main operations floor and interviewed senior commanders, intelligence officials, legal advisers, and civilian-casualty assessment experts. We provided their analysts with the coordinates and date ranges of every airstrike—103 in all—in three ISIS-controlled areas and examined their responses. The result is the first systematic, ground-based sample of airstrikes in Iraq since this latest military action began in 2014.

We found that one in five of the coalition strikes we identified resulted in civilian death, a rate more than thirty-one times that acknowledged by the coalition. It is at such a distance from official claims that, in terms of civilian deaths, this may be the least transparent war in recent American history. Our reporting, moreover, revealed a consistent failure by the coalition to investigate claims properly or to keep records that make it possible to investigate the claims at all. While some of the civilian deaths we documented were a result of proximity to a legitimate ISIS target, many others appear to be the result simply of flawed or outdated intelligence that conflated civilians with combatants. In this system, Iraqis are considered guilty until proved innocent. Those who survive the strikes, people like Basim Razzo, remain marked as possible ISIS sympathizers, with no discernible path to clear their names.

.        .        .

Basim woke up in a ward at Mosul General Hospital, heavy with bandages. He was disoriented, but he remembered being pried loose from the rubble, the neighbors' hands all over his body, the backhoe serving him down to the earth, the flashing lights of an ambulance waiting in the distance. The rescuers worked quickly. Everyone knew it had been an airstrike; the planes could return at any minute to finish the job.

In the hospital, Basim was hazily aware of nurses and orderlies, but it was not until morning that he saw a familiar face. Mayada's brother placed a hand on his shoulder. When Basim asked who in his home survived, he was told: nobody. The blast killed Mayada and Tuqa instantly. A second strike hit next door, and Mohannad and Najib were also dead. Only Azza, Najib's mother, was alive, because the explosion had flung her through a second-story window.

With his hip shattered, his pubic bone broken, and his back and the sole of his left foot studded with shrapnel, Basim would need major surgery. But no hospital in Mosul, or anywhere in the caliphate, had the personnel or equipment to carry it out. The only hope was to apply for permission to temporarily leave ISIS territory, which required approval from the surprisingly complex ISIS bureaucracy. A friend put in the paperwork, but the ISIS representative denied the request. "Let him die," he told Basim's friend. "There were four martyrs. Let him be the fifth."

Basim was moved to his parents' home on the city's southern side. For two days, close friends and family members streamed in, but he hardly registered their presence. On the third day, he found himself able to sit up, and he began flipping through the pictures on his phone. One of the last was taken the evening before the attack: Tuqa grinning in the kitchen, clutching a sparkler. For the first time, he began to sob. Then he gathered himself and opened Facebook. "In the middle of the night," he wrote, "coalition airplanes targeted two houses occupied by innocent civilians. Is this technology? This barbarian attack cost me the lives of my wife, daughter, brother and nephew."

Suddenly, it was as if the whole city knew, and messages poured in. Word filtered to local sheikhs, imams, and businessmen. Basim's own fate was discussed. Favors were called in, and a few

weeks later, ISIS granted Basim permission to leave the caliphate. There was one condition: He must put up the deed to some
of his family's property, which would be seized if he did not
return. Basim feared traveling to Baghdad; whoever targeted his
home might still believe him to be part of ISIS. Turkey seemed
like his only option, and the only way to get there was to cross
the breadth of Islamic State lands, through Syria.

For Basim, the next few days passed in a haze. A hired driver
lowered him into a GMC Suburban, its rear seats removed to
accommodate the mattress on which he reclined. They drove
through the Islamic State countryside, past shabby villages and
streams strewn with trash. In the afternoon, they reached
Mount Sinjar, where a year earlier, Yazidi women were carted
off by ISIS and sold into slavery. "I'm sorry, I have to go fast
now," the driver said, revving up the engine until they were
tearing through at 100 m.p.h. Yazidi guerrillas were now taking
refuge in the highlands and were known to take aim at the traffic down below.

The country opened up into miles and miles of featureless desert. Basim could not distinguish the small Syrian towns they
passed but was aware of reaching Raqqa, the capital of the caliphate, and being lifted by a team of pedestrians and moved to a
second vehicle. Soon a new driver was rushing Basim along darkened fields of wheat and cotton on narrow, bone-jarring roads.
At times, the pain in his hip was unbearable. They stopped to
spend the night, but he did not know where. At dawn, they set
out again. After a while, the driver reached under his seat and
produced a pack of cigarettes, forbidden in the caliphate. Basim
was alarmed, but the driver began to laugh. "Don't worry," he
said. "We're now in Free Syrian Army territory."

Before long, the traffic slowed, and they were weaving through
streets crowded with refugees and homeless children and Syrian
rebels. Basim was pushed across the border on a wheelchair. Waiting on the Turkish side, standing by an ambulance, was his son.

Weeping, Yahya bent down to embrace his father. They had not seen each other in a year.

Basim spent the next two months in and out of a bed at the Special Orthopedic Hospital in Adana, Turkey. In the long hours between operations, when the painkillers afforded moments of lucidity, he tried to avoid ruminating on his loss. He refused to look at photos of his house, but occasionally at first, and then obsessively, he began replaying his and Mayada's actions in the days and weeks before the attack, searching for an explanation. Why was his family targeted? Some friends assumed that an ISIS convoy had been nearby, but the video showed nothing moving in the vicinity. What it did show was two direct hits. "OK, this is my house, and this is Mohannad's house," he recalled. "One rocket here, and one rocket there. It was not a mistake."

Basim's shock and grief were turning to anger. He knew the Americans; he had lived among them. He had always felt he understood them. He desperately wanted to understand why his family was taken from him. "I decided," he said, "to get justice."

·　　·　　·

Basim belongs to one of Mosul's grand old families, among the dozens descended—the story goes—from forty prophets who settled the baking-hot banks of the Tigris, opposite the ancient Assyrian metropolis of Nineveh. Though the city they founded has since acquired a reputation for conservatism, Basim could remember a time of cosmopolitan flair. When he was growing up, domed Yazidi shrines and arched Syriac Orthodox churches stood nearly side by side with mosques and minarets; cafes in the evenings filled with hookah smoke and students steeped in Iraq's burgeoning free-verse poetry movement. On Thursdays, visitors could find bars, clubs, and raucous all-night parties or head to the Station Hotel, built in the central railway depot, where travelers liked to congregate for a drink (and where, to her eternal amusement, Agatha Christie once met the manager, a Syrian Christian named Satan). The wealthy tended to sympathize with the old monarchy or nationalist causes, but the working-class neighborhoods, particularly the Kurdish and Christian quarters, were bastions of communist support. Islamic fundamentalism was nearly unheard-of, a bizarre doctrine of the fringe.

In the 1970s, as Saddam Hussein consolidated power, Mosul's pluralism began to erode, but Basim would not be around long enough to witness its disappearance. He left for England in 1979 and soon made his way to the United States. Settling into Michigan life was easy. Basim bought a Mustang, figured out health insurance, barbecued, went to cocktail parties, and dated a woman he met in England. This development alarmed his parents, who began to pester him to settle down and suggested that he marry his cousin Mayada. He resisted at first, but the allure of making a life with someone from back home proved too great. He married Mayada in 1982, in a small ceremony at his uncle's home in Ann Arbor, Mich., in front of a dozen people.

As the oldest son, Basim felt increasingly concerned about his aging parents, so in 1988, he and Mayada made the difficult decision to move back home permanently. The city they returned to had undergone a shocking transformation. The Iran-Iraq war was winding down, but at a cost of as many as half a million dead Iraqis. The political alternatives of Basim's youth were gone: Communism had long since been crushed, and Arab nationalism had lost its luster under Hussein's Baathist dictatorship.

Instead, people increasingly described their suffering in the language of faith. The culture was transforming before Basim's eyes; for the first time, Mayada wrapped herself in a head scarf. Not long after, small networks of religious fundamentalists began appearing in Mosul, preaching to communities devastated by war and United Nations sanctions.

Then, in 2003, the United States invaded. One night just a few months afterward, the Americans showed up at the Woods and took over a huge abandoned military barracks across the street from Basim's property. The next morning, they started cutting down trees. "They said, 'This is for our security,'" Basim recalled. "I said, 'Your security doesn't mean destruction of the forest.'" Walls of concrete and concertina wire started to appear amid the pine and chinar stands. The barracks became a joint coordination center, or JCC, where American troops worked with local security forces. Basim came to know some of the Americans; once, before the center acquired internet access, he helped a soldier send e-mail to his mother back home. Sometimes he would serve as an impromptu translator.

Across Iraq, the American invasion had plunged the country into chaos and spawned a nationalist resistance—and amid the social collapse, the zealots seized the pulpit. Al-Qaeda in Iraq recruited from Mosul's shanty towns and outlying villages and from nearby provincial cities like Tal Afar. By 2007, sections of Mosul were in rebellion. By then, the Americans had expanded the mission of the JCC, adding a center where Iraqis could file compensation claims for the injury or death of a loved one at the hands of American forces.

When the Americans withdrew in 2011, Basim felt as if almost everyone he knew harbored grievances toward the occupation. That same year, on one of his customary rambles around the internet, Basim came upon a TEDx Talk called "A Radical Experiment in Empathy," by Sam Richards, a sociology professor at Penn State. Richards was asking the audience to imagine that China had invaded the United States, plundered its coal and propped up a kleptocratic government. Then he asked the audience to put themselves in the shoes of "an ordinary Arab Muslim living in the Middle East, particularly in Iraq." He paced across the stage, scenes from the Iraq conflict playing behind him.

"Can you feel their anger, their fear, their rage at what has happened to their country?"

Basim was transfixed. He'd never seen an American talk this way. That night, he wrote an e-mail. "Dear Dr. Richards, my name is Basim Razzo, and I am a citizen of Iraq," he began. He described how Iraqis had celebrated the overthrow of Hussein but then lost hope as the war progressed. "Radical Islamists grew as a result of this war, and many ideas grew out of this war which we have never seen or heard before," he said. "I thank you very much for your speech to enlighten the American public about this war."

Richards invited Basim to begin speaking to his classes over Skype, and a friendship blossomed. Years later, Richards saw Basim's Facebook post describing the attack and ran it through Google Translate. He and his wife spent hours messaging with Basim, trying to console him. In the end, Richards had signed off, "This American friend of yours, this American brother, sends you a virtual hug."

Now, as Basim lay in bed in the Special Orthopedic Hospital in Adana, he found his thoughts returning to the old joint coordination center next to his house in Mosul and the condolence payments they used to offer. He knew that he would never recover the full extent of his losses, but he needed to clear his name. And he wanted an accounting. He decided that as soon as he recuperated, he would seek compensation. It was the only way he could imagine that an Iraqi civilian might sit face to face with a representative of the United States military.

·      ·      ·

The idea that civilian victims of American wars deserve compensation was, until recently, a radical notion floating on the edges of military doctrine. Under international humanitarian law, it is legal for states to kill civilians in war when they are not specifically targeted, so long as "indiscriminate attacks" are not used and the number of civilian deaths is not disproportionate to the military advantage gained. Compensating victims, the argument went, would hinder the state's ability to wage war. Even the Foreign Claims Act, the one American law on the books that allows civilians to be compensated for injury or death at the hands of United States military personnel, exempts losses due to combat.

Over the years, however, war planners have come to see strategic value in payments as a goodwill gesture. During the Korean War, American commanders sometimes offered token cash or other gifts to wronged civilians, in a nod to local custom. These payments were designed to be symbolic expressions of condolence, not an official admission of wrongdoing or compensation for loss. During the Iraq and Afghanistan conflicts, war planners began to focus more seriously on condolence payments, seeing them as a way to improve relations with locals and forestall revenge attacks. Soon, American forces were disbursing thousands of dollars yearly to civilians who suffered losses because of combat operations, for everything from property damage to the death of a family member.

Because the military still refused to consider the payments as compensation for loss, the system became capricious almost by design. Rebuilding a home could cost hundreds of thousands of dollars, on top of several thousands' worth of furniture and other possessions. Medical bills could amount to thousands of dollars, especially for prostheses and rehabilitation. Losing government documents, like ID cards, could mean years of navigating a lumbering bureaucracy. The American condolence system addressed none of this. Payouts varied from one unit to the next, making the whole process seem arbitrary, mystifying, or downright cruel to recipients: payouts in Afghanistan, for example, ranged from as little as $124.13 in one civilian death to $15,000 in another.

In 2003, an activist from Northern California named Marla Ruzicka showed up in Baghdad determined to overhaul the system. She founded Civic, now known as the Center for Civilians in Conflict, and collected evidence of civilians killed in American military operations. She discovered not only that there were many more than expected but also that the assistance efforts for survivors were remarkably haphazard and arbitrary. Civic championed the cause in Washington and found an ally in Senator Patrick J. Leahy of Vermont. In 2005, Ruzicka was killed by a suicide blast in Baghdad, but her efforts culminated in legislation that established a fund to provide Iraqi victims of American combat operations with nonmonetary assistance—medical care, home reconstruction—that served, in practice, as compensation.

When the Americans withdrew in 2011, however, all condolence programs went defunct, and they were not revived when the United States began the war against ISIS in 2014. The Marla Ruzicka Iraqi War Victims Fund itself—the only program specifically designed to aid war victims still in effect—has turned to other priorities and no longer provides assistance to civilian survivors of American combat operations. When we asked the State Department whether civilian victims of American airstrikes could turn to the Marla Fund for assistance, they were unable to provide an answer.

The two most recent military spending bills also authorized millions of dollars for condolence payments, but the Defense Department has failed to enact these provisions or even propose a plan for how it might disburse that money. In fact, in the course of our investigation, we learned that not a single person in Iraq or Syria has received a condolence payment for a civilian death since the war began in 2014. "There really isn't a process," a senior Central Command official told us. "It's not that anyone is against it; it just hasn't been done, so it's almost an aspirational requirement."

With Mosul and Raqqa now out of ISIS control, the coalition is "not going to spend a lot of time thinking about" condolence payments, said Col. John Thomas, a spokesman for Central Command. "We're putting our efforts into community safety and returning refugees to some sort of home." While assisting civilian victims is no longer a military priority, some authorities appear to remain concerned about retaliation. About a year after the strike on Basim's house, his cousin Hussain Al-Rizzo, a systems-engineering professor at the University of Arkansas at Little Rock, received a visit from an FBI agent. The agent, he said, asked if the deaths of his relatives in an American airstrike made him in his "heart of hearts sympathize with the bad guys." Hussain, who has lived in the United States since 1987, was stunned by the question. He said no.

.        .        .

In late December 2015, after three operations, Basim moved to Baghdad to live with Yahya in a five-bedroom house next door to his nephew Abdullah, Mohannad's oldest son. Eight screws were drilled into his left hip, a titanium plate stabilized his right hip and a six-inch scar mapped a line across his abdomen. His pain was unremitting. He was out of work and had little more than the clothes he took when escaping Mosul. His computer, the photo albums, the wedding gifts Mayada had packed for Yahya—all of it was buried under rubble.

Basim channeled his frustrations into proving his case to the Americans. With a quiet compulsiveness, he scoured the web, studying Google Earth images. He asked a niece, still living inside Mosul, to take clandestine photographs of the site, including close-ups of bomb fragments. He inventoried his lost possessions. He contacted everyone he'd met who might have links to the American authorities: acquaintances from Michigan, his cousins in Arkansas, a relative who was an assistant professor at Yale University. His best hope was Sam Richards, the professor at Penn State: one of his former students was an adviser to Hillary Clinton's presidential campaign, and she helped him get an appointment at the United States Embassy in Baghdad.

On a rainy Sunday in February 2016, Yahya drove Basim to the perimeter of the Green Zone in downtown Baghdad. He proceeded into the fortified compound by walker and then boarded a minibus for the embassy, carrying a nine-page document he had compiled. Because there was no established mechanism for Iraqi victims to meet American officials, his appointment was at the American Citizen Services section. He pressed against the window and showed the consular officer his dossier. One page contained satellite imagery of the Razzo houses, and others contained before-and-after photos of the destruction. Between them were photos of each victim: Mayada sipping tea, Tuqa in the back yard, Najib in a black-and-white self-portrait and a head shot of Mohannad, an engineering professor, his academic credentials filling the rest of the page. The most important issue, Basim had written, was that his family was now "looked at as members of ISIS" by the Iraqi authorities. This threatened to be a problem, especially after the city's liberation.

The consular officer, who spoke to us on the condition of anonymity, was moved. "I have people coming in every day that lie to me, that come with these sob stories," the officer remembered telling him, "but I believe you." When Basim emerged onto the street, the rain was beating down, and a passer-by held out an umbrella as he hobbled to a taxi.

Two months passed, and Basim heard nothing. He wrote to the officer and reattached the report, asking for an update, but he received no reply. He tried again the next month and was told that his case had been "forwarded." Then more silence.

We first met Basim not long after, in the spring of 2016, in a quiet cafe in Baghdad's Mansour district. Basim's cousin's wife, Zareena Grewal, the Yale professor, had written an op-ed in the *New York Times* about the attack. We had already been investigating the larger problem of civilian airstrikes for several months, so we contacted him to learn more about his story. Nearly half the country was still under ISIS control, and all along Mansour's palm-shaded sidewalks were the resplendent bursts of militia flags and posters of angelic-looking young men who had fallen on the front. Around the city, residents were living under a pall of suspicion that they were Islamic State sympathizers, a target for rogue militias and vengeful security forces, and Basim was eager to move north to Erbil. This was another reason he was determined to meet the Americans—not only for compensation but also for a letter attesting to their mistake, to certify that he did not belong to ISIS. "We'll hear something soon," Basim assured us.

But as the summer months came and went, still without word, Basim's confidence began to waver. In September, nearly a year after the airstrike, he tried e-mailing the embassy again. This time he received a response: "The recipient's mailbox is full and can't accept messages now. Please try resending this message later, or contact the recipient directly." (The consular officer later told us that when Basim's case was referred to a military attorney, the attorney replied, "There's no way to prove that the U.S. was involved.")

In November, we wrote to the coalition ourselves, explaining that we were reporters working on an article about Basim. We provided details about his family and his efforts to reach someone in authority and included a link to the YouTube video the coalition posted immediately after the strike. A public-affairs officer responded, "There is nothing in the historical log for 20 SEP 2015," the date the coalition had assigned to the strike video. Not long after, the video disappeared from the coalition's YouTube channel. We responded by providing the GPS coordinates of Basim's home, his e-mails to the State Department and an archived link to the YouTube video, which unlike the videos on the Pentagon's website allow for comments underneath—including those that Basim's family members left nearly a year before.

"I will NEVER forget my innocent and dear cousins who died in this pointless airstrike," wrote Aisha Al-Rizzo, Tuqa's sixteen-year-old cousin from Arkansas.

"You are murderers," wrote Basim and Mohannad's cousin Hassan al-Razzo. "You kill innocents with cold blood and then start creating justification."

"How could you do that?" wrote another relative. "You don't have a heart."

Over the coming weeks, one by one, the coalition began removing all the airstrike videos from YouTube.

.        .        .

The Coalition's air war in Iraq is directed largely from the Combined Air Operations Center, quartered inside Al-Udeid Air Base in the desert outskirts of Doha, Qatar. As a shared hub for the Qatari Air Force, the British Royal Air Force and the United States Air Force and Central Command, among others, Udeid hosts some of the longest runways in the Middle East, as well as parking lots full of hulking KC-135 Stratotanker refueling planes, a huge swimming pool, and a Pizza Hut. An alarm blares occasional high-temperature alerts, but the buildings themselves are kept so frigid that aviators sometimes wear extra socks as mittens.

When we visited in May, several uniformed officials walked us through the steps they took to avoid civilian casualties. The process seemed staggeringly complex—the wall-to-wall monitors, the soup of acronyms, the army of lawyers—but the impressively choreographed operation was designed to answer two basic questions about each proposed strike: Is the proposed target actually ISIS? And will attacking this ISIS target harm civilians in the vicinity?

As we sat around a long conference table, the officers explained how this works in the best-case scenario, when the coalition has weeks or months to consider a target. Intelligence streams in from partner forces, informants on the ground, electronic surveillance, and drone footage. Once the coalition decides a target is ISIS, analysts study the probability that striking it will kill civilians in the vicinity, often by poring over drone footage of patterns of civilian activity. The greater the likelihood of civilian harm, the more mitigating measures the coalition takes. If the target is near an office building, the attack might be rescheduled for nighttime. If the area is crowded, the coalition might adjust its weaponry to limit the blast radius. Sometimes aircraft will even fire a warning shot, allowing people to escape targeted facilities before the strike. An official showed us grainy night-vision footage of this technique in action: Warning shots hit the ground near a shed in Deir al-Zour, Syria, prompting a pair of white silhouettes to flee, one tripping and picking himself back up, as the cross hairs follow.

Once the targeting team establishes the risks, a commander must approve the strike, taking care to ensure that the potential civilian harm is not "excessive relative to the expected military advantage gained," as Lt. Col. Matthew King, the center's deputy legal adviser, explained.

After the bombs drop, the pilots and other officials evaluate the strike. Sometimes a civilian vehicle can suddenly appear in the video feed moments before impact. Or, through studying footage of the aftermath, they might detect signs of a civilian presence. Either way, such a report triggers an internal assessment in which the coalition determines, through a review of imagery and testimony from mission personnel, whether the civilian-casualty report is credible. If so, the coalition makes refinements to avoid future civilian casualties, they told us, a process that might include reconsidering some bit of intelligence or identifying a flaw in the decision-making process.

Most of the civilian deaths acknowledged by the coalition emerge from this internal reporting process. Often, though, watchdogs or journalists bring allegations to the coalition, or officials learn about potential civilian deaths through social media. The coalition ultimately rejects a vast majority of such external reports.

It will try to match the incident to a strike in its logs to determine whether it was indeed its aircraft that struck the location in question (the Iraqi Air Force also carries out strikes). If so, it then scours its drone footage, pilot videos, internal records, and, when they believe it is warranted, social media and other open-source information for corroborating evidence. Each month, the coalition releases a report listing those allegations deemed credible, dismissing most of them on the grounds that coalition aircraft did not strike in the vicinity or that the reporter failed to provide sufficiently precise information about the time and place of the episode. (The coalition counts both aircraft and artillery attacks in its strike figures; we excluded artillery attacks.)

In the eyes of the coalition, its diligence on these matters points to a dispiriting truth about war: Supreme precision can reduce civilian casualties to a very small number, but that number will never reach zero. They speak of every one of the acknowledged deaths as tragic but utterly unavoidable. "We're not happy with it, and we're never going to be happy with it," said Thomas, the Central Command spokesman. "But we're pretty confident we do the best we can to try to limit these things."

Because so much of this process is hidden—through March, the coalition released only one internal investigation from Iraq, a strike that hit a civilian vehicle in the Hatra district southwest of Mosul—its thoroughness is difficult to evaluate independently. The preeminent organization that seeks to do so is Airwars, a nonprofit based in London that monitors news reports, accounts by nongovernmental organizations, social-media posts, and the coalition's own public statements. Airwars tries to triangulate these sources and grade each allegation from "fair" to "disputed." As of October, it estimates that up to 3,000 Iraqi civilians have been killed in coalition airstrikes—six times as many as the coalition has stated in its public summaries. But Chris Woods, the organization's director, told us that Airwars itself "may be significantly underreporting deaths in Iraq," because the local reporting there is weaker than in other countries that Airwars monitors.

The coalition sees the same problem but draws the opposite conclusion. In a September opinion article in *Foreign Policy*, with the headline "Reports of Civilian Casualties in the War Against ISIS Are Vastly Inflated," Lt. Gen. Stephen J. Townsend, the coalition's former top commander, wrote: "Our critics are unable to conduct the detailed assessments the coalition does. They arguably often rely on scant information phoned in or posted by questionable sources."

Counting civilian deaths in war zones has always been a difficult and controversial endeavor. The Iraq Body Count project, which sought to record civilian deaths after the 2003 invasion using techniques similar to Airwars, was flooded with criticism for both undercounting and overcounting. *The Lancet*, a medical journal, published studies based on surveys of Iraqi households that detractors alleged were not statistically sound. Human Rights Watch and Amnesty International have conducted ground investigations but usually for only a handful of strikes at a time. Yet the coalition, the institution best placed to investigate civilian death claims, does not itself routinely dispatch investigators on the ground, citing access and security concerns, meaning there has not been such a rigorous ground investigation of this air war—or any American-led air campaign—since Human Rights Watch analyzed the civilian toll of the NATO bombing in Kosovo, a conflict that ended in 1999.

In our interview at the base, Lt. Gen. Jeffrey Harrigian, commander of the United States Air Forces Central Command at Udeid, told us what was missing. "Ground truth, that's what you're asking for," he said. "We see what we see from altitude and pull in from other reports. Your perspective is talking to people on the ground." He paused, and then offered what he thought it would take to arrive at the truth: "It's got to be a combination of both."

•     •     •

Investigating civilian harm on the ground is difficult but not impossible. In the spring of 2016, we began our own effort, visiting Iraqi cities and towns recently liberated from ISIS control. Ultimately, we selected three areas in Nineveh Province, traveling to the location of every airstrike that took place during ISIS control in each—103 sites in all. These areas encompassed the range of ISIS-controlled settlements in size and population makeup: downtown Shura, a small provincial town that was largely abandoned during periods of heavy fighting; downtown Qaiyara, a suburban municipality; and Aden, a densely packed city neighborhood in eastern Mosul. The sample would arguably provide a conservative estimate of the civilian toll: It did not include western Mosul, which may have suffered the highest number of civilian deaths in the entire war. Nor did it include any strikes conducted after December 2016, when a rule change allowed more ground commanders to call in strikes, possibly contributing to a sharp increase in the death toll.

The areas we visited had undergone intense attacks of all kinds over the previous two years: airstrikes, sniper fire, mortars, rockets, improvised explosive devices, demolitions by ISIS, demolitions by anti-ISIS vigilantes, and more. Our approach required mapping each area, identifying the sites that had been struck from the air, and excluding those damaged by Iraqi forces in close-quarters ground combat.

Finally, we determined who or what had been hit. In addition to interviewing hundreds of witnesses, we dug through the debris for bomb fragments, tracked down videos of airstrikes in the area and studied before-and-after satellite imagery. We also obtained and analyzed more than one hundred coordinate sets for suspected ISIS sites passed on by intelligence informants. We then mapped each neighborhood door to door, identifying houses where ISIS members were known to have lived and locating ISIS facilities that could be considered legitimate targets. We scoured the wreckage of each strike for materials suggesting an ISIS presence, like weapons, literature, and decomposed remains of fighters. We verified every allegation with local administrators, security forces, or health officials.

In Qaiyara's residential district, where small wheat-colored homes sit behind low concrete walls, one or two structures had been reduced to rubble on almost every block. We went to all of them. A significant part of our efforts involved determining which air force—Iraqi or coalition—carried out each strike. Either way, according to official accounts, the air war in Qaiyara was remarkably precise: The coalition has stated that it killed only one civilian in or near the town while the Iraqi Air Force has not acknowledged any civilian deaths in the area.

It was soon clear that many more had died. We visited one house that stood partly intact but for the rear alcove, which had been pancaked. A woman stepped out from the front of the structure, three children orbiting her. She told us her name, Inas Hamadi. "My children died here," she said. "It happened so quickly." One of the surviving children, Wiham, eleven, remembered waking up to the sound of aircraft and running under the stairs to hide with her six siblings and cousins. Then the house was struck, collapsing the staircase onto them. Riam, eight, and Daoud, five, did not survive. "Daoud's body was full of shrapnel," Wiham said. "Riam had a hole beside her ear and a hole in her brain. She looked around and was dizzy."

The strike was witnessed by neighbors, who helped rescue the children. Everyone agreed that the target was most likely the hospital or a pair of homes on the next street, all of which had been commandeered by ISIS. We collected the names and photographs of the dead and checked satellite imagery to confirm the date range of the strike. The deaths were never reported, were never recorded in any public database, and were not investigated by the coalition.

We continued in this fashion, door to door. What we found was sobering: During the two years that ISIS ruled downtown Qaiyara, an area of about one square mile, there were forty air-strikes, thirteen of which killed forty-three civilians—nineteen men, eight women, and sixteen children, ages fourteen or younger. In the same period, according to the Iraqi federal police, ISIS executed eighteen civilians in downtown Qaiyara.

In Shura and Aden, we found a similar discrepancy between the number of civilian deaths on the ground and the number reported by the coalition. Through dozens of interviews at each site in all three locations, along with our house-to-house mapping, we tried to determine the reasons behind each airstrike that killed civilians. Coalition officials say ISIS fighters embedded in the population, making it difficult to avoid hitting civilians nearby. This appeared to be the case for about one-third of the deadly strikes—for example, a September 2016 strike on an ISIS-occupied primary school in Shura that killed three civilians in the vicinity.

But in about half of the strikes that killed civilians, we could find no discernible ISIS target nearby. Many of these strikes appear to have been based on poor or outdated intelligence. For example, last fall we visited a bombed-out house on the edge of Qaiyara, near the rail yard. It belonged to the family of Salam al-Odeh; neighbors and relatives told us the family had been sleeping one night when they awoke to the shudder of an airstrike nearby. Sometimes strikes came in pairs, so Salam's wife, Harbia, scooped up their baby, Bara, and ran out the door. Salam scrambled to save his other children—his daughter, Rawa, and his sons, Musab and Hussein. But then a second strike hit. Salam, the baby, and Hussein were killed instantly. His wife hung on until she reached the hospital, where she told her relatives what happened but then died from her injuries. A few weeks later, Musab died of his wounds too. Only Rawa, who was two, survived. Several months later, we found the person who called in the strike, one of the coalition's main sources in Qaiyara, a local Iraqi official we are not identifying for his safety. He told us that while on a walk one day, he spotted an ISIS mortar under a clump of trees near the rail yard and transmitted the coordinates. (Neighbors also told us that ISIS had occupied and then abandoned a house in the area a year earlier, which a different informant may have told the coalition about.) By the time the information made its way to the coalition and it decided to act, the mortar had been moved.

Such intelligence failures suggest that not all civilian casualties are unavoidable tragedies; some deaths could be prevented if the coalition recognizes its past failures and changes its operating assumptions accordingly. But in the course of our investigation, we found that it seldom did either.

In June, for example, we visited an electrical substation occupying several blocks of the Aden neighborhood in eastern Mosul. On the evening of April 20, 2015, aircraft bombed the station, causing a tremendous explosion that engulfed the street. Muthana Ahmed Tuaama, a university student, told us his brother rushed into the blaze to rescue the wounded, when a second blast shook the facility. "I found my brother at the end of the street," he said. "I carried him." Body parts littered the alleyway. "You see those puddles of water," he said. "It was just like that, but full of blood." We determined that at least eighteen civilians died in this one attack and that many more were grievously wounded. News of the strike was picked up by local bloggers, national Iraqi outlets, and ISIS propaganda channels and was submitted as an allegation to the coalition by Airwars. Months later, the coalition announced the results of its investigation, stating that there was "insufficient evidence to find that civilians were harmed in this strike." Yet even a cursory internet search offers significant evidence that civilians were harmed: We found disturbingly graphic videos of the strike's aftermath on YouTube, showing blood-soaked toddlers and children with their legs ripped off.

A key part of the coalition's investigation process is to match civilian casualty accusations against its own logs. Chris Umphres, an Air Force captain at Udeid who assesses allegations of civilian casualties, told us that military investigators possess the coordinates of "every single strike conducted by coalition forces," crucial information unavailable to the typical journalist. "We have 100 percent accountability of where all of our weapons are employed."

We found this to not always be the case. For every location we visited, we submitted GPS coordinates to determine whether it was the coalition or the Iraqi Air Force that bombed the site. At first, the coalition told us it did not have the time or the staff to check more than a handful of the coordinates. But eventually, a team of Air Force analysts at Udeid agreed to compare the dates and coordinates of each of the 103 sites in our sample with those the coalition had recorded in its airstrike log. If a strike in our sample occurred within 50 meters of a strike that was recorded in the logs, they classified it as a "probable coalition airstrike," while assessing those outside this range—that is, anything more than a couple of house-lengths away—as "unlikely."

By this measure, 30 of the 103 strike sites in the sample we submitted are probable coalition strikes. But other evidence suggests that the coalition was responsible for many more. Human rights organizations have repeatedly found discrepancies between the dates or locations of strikes and those recorded in the logs. In one instance, the coalition deemed an allegation regarding a strike in the al-Thani neighborhood of Tabqa, Syria, on December 20, 2016, as "not credible," explaining that the nearest airstrike was more than a kilometer away. After Human Rights Watch dispatched researchers to the ground and discovered evidence to the contrary, the coalition acknowledged the strike as its own.

We found many such discrepancies. For instance, the Air Force analysts said it was unlikely that the coalition had struck Qaiyara's water-sanitation facility because the logs recorded the nearest strike as 600 meters away, which would place it outside the compound entirely. Yet we discovered a video—uploaded by the coalition itself—showing a direct strike on that very facility. (When we asked Lt. Col. Damien Pickart, director of public affairs at Udeid, about this discrepancy, he said he could only report "what the strike log shows.") Similarly, we were told that a strike we identified on Qaiyara's main bridge was unlikely to be by the coalition, because the nearest strike was on a truck 150 meters away. We again found a coalition video showing a direct hit on the structure. Pickart explained the inconsistency by saying the coalition had conducted multiple strikes on various targets within an hour-long period, only one of which was included in the official log.

The most common justification the coalition gives when denying civilian-casualty allegations is that it has no record of carrying out a strike at the time or area in question. If incomplete accounts like these are standard practice, it calls into question the coalition's ability to determine whether any strike is its own. Still, even using the most conservative rubric and selecting only those thirty airstrikes the Air Force analysts classified as "probable" coalition airstrikes, we found at least twenty-one civilians had been killed in six strikes. Expanding to the sixty-five strikes that fell within 600 meters—for example, the strikes on the home of Inas Hamadi in Qaiyara and the electrical substation in Aden—pushed that figure to at least fifty-four killed in fifteen strikes. No matter which threshold we used, though, the results from our sample were consistent: One of every five airstrikes killed a civilian.

To understand how radically different our assessment is from the coalition's own, consider this: According to the coalition's available data, 89 of its more than 14,000 airstrikes in Iraq have resulted in civilian deaths, or about one of every 157 strikes. The rate we found on the ground—one out of every five—is thirty-one times as high.

.     .     .

Last December, fifteen months after the attack, following a long, tangled chain of e-mails and phone calls, the coalition confirmed that it had indeed carried out an airstrike on Basim and Mohannad's homes. It acknowledged that it had, in fact, conducted an internal inquiry—a "credibility assessment"—the previous autumn after Zareena Grewal, Basim's relative at Yale, wrote the op-ed in the *Times*. The assessment, completed on October 30, 2015, concluded that the allegation was "credible"; this meant the coalition had known for more than a year that it had "more likely than not" killed civilians and that it had recommended a full investigation into the strike, even as Basim's attempts to reach the coalition were being ignored. Despite this finding, the coalition neglected to include the incident in its public tally of deaths—which, in Iraq at that time, stood at seventy-six civilians—because of what Col. Joseph Scrocca, a coalition spokesman, called "an administrative oversight."

Basim's case had now become impossible to ignore. Based on the evidence we provided, Maj. Gen. Scott Kindsvater, then an Air Force deputy commander, ordered an internal investigation to determine what might have gone wrong on the night of the strike. And then, on February 14, for the first time in the seventeen months since the attack, Basim received an e-mail from the coalition. "We deeply regret this unintentional loss of life in an attempt to defeat Da'esh," Scrocca wrote, using another term for ISIS. "We are prepared to offer you a monetary expression of our sympathy and regret for this unfortunate incident." He invited Basim to come to Erbil to discuss the matter. Basim was the first person to receive such an offer, in Iraq or Syria, during the entire anti-ISIS war.

Early in the morning of his scheduled meeting, Basim dreamed about Mayada. He could feel her skin next to his. He suddenly felt a surge of regret for things said and left unsaid, accrued over a lifetime together. He awoke in tears. "I washed my face," he said, "did my morning prayer and sent her my prayers. It made me calmer."

It was March 17. The air outside was soft and cool; Erbil had finally experienced rainfall after a parched winter. The coalition had asked Basim to go to Erbil International Airport, where he would be picked up and taken to meet coalition representatives and receive a condolence payment. He invited us to join him, and we agreed. Basim did not know how much money the Americans would offer, but he had spent hours calculating the actual damages: $500,000 for his and Mohannad's homes, furnishings and belongings; $22,000 for two cars; and $13,000 in medical bills from Turkey. We stood waiting in the parking lot. A white SUV with tinted windows rolled by. A family emerged from a taxi, the father juggling two suitcases and a toddler, heading off on what appeared to be a vacation.

Basim checked his phone to see the latest messages from friends in Mosul. It had been a month since Iraqi forces seized the eastern half of the city, but the Woods were still too dangerous to visit because ISIS controlled the opposite bank and was lobbing mortars across the river. On the west side, thousands were trapped in the Old City, and Basim heard stories that ISIS was welding doors shut to keep people in their homes, holding them hostage against heavy artillery and air power. That morning, an airstrike flattened almost an entire city block in the Mosul Jidideh neighborhood—killing 105 civilians, according to the coalition, or possibly double that number, according to Airwars, in either case making it one of the largest aerial massacres since the war began.

It was late afternoon, thirty minutes past the meeting time, when an SUV rolled up, an American in army fatigues behind the wheel. We climbed in, and the truck moved off through the sprawling airfield, past rows of parked helicopters, toward a set of hangars. Basim struggled to maintain his composure. He'd imagined this day a hundred times, but now he wasn't sure what to say, how to act. The driver made small talk about the weather, the winter drought, the needs of farmers. He pulled the truck around to a prefab trailer ringed by blast walls. Inside, sitting around a large wooden table, were more American soldiers. Capt. Jaclyn Feeney, an army attorney, introduced herself and invited Basim to be seated.

"We just wanted to start by expressing our deepest sympathies, not only on behalf of the army but on behalf of myself," she said. "We do take the closest care in what we do here, but it's high risk, and sometimes we make mistakes. We try our best to prevent those mistakes, but we hope that since we did make a mistake here, we can do everything that we can to right it, as best we can. I know there's nothing that I can say that can make up for the loss that you've—"

"The only thing that cannot be returned is the loss of life," Basim said. His hands gripped the armrests, as if he were using every ounce of energy to stay seated. He struggled to keep his voice steady. "Everything else could be redone or rebuilt. The loss of life is unrepairable."

"Certainly. We are prepared to offer you a condolence payment," Feeney replied. "It's not meant to recompensate you for what you've lost, or for rebuilding or anything like that. It's just meant to be an expression of our sympathy, our apologies for your loss."

Outside, a plane lifted off, and the room trembled. Feeney was holding documents in her hand. "And so for that reason, we are capped in the amount that we can give you. So the amount in U.S. dollars is $15,000, which we will be paying you in Iraqi dinars, so 17,550,000 dinars. And so, if you're willing to accept that—"

Basim looked at her in disbelief. "No."

"You're not willing to accept that?"

"This is—this is an insult to me. No, I will not accept it. I'm sorry."

Feeney looked stunned. "I'm sorry also," she said.

Moments passed, and everyone sat in silence. Feeney explained again that they were capped by their own regulations. Basim replied, "This is, I have to say, I'm sorry to say, ridiculous." Basim said he wanted official documentation proving his innocence, so that he could return safely to Mosul one day. Feeney promised to make some calls. The meeting quickly came to an end.

Basim walked out into the late-afternoon air. Traffic at the air-port had picked up: buses overloaded with families, children sticking their elbows out of taxis. Basim drove home in disbelief, as if he were living through an elaborate hoax and the Americans would call back any minute with a serious offer. The truth was, he never expected to recover the full extent of his material losses, and he knew the military was not in the business of compensa-tion, only condolence, but after so many months, so much back and forth, the humiliation burned. "This is what an Iraqi is worth," he said.

At home, he considered his options. He wanted a lawyer—but from where? Could an Iraqi find an American attorney? The amount the coalition had offered exceeded its own guidelines, which stipulated $2,500 per Iraqi, but did not cover Mohannad and Najib, which meant he—or his sister-in-law—would poten-tially have to endure this process again. He considered traveling to the United States to find an advocate, but getting a visa was almost impossible. Once, in the first months after the attack, he even wanted to move there, seek asylum. Now the thought seemed absurd.

Despite everything, Basim could not bring himself to hate Americans. In fact, this experience was further evidence for a theory he had harbored for a while: that he, fellow Iraqis, and even ordinary Americans were all bit players in a drama bigger than any of them. A few weeks later, he spoke to Sociology 119, Sam Richards's Race and Ethnic Relations class at Penn State. "I have nothing against the regular American citizen," he told the class of some 750 students. "I lived among you guys for eight years. I was never bothered by any person—in fact, many of them were very helpful to me."

"This situation of war," he continued, "big corporations are behind it." This is where the real power lay, not with individual Americans. He'd come to believe that his family, along with all Iraqis, had been caught in the grinder of grand forces like oil and empire and that the only refuge lay in something even grander: faith. He had rediscovered his religion. "There was some bond that grew between me and my God. I thanked him for keeping my son alive. I thanked him that my operation was successful. Now I can walk."

It was the same God who had written out his whole life from the fortieth day in the womb. Basim's faith in this divinely authored fate had become a calming current, coursing through his every waking moment. "Sometimes I go out with my friends," Basim told the students. "But when I come back home, when I go to bed and thoughts start coming into my head about my wife, what would have happened probably five years from now, my daughter would be in college, she wanted to study this and that— there isn't a day that goes by that I don't think about them. But in the end, life goes on."

.        .        .

This spring, Iraqi forces pushed deeper into western Mosul, into the Old City, a hive of stacked houses that lean over narrow streets. The neighborhood was being pounded with airstrikes and mortars, while ISIS was refusing to allow people to leave. Basim learned that three in-laws of Abdullah, Mohannad's son—a pregnant woman, her husband, and his father—had tried to bribe their way to the east side but were caught and beheaded. Nearly everyone was telling such stories. Meanwhile, word spread that Basim had taken his case to the coalition, and aggrieved families started to reach out for advice. Basim felt like an elder statesman of heartbreak, and he offered whatever counsel he could. The strike on his house remained a great mystery, though, and not a day passed when he did not retrace the hours and days before the attack, wondering what could have brought it on.

In April, through the Freedom of Information Act, we finally obtained a portion of the coalition's internal probe of the strike on the Razzo homes. As Basim read though a dozen partly redacted pages, a story began to emerge—the coalition had been receiving intelligence that his and Mohannad's houses were an ISIS command center. The report suggests that this may have been because of the JCC next door; Basim recalled that ISIS briefly occupied the JCC when it first conquered Mosul but had long since abandoned the facility. Yet the coalition's intelligence source apparently passed along this outdated information and in the process confused his house with the JCC.

Next, according to the report, the coalition dispatched a drone to surveil the property. Over three days, in fifteen-to-thirty-minute windows, his house was filmed. The investigation acknowledged that "no overtly nefarious activity was observed," but nonetheless everything the coalition witnessed confirmed its conviction that it was filming a terrorist headquarters. No weapons were visible, but the report noted that ISIS "does not obviously brandish weapons," so as to go undetected. Occasionally Basim or Mohannad would open their shared gate to the street, allowing a guest to enter. The coalition simply saw men opening a gate, an action that it determined was consistent with the activity of an ISIS headquarters. And, perhaps most important, the report stated that the coalition did not observe any women or children outdoors—although in the ISIS-controlled city, women rarely left the house to avoid the religious police, and most filming had occurred under the blistering afternoon sun, when almost everyone stayed indoors.

Though the Razzos hadn't known it, the burden of proof had been on them to demonstrate to a drone watching them from above that they were civilians—guilty until proved innocent. In the end, ninety-five minutes of unremarkable footage had sealed the fate of Mayada, Tuqa, Mohannad, and Najib. The report concluded that there was "no evidence indicating carelessness or bad faith" on the part of the coalition and that its targeting process "remains sound." (It also declared that because of an equipment error, the drone footage no longer existed for investigators to review.) Yet to Basim, the truth seemed just the opposite: The coalition had disregarded ground realities and acted on flimsy intelligence.

Not long after receiving the report, Basim decided to return to the Woods. It was risky to visit—ISIS was still controlling neighborhoods on the opposite bank—but he wanted to see, to touch, what was left, and he took us along. We set out in the early morning, driving past dusty abandoned villages, through checkpoints sporting brilliant hoists of red, blue, and green militia flags and onto a broad boulevard, teeming with pushcart vendors and street children. Whole city blocks were flattened. Basim was not caught off guard by the destruction, which he expected based on the videos he'd seen, but he was surprised by the traffic. He regarded the passing scenes as if he were a tour guide, recounting the history of each neighborhood. It appeared to be an affectation of calm, a studied attempt to withstand the torment of return, but the truth eventually surfaced. "I'm numb," he said. "I'm just numb."

We drove past more ruined buildings. Around the wreckage of one stood a concrete wall, still intact, where ISIS had painted two hands open in supplication. Basim translated the inscription: THANK GOD FOR EVERYTHING YOU HAVE. IF YOU DO, HE WILL GIVE YOU MORE.

We headed toward the Tigris River. As we approached, we could see the apartments, houses and minarets on the other side, still under ISIS control. And then suddenly, the city was gone. We entered the Woods, which remained a bucolic oasis.

The trees were heavy with figs, apricots, and lemons, and the air buzzed with mosquitoes. We pulled up to a pale yellow gate. Basim lingered outside for a moment, afraid to approach. He then opened it and stepped onto his property for the first time in eighteen months. We followed him along an overgrown stone path. He stopped in front of a smashed-up wall surrounded by chunks of concrete. Rebar snaked out like hairs. "This was the laundry room," he said.

To the right stood what was once his kitchen. A faint rotten odor emerged from within. The remnants of a table and three chairs were visible. Scattered amid the shattered glass and charred metal bars were pages of recipes: Cookies & Cream Freeze, Chocolate Mousse Torte.

We moved over the rest of the debris. Marble shards, concrete blocks, several mattresses, two satellite dishes, a Spalding tennis racket, an iron, a book of equations, a bathroom sink. The backyard was intact. "At least we still have a swimming pool!" Basim said, laughing absently.

He circled back to the laundry room. There he spotted in a corner, poking out of the rubble, a white platform heel. It belonged to Tuqa. "I told her they were too high and that she would fall," he said. He could picture her wearing them, coming down the stairs.

## National Geographic and *ProPublica*

FINALIST—REPORTING

*This is an extraordinary account of nightmarish violence. In March 2011, dozens, perhaps hundreds of men, women, and children were murdered in and around the town of Allende, Mexico, not far from Texas. They were killed during the course of the month by members of the drug cartel known as the Zetas after information about their leaders was given to the U.S. Drug Enforcement Agency, which in turn shared it with a Mexican police unit known to be unreliable. Copublished by* ProPublica *and* National Geographic, *"How the U.S. Triggered a Massacre in Mexico" was described by the Ellie judges as "deeply sourced and beautifully written." Weaving together the voices of witnesses with her own reporting, Ginger Thompson's account stands on its own in print but was enriched online by evocative audio and striking photography.*

Ginger Thompson

# How the U.S. Triggered a Massacre in Mexico

We have testimony from people who say they participated in the crime. They described some 50 trucks arriving in Allende, carrying people connected to the cartel. They broke into houses, they looted them and burned them. Afterward, they kidnapped the people who lived in those houses and took them to a ranch just outside of Allende.

First they killed them. They put them inside a storage shed filled with hay. They doused them with fuel and lit them on fire, feeding the flames for hours and hours.

—José Juan Morales, investigative director for the disappeared in the Coahuila State Prosecutor's Office

There's no missing the signs that something unspeakable happened in Allende, a quiet ranching town of about 23,000, just a forty-minute drive from Eagle Pass, Texas. Entire blocks of some of the town's busiest streets lie in ruins. Once-garish mansions are now crumbling shells, with gaping holes in the walls, charred ceilings, cracked marble countertops and toppled columns. Strewn among the rubble are tattered, mud-covered remnants of lives torn apart: shoes, wedding invitations, medications, television sets, toys.

In March 2011 gunmen from the Zetas cartel, one of the most violent drug-trafficking organizations in the world, swept through

Allende and nearby towns like a flash flood, demolishing homes and businesses and kidnapping and killing dozens, possibly hundreds, of men, women and children.

The destruction and disappearances went on in fits and starts for weeks. Only a few of the victims' relatives—mostly those who didn't live in Allende or had fled—dared to seek help. "I would like to make clear that Allende looks like a war zone," reads one missing-person report. "Most people who I questioned about my relatives responded that I shouldn't go on looking for them because outsiders were not wanted, and were disappeared."

But unlike most places in Mexico that have been ravaged by the drug war, what happened in Allende didn't have its origins in Mexico. It began in the United States, when the Drug Enforcement Administration scored an unexpected coup. An agent persuaded a high-level Zetas operative to hand over the trackable cell phone identification numbers for two of the cartel's most wanted kingpins, Miguel Ángel Treviño and his brother Omar.

Then the DEA took a gamble. It shared the intelligence with a Mexican federal police unit that has long had problems with leaks—even though its members had been trained and vetted by the DEA. Almost immediately, the Treviños learned they'd been betrayed. The brothers set out to exact vengeance against the presumed snitches, their families, and anyone remotely connected to them.

Their savagery in Allende was particularly surprising because the Treviños not only did business there—moving tens of millions of dollars in drugs and guns through the area each month—they'd also made it their home.

For years after the massacre, Mexican authorities made only desultory efforts to investigate. They erected a monument in Allende to honor the victims without fully determining their fates or punishing those responsible. American authorities eventually helped Mexico capture the Treviños but never acknowledged the devastating cost. In Allende, people suffered mostly in silence, too afraid to talk publicly.

A year ago *ProPublica* and *National Geographic* set out to piece together what happened in this town in the state of Coahuila—to let those who bore the brunt of the attack, and those who played roles in triggering it, tell the story in their own words. They did so often at great personal risk. Voices like these have rarely been heard during the drug war: local officials who abandoned their posts; families preyed upon by both the cartel and their own neighbors; cartel operatives who cooperated with the DEA and saw their friends and families slaughtered; the U.S. prosecutor who oversaw the case; and the DEA agent who led the investigation and who, like most people in this story, has family ties on both sides of the border.

When pressed about his role, the agent, Richard Martinez slumped in his chair, his eyes welling with tears. "How did I feel about the information being compromised? I'd rather not say, to be honest with you. I'd kind of like to leave it at that. I'd rather not say."

## The Massacre

As sundown approached on Friday, March 18, 2011, gunmen from the Zetas cartel began pouring into Allende.

> We were eating at Los Compadres, and two guys came in. We could tell they weren't from here. They looked different. They were kids—eighteen to twenty years old. They ordered fifty hamburgers to go. That's when we figured something was going on, and we decided we'd better get home.
> —Guadalupe García, retired government worker

Things began happening in the evening. Armed men began arriving. They were going house to house, looking for the people who had done them wrong. At eleven at night there was no traffic on the streets. There was no movement of any kind.

—Martín Márquez, hot dog vendor

My husband, Everardo, usually came home between 7 and 7:30 at night. I was waiting for him. Time passed—7, 7:30, 8, 9. I began calling him. The phone was not in service. I thought maybe he was at his mother's house and his battery had died. I called his mother. She told me that she hadn't seen him and that maybe he was out with friends. But that didn't make sense to me. He would have called. So I went out looking for him.

—Etelvina Rodríguez, middle-school teacher and wife of victim Everardo Elizondo

The atmosphere felt tense. It was nine at night, which was not very late, not on a Friday. The town was completely deserted.

A few miles outside of town, the gunmen descended on several neighboring ranches along a dimly lit two-lane highway. The properties belonged to one of Allende's oldest clans, the Garzas. The family mostly raised livestock and did odd contracting jobs, including coal mining. But according to family members, some of them also worked for the cartel.

Now those connections were proving deadly. Among those the Zetas suspected of being a snitch—wrongly, it turns out—was José Luis Garza Jr., a relatively low-level cartel operative, whose father, Luis, owned one of the ranches. It was payday, and several workers had gone to the ranch to pick up their money. When the gunmen showed up, they rounded up everyone they could find and took them hostage. After nightfall, flames began rising from one of the ranch's large cinder-block storage sheds. The Zetas had begun burning the bodies of some of those they'd killed.

My husband, Rodolfo, arrived. He told me, "My head is killing me. I'm going to take a shower." He was completely covered in soot because he was opening a new coal mine. After a while his phone started ringing. I thought he had gone to lie down, but he came out of the bedroom, fully dressed, and he looked me in the eye in a way I had never seen before. "Don't leave the house," he told me. "There's something going on. I don't know what it is. But don't leave the house. I'll be back."

After a while, Rodolfo called me. "Get out of the house," he said. "And don't go in our truck." He told me to ask my cousin to take our daughter, Sofía, and me to my mother's house.

His uncle Luis's ranch was on fire. And there were a lot of armed men standing outside the gate. His sister wasn't answering her phone. His father wasn't answering either. He sent one of his workers, Pilo, to the gate to see what was going on. Pilo had been in the military. The gunmen opened the gate. Pilo went in. But he never came out.

Rodolfo was inconsolable. He couldn't find his parents. He couldn't find his sister. And now his best worker was gone. He told me he was going to try to sneak onto the ranch through the back.

A few minutes later, he called again. He was speaking so softly I could barely hear him. He told me to get out of Allende. "Tell your cousin to take you to Eagle Pass. Don't pack. Just go."

—Sarah Angelita Lira, pharmacist and
wife of victim Rodolfo Garza Jr.

Officers under my command responded to reports of a fire at one of the Garza ranches. We're talking about less than three kilometers away from Allende. It appeared that the Garza family was having some kind of gathering. Among the first responders was a group of firefighters with a backup engine. They noticed there were certain people connected to criminal organizations, who told them, in vulgar terms and at gunpoint, to withdraw. They said there were going to be numerous incidents. We were going to get numerous emergency calls about gunshots, fires, and things like that. They told us we were not authorized to respond.

In my capacity as fire chief, what I did was to advise my boss, who in this case was the mayor. I told him that we were facing an impossible situation and that the only thing we could do was to stand down, out of fear of the threats we faced. There were too many armed men. We were afraid for our lives. We couldn't fight bullets with water.

—Evaristo Treviño, former fire chief,
no relation to Zetas leaders

From Allende the gunmen moved north along the dry, flat landscape, rounding up people as they covered the thirty-five miles to the city of Piedras Negras, a grimy sprawl of assembly factories on the Rio Grande. The attackers drove many of their victims to one of the Garza ranches, including Gerardo Heath, a fifteen-year-old high school football player, and Edgar Ávila, a thirty-six-year-old factory engineer. Neither had anything to do with the cartel or with those the cartel believed were working with the DEA. They just happened to be in the way.

I was packing because we were leaving for San Antonio at five the next morning to go to a football game. Gerardo was playing, so we needed to be there early. Gerardo and his sister were horsing around outside. I looked out the window and saw two of Gerardo's friends drive up. They were our neighbors.

Gerardo came inside and asked if he could go out with his friends. I said, "No, Gerardo. We've got to pack." Next thing I knew, Gerardo had on the clothes we had bought him for his birthday. He had just turned fifteen. The shirt was blue, and it matched his eyes. He told me, "Come on, Mom. I won't be late."

I said, "Fine, Gerardo, don't be late."

At around ten that night, my husband called Gerardo's cell phone to see what time he'd be coming home. Gerardo didn't answer. My husband called again. No answer. A while later someone knocked on our door. It was a couple of friends of Gerardo's from school. They looked terrified. I asked them, "What's the matter? Where's Gerardo?"

The boys said, "They took him."

I asked, "What are you talking about? Who took him?"

The boys said they saw Gerardo and our neighbors in front of the neighbors' house. A truck came, carrying a lot of men with guns. The men forced the neighbors and Gerardo into the truck and drove away. The boys told me they didn't recognize the men. And since they had weapons, the boys didn't dare say anything.

Within minutes, we called the mayor of Piedras Negras. He was at a wedding. He said that he felt terrible about what had happened to us, but there wasn't anything he could do. Not a single police car came.

> —Claudia Sánchez, cultural affairs director and
> mother of victim Gerardo Heath

I was at work, waiting for the judge to sign off on two sentencing reports I had written, when Edgar called to say his friend Toño had invited him over to watch a soccer match. I was pregnant, and by the time I got home, I was super tired. Edgar had fed our daughter and given her a bath. I asked him to pick up some empanadas for me before he went out. He brought them to me and gave me a kiss.

It wasn't until I woke up at two in the morning that I noticed Edgar wasn't home. None of my calls went through. I said to myself, "How strange that he hasn't called." Edgar always called.

I sat in an armchair the rest of the night and waited for him until about six-thirty a.m. Then I called my sister. I told her he hadn't come home. So she came over, and wearing my pajamas, I went with her and my brother-in-law to Toño's house. There was no one there, but there were signs of a struggle. Everything had been thrown around.

—María Eugenia Vela, lawyer and wife of
victim Edgar Ávila

The next morning, Saturday, March 19, the gunmen summoned several heavy-equipment operators and ordered them to tear down dozens of houses and businesses across the region. Many of the properties were in busy, well-to-do neighborhoods within sight or earshot not only of passersby but also of government offices, police stations, and military outposts. The gunmen invited townspeople to take whatever they wanted, triggering a free-for-all of looting.

Government records obtained by *ProPublica* and *National Geographic* indicate that state emergency-response authorities were deluged that Saturday with some 250 calls from people reporting general disorder, fires, fights, and home invasions throughout the region. But numerous people interviewed said no one came to help.

Saturday is when everything began. Houses began exploding. People began breaking in and looting, and all I could think about was where Everardo might be. All day Saturday I spent searching and calling people to ask, "What have you heard?"

One person told me, "I saw armed men." Another told me, "The warehouses are still on fire. The smoke is really black, as if someone's burning tires. It's black, scary smoke."

I got a call from a man who worked with my husband. My husband raised fighting cocks. In this region cockfighting is very popular. He worked for José Luis Garza, but not full time. In the mornings and in the afternoons, he would go to the ranch to feed the animals.

The man told me, "There's something bad going on at the ranch. We don't know what's happened to all the people." I asked, "What do you mean? What people?"

He said that several of the men who worked with my husband had not arrived home the previous night. One was a tractor driver. Another watered the fields. None had arrived home.

I asked him, "OK, what do we do? Let's go look for them." He said, "Don't go anywhere near there, or else they'll take you too."

The image of one thing that happened is still with me: people breaking into supply stores and carrying away sacks of animal feed, parrots, and cages. They were taking lamps and dining-room sets.

The image that sticks with me most is of a tiny motorcycle with a woman riding on the back. She had turned a bed sheet into a sack. She had stuffed it full of things and was carrying it like Santa Claus, with one hand. And with the other she was holding a lamp. The motorcycle looked like it was going to tip over, but they looked happy with all the stuff they had taken.

—Rodríguez, victim's wife

I had two friends who collected and sold junk. They heard that the ranch was burning and that the owners had left, so they went—a father and son—to see if there was anything worth taking. They said they saw a freezer off the highway, a big one. And they wanted to take it. But it was really heavy. So the father told the son, "Let's dump what's inside." They opened it and saw two bodies. They ran away.

—Márquez, hot dog vendor

All the members of the town council met, not in formal session, but we all gathered—the council members, the public-security director. There were a lot of questions. The main one was, "What's happening?" But what everyone really wanted to know was why. We already knew there had been gunfire and that there were cases of disappearances and deaths.

There were a lot of questions about what we should do, but no one wanted to take charge. One of the council members even said, "Let's just get out of here, before something happens to us."

I didn't want to be a hero, but I thought at the very least we should stay in our offices so that people would see that we had not abandoned them. But all the staff wanted to leave. Everyone was focused on their own families.

With all that we were going through, we distrusted everyone. We realized that there was a two-sided government, the official one and the criminal one that was in charge. We knew that the police were controlled by criminals.

The director of public security told us, "These are *their* affairs." He didn't say any more. He didn't need to. I understood: "Don't investigate or intervene, or else."

—Evaristo Rodríguez, a veterinarian and
Allende's deputy mayor at the time

The last phone call with Rodolfo was at a quarter to noon. He sounded exhausted. He still hadn't heard anything from his parents. I told him he had done everything he could for them, and now it was time to think about Sofía and me. I begged him to come meet us in Eagle Pass. He said, "OK. I'm on my way."

I never heard from him again.

—Lira, victim's wife

There's no playbook to tell you what to do when someone steals your child. There is no first step. You go crazy. You want to run, but you don't know where. You want to scream, but you don't know whether anyone is listening. One of my cousins suggested I put it on Facebook. So I wrote, "Give me back my son. If anyone knows where he is, bring him back to me."

—Sánchez, victim's mother

How can I explain how I felt? It was as if they had kidnapped me that day too. In some ways I died. They killed the future we had, the plans, the dreams, the illusions, the peace, everything. At that time I had lived longer with Edgar than I had lived without him. Just think about that. On top of that I was pregnant, so I couldn't even think of taking any kind of sedative. I had to try to stay composed, very calm, but I'd come home and feel like the house was caving in on me. I couldn't find a place to sit down without feeling like the walls were falling. I couldn't make sense of this. Despite being a lawyer, I couldn't make sense of what had happened.

—Vela, victim's wife

## The Operation

Several months earlier, in the Dallas suburbs, the DEA had launched Operation Too Legit to Quit after some surprising busts. In one, police had found $802,000, vacuum-packed and hidden in the gas tank of a pickup. The driver said he worked for a guy he knew only as "El Diablo," the Devil.

After more arrests, DEA Agent Richard Martinez and Assistant U.S. Attorney Ernest Gonzalez determined that El Diablo was thirty-year-old Jose Vasquez Jr., a Dallas native who'd started selling drugs in high school and was now the leading Zetas cocaine distributor in east Texas, moving truckloads of drugs, guns, and money each month.

As they prepared to arrest him, Vasquez slipped across the border to Allende, where he sought protection from members of the cartel's inner circle.

But Martinez and Gonzalez saw an opportunity in his escape. If they could persuade Vasquez to cooperate, it would give them rare access to the senior ranks of the notoriously impenetrable cartel and a chance to capture its leaders, particularly the Treviño brothers, who had killed their way onto the list of the DEA's top targets. Miguel Ángel Treviño was known as Z-40, Omar as Z-42.

What Martinez wanted were the trackable PINs, or personal identification numbers, of the Treviños' BlackBerry phones. Vasquez had left the agent plenty of leverage. His wife and mother were still living in Texas.

> My wife calls me at like 6 o'clock in the morning. She tells me, "Hey, the house is surrounded."
>
> I said, "What do you mean, it's surrounded?"
>
> She said, "Yeah, there's a lot of cops outside."
>
> I said, "Well, listen, they're probably going to arrest you. Let me call [my lawyer]. Just make sure you don't tell them nothing. Just try to relax. We'll get you out on bond."
>
> I told her, "Break the phones." We had toilets in the house that flush real strong, so she broke them and flushed the phones down the toilet.
>
> Then Richard [Martinez] called me from there. He put me on speakerphone, so my wife could hear.
>
> He told me he was going to arrest her. I thought he was bluffing, so I said, "Do what you got to do."
>
> —Jose Vasquez Jr., convicted Zetas operative

At the beginning all we wanted was for Jose to turn himself in and cooperate, so that he could tell us the structure of the Zetas organization. I think that would have appeased us at that point because we really didn't know how close—how near—he was to Miguel and Omar. We didn't know—until he started saying who he was talking to, who he was seeing—what they were doing. That's when our perspective of what we could do, and how, began to change. We started to try to come up with ideas about how to capture them.

When Jose didn't turn himself in, and we saw that he was willing to sacrifice his wife, we knew we needed to turn the screws even harder, or put more leverage on him.

Richard tells him, "Your mom's going to be charged."

—Ernest Gonzalez, assistant U.S. attorney


I told him, "Man, listen, man, I'll go to the border right now, walk over and turn myself in. I won't fight you for nothing. I'll sign all your seizure papers. Give me a life sentence. Throw away the key. I don't care. But leave my wife alone. Leave my mother alone."

He's like, "Listen, the only way your wife doesn't do no jail time or your mom doesn't do no jail time is if you cooperate with us."

I said, "Richard, I don't want to cooperate, man. There's going to be a lot of murders that come behind this."

He was like, "All I have to tell you is if you don't cooperate, they're going to do time with you."

I asked Richard, "What do you want?"

—Vasquez, convicted Zetas operative


I wanted the numbers. Our hope was to get the Zetas leadership. I figured that those numbers gave us the best chance to get them. I knew Jose was in a position to help us.

When it comes down to it, a lot of these guys flee the United States. But if you grew up here, it's still America, the best country in the world. You still want to eventually come back to America. If your family is here, you still want to be around them. I thought that once Jose realized that the jig was up, he was going to do whatever he had to do to help us. I was going to push him to do that while I had the opportunity.

This is kind of getting off subject, but I remember going to Mexico as a kid. My mother is from Mexico—Monterrey. I've been to Coahuila. I've got family in Coahuila. You can't go back there right now. It's sad to say. But you can't go down these rural roads. I would love for my family to go back there, but they can't.

I saw these numbers as a key. They're very significant. I saw it as an opportunity to stop the Miguel and Omar Treviño reign.

—Richard Martinez, DEA agent

It was something personal, absolutely. It was important because of my background, because of my own personal heritage, and of knowing what [the Zetas] were doing to Mexico. I spent my summers with my grandparents in Mexico. They had farms and ranches. I enjoyed my youth in Mexico. This organization was destroying all that with their greed and their violence.

—Gonzalez, assistant U.S. attorney

To avoid capture, the Zetas had their closest lieutenant in Coahuila, Mario Alfonso "Poncho" Cuéllar, provide them new cell phones every three or four weeks. Cuéllar assigned the job of buying the phones to his right-hand man, Héctor Moreno.

Under pressure to get the phones' PINs, Vasquez turned to Moreno, using a little leverage of his own. It was Moreno's brother, Gilberto, who had been caught driving the truck with $802,000 in the gas tank. Facing twenty years in prison, Gilberto had confessed that he was working for the Zetas and that the cash belonged to the Treviño brothers.

Vasquez arranged for his lawyer in Dallas to represent Gilberto and promised not to let anyone else in the cartel know about Gilberto's incriminating statements. Moreno repaid the favor by agreeing to get Vasquez the numbers. But when the time came, Moreno had second thoughts.

> The Zetas controlled everything. They did whatever they wanted. When soldiers were going to come to the area, someone from the military would notify us in advance.
>
> Sometimes planeloads of federal police would arrive, with 200 officers. But we'd get a call a week ahead of time: "Are you stashing anything in such and such a house?"
>
> We'd say, "No, there's nothing there."
>
> They'd say, "Good, because there is a search warrant for that location, and agents are going to arrive on Thursday."
>
> The government told us everything. So I knew that if the government got those numbers, the Zetas would find out.
>
> —Héctor Moreno, former Zetas operative

The day Héctor was supposed to give me the numbers, I called him. He said, "I got the numbers, but I threw them out."

I said, "What happened? You said you were going to give them to me."

He told me, "These numbers could get us in a lot of trouble, so I threw them out the window."

I told him, "I have these guys waiting for me. I told them I was going to give them the numbers. What about my family?"

After a while, I talked him into driving back to the road where he threw the numbers out. We drove up and down that road for like an hour or two, until we found the slip of paper.

I got all the numbers—for 40, and 42, and all of them. I didn't know what they were going to do with them. I thought they were going to try to wiretap them or something like that. I never thought they were going to send the numbers back to Mexico. I told them not to do that, because it was going to get a lot of people killed. Not only that, I was still there. I was still hanging around those people. They said they wouldn't. Richard told me I had to trust him.

—Vasquez, convicted Zetas operative

## The Takeover

Lawlessness was not unfamiliar to people in Allende. Because of its proximity to the U.S. border—residents do their weekend shopping in Texas—there had long been families engaged in smuggling who lived quietly within their communities. But by 2007 the Zetas moved in with the money and muscle of a hostile occupation. They vanquished rivals, took control of critical government agencies, turned local police into their henchmen, and transformed the region into a haven for all kinds of criminality.

Then the traffickers embedded themselves in society—buying businesses, staging galas, recruiting from or marrying into local families.

The violence that exploded here in 2011 didn't just happen from one day to the next. There had already been drug trafficking for a long time. And for a long time, there was only one boss, named Vicente Lafuente Guereca. Everyone knew who he was and what he did for a living. But there was mutual respect. He respected society, and society respected him. And in that spirit, life carried on with a certain normalcy. Drugs passed through, but society didn't intervene. And Lafuente didn't interfere with the government or with civil society. There were no kidnappings. There was nothing like that.

But that peaceful coexistence ended when Lafuente was murdered.

—Carlos Osuna, retired businessman and<br>organizer for the National Action Party

When the Zetas arrived, they recruited everyone to work for them. All the narcos in the area had to work for the Zetas. There were no more independent groups. Before they came, Coahuila had been a kind of free market. Anyone who wanted to could operate there. The Tejas [a gang based in Nuevo Laredo] were there. Chapo [Joaquín Guzmán, head of the Sinaloa cartel] was there. It was wide open. But the Zetas arrived, and they killed Omar Rubio, of the Tejas. They killed Vicente Lafuente. They killed a few other important people. And everyone who was left joined them.

My family had been in the area for a long time. On my mother's side, I had relatives who ran funeral homes and hardware stores. On my father's side, they owned ranches. But the truth is, none of that offered as much money as drug trafficking. That's why I got involved.

—Moreno, former Zetas operative

When I was a member of Congress, ranchers and farmers from Allende began coming to see me. They were terrified because their lives were being threatened. They said that criminals were taking over their properties. Some of them told me that the only way they could get onto their own land was if they asked for permission from the criminals.

One of them was José Piña. He told me he had gone to the police for help, and they told him there was nothing they could do. There was a military checkpoint a few meters away from his property, so I asked him, "What about the soldiers?" He told me, "I've told the soldiers, and—nothing." I said, "What do you mean, nothing?" He said, "They won't do anything."

He said [the Zetas] had offered him money for his ranch, but he wouldn't take it. He had complained to the mayor and the governor, but he couldn't get anyone to listen. So he came to me, and he gave me a handwritten letter for the president.

Two days later, Mr. Piña was dead.

—Ángel Humberto García, medical doctor
and former legislator

The Mexican newspaper *El Universal* published a story about the 2009 murder. It reported that Piña's body, found behind a Catholic elementary school, had been "riddled with bullets." The story said the rancher's tongue had been cut out, his fingers cut off, and one of them was stuffed inside his mouth. The killers attached a written missive: "We don't mess with you. Don't mess with us."

The Zetas killed Piña because his ranch was set on the Río Bravo [Rio Grande]. 40 and 42 used to pass through there every day. They would leave his gates open, so his cattle would escape. He complained about it to the military. The soldiers told the Zetas. And because of that they went and killed him.

—Moreno, former Zetas operative

One night, [the Zetas] beat my son. It was really bad. He had bruises all over his body. His face was swollen. They had put a machine gun to his head and threatened to shoot him. He had been drinking with his friends. They stopped at a gas station. [The Zetas] beat him there, in front of the police.

I went to the police and asked, "Why in the hell did you let those assholes beat my son?" I took the keys to their patrol cars. I told them, "What good is it to have officers on the streets who won't protect people?"

They told me, "They'd have killed us if we'd tried to stop them."

Later I went out and had too much to drink. As I walked to my car, I saw some police officers nearby. I shouted at them, "Tell the [Zetas] boss I want to see him."

The next day, I was running errands in town, and I saw a line of cars heading toward me. The cars pulled in front of me and stopped. "The boss wants to speak with you." They walked me over to one of the cars. I got in, next to the driver. It was 42.

He said, "What can I do for you, Mr. Mayor?"

I told him, "Listen, how would you feel if someone beat the shit out of your kid? Wouldn't that piss you off?"

"Of course it would," he said.

"Well I'm pissed," I said. "You guys think that you're so tough because you've got weapons, and that there's nothing we can do about it. You might be right. But as for my family, if you want to touch anyone, you come to me. If you want to kill someone, kill me."

He said, "I'm not going to kill you. You are not my enemy, as long as you mind your affairs and let us handle ours. But please keep your son home at night. If he wants to drink with his friends, let them do that at home. The night belongs to us."

—Ricardo Treviño Guevara, a former mayor of Allende

There was a point at which we started to see signs that [the Zetas] had begun a kind of hegemonic takeover of all commercial activities. In addition to trafficking drugs and weapons, they began to start companies and businesses in the service sector, in real estate, in construction.

For example, they began operating money-exchange houses at the border, to exchange dollars for pesos. They staged concerts and dances. They opened restaurants, bars, and red-light districts. They got into buying and selling used cars. Then they turned to bigger businesses. They began building shopping malls, hotels, and casinos.

And they began living here. After a while, their children began attending schools with your children.

Don't think they were living on the outskirts in some ranch. They lived right here in front of city hall. In fact, from this balcony I can point to one of the houses where they lived.

Everyone was afraid of them. The Zetas were stronger than the government. You understand? They were economically stronger. They were better organized. They were better armed. Everyone was afraid of them, and those who weren't afraid had been bought by them.

—Fernando Purón, mayor of Piedras Negras

The biggest impact on society was on our sense of freedom. I could no longer go out to my ranch, or even to the corner without fear that someone would mistake me for someone else and beat me, or worse. That loss was what we felt most.

And then, even if we weren't involved with [the cartel], they would establish ties to our families. One of them would marry a cousin or the daughter of a close friend, and suddenly they're at the same parties or holiday dinners.

At the beginning we simply kept quiet out of fear. But unfortunately, drug trafficking brings a lot of money with it. And we all like money. So these guys show up with it, and they start spreading it around, and before you know it they're members of the Lions Club.

It wasn't hard to spot. We are a small community. Everyone knows one another's income levels. So when someone is living on a thousand pesos one day, and 3 million pesos the next, you have to say, wait a minute, something's going on there. Unfortunately, we all accepted it.

—Osuna, retired businessman

## The Leak

About three weeks after Vasquez provided the PIN numbers to the DEA, the cartel's leaders got word that one of their own had betrayed them and launched a frenzy of retribution.

Law enforcement sources close to the case said that after Martinez gave the intelligence to his superior, it was passed to a DEA supervisor in Mexico City. He, in turn, shared it with a Mexican federal police unit that had been specially created to conduct operations under the DEA's direction.

Most members of the Sensitive Investigative Unit receive mandatory training and vetting by the DEA. But several current and former DEA agents said despite that vetting, the unit has long had a poor record of keeping information out of the hands of criminals. Among the most glaring problems, they say, is that Mexico doesn't allow the DEA to scrutinize the unit's supervisors in the same way as it does the unit's members. Two law-enforcement officials close to the Zetas case said their own inquiries revealed that a supervisor in the SIU was responsible. Former senior members of the Mexican Federal Police who worked closely with the unit did not respond to multiple requests for interviews.

Earlier this year, one of the unit's supervisors, Iván Reyes Arzate, turned himself in to U.S. federal authorities to face charges of sharing information about the DEA's investigations with drug traffickers. It's unclear if Reyes was the source of the leak in the Allende case.

As for the Zetas, it wasn't hard for them to identify who within the cartel may have betrayed them since very few people had access to their PIN numbers.

How did I know there was trouble? Because I was holding 596 kilos of cocaine for the cartel, and 40 sent a guy to take it back from me. That's something I had seen them do many times before. Every time 40 planned to kill someone in the organization, he would first make sure he had taken back their merchandise.

He sent me a photo of himself, with drawings of frogs all over it. At the bottom of the photo he wrote, "Look, the damned frogs had me shot." "Frogs" is their word for snitches.

I called 40 and asked him, "Hey, what's this about?" He didn't answer. All he said was, "I need to see you. Where are you going to be later?"

I told him I was going to be at the horse track. But I didn't go. I called a couple of my guys, and I told them to go see what was going on. After they got there, they called me and said, "You're screwed." One of 40's guys was there, cursing my name because I hadn't shown up. That's when I knew I had to leave.

I began calling my friends, warning them to get out too. Unfortunately, none of them listened to me. When 40 couldn't find me, he went after them.

—Mario Alfonso "Poncho" Cuéllar,
convicted Zetas operative

Héctor [Moreno] called me and told me that all hell was breaking loose. He asked me what I had done with the numbers. I told him that I had turned them in to the DEA. He told me, "Well something's going on. Somehow the Zetas found out."

I called Richard [Martinez] and said, "What'd you do with the numbers?" He said, "Man, they went to Mexico."

I said, "Man, how did you let that happen? I told you what would happen if those numbers came to Mexico."

Richard said, "Man, it wasn't me. It wasn't my call. It was above me. The boss did it. They sent the numbers to Mexico, thinking they had a friend over there they could trust."

—Vasquez, convicted Zetas operative

Richard called and said we got the numbers, but they've been sent to Mexico. I said, "What?" We hadn't had a meeting to discuss how to handle them. I got angry. I think Richard was of the same mindset. He didn't want it done that way either, but it was out of his hands. He said, "It's the bosses. It's management."

I knew well that there were issues with secrecy in Mexico. When information was passed on previous occasions, it always seemed that something would happen.

We had been trying forever to find the best way to locate the Treviños. What would be the best mechanism where we could definitively say, "This is where they are at this time." We knew they moved around a lot. This was one of those opportunities where you could do that. It was something we had struggled for a long time to achieve. We had put pressure on people to cooperate. We had arrested wives and mothers, and had all these great seizures.

It was a great opportunity. But it was squandered because it wasn't done correctly, and it got compromised.

—Gonzalez, assistant U.S. attorney

Vasquez, Moreno, Cuéllar, and Garza, whose family's ranch was the scene of many of the killings, fled to the United States when the massacre began and agreed to cooperate with U.S. law enforcement in exchange for leniency. Their horrifying accounts of what was going on in Allende made American authorities aware of what they had unleashed.

I remember my first meeting with the DEA. I was telling them what was happening in Coahuila, about all the violence. I remember Ernest [Gonzalez] getting up from the table, going outside, and confronting one of the DEA bosses. He started shouting at him. He said something like, "Did you hear what's going on? All this because you sent those numbers to Mexico."

—Cuéllar, convicted Zetas operative

I told him this was bullshit. Things should have never happened this way. We had information that could have helped us capture these guys, but because of the way it was handled, the whole thing had unraveled. And now it was a goddamned mess.

—Gonzalez, assistant U.S. attorney

## The Aftermath

For years state and federal authorities in Mexico didn't appear to make a real effort to delve into the attack. Mexican federal authorities said their predecessors didn't investigate because the killings couldn't be linked to organized crime but acknowledged that they also have not investigated.

Estimates of the number of dead and missing vary wildly between the official count, 28, and the one from victims associations, about 300. *ProPublica* and *National Geographic* have identified about 60 people whose deaths or disappearances have been linked by relatives, friends, victims' support groups, court files, or news reports to the Zetas siege that year.

Relatives were left on their own to try to piece together what had happened and to rebuild their lives.

In May 2011 Héctor Reynaldo Pérez filed a missing-person report with state authorities. His sister, who had married a Garza, had disappeared along with her entire family. Less than a year later, Pérez himself disappeared. A report by independent human rights investigators at the Colegio de México found evidence that Pérez was last seen in the custody of Allende police officers.

After that, few victims' relatives dared to turn to authorities for help, much less talk publicly about their ordeal. Several moved to the United States.

No family lost more members than the Garzas. Nearly twenty are believed dead, including eighty-one-year-old Olivia Martínez de la Torre and her seven-month-old great-grandson, Mauricio Espinoza. The baby's siblings, Andrea and Arturo Espinoza, five and three at the time, turned up at a Piedras Negras orphanage after their parents had been killed.

Their paternal grandmother, Elvira Espinoza, a hotel housekeeper in San Antonio, went with her husband to fetch them.

Andrea says they drove to a place where the houses didn't have roofs. She said the men took her mother, her grandmother, and her great-grandmother out of the car. They told the children, "Stay here. We're just going to talk."

The men kept them there and told them to stay quiet. No crying. Andrea said she changed the baby's diapers and made his bottles.

She doesn't remember how many days they were there before the men took her, Arturo, and Mauricio to Piedras Negras. Andrea said the men dropped her and Arturo in a park, but they took Mauricio with them.

She said that she begged them to leave the baby with her. But the men told her that the baby was too little and cried too much to leave him there with them.

Andrea blames herself for what happened to him. She says, "If I had been stronger, Mauricio would still be with us."

—Elvira Espinoza, hotel housekeeper and
grandmother of the Espinoza children

I filed a missing-person report. The investigator told me it would be confidential. He promised to keep my identity anonymous. Then a few days later I received a threat. Someone called my cell phone and told me that if I went forward with the complaint, the same thing that happened to my husband would happen to the rest of my family. My mother and father still lived in Allende. I would have never forgiven myself if something had happened to them.

I called the investigator that same day. I told him he had lied to me about keeping my name a secret and that I wanted to withdraw my complaint.

I also went to the Mexican Consulate in San Antonio. You won't believe what they said. They blamed me. They said, "Ah, you come crying now that your husband is missing. All this time, you knew what kind of business your relatives were in. But you didn't seem to mind until you were personally affected."

I never asked the government for anything again.

—Lira, victim's wife

Three years after the Zetas' rampage, Coahuila's governor, Rubén Moreira, announced that state officials would investigate what happened in Allende. With great fanfare, officials launched a "mega-operation" to collect evidence and find the truth. Victims' families and Allende residents say it has been little more than a publicity stunt. The inquiry has produced no conclusive DNA results, nor a final tally of the dead and missing.

Fewer than a dozen suspects have been arrested—most of them former local police and cartel grunts who followed orders. No one has been charged with murder. In 2015 the Coahuila State Prosecutors' Office began a series of meetings with relatives of those victims whom investigators believed—based on confessions— were dead. They handed out death certificates, despite having no bodies, that listed such causes of death as "neurogenic shock" and "total combustion due to direct exposure to fire."

When they gave me the news, my body went limp. They told me Gerardo had been taken to a ranch and killed. Something inside told me that it was true. But I asked, "Are you sure it was him?"

They told me that the witnesses had said that among the victims there was a family with three boys, and that one of the boys was my son. They said he had started to cry. It was stressing them out, so they killed him. That's when I lost it. How could anyone kill a fifteen-year-old boy who's afraid and crying?

The officials asked me what I wanted. I told them I wanted his remains. They said that would be difficult, since my son was incinerated along with a lot of other people. Instead they brought me ashes and dirt from the place where he died. I asked them if I could go there. They told me it wasn't safe. I told them I wanted to go anyway. So they escorted us in a caravan.

I was struck by how close it was. I thought to myself, Gerardo was so strong that if only he could have gotten away and made it to the highway, he would have easily managed to make it home.

—Sánchez, victim's mother

The prosecutor and his team were supposed to arrive in the afternoon, but they didn't arrive until that night. We waited more than five hours for them. And when they finally got there, all they offered were symbolic gestures. They told us they were going to hand out death certificates, with information based on the statements that had come from the people who had been arrested. And they had small boxes of dirt for any relatives who wanted them. That was it.

I told them, "Hold on. I didn't wait here for six hours to have you come and offer me a death certificate and this box. We're human. How can you possibly think this is the right way to help bring us closure? I want to know what you learned and where you learned it. Where is the person who killed [my husband]? How did they kill him?"

They said that the answers might be hard to hear. They didn't want to be cruel. I told them nothing could be worse than the 20,000 things I had already imagined on my own.

How would the suspects know my husband's name, if they weren't from here? We had believed all this time that the people who did this had been brought from another state.

In the end we learned they were people from here. The monsters we thought had come from who knows where were monsters who had lived among us and who were supposed to protect us.

—Rodríguez, victim's wife

They gave me a death certificate dated the 19th of March, 2011—the day after he disappeared. The only thing I asked them was whether they were certain they were right. They told me that the forensic specialists had not been able to test the fragments that had been recovered, so they couldn't be 100 percent sure. But they told me they were confident that Edgar was there at the time of the massacre. I think it's because they had witness statements.

I still don't know what to believe. I hadn't heard anything from them in five years; then, out of nowhere, they ask me to believe the case is solved.

I bet that if you were able to get a look at my husband's case file, you'd see it's empty.

Still, with the death certificate I began to make the changes that were long overdue. I moved out of our house. I left with only our clothes and [my daughter's] bedroom furniture. All of Edgar's clothes are still back there, hanging in the closet, exactly as he left them.

I could finally speak openly with my daughter about what had happened. I hadn't been able to tell her that her father was dead, because, what if he returned? I think in some ways she had already figured it out.

—Vela, victim's wife

The Treviño brothers were eventually captured, Miguel in 2013 and Omar in 2015, in operations led by Mexican marines. Since then, the cartel's hold on Coahuila has weakened, and nightlife has returned to Allende, though many residents remain emotionally scarred and leery of strangers. They fixate on reports of drug-related violence, worrying that the Treviños are exerting control over the drug trade from prison.

The DEA takes credit for the captures but won't say what, if anything, it did to investigate how the information about the PIN numbers wound up in the hands of the Zetas. Terrance Cole, Martinez's supervisor in Dallas, and Paul Knierim, then a DEA supervisor in Mexico City who served as a liaison with the DEA-trained Mexican federal police unit, declined to be interviewed.

Knierim has since been promoted and is now the agency's deputy chief of operations in Washington.

But Martinez agreed to speak, briefly choking up when asked about his role in the massacre. Named agent of the year in 2011, he is now battling kidney cancer, and so far aggressive treatment has failed. Russ Baer, a DEA spokesman, twice flew from Washington, D.C., to Texas to monitor interviews with Martinez and another agent there. As Martinez spoke, Baer interrupted to stress that the top Zetas were in prison and the agency's investigation was ultimately a success.

> Obviously I'm devastated by it. You know that in this line of work, there are going to be consequences. The potential for someone to get killed is always there. But to actually be involved in something like that and not being able to do anything is devastating.
>
> The goal was an honorable goal: to try to get these guys arrested and put in jail so that they would stop killing people. But at that point in the investigation, it had the opposite effect.

I had heard about the brutality of Miguel and Omar Treviño and the senseless violence they had perpetrated in the past, but it didn't register with me that it could be that way, that anybody that was even remotely linked to you, even if it was outside the drug trade, would be picked up and killed. That just didn't seem possible. It probably should have. But it didn't, until it was happening, until it happened.

—Gonzalez, assistant U.S. attorney:

I got the numbers. I passed them to our people. As far as that, I don't have anything to do with anything else.

We all knew the numbers were dangerous. If I just sat on a number—what am I going to do with them here in Dallas? The wiretap is not as easy as people say it is. I have to have probable cause.

To me, I got the numbers, and I passed them on. That's my job.

I can't speak for the agency, other than I just know what I did. I did all I could do.

I gave it a shot. That's the way I felt. I did the best I could do that day. I had the opportunity to get the intelligence and pass it on. I got it. I can't very well go into Mexico and try to handle it myself.

—Martinez, DEA agent

Listen to this guy. He's got family that's from Mexico. He talked about health problems. He's talking about this almost tearing up at times because he's so emotionally invested in this. This is a guy who started by watching the glamour of *Miami Vice*,' dedicated his life as a public servant to work for DEA, and ultimately took down the Zetas cartel. That personal story, it doesn't get much better than that. It sends chills up my spine.

As far as what happened in Mexico and the aftermath of the compromise, the DEA's official position is: That's squarely on Omar and Miguel Treviño. They were killing people before that happened, and they killed people after the numbers were passed. DEA did our job to target them and to try to focus and dedicate our resources to put them out of business. We were eventually successful in that regard.

Our hearts go out to those families. They're victims, unfortunately, of the violence perpetrated by the Treviño brothers and the Zetas. But this is not a story where the DEA has blood on its hands.

—Russ Baer, DEA spokesman

## Voices

### Informants

- Jose Vasquez Jr., convicted Zetas operative

    A Dallas native, he began selling drugs in high school and went on to become the Zetas' leading cocaine distributor in East Texas. According to court records, each month he moved 3,000 to 4,000 kilos of cocaine—valued at $12 million to $16 million—through Dallas to different points across the country. Vasquez, a husband and father of three, gave the DEA the Zetas leaders' trackable cell phone PIN numbers.

- Mario Alfonso "Poncho" Cuellar, convicted Zetas operative and former Mexican Highway Patrol officer

    A father of four and avid body builder, Cuellar controlled most of the Zetas' operations in and around Allende and Piedras Negras, which sits across the border from Eagle Pass, Texas. In the northern Mexican state of Coahuila, he was the Treviño brothers' right hand and even godfather to some of the traffickers' children.

- Hector Moreno, former Zetas operative

    He was Cuellar's top lieutenant, managing day-to-day trafficking operations in and around Piedras Negras. One of his responsibilities was handling the cartel's communications, which gave him access to the trackable cell phone PIN numbers for the group's leaders. He was involved with providing those numbers to the DEA.

## American Law Enforcement

- Richard Martinez, DEA agent

  A twelve-year veteran of the agency, he led Operation Too Legit to Quit. Martinez obtained the trackable cell phone identification numbers for the leaders of the Zetas cartel and gave them to his superiors. He is a Texas native and has family in Coahuila.

- Ernest Gonzalez, assistant U.S. attorney in the Eastern District of Texas

  He worked closely with the DEA on Too Legit to Quit and later prosecuted several Zetas operatives in a case tracing the cartel's drug supply chain from Mexico through Guatemala to Colombia. He previously worked along the U.S.-Mexico border, but had to move in 2004 after traffickers threatened to kidnap his wife and child. He was born in the United States but has family in Mexico.

## Victims' Relatives

- Claudia Sánchez, a cultural affairs director and mother of victim Gerardo Heath

  Sanchez's son Gerardo, fifteen, a high-school football player who had nothing to do with the Zetas or the drug trade, has become a symbol of the brutal attack. Before authorities told her that eyewitnesses confirmed Gerardo's death, she had fallen prey to scam artists who offered to track down her son for a fee. For several years, Sanchez staged prayer rallies at a local stadium calling for an end to cartel violence.

- Sarah Angelita Lira, a pharmacist and wife of victim Rodolfo Garza Jr.

  Lira and her daughter fled to the United States as the massacre began and have never returned to live in Allende. Her husband, a contractor at a coal mine, was a member of the Garza family, but Lira said he didn't work for the Zetas like some family members. She said she warned him that his relatives' ties to the cartel could prove deadly. Nearly twenty members of the Garza family are dead or missing.

- Etelvina Rodríguez, middle-school teacher and wife of victim Everardo Elizondo

  Rodriguez's husband raised fighting cocks for the Garza family. He was at one of the Garza ranches when the massacre began and is presumed dead. She has traveled to the United States and Europe to denounce drug violence and to seek support for Mexican crime victims.

- Maria Eugenia Vela, lawyer and wife of victim Edgar Avila

  Vela's husband, a factory engineer, was watching a soccer match on television at a friend's home when Zetas gunmen arrived looking for the friend's brother, who was connected to the cartel. The brother wasn't there, but the gunmen took everyone else away. Avila has never been seen since. Vela was pregnant at the time with the couple's second child.

## Smithsonian

FINALIST—ESSAYS
AND CRITICISM

*The Ellie judges described "Whatever Happened to the Russian Revolution?" as "a masterful combination of travel writing and historical investigation."* Ian Frasier begins this journey through Russia not at a place but in the past—at the Decembrist uprising in 1825— then explores the lasting impact of the October Revolution of 1917. "Yet," the judges continued, "this is also an alarmingly relevant political essay about a populist uprising hijacked by disciplined, ruthless and uncompromising ideologues." *A longtime contributor to* The New Yorker, *Frasier first explored Russia in* Travels in Siberia, *published in 2010. Earlier books include his account of the American West,* Great Plains, *and the collection* Dating Your Mom. *An official publication of the Smithsonian Institution,* Smithsonian *along with Smithsonian.com provides a singular chronicle of the everyday richness of our past and future.*

Ian Frazier

# What Ever Happened to the Russian Revolution?

## 1

Russia is both a great, glorious country and an ongoing disaster. Just when you decide it is the one, it turns around and discloses the other. For a hundred years before 1917, it experienced wild disorders and political violence interspersed with periods of unquiet calm, meanwhile producing some of the world's greatest literature and booming in population and helping to feed Europe. Then it leapt into a revolution unlike any the world had ever seen. Today, a hundred years afterward, we still don't know quite what to make of that huge event. The Russians themselves aren't too sure about its significance.

I used to tell people that I loved Russia because I do. I think everybody has a country not their own that they're powerfully drawn to; Russia is mine. I can't explain the attraction, only observe its symptoms going back to childhood, such as listening over and over to Prokofiev's *Peter and the Wolf*, narrated by Peter Ustinov, when I was six, or standing in the front yard at night as my father pointed out *Sputnik* crossing the sky. Now I've traveled enough in Russia that my affections are more complicated. I know that almost no conclusion I ever draw about it is likely to be right. The way to think about Russia is without thinking about it. I just try to love it and yield to it and go with it while also paying vigilant attention—if that makes sense.

I first began traveling to Russia more than twenty-four years ago, and in 2010 I published *Travels in Siberia*, a book about trips I'd made to that far-flung region. With the fall of the Soviet Union, areas previously closed to travelers had opened up. During the 1990s and after, the pace of change in Russia cascaded. A harsh kind of capitalism grew; democracy came and mostly went. Then, two years ago, my son moved to the city of Yekaterinburg, in the Ural Mountains, on the edge of Siberia, and he lives there now. I see I will never stop thinking about this country.

As the 1917 centennial approached, I wondered about the revolution and tangled with its force field of complexity. For example, a question as straightforward as what to call certain Russian cities reveals, on examination, various options, asterisks, clarifications. Take St. Petersburg, whose name was changed in 1914 to Petrograd so as not to sound too German (at the time, Russia was fighting the Kaiser in the First World War). In 1924 Petrograd became Leningrad, which then went back to being St. Petersburg again in 1991. Today many of the city's inhabitants simply call it "Peter." Or consider the name of the revolution itself. Though it's called the Great October Revolution, from our point of view it happened in November. In 1917, Russia still followed the Julian calendar, which lagged thirteen days behind the Gregorian calendar used elsewhere in the world. The Bolshevik government changed the country to the Gregorian calendar in early 1918, soon after taking control. (All this information will be useful later on.)

In February and March I went to Russia to see what it was like in the centennial year. My way to travel is to go to a specific place and try to absorb what it is now and look closer, for what it was. Things that happen in a place change it and never leave it. I visited my son in Yekaterinburg, I rambled around Moscow, and I gave the most attention to St. Petersburg, where traces of the revolution are everywhere. The weather stayed cold. In each of the cities, ice topped with perfectly white snow locked the rivers. Here and there, rogue footprints crossed the ice expanses with their brave or heedless dotted lines. In St. Petersburg, I often passed Senate Square, in the middle of the city, with Étienne Falconet's black statue of Peter the Great on his rearing horse atop a massive rock. Sometimes I saw newlyweds by the statue popping corks as an icy wind blew in across the Neva River and made the champagne foam fly. They were standing at a former pivot point of empire.

·　　·　　·

I'll begin my meditation in 1825, at the Decembrist uprising. The Decembrists were young officers in the czar's army who fought in the Napoleonic wars and found out about the Enlightenment and came home wanting to reform Russia. They started a secret society, wrote a constitution based on the U.S. Constitution, and, on December 14, at the crucial moment of their coup attempt, lost their nerve. They had assembled troops loyal to them on Senate Square, but after a daylong standoff Czar Nicholas I dispersed these forces with cannon fire. Some of the troops ran across the Neva trying to escape; the cannons shot at the ice and shattered it and drowned them. The authorities arrested a hundred-some Decembrists and tried and convicted almost all. The czar sent most to Siberia; he ordered five of the leaders hanged. For us, the Decembrists' example can be painful to contemplate—as if King George III had hanged George Washington and sent the other signers of the Declaration of Independence to hard labor in Australia.

One good decision the Decembrists made was to not include Alexander Pushkin in their plot, although he was friends with more than a few of them. This spared him to survive and to become Russia's greatest poet.

Tolstoy, of a younger generation than theirs, admired the Decembrists and wanted to write a book about their uprising. But the essential documents, such as the depositions they gave after their arrests, were hidden away under czarist censorship, so instead he wrote *War and Peace*. In Tolstoy's lifetime the country's revolutionary spirit veered into terrorism. Russia invented terrorism, that feature of modern life, in the 1870s. Young middle-class lawyers and university teachers and students joined terror groups of which the best known was Naródnaya Volia, or People's Will. They went around shooting and blowing up czarist officials and killed thousands. Alexander II, son of Nicholas I, succeeded his father in 1855, and in 1861 he emancipated the serfs. People's Will blew him up anyway.

When Tolstoy met in 1886 with George Kennan, the American explorer of Siberia (and a cousin twice removed of the diplomat of the same name, who, more than a half-century later, devised Truman's Cold War policy of "containment" of the Soviet Union), Kennan pleaded for support for some of the Siberian exiles he had met. But the great man refused even to listen. He said these revolutionaries had chosen violence and must live with the consequences.

Meanwhile Marxism was colonizing the brains of Russian intellectuals like an invasive plant. The *intelligentsia* (a word of Russian origin) sat at tables in Moscow and St. Petersburg and other cities in the empire or abroad arguing Marxist doctrine and drinking endless cups of tea, night after night, decade after decade. (If vodka has damaged the sanity of Russia, tea has been possibly worse.) Points of theory nearly impossible to follow today caused Socialist parties of different types to incubate and proliferate and split apart. The essential writer of that later-nineteenth-century moment was Chekhov. The wistful, searching characters in his plays always make me afraid for them. I keep wondering why they can't do anything about what's coming, as if I'm at a scary movie and the teenage couple making out in the car don't see the guy with the hockey mask and chain saw who is sneaking up on them.

The guy in the hockey mask was Vladimir I. Lenin. In 1887, his older brother, Aleksandr Ulyanov, a sweet young man by all accounts, joined a plot to assassinate Czar Alexander III. Betrayed by an informer (a common fate), Ulyanov was tried and found guilty, and he died on the gallows, unrepentant. Lenin, seventeen at the time, hated his family's liberal friends who dropped the Ulyanovs as a consequence. From then on, the czar and the bourgeoisie were on borrowed time.

·　　·　　·

The Romanov dynasty stood for more than 300 years. Nicholas II, the last czar, a Romanov out of his depth, looked handsome in his white naval officer's uniform. He believed in God, disliked Jews, loved his wife and five children, and worried especially about his youngest child, the hemophiliac only son, Alexei. If you want a sense of the last Romanovs, check out the Fabergé eggs they often gave as presents to each other. One afternoon I happened on a sponsored show of Fabergé eggs in a St. Petersburg museum. Such a minute concentration of intense, bejeweled splendor you've never seen. The diamond-encrusted tchotchkes often opened to reveal even littler gem-studded gifts inside. The eggs can stand for the czar's unhelpful myopia during the perilous days of 1917. Viewers of the exhibit moved from display case to display case in reverent awe.

One can pass over some of the disasters of Nicholas' reign. He was born unlucky on the name day of Job, the sufferer. On the day of his coronation, in 1896, a crowd of half a million, expecting a special giveaway in Moscow, panicked, trampling to death and suffocating 1,400 people. Nicholas often acted when he should have done nothing and did nothing when he should have acted. He seemed mild and benign, but after his troops killed hundreds of workers marching on the Winter Palace with a petition for an eight-hour workday and other reforms—the massacre was on January 9, 1905, later known as Bloody Sunday—fewer of his subjects thought of him as "the good czar."

The 1905 protests intensified until they became the 1905 Revolution. The czar's soldiers killed perhaps 14,000 more before it was under control. As a result, Nicholas allowed the convening of a representative assembly called the State Duma, Russia's first parliament, along with wider freedom of the press and other liberalizations. But the Duma had almost no power, and Nicholas kept trying to erode the little it had. He did not enjoy being czar but believed in the autocracy with all his soul and wanted to bequeath it undiminished to his son.

It's July 1914, just before the beginning of the First World War: The czar stands on a balcony of the Winter Palace, reviewing his army. The whole vast expanse of Palace Square is packed with people. He swears on the Bible and the holy icons that he will not sign for peace so long as one enemy soldier is standing on Russian soil. Love of the fatherland has its effect. The entire crowd, tens of thousands strong, falls to its knees to receive his blessing. The armies march. Russia's attacks on the Eastern Front help to save Paris in 1914. Like the other warring powers, Russia goes into the trenches. But each spring, in 1915 and 1916, the army renews its advance. By 1917 it has lost more than three million men.

In America we may think of disillusionment with that war as a quasi-literary phenomenon, something felt by the writers of the Lost Generation in Paris. Long before America entered the war, Russian soldiers felt worse—disgusted with the weak czar and the German-born czarina, filled with anger at their officers, and enraged at the corruption that kept them poorly supplied. In the winter of 1916–17, they begin to appear in Petrograd as deserters and in deputations for peace, hoping to make their case before the Duma. The czar and the upper strata of Russian society insist that the country stay in the war, for the sake of national honor and for their allies, some of whom have lent Russia money. Russia also hopes to receive as a war prize the Straits of Bosporus and the Dardanelles, which it has long desired. But the soldiers and common people see the idiocy of the endless, static struggle and the unfair share they bear in it, and they want peace.

The absence of enough men to bring in the harvests, plus a shortage of railroad cars, plus an unusually cold winter, lead to a lack of bread in Petrograd. In February many city residents are starving. Women take to the streets and march on stores and bakeries crying the one word: "*Khleb!*" Bread! Striking workers from Petrograd's huge factories, like the Putilov Works, which employs 40,000 men, join the disturbances. The czar's government does not know what to do. Day after day in February the marches go on. Finally, the czar orders the military to suppress the demonstrations. People are killed. But now, unlike in 1905, the soldiers have little to lose. They do not want to shoot; many of the marchers are young peasants like themselves, who have recently come to the city to work in the factories. And nothing awaits the soldiers except being sent to the front.

So, one after another, Petrograd regiments mutiny and join the throngs on the streets. Suddenly the czar's government can find no loyal troops willing to move against the demonstrators. Taking stock, Nicholas's ministers and generals inform him that he has no choice but to abdicate for the good of the country. On March 2 he complies, with brief complications involving his son and brother, neither of whom succeeds him.

Near-chaos ensues. In the vacuum, power is split between two new institutions: the Provisional Government, a cabinet of Duma ministers who attempt to manage the country's affairs while waiting for the first meeting of the Constituent Assembly, a nationwide representative body scheduled to convene in the fall; and the Petrograd Soviet of Workers' and Soldiers' Deputies, a somewhat amorphous collection of groups with fluid memberships and multi-socialist-party affiliations. (In Russian, one meaning of the word "soviet" is "council"—here, an essentially political entity.) The Petrograd Soviet is the working people's organization while the Provisional Government mostly represents the upper bourgeoisie. This attempt at dual governance is a fiction because the Petrograd Soviet has the support of the factory workers, ordinary people, and soldiers. In other words, it has the actual power; it has the guns.

The February Revolution, as it's called, is the real and original Russian revolution. February supplied the raw energy for the rest of 1917—energy that Lenin and the Bolsheviks would co-opt as justification for their coup in October. Many classic images of the people's struggle in Russia derive from February. In that month red became the color of revolution: Sympathetic onlookers wore red lapel ribbons, and marchers tore the white and blue stripes from the Russian flag and used the red stripe for their long, narrow banner. Even jaded Petrograd artistic types wept when they heard the self-led multitudes break into "The Marseillaise," France's revolutionary anthem, recast with fierce Russian lyrics. Comparatively little blood was shed in the February Revolution, and its immediate achievement—bringing down the Romanov dynasty—made a permanent difference. Unlike the coup of October, the February uprising had a spontaneous, popular, tectonic quality. Of the many uprisings and coups and revolutions Russia has experienced, only the events of February 1917 seemed to partake of joy.

## 2

The city of St. Petersburg endlessly explains itself, in plaques and monuments everywhere you turn. It still possesses the majesty of an imperial capital, with its plazas, rows of eighteenth- and nineteenth-century government buildings receding to a vanishing point, glassy canals, and towering cloudscapes just arrived from the Baltic Sea. The layout makes a grand backdrop, and the revolution was the climactic event it served as a backdrop for.

A taxi dropped me beside the Fontanka Canal at Nevskii Prospekt, where my friend Luda has an apartment in a building on the corner. Luda and I met eighteen years ago, when Russian friends who had known her in school introduced us. I rented one of several apartments she owns in the city for a few months in 2000 and 2001. We became friends despite lack of a common language; with my primitive but slowly improving Russian and her kind tolerance of it, we made do. Now I often stay with her when I'm in the city.

When we first knew each other Luda worked for the local government and was paid so little that, she said, she would be able to visit the States only if she went a year without eating or drinking. Then she met a rich Russian American, married him, and moved to his house in Livingston, New Jersey, about ten miles from us. After her husband died she stayed in the house by herself. I saw her often, and she came to visit us for dinner. The house eventually went to her husband's children, and now she divides her time between St. Petersburg and Miami. I have more phone numbers for her than for anyone else in my address book.

Her Nevskii apartment's midcity location is good for my purposes because when I'm in St. Petersburg I walk all over, sometimes fifteen miles or more in a day. One morning, I set out for the Finland Station, on the north side of the Neva, across the Liteynyi Bridge from the city's central district. The stroll takes about twenty minutes. As you approach the station, you see, on the square in front, a large statue of Lenin, speaking from atop a stylized armored car. One hand holds the lapel of his greatcoat, the other arm extends full length, gesturing rhetorically. This is your basic and seminal Lenin statue. The Finlandskii Voksal enters the story in April of 1917. It's where the world-shaking, cataclysmic part of the Russian Revolution begins.

·　　·　　·

Most of the hard-core professional revolutionaries did not participate in the February Revolution, having been earlier locked up, exiled, or chased abroad by the czar's police. (That may be why the vain and flighty Alexander Kerensky rose to power so easily after February: The major-leaguers had not yet taken the field.)

Lenin was living in Zurich, where he and his wife, Nadezhda Krupskaya, had rented a small, disagreeable room. Awaiting developments, Lenin kept company with other expatriate socialists, directed the Petrograd Bolsheviks by mail and telegram, and spent time in the public library. He did not hear of the czar's abdication until some time after the fact. A Polish socialist stopped by and brought news of revolution in Russia in the middle of the day, just after Krupskaya had finished washing the lunch dishes. Immediately Lenin grew almost frantic with desire to get back to Petrograd. His wife laughed at his schemes of crossing the intervening borders disguised as a speech- and hearing-impaired Swede or of somehow obtaining an airplane.

Leon Trotsky, who would become the other major Bolshevik of the revolution, was then living in (of all places) the Bronx. With his wife and two young sons he had recently moved into a building that offered an elevator, garbage chute, telephone, and other up-to-date conveniences the family enjoyed. Trotsky hailed the February Revolution as a historic development and began to make arrangements for a transatlantic voyage.

Both Trotsky and Lenin had won fame by 1917. Lenin's Bolshevik Party, which emerged from the Russian Social-Democratic Labor Party in 1903, after splitting with the more moderate Mensheviks, kept its membership to a small group of dedicated followers. Lenin believed that the Bolsheviks must compromise with nobody. Since 1900, he had lived all over Europe, spending more time outside Russia than in it, and emphasized the international aspect of the proletariat revolution. Lenin wrote articles for socialist journals and he published books; many devotees knew of him from his writings. Trotsky also wrote, but he was a flashier type and kept a higher public profile. Born Lev Davidovich Bronstein in the Ukraine, he had starred in the 1905 Revolution: At only twenty-six he organized a Soviet of Workers' Deputies that lasted for fifty days before the government crushed it.

Lenin's return to Russia required weeks of arrangements. Through German contacts he and a party of other exiled revolutionaries received permission to go by train via Germany, whose government encouraged the idea in the hope that Lenin and his colleagues would make a mess of Russia and thereby help Germany win the war. In pursuit of their political ends Lenin and the Bolsheviks acted as German agents and their policy of "revolutionary defeatism" strengthened the enemy. They went on to receive tens of millions of German marks in aid before the Kaiser's government collapsed with the German defeat, although that collusion would not be confirmed until later.

The last leg of Lenin's homeward journey led through Finland. Finally, at just after eleven on the night of April 16, he arrived in Petrograd at the Finland Station. In all the iconography of Soviet communism few events glow as brightly as this transfiguring arrival. Lenin and his fellows assumed they would be arrested upon stepping off the train. Instead, they were met by a band playing "The Marseillaise," sailors standing in ranks at attention, floral garlands, a crowd of thousands, and a searchlight sweeping its beam through the night. The president of the Petrograd Soviet, a Menshevik, welcomed Lenin with a condescending speech and reminded him that all socialists now had to work together. Lenin listened abstractedly, looking around and toying with a bouquet of red roses someone had given him. When he responded, his words "cracked like a whip in the face of the 'revolutionary democracy,'" according to one observer. Turning to the crowd, Lenin said,

> Dear comrades, soldiers, sailors, and workers!
> I am happy to greet in your persons the victorious Russian revolution, and to greet you as the vanguard of the worldwide

proletarian army . . . the hour is not far distant when at the call of our comrade Karl Liebknecht, the people of Germany will turn their arms against their own capitalist exploiters. . . . The worldwide socialist revolution has already dawned . . . the Russian revolution accomplished by you has prepared the way and opened a new epoch. Long live the worldwide socialist revolution!

A member of the Petrograd Soviet named Nikolai Sukhanov, who later wrote a seven-volume memoir of the revolution, heard Lenin's speech and was staggered. Sukhanov compared it to a bright beacon that obliterated everything he and the other Petrograd socialists had been doing. "It was very interesting!" he wrote, though he hardly agreed with it. I believe it affected him—and all of Russia, and the revolution, and a hundred years of subsequent history—because not since Peter the Great had anyone opened dark, remote, closed-in Russia so forcefully to the rest of the world. The country had long thought of itself as set apart, the "Third Rome," where the Orthodox faith retained its original and unsullied purity (the Second Rome having been Constantinople). But Russia had never spread that faith widely abroad.

Now Lenin informed his listeners that they had pioneered the international socialist revolution and would go forth into the world and proselytize the masses. It was an amazing vision, Marxist and deeply Russian simultaneously, and it helped sustain the despotic Bolsheviks, just as building St. Petersburg, no matter how brutal the cost, drove Peter the Great 200 years before. After Lenin, Russia would involve itself aggressively in the affairs of countries all over the world. That sense of global mission, soon corrupted to strategic meddling and plain troublemaking, is why America still worries about Russia today.

Making his ascension to the pantheon complete, Lenin then went out in front of the station and gave a speech from atop an armored car. It is this moment that the statue in the plaza refers to. Presumably, the searchlight illuminated him, film-noirishly. As the armored car slowly drove him to Bolshevik headquarters he made more speeches standing on the vehicle's hood. Items associated with this holy night have been preserved as relics. The steam engine that pulled the train that Lenin arrived in resides in a glass enclosure next to the Finland Station's Platform Number 9. And an armored car said to be the same one that he rode in and made the speeches from can be found in an unfrequented wing of the immense Artillery Museum, not far away.

Guards are seldom in evidence in the part of the museum where the historic *bronevik* sits permanently parked. Up close the armored car resembles a cartoon of a scary machine. It has two turrets, lots of rivets and hinges, flanges for the machine guns, solid rubber tires, and a long, porcine hood, completely flat and perfect for standing on. The vehicle is olive drab, made of sheet iron or steel, and it weighs about six tons. With no guard to stop me I rubbed its cold metal flanks. On its side, large, hand-painted red letters read: *VRAG KAPITALA*, or "Enemy of Capital."

When Lenin mounted this metal beast, the symbolic connection to Peter the Great pulled tight. Falconet's equestrian Peter that rears its front hooves over Senate Square—as it reared over the dead and wounded troops of the Decembrists in 1825—haunts the city forever. It's the dread "Bronze Horseman" of the Pushkin poem. Gesturing dramatically from atop his armored beast-car, Lenin can be construed as reenacting that statue, making it modernist, and configuring in his own image the recently deposed Russian autocracy.

Alone with the beast in the all-but-deserted Artillery Museum, I went over it again. At its back, on the lower corners on each side, two corkscrew-shaped iron appendages stuck out. I could not imagine what they were for. Maybe for attaching to something? But then why not use a simple metal hitch or loop? I still don't know. And of course the appendages looked exactly like the tails of pigs. Russia is an animist country. In Russia all kinds of objects have spirits. Nonanimal things are seen as animals, and often the works of men and women are seen as being identical with the men and women themselves. This native animism will take on special importance in the case of Lenin.

·　　　·　　　·

Bolshevik headquarters occupied one of the city's fanciest mansions, which the revolutionaries had expropriated from its owner, a ballerina named Matilda Kshesinskaya. Malice aforethought may be assumed because Kshesinskaya had a thing for Romanovs. After a performance when she was seventeen, she met Nicholas, the future czar, and they soon began an affair that lasted for a few years, until Alexander III died. Nicholas then ascended the throne and married the German princess Alix of Hesse (thenceforth to be known as Empress Alexandra Feodorovna). After Nicholas, the ballerina moved on to his father's first cousin, Grand Duke Sergei Mikhailovich. During her affair with that grand duke, she met another one—Grand Duke Andrei Vladimirovich, Nicholas's first cousin. They also began an affair. Such connections helped her to get good roles in the Imperial Ballet, although, in fairness, critics also regarded her as an outstanding dancer.

Whom she knew came in handy during the hard days of the war. In the previous winter the British ambassador, Sir George Buchanan, had been unable to find coal to heat his embassy. He even asked the head of the Russian Navy, who said there was none. While out on a walk with the French ambassador, Buchanan happened to see four military lorries at Kshesinskaya's house and a squad of soldiers unloading sacks of coal. "Well, if that isn't a bit too thick!" Buchanan remarked. Good contacts kept her a step ahead of events in 1917. Warned, Kshesinskaya fled with her more portable valuables before the Bolsheviks arrived. Later she and her son and Grand Duke Andrei emigrated to Paris, where she ran a ballet school and lived to be almost one hundred years old. A movie, *Matilda*, based on her affair with Nicholas, is due to be released in Russia on October 25, 2017. Admirers of Nicholas have sought to ban it, arguing that it violates his privacy.

The mansion, an example of the school known as *style moderne*, won a prize for the best building facade in St. Petersburg from the City Duma in 1910, the year after its construction. It sits on a corner near Trinity Square, and from a second-story French window a balcony with decorative wrought-iron grillwork extends above the street. In Soviet times the mansion became the Museum of the October Revolution, said to be confusing for its many omissions, such as not showing any pictures of Trotsky. Today the building houses the Museum of Russian Political History, which tells the story of the revolution in clear and splendid detail, using text, photos, film, sounds, and objects.

I have spent hours going through its displays, but my favorite part of the museum is the balcony. I stand and stare at it from the sidewalk. Upon his arrival from the Finland Station, Lenin made a speech from this balcony. By then he had grown hoarse. Sukhanov, who had followed the armored car's procession, could not tear himself away. The crowd did not necessarily like what it heard, and a soldier near Sukhanov, interpreting Lenin's internationalist sentiments as pro-German, said that he should be bayoneted—a reminder that although "Bolshevik" meant, roughly, "one of the majority," not many ordinary Russians or a majority of socialists or even all Bolsheviks shared Lenin's extreme views.

Lenin gave other speeches from the balcony during the three months more that the Bolsheviks used the mansion. Photographs show him speaking from it, and it appears in socialist-realist paintings. A plaque notes the balcony's revolutionary role, but both plaque and subject are above eye level, and no passersby stop to look. In fact, aside from the pope's balcony in Rome, this may be the most consequential balcony in history. Today the ground where the listeners stood holds trolley-bus tracks, and cables supporting the overhead electric wires attach to bolts in the wall next to the balcony.

I can picture Lenin: hoarse, gesticulating, smashing the universe with his incisive, unstoppable words; below him, the sea of upturned faces. Today an audience would not have much room to gather here, with the trolley buses, and the fence enclosing a park just across the street. Like a formerly famous celebrity, this small piece of architecture has receded into daily life, and speeches made from balconies no longer rattle history's windowpanes.

.     .     .

In the enormous three-ring shouting match and smoke-filled debating society that constituted revolutionary Petrograd during the months after the czar's removal, nobody picked the Bolsheviks to win. You had parties of every political ilk, from far left to far right, and schismatic groups within them, such as the Social-Democratic Labor Party's less radical wing (the Mensheviks); another powerful party, the Socialist-Revolutionaries, had split contentiously into Left SR's and Right SR's. Added to these were many other parties, groups and factions—conservatives, populists, moderates, peasant delegations, workers' committees, soldiers' committees, Freemasons, radicalized sailors, Cossacks, constitutional monarchists, wavering Duma members. Who knew what would come out of all that?

Under Lenin's direction the Bolsheviks advanced through the confusion by stealth, lies, coercion, subterfuge, and finally violence. All they had was hard-fixed conviction and a leader who had never been elected or appointed to any public office. Officially, Lenin was just the chairman of the "Central Committee of the Russian Social-Democratic Labor Party (Bolsheviks)," as their banner read.

The dominant figure of Alexander Kerensky, a popular young lawyer, bestrode these days like a man with one foot on a dock and the other on a leaky skiff. He came from the city of Simbirsk, where his family knew the Ulyanovs. His father had taught Lenin in high school. Kerensky had defended revolutionaries in court and sometimes moved crowds to frenzy with his speeches. As the vice chairman of the Petrograd Soviet and, simultaneously, the minister of war (among other offices) in the Provisional Government, he held unique importance. Dual government, that practical implausibility, embodied itself in him.

Some participants in the Russian Revolution could not get the fate of the French Revolution out of their heads, and Kerensky was among them. When spring moved toward summer, he ordered a new, make-or-break offensive in the war, and soon mass demonstrations for peace boiled over again in Petrograd. The Bolsheviks, seeing advantage, tried to seize power by force in April and again in early July, but Kerensky had enough troops to shut these tentative coup attempts down. Also, Lenin's traitorous connection to the Germans had begun to receive public attention. Concerned about being arrested or lynched, he hurried back to Finland. But Kerensky felt only contempt for the Bolsheviks. Thinking of Napoleon's rise, he mainly dreaded a counterrevolution from the right.

This predisposition caused him to panic in August while trying to keep the war going and supply himself with loyal troops in the capital. After giving ill-considered and contradictory orders that caused one general, fearing arrest, to shoot himself, Kerensky then accused the commanding general, Lavr Kornilov, of mutiny. Kornilov, who had not, in fact, mutinied, became enraged by the charge and decided to mutiny for real. He marched on Petrograd, where a new military force, the Red Guards, awaited him. This ad hoc people's militia of young workers and former Russian Army soldiers carried weapons liberated in the February mutinies. Rallied by the Bolsheviks, the Red Guards stopped

Kornilov before he reached the capital. The Kornilov episode strengthened the Bolsheviks' credibility and destroyed Kerensky's support among the regular military. Now he would not have an army when he needed one.

With Lenin in hiding, Trotsky kept the Bolsheviks on message with their promise of "Bread, Peace, and Land." The first two watchwords were self-explanatory, and the third went back to a hope the peasants had nourished since before emancipation in the nineteenth century. Their wish that all privately held lands would be distributed to the smaller farmers ran deep. The slogan's simplicity had an appeal; none of the promises would be fulfilled, but at least the party knew what people wanted to hear. In September, for the first time, the Bolsheviks won a majority of seats in the Petrograd Soviet. Responding to perceived threats from "Kornilovites" and other enemies of the revolution, the Petrograd Soviet also established its Military Revolutionary Committee, or MRC. For the Bolsheviks, this put an armed body of men officially at their command.

Lenin sneaked back from Finland but remained out of sight. Kerensky now held the titles of both prime minister and commander in chief but had lost most of his power. The country drifted, waiting for the Second All-Russian Congress of Soviets that was set to meet in October and, beyond that, for the promised first gathering of the Constituent Assembly. Both these bodies would consider the question of how Russia was to be governed. Lenin knew that no better time for a takeover would ever present itself. He wanted to act quickly so as to hand the upcoming assemblies a fait accompli. Through the night of October 10, in the apartment of a supporter, Lenin argued with the other eleven members of the party's Central Committee who were there. Relentlessly, he urged an immediate armed takeover. Several of the dissenters thought he was moving too fast.

By morning the committee voted in his favor, 10 to 2.

**3**

One can read about these events in Sukhanov's *The Russian Revolution, 1917: A Personal Record* (a good abridgment came out in 1984); or in Richard Pipes's classic, *The Russian Revolution*; or in Edmund Wilson's fascinating intellectual history, *To the Finland Station*; or in Trotsky's extensive writings on the subject; or in many other books. For the coup itself I rely on my hero, John Reed.

I first became swept up in the story of the Russian Revolution when I read Reed's landmark eyewitness account, *Ten Days That Shook the World*. Reed went to Harvard, class of 1910, and joined the humor magazine, the *Lampoon*. He had the college-boy hair of that era, the kind that went up and back, in waves—Mickey Rooney hair. None of the fancier clubs asked him to join, and I wouldn't wonder if the pain of that, for a young man whose family had some standing in far-off Portland, Oregon, didn't help make him a revolutionary. When I joined the *Lampoon*, fifty-nine years later, a member pointed out to me the building's stained-glass window in memory of Reed. It shows a silver hammer and sickle above Reed's name and year, on a communist-red background. Supposedly the window had been a gift from the Soviet Union. The strangeness of it gave me shivers. At that stage of the Cold War, Russian missiles were shooting down American jets in Vietnam. How had this man come to be revered by the other side?

Reed dwelt in romance. Everything he did had style. In college he cut a wide swath, leading the cheers at football games, writing plays, publishing poetry, and tossing off grand gestures, like hopping a ship for Bermuda during spring break and returning to campus late and getting in trouble with the dean. Three years after graduation he was riding with Poncho Villa's rebels in Mexico. *Insurgent Mexico*, the book he wrote about the experience, made him famous at twenty-seven. When the First World

War started he decamped to Europe. On a tour of the front lines he somehow managed to cross over to the entrenchments of the Germans, where, at the invitation of a German officer, he fired a couple of shots in the direction of the French. When he returned to New York, news of this exploit got out, and afterward the French quite understandably refused to let him back into France.

So he made his next trip to the Eastern Front instead. The journey brought him to Russia, and to a passion for the country that would determine the rest of his life. In his 1916 book *The War in Eastern Europe*, Reed wrote:

> [Russia is] an original civilization that spreads by its own power. . . . And it takes hold of the minds of men because it is the most comfortable, the most liberal way of life. Russian ideas are the most exhilarating, Russian thought the freest, Russian art the most exuberant; Russian food and drink are to me the best, and Russians themselves are, perhaps, the most interesting human beings that exist.

Yikes! As an intermittent sufferer of this happy delusion myself, I only note that it may lead a person astray. In 1917, paying close attention to events, Reed knew he had to return to Russia. He arrived in Petrograd in September, not long after the Kornilov mutiny. (With him was his wife, the writer Louise Bryant.) What he saw around him thrilled him. He had participated in strikes and protests in the United States, gone to jail, and shared in the hope of an international socialist revolution. "In the struggle my sympathies were not neutral," he wrote in the preface to *Ten Days*. With the unsleeping strength of youth he went everywhere in Petrograd and saw all he could. By limiting a vast historical movement to what he experienced over just a short period (in fact, a span somewhat longer than ten days), he allowed his focus to get up-close and granular.

St. Petersburg has not changed much from when it was revolutionary Petrograd. The Bolsheviks' move of the government to Moscow in 1918 exempted the former capital from a lot of tearing-down and rebuilding; becoming a backwater had its advantages. In places where Reed stood you can still picture how it looked to him. He wrote:

> What a marvelous sight to see Putilovsky Zavod [the Putilov Factory] pour out its forty thousand to listen to Social Democrats, Socialist Revolutionaries, anarchists, anybody, whatever they had to say, as long as they would talk!

Today that factory is called Kirovsky Zavod and it has its own metro station of that name, on the red line, southeast of the city center. Photographs from 1917 show the factory with a high wall along it and big crowds of people on the street in front. Now the wall and the factory's main gate are almost the same as then. Next to the gate a big display highlights some of what is built here—earthmovers, military vehicles, atomic reactor parts. The factory wall, perhaps fifteen feet high, runs for half a mile or more next to the avenue that adjoins it. Traffic speeds close by; no large crowds of workers could listen to speakers here. Like many of the public spaces important in the revolution this one now belongs to vehicles.

At a key moment in the Bolsheviks' takeover, Reed watched the army's armored-car drivers vote on whether to support them. The meeting took place in the Mikhailovsky Riding School, also called the Manège, a huge indoor space where "some two thousand dun-colored soldiers" listened as speakers took turns arguing from atop an armored car and the soldiers' sympathies swung back and forth. Reed observes the listeners:

> Never have I seen men trying so hard to understand, to decide. They never moved, stood staring with a sort of terrible

intentness at the speaker, their brows wrinkled with the effort of thought, sweat standing out on their foreheads; great giants of men with the innocent clear eyes of children and the faces of epic warriors.

Finally the Bolshevik military leader, N. V. Krylenko, his voice cracking with fatigue, gives a speech of such passion that he collapses into waiting arms at the end. A vote is called: those in favor to one side; those opposed, to the other. In a rush almost all the soldiers surge to the Bolshevik side.

The building where this happened is on Manège Square; Luda's apartment is just around the corner. Today the former riding academy has become the Zimnoi Stadion, the Winter Stadium, home to hockey matches, skating competitions, and non-ice events like track meets. The last time I saw it the nearby streets were filled with parents and little kids carrying balloon animals and other circus souvenirs.

I think of the scene from Reed's book whenever I pass by. He caught the details, large and small—the dreary, rainy November weather, with darkness coming at three in the afternoon; the posters and notices and manifestoes covering the city's walls; the soldier who was putting up some of the notices; and the little boy who followed behind him, with a bucket of paste. And the mud. Reed observed it on greatcoats, boots, floors, stairways. I have often marveled at the big patches of mud that suddenly appear in the middle of completely paved St. Petersburg avenues. Then I remember the swamp the city was built on. The February Revolution happened in the snow, but in swampy Russia, the glorious October Revolution happened in the mud.

• • •

*Ten Days That Shook the World* is a rare example of a book that is better for being more complicated. Reed could have spared his readers the effort of figuring out who was who among (as he put it) "the multiplicity of Russian organizations—political groups, Committees and Central Committees, Soviets, Dumas, and Unions." Instead he begins the book with a detailed list, including the subdistinctions among them. It's like a speed bump to slow the reader down, but it's also respectful. The care he took kept his book alive even after Soviet censors banned it during the Stalin era. (Stalin has basically no role in *Ten Days*, and his name appears only twice.)

The book returned to publication during the Khrushchev period, after Stalin's death, though even then it was not much read. Boris Kolonitsky, a leading historian of the revolution, found his vocation when he happened on a copy of the book at the age of fourteen. Today Kolonitsky is first vice rector and professor of history at the European University at St. Petersburg and has been a visiting professor at Yale, Princeton, and the University of Illinois. I met him at his university office in a building near the Kutuzov Embankment of the Neva.

Kolonitsky looks like a professor, with a beard and round glasses and quick, dark-blue eyes, and his jacket and tie reinforce a courteous, formal manner. I asked how he had first discovered Reed's book.

"I was born in Leningrad, my early schooling was here, and I graduated from the history department of the Hertzen State Pedagogical University in Leningrad," he said. "So I am a Leningrad animal from a long way back, you might say. The fact that Reed's book takes place mostly in this city made a connection for me. I first read it when I was in middle school, and of course at that time it was impossible not to know the Soviet story of the glorious October—the volley from the cruiser *Aurora*, the storming of the Winter Palace, and so forth. For me reading Reed was very much a cultural shock. Suddenly here before me was a complicated and contradictory story. Reed was greatly in sympathy with the Bolsheviks but also a very good journalist, and his picture is multidimensional, not just black and white—or Red and White. Trotsky, for example, who had become a nonperson, is vivid in the book. Also the opponents of the Bolsheviks were much more complicated than in Soviet iconography. Later, when I became a teacher (still in Soviet times), I assigned this book to my students and they came back to me with their eyes wide and said, 'Boris Ivanovich, this is an anti-Soviet book!'"

I mentioned Reed's courage. "Yes, at one point in the book they are going to shoot him on the spot!" Kolonitsky said. "He is near the front at Tsarskoe Selo"—a village about fifteen miles south of Petrograd—"where the Whites are making an attack, and he becomes separated from the soldiers who brought him; and then other Red Guards, who are illiterate, cannot read the journalist's pass he has from the Bolshevik leadership, and they tell him to stand by a wall, and suddenly he realizes they are about to shoot him. He persuades them to find someone who can read."

"And afterward he does not make any big production about it," I said. "He just goes on reporting."

"It was not a rational time, not a conscious time," Kolonitsky said. "Reed did not speak much Russian and what surrounded him often was simply chaos."

I had noticed, at the Museum of Russian Political History, that Kolonitsky was scheduled to lecture on "Rumor in Revolutionary Petrograd in October of 1917." I asked about his work on rumor and the popular culture of the revolution.

"Well, this subject had not been too much written on before. Rumor and street culture—jokes, postcards, sayings, bawdy plays performed in saloons—changed the image of the czar and the czarina, desacralized them, before and during the war. Empress Alexandra's dependence on Rasputin, the so-called crazed monk, had catastrophic consequences. Tales of the czarina's debauchery with Rasputin (completely untrue), and rumors of the czar's impotence, and her supposed sabotage of the war effort because she was born in Germany, all undermined the Romanovs, until finally nobody could be too sad when the monarchy went away. People sent each other erotic postcards of the czarina with Rasputin, audiences howled laughing at plays about his supposed sexual power. It resembled modern defamation by social media, and it did great damage. I call it the 'tragic erotics' of Nicholas's reign. If you loved Russia you were obliged to love your czar. People were saying, 'I know I must love my czar, but I cannot.'"

He went on, "Rumor also had a very big role in October of 1917, of course. Kerensky, whom many people almost worshiped, was damaged by rumors about his affair with his wife's cousin or about his fantasies of his own greatness or his supposed plan to abandon Petrograd to the Germans. Many such rumors spread through the crowds on the streets. It caused a highly unstable atmosphere."

.        .        .

Everybody knew that the Bolsheviks were planning an overthrow. In the Duma, Kerensky reassured its members that the state had sufficient force to counter any Bolshevik action. Reed obtained an interview with Trotsky, who told him that the government had become helpless. "Only by the concerted action of the popular mass," Trotsky said, "only by the victory of proletarian dictatorship, can the Revolution be achieved and the people saved"—that is, a putsch would come soon. The Bolshevik-run Military Revolutionary Committee began making demands for greater control of the army, and the Petrograd garrison promised to support the MRC. In response, Kerensky ordered loyal army units to occupy key points in the city.

Lenin, who had not appeared in public since July, narrowly escaped arrest as he made his way in disguise to Bolshevik headquarters, now at the Smolny Institute, a vast building that had formerly housed a school for noble-born girls. In meetings of the Petrograd Soviet and of the long-awaited Second All-Russian

Congress of Soviets (both also housed in Smolny) and in the State Duma, thunderous arguments raged about the course the Bolsheviks were taking. Defending his party before the Petrograd Soviet, Trotsky stepped forward, "his thin, pointed face," Reed wrote, "positively Mephistophelian in its expression of malicious irony." On a stairway at Smolny in the early morning of October 24, Reed ran into Bill Shatov, an American acquaintance and fellow communist, who slapped him on the shoulder exultantly and said, "Well, we're off!" Kerensky had ordered the suppression of the Bolsheviks' newspapers and the MRC was moving "to defend the revolution."

On that day and the next, Reed ranged widely. He had tickets to the ballet at the Mariinsky Theater—regular life went on in Petrograd, revolution or no—but he decided against using them because "it was too exciting out of doors." On the night of the twenty-fifth he made his way to Smolny and found the building humming, with bonfires burning at the gates out front, vehicles coming and going, and machine guns on either side of the main entryway, their ammunition belts hanging "snake-like from their breeches." Feet were pounding up and down Smolny's hallways. In the crowded, stuffy, smoke-filled assemblies, as the arguments raged on and on, a deeper sound interrupted—the "dull shock" of cannon fire. Civil war had begun. With a reporter's instinct Reed ventured out again into the city.

One morning I decided to trace part of the route he took that night. Leaving Luda's apartment I walked the couple of miles to Smolny, a multi-block-long building that now houses St. Petersburg's city government. The front of the pale yellow imperial structure looms high, and its tall, narrow windows give passersby a view of the interior ceilings and chandeliers. "The massive facade of Smolny blazed with light," Reed wrote; and indeed from every window the chandeliers were shining down on the gloomy sidewalk I stood on. Arriving office workers passed by. Black limousines pulled up at the inner gate, drivers opened the back doors, and dark-suited men with briefcases strode through the security station, past the Lenin statue and into the building.

The immense park in front of Smolny is a quiet place, with asphalt pathways and drastically pruned trees whose stubby branches jut like coral. People walk their dogs. I saw a bulldog wearing a jumpsuit that had a buttoned pocket on one side and a white Labrador in four-legged pants with the cuffs rolled up.

When Reed came out of Smolny the night was chilly. "A great motor truck stood there, shaking to the roar of its engine. Men were tossing bundles into it, and others receiving them, with guns beside them." Reed asked where they were going. A little work-man answered, "Downtown—all over—everywhere!" Reed, with his wife, Bryant, and several fellow correspondents, jumped in. "The clutch slid home with a raking jar, the great car jerked forward." They sped down Suvorovsky Prospekt tearing open the bundles and flinging printed announcements that read: "TO THE CITIZENS OF RUSSIA! The State Power has passed into the hands of the organ of the Petrograd Soviet of Workers' and Soldiers' Deputies, the Military Revolutionary Committee, which stands at the head of the Petrograd proletariat and garri-son," and so on. The vehicle soon had "a tail of white papers floating and eddying out behind."

Today Suvorovsky Prospekt presents the usual upscale urban Russian avenue. Reed saw bonfires and patrols gathered on the corners. Bus shelters featuring ads for concerts, cruises, taxi com-panies, and Burger King have taken their place. His fellow pas-sengers looked out for snipers; men at checkpoints stepped toward them from the darkness with upraised weapons. Now a Ralph Lauren Home store with window mannequins in pastels came as no surprise on one of the tonier blocks.

Suvorovsky runs into Nevskii Prospekt near a hub with six major streets radiating from it. Reed wrote, "We turned into Zna-mensky Square, dark and almost deserted, careened around Trubetskoy's brutal statue and swung down the wide Nevsky."

Today this hub is called Ploshchad Vosstaniya, Uprising Square. The "brutal statue" was of Alexander III on horseback. Horse and rider together evoked a hippo, with their breadth and squatness. Revolutionaries often used the statue's plinth for an orator's platform, and crowds gathered here; photographs of that time show the square teeming with people. The statue has been moved to a museum courtyard, and an obelisk stands at the center of the square now. I wanted to see the obelisk close up but walking into the square is almost impossible. Endless cars and buses swirl around its rotary, and waist-high metal barriers keep pedestrians out.

A loudspeaker somewhere on the square was playing "It's Beginning to Look a Lot Like Christmas." Russian public spaces sometimes emit American Christmas music at odd times of year, such as early March. This was my first St. Petersburg neighborhood, back when I used to stay at the nearby Oktyabrskaya Hotel. There's a florist across the street from it, and I stopped to buy Luda some flowers, considering some roses for 2,500 rubles but settling instead on a bouquet of yellow chrysanthemums for 2,000 rubles (about $30).

Reed's conveyance swayed and bounced along Nevskii Prospekt toward the city center then slowed at a crowded bottleneck before the bridge over the Ekaterina Canal (now the Gribodeyeva Canal). He and his companions climbed out. A barrier of armed sailors was blocking the passage of a group of 300 or 400 well-dressed people lined up in columns of four, among whom Reed recognized Duma members, prominent non-Bolshevik socialists, the mayor of Petrograd, and a Russian reporter of Reed's acquaintance. "Going to die in the Winter Palace!" the reporter shouted to him. The ministers of the Provisional Government were meeting in emergency session in the Winter Palace, and these unarmed citizens intended to defend the building with their bodies. The mayor and other eminences demanded that the sailors let them through. The sailors refused. After some further arguing the eminences about-faced and, still in columns of four, marched off in the opposite direction. Meanwhile Reed and his companions slipped by.

At Luda's apartment, where I took a break on my hike, she admired the flowers and put them in water. I explained that I was retracing Reed's route during the night of Glorious October and asked her if she wanted to come along to the Winter Palace. She said yes, and after some kielbasa and tea we left. Because she had been sick she preferred not to walk. We decided to take a trolley bus.

The Number 1 Nevskii Prospekt trolley bus pulled up. As we boarded, several dark-haired guys, all similarly dressed in jackets and sweats, crowded around and pushed and shoved through the door. Once inside they stood close to me. I couldn't even see Luda. The fare lady came and I took out my wallet and paid my forty rubles. The fare lady looked at me for a too-long moment, with a weird smile. The door opened at the next stop and the guys suddenly all crowded out, bumping and pushing even more. After they left I sat down next to Luda, wondering what that had been all about. Then I felt in the back pocket of my jeans.

Losing my wallet to these thieves temporarily derailed my purpose. I completed it the next day. I had been robbed of credit cards and rubles, but not my passport, which I kept in a separate pocket. I wished I had spent more of the now-vanished rubles on the flowers. Luda, for her part, berated me up and down for being a naive, trusting, stupid American and moved on to criticisms of my worldview in general. I kept silent. Some years ago she took care of me when I had dysentery and since then she can do no wrong.

Beyond the sailors' checkpoint, Reed and company got in with a throng that flowed to Palace Square, ran halfway across it, and sheltered behind the Alexander Column in its center. Then the attackers rushed the rest of the distance to the firewood barricades around the Winter Palace, jumped over them, and whooped when they found the guns the defenders had left behind. From there the miscellaneous assault, mostly composed of young Red Guards, walked into the building unopposed. There was no "storm-ing" of the Winter Palace, then or earlier, Sergei Eisenstein's celebratory 1928 film notwithstanding. The building's defenders had mostly disappeared. As Reed went in, he saw the ministers of the Provisional Government being led out under arrest. Kerensky was not among them; he had left the city the day before in search of loyal troops at the front.

Reed and his companions wandered up into the huge building, through rooms whose liveried attendants were saying helplessly, "You can't go in there, *barin*! It is forbidden . . ." Finally he came to the palace's Malachite Room, a chamber of royal splendor, with walls of gold and deep-green malachite. The Provisional Government ministers had been meeting there. Reed examined the long, baize-topped table, which was as they had just left it:

> Before each empty seat was pen, ink, and paper; the papers were scribbled over with beginnings of plans of action, rough drafts of proclamations and manifestoes. Most of these were scratched out, as their futility became evident, and the rest of the sheet covered with absent-minded geometrical designs, as the writers sat despondently listening while Minister after Minister proposed chimerical schemes.

An ambient crowd of soldiers grew suspicious and gathered around Reed's small group, asking what they were doing there. Reed produced his pass, but again, no luck: The soldiers could not read. This time a savior appeared in the form of an MRC officer whom Reed knew and who vouched for him and his companions. Gratefully back on the street, in the "cold, nervous night," they stepped on broken pieces of stucco—the result of a brief bombardment of the palace by mutinous cannoneers. By now it was after three in the morning. Along the Neva, the city was quiet, but elsewhere frenzied meetings were going on. Reed, sleepless, hurried to them.

As for my own storming of the Winter Palace, I took the conventional route of paying the entrance fee to the Hermitage Museum, of which the palace is now a part. (I had the funds thanks to a loan from Luda. "*Ne bespokoisya*," she said. "Do not disquiet yourself. I am not a poor woman.") Following a stochastic path through the multitude of galleries I soon hit upon the Malachite Room, which is Room 189. Like many of the Hermitage's interiors, it brims with light reflected from the Neva. The river's ice was solid except in the middle, where a procession of jumbled-up blue-white chunks moved slowly across the windows' view. An informational sign announced that in this hall revolutionary workers and soldiers "arrested members of the counter-revolutionary Provisional Government." Evidently the sign's angle of interpretation has not been recently revised.

The handles of the Malachite Room's four sets of tall double doors are in the shape of bird feet, with each foot clutching a faceted sphere of red translucent stone. The doors were open. Holding the handles felt strange—like grabbing the scaly foot of a large bird that's clutching a rock. The museum guard told me not to touch. She said the door handles were the originals. Tourists came through in a constant stream. Nearly all were holding up their phones and taking videos or photographs. Sometimes a tourist would stop in the middle of the room, hold the phone up with both hands in the air, and slowly turn in a circle so the video could pan the entire room. This slow, un-self-conscious video-making rotation in the room's center with arms upstretched happened over and over, a new century's new dance.

When daylight arrived on the morning after the takeover, Reed took note of the dueling posters all over the city. An order from Kerensky denounced "this insane attempt of the Bolsheviki [to] place the country on the verge of a precipice" and called on all army personnel and other officials to remain at their posts.

A placard of Bolshevik origin ordered the army to arrest Kerensky. A group called the Committee for the Salvation of the Fatherland, recently created, rallied citizens to resist the Bolsheviks' "indescribable crime against the fatherland." At a session of the Duma, the mayor of Petrograd decried the coup's imposition of "Government by the bayonet," an accurate description that offended the Bolshevik delegates and caused them to walk out.

The Congress of Soviets, which the party had packed with its own people, scheduled a meeting at Smolny. Beforehand many Bolsheviks said they should agree to go along with the other socialist parties because too many people were against them. Lenin and Trotsky declared they would not give an inch. At eight-forty in the evening, Lenin entered the Congress to a "thundering wave of cheers." (In *Ten Days*, this is the first time he appears in person.) Reed noted his shabby clothes and too-long trousers but praised his shrewdness, powers of analysis, "intellectual audacity," and ability to explain complicated ideas.

Lenin took the stage, gripped the edge of the reading stand, and waited for the long ovation to die down. Then he said, "We shall now proceed to construct the socialist order!" That evening and into the next morning, with the Congress of Soviets' enthusiastic approval, the Bolsheviks began to put in place the basic system by which they would rule unchallenged for the next seven decades.

**4**

In 1967, a *New York Times* editorial titled "Russia's Next Half-Century" congratulated the Soviet Union for becoming "one of the world's foremost economic, scientific, and military powers." The *Times* said it looked forward to a prosperous future for the country, but added, "Russia's leaders, surveying the changes of fifty hectic years, surely understand that the vision of a monolithic, uniform world—whether Communist or capitalist—is a fantasy."

I wonder if any readers of this editorial stopped and asked themselves: "fifty *hectic* years"? Was "hectic" really the right word for the Soviet state's first half century?

In December 1917, little more than a month after the coup, Lenin established the department of secret police, called the Cheka. Its name, from Chrezvychaina Kommissia—Emergency Committee—would change through the years, to GPU, to NKVD, to KGB, to FSK, to today's FSB. When the Cheka was founded, its purpose was to persuade white-collar employees, specifically bankers, who hated the Bolsheviks, to cooperate with administrative measures of the new government. The Cheka's mission and mandate soon expanded enormously. Its first leader, Felix Dzerzhinsky, earned a reputation for implacable fierceness, along with the nickname "Iron Felix."

Some years ago, I slightly knew the art critic Leo Steinberg, who happened to be the son of I. N. Steinberg, the first people's commissar of justice in the Bolshevik regime. By way of Leo, I received a copy of his father's book, *In the Workshop of the Revolution*, which describes Steinberg's attempts to preserve rule of law in the Cheka's policing methods during the government's early period. Once, when he heard that Dzerzhinsky planned to execute an imprisoned officer without trial for possessing a gun, Steinberg and a colleague rushed to find Lenin and have Dzerzhinsky stopped. Lenin was at Smolny, in a meeting of the party's Central Committee. They summoned him from it and urgently explained the situation. At first Lenin could not understand what they were upset about. When it finally sank in, his face became distorted with rage. "Is this the important matter for which you called me from serious business?" he demanded. "Dzerzhinsky wants to shoot an officer? What of it? What else would you do with these counter-revolutionaries?"

Lenin saw the world as divided between allies and enemies. The latter had to be suppressed or killed. Even before their takeover, the Bolsheviks had promised to safeguard the elections for the Constituent Assembly, which the Provisional Government had set for November. After the coup the election went forward. Forty-four million Russians voted, and the elected delegates showed up in Petrograd in early January 1918. Unfortunately for the Bolsheviks, their candidates had lost badly. Lenin's government called for new elections. Then it ordered troops to disperse a crowd of perhaps 50,000 who marched in support of the assembly. The soldiers opened fire on the demonstrators, killing eight or more. Russian troops had not shot unarmed demonstrators since the February Revolution. The next day the new government closed the assembly permanently. This was the Bolsheviks' third month in power.

Ex-czar Nicholas and his family, under house arrest since soon after his abdication, had been moved to Yekaterinburg, a thousand miles east of Petrograd. The Provisional Government had treated him decently, and Kerensky thought he and his family would be safer far away from the capital. But the Bolshevik coup spelled their end. After civil war broke out and White Army forces began to approach Yekaterinburg, Lenin decided that Nicholas must be killed. On the night of July 16, 1918, an execution squad of maybe a dozen men gathered the seven Romanovs, their doctor, and three servants in the basement of the house where they were being held. Early the next morning the executioners slaughtered them all.

The pattern had been set. The secret police would kill whom they chose, Bolshevik power would be absolute, and violence would be used not just for strategic purposes but to terrify. The murder of the Romanovs upped the ante for the new government; now there could be no return. The ghastly way forward led through the grain requisitions of the next few years and the bloody suppression of the sailors' rebellion at the Kronstadt naval base in 1921 and the war on the peasants and the forced mass starvations and the rise of Stalin's terror in the thirties and the one million who died in the labor camps in 1937–38 alone. Historians estimate that before the end of the Soviet Union the Bolshevik revolution resulted in the deaths of perhaps 60 million people.

The Bolsheviks changed their name to the Russian Communist Party in 1918. Though the Communist regime remained obsessively secretive, much information about its crimes had come out by 1967, when the *Times* published the editorial. Whoever wrote it must have known that as an adjective to describe the Soviet half century, "hectic" did not suffice. But you can also see the problem the editorial writer faced. What could be said about such horrors? The United States had never known what to make of its cruel, sly, opaque World War II ally turned Cold War enemy. America even tried to like Stalin for a while. He appeared on the cover of *Time* magazine twelve times.

·　　·　　·

Of those few individuals who can place Yekaterinburg on a map, even fewer know that it has a population of 1.4 million. When the missionary sitting next to me on the plane asked why I was going there, I told her, "To visit family." My son, Thomas, lives in that city because of his girlfriend, Olesya Elfimova, who grew up there. The two met at Vassar College when he was studying Russian and she was taking time from her studies at Moscow University to be a language instructor. After graduating he moved with her to Yekaterinburg and taught English. Now they both work for a Swiss computer company that's based there, and he also writes fiction and articles.

I had stopped in Yekaterinburg during my Siberian travels in 2001; one of my goals then had been to find the house where the Romanovs were murdered. After some searching I located the address. But the house, known as the Ipatiev Mansion, had been torn down in 1977. I could not evoke much from what remained—it was just an empty half-acre lot of bulldozed dirt and gravel.

On this trip, Olesya's father, Alexei, a slim, athletic building contractor twenty years my junior who drives a Mercedes SUV, brought me to the site. I had forgotten it's in the center of the city. Now when I got out of the car, I was stunned. An Orthodox church perhaps fifteen stories high, topped with five golden domes, occupies the same piece of ground. It's called Khram na Krovi, the Church on the Blood. The cathedral venerates Nicholas and his wife and five children, who are now saints of the Orthodox Church. Above the main entryway a giant statue of Nicholas strides into the future, with his son in his arms and his wife and their daughters behind him. Inside, depictions of other saints cover the walls all the way to the distant top, where a portrait of a dark-browed, angry Jesus stares down.

Viewed from a distance, the church provides a strong addition to the city's skyline, a radiance in white and gold. The name of the street that the church is on—Karl Liebknecht Street—has not been changed since Soviet times. Liebknecht, a leader of the German Social-Democratic Labor Party, was killed by right-wing militia after participating in a communist uprising in Berlin in 1919. Thus history makes its juxtapositions: a church in memory of sanctified royal martyrs gilds a street named for a martyr of international communism.

Because I wanted to see other local sites associated with the Romanov murders—the place where the bodies were doused with acid and burned and the swampy lane where they were buried—Alexei obligingly brought me to them, overlooking the gloominess and even creepiness of my quest. The first place, known as Ganyna Yama, is now a monastery and complex of churches and pathways in a forest outside the city. The tall firs and birches stood distinct and quiet, and deep snow overhung the church roofs. A granite marker quoted a biblical verse, from Amos 2:1—

Thus says the Lord:
"For three transgressions of Moab, and for four, I will not revoke the punishment, because he burned to lime the bones of the King of Edom."

The story is that a bookmark in Nicholas's Bible indicated these as the last verses he happened to read on the night that he was murdered.

Many people come to pay homage to Nicholas and his family, walking single file on the paths in the snow, their steaming breath visible as they cross themselves and light candles and pray in the unheated churches. A factotum of the monastery seized on Thomas and me as Americans and introduced us to the Metropolit, the head of the Orthodox Church in the region, who was at Ganyna Yama that morning. The high priest wore a black cassock and dark-rimmed glasses and he had a mustache and a large gray-black beard. Taking my hand in both of his he focused on me for a moment his powerful, incense-scented aura of kindness and sanctity.

The Romanovs' burial site is out in the woods and next to some railroad tracks. A more nondescript location cannot be imagined. It was marked with several small obelisks; a blue-and-yellow banner that said "Video Surveillance in Progress" hung from ropes in the birch trees. The bodies themselves are no longer there. In 1998, the family's remains were reinterred, and those of Nicholas and Alexandra are now entombed with his forebears in the Peter and Paul Fortress in St. Petersburg.

·　　·　　·

In addition to exploring Yekaterinburg with Thomas and meeting Olesya's mother and grandmother and two sisters and admiring how well Thomas speaks Russian, my main occupation was visiting the Boris Yeltsin Presidential Center, which includes a museum. I spent whole afternoons there.

Yeltsin came from a village near Yekaterinburg. The museum, overlooking the Iset River, is the country's first presidential museum, in honor of the Russian Federation's first freely elected president. It features a wide-screen film explaining Russian history in semirealistic motion-capture animation that ends with Yeltsin defying the Generals' Putsch in 1991—an attempted coup by hardline Communist Party leaders who opposed the Soviet Union's accelerating reforms. The movie portrays his triumph as the beginning of a new and ongoing era of Russian freedom. Other exhibits then take you through Yeltsin's whole career and its successes and defeats up to his eventual resignation in favor of Vladimir Putin, his then mild-seeming protégé. The overall impression is of Yeltsin's bravery, love of country, and basic humanity fading to weakness after a heart attack in 1996.

In fact, most Russians regard the Yeltsin years as miserable ones. Remembering the food shortages, lack of services, plundering of public wealth, and international humiliations of the 1990s and early 2000s, more than 90 percent of Russians, according to some opinion surveys, view Yeltsin unfavorably. Video interviews with people who feel this way round out the museum's picture of him. Some interviewees say they consider the museum itself an insult to Russians who lived through those times. Here the museum impressed me with its candor. But the Russian sense of history often shifts like sand. A Yeltsin-centered view deemphasizes the century's earlier upheavals. The museum made only brief mention of 1917, and it will have no special exhibit to celebrate the revolution.

If you could somehow go back in time and tell this to the Soviet citizens of 1967, none would believe you. They would expect that such an important new museum—as well as every museum and municipality in the country—would devote itself on a vast scale to the jubilee. In 1967, the half centennial was a huge deal not only in Russia but around the world. On April 16, 1967, ten thousand people (according to Soviet sources) reenacted Lenin's return to the Finland Station; some even wore period costumes. In May, 2,000 Soviet mountaineers climbed Mount Elbrus, in the Caucasus, and placed busts of Lenin at the top. Anticipating the half centennial's high point, 6,500 couples applied to have their marriages performed in Moscow on the eve of November 7. Babies born in that year were named Revolutsia.

The commemorative celebrations in Moscow and Leningrad rated front-page coverage in the United States. Over-the-top extravaganzas went on for days. Only a few flaws showed in the facade. Other communist nations sent representatives—with the exception of Albania and of China, which did not approve of Brezhnev's policies of peaceful coexistence. Cuba sent only low-level officials because Castro had been wanting to overthrow some Latin American governments and Brezhnev wouldn't let him. Ho Chi Minh, worrying about offending either China or Russia, also stayed away, but he did contribute a special gift: a piece of a recently shot down American jet.

Reporters asked Alexander Kerensky to comment on the historic milestone. Having escaped the Bolsheviks via the northern port of Murmansk, the former Provisional Government prime minister now lived on the Upper East Side of Manhattan. At eighty-six he had only recently stopped taking regular walks around the Central Park Reservoir. Few of his contemporaries of '17 had been so lucky. Almost none of the original Bolsheviks whom the jubilee might have honored still survived; Stalin, or time, had done away with the others. John Reed had died of typhus in Moscow in 1920, before he turned thirty-three. Lenin very much admired his book and gave it what today would be called a blurb. Reed received a state funeral and was buried in the Kremlin Wall.

The *Times*'s Harrison Salisbury, reporting from Russia, noted a certain lack of enthusiasm about the half centennial. He interviewed a lot of young Soviets who couldn't seem to get excited about anything except jazz. In 1967 observers said that you could see the number "50" all over Russia—on posters and signs and fences and product labels. There was a fiftieth-anniversary beer. You could buy a kind of kielbasa that, when cut into, revealed the number "50" formed in fat in each slice. I figured that somewhere in my 2017 travels I had to run into a sign with "100" on it for the centennial. Finally, in a metro station, I spotted it—the number "100" on a poster down the platform. But when I got closer I saw that it was an advertisement for a concert celebrating the hundredth anniversary of the birth of Ella Fitzgerald. Perhaps Salisbury had a prophetic streak.

This November, instead of glorifying the Centennial Jubilee of the Great October Revolution, Russia will observe a holiday called the Day of People's Unity, also called National Unity Day. It commemorates a popular uprising that drove Polish occupiers from Moscow in 1613, at the end of a period of strife known as the Time of Troubles. That victory led directly to the founding of the Romanov dynasty. The Day of People's Unity had existed as a holiday until the Bolsheviks got rid of it. Before Putin reinstituted it in 2005, none of the Russians I know had ever heard of it.

As the current president of the Russian Federation, Putin has good reason not to be crazy about the idea of revolution. The example of, say, the civil unrest of early February 1917 may not appeal to a leader who faced widespread protests against his own autocratic rule in 2011, as well as earlier this year. When speaking about the centennial, Putin has made gestures toward "reconciliation" and "consolidating the social and political unanimity that we have managed to reach today." The supposed unanimity he referred to, of course, reflects favorably on himself.

When I talked to Boris Kolonitsky, the professor of Russian history, I asked him what his fellow citizens thought about the centennial and what the revolution means for them today. "You have to remember that adults in Russia have their own experience of civil disturbance, they have seen a coup and an attempted coup," he told me. "After the generals' coup against Gorbachev, when he was removed from power in '91, we saw Yeltsin defy the conspirators and overcome them. When he stood on top of the tank addressing the crowd in front of the White House"—then Russia's new Parliament building—"that image was a clear quotation of a famous romantic image from the Russian Revolution: Lenin on the armored car at Finland Station.

"Yeltsin's victory was the beginning of a period of relative democracy," he went on. "Expectations were high. But everyone also remembers the rest of the nineties, the years that followed, which were quite terrible. Therefore we became less excited about romantic images of revolution. Two years after Yeltsin stood on the tank, he ordered tanks to fire at the Parliament building, to resolve the constitutional crisis brought on by those trying to overthrow him. As Putin himself said, 'In Russia we have overfulfilled our plans in revolutions.'

"Now an important value in Russia is peace," Kolonitsky continued. "Stability also—and therefore revolution loses its appeal. I think the country will observe the centennial with reflection and discussion, but without celebration."

## 5

The oldest person I know was born before the Bolsheviks changed Russia to the Gregorian calendar. Lyudmila Borisovna Chyernaya came into the world on December 13, 1917—after the Bolshevik coup and a week before the founding of the Cheka. This December she will celebrate her hundredth birthday. Lyudmila Borisovna (the polite form of address is to use both the first name and patronymic) is the mother of my longtime friend, the artist Alex Melamid. I first met her twenty-four years ago when Alex and his wife, Katya, and I stayed in her apartment on my first trip to Russia. Last March I made a detour to Moscow, to see her again.

For my visit to her apartment one Saturday afternoon I brought along my friend Ksenia Golubich, whom I got to know when she translated for me at a Russian book fair in 2013. Lyudmila Borisovna shows almost no disabilities of age. In 2015, she published a much-praised memoir, *Kosoi Dozhd* (or *Slanting Rain*). Now she is working on a sequel. She talks quickly and in long, typographical paragraphs. I was glad I had Ksenia to help me keep up. On the wall of the apartment are paintings by Alex and portraits of her late husband, Daniil Elfimovich Melamid, an author, professor, and expert on Germany. She showed us photographs of her great-grandchildren, Lucy and Leonard, who are five and two and live in Brooklyn. They come to Moscow to visit her because at almost one hundred years old she can no longer travel easily to America.

Lyudmila Borisovna was born in Moscow. Her parents had moved here, in 1914, to a pleasant, small apartment with five rooms on a classic Moscow courtyard. They were educated people; her mother was one of the first women admitted to a university in Russia and later translated all of Stalin's speeches into German for TASS, the Soviet international news agency. Lyudmila Borisovna first experienced the revolution, indirectly, at the age of three or four; she had to give up her own room, the nursery, when their apartment became communal and two communists moved in. Later more new residents took over other rooms, but her parents did not mind because they believed in the revolution and wanted to do their part.

Lyudmila Borisovna had a distinguished career as a journalist, author, translator, and German-language counterpropagandist on the radio during the Second World War. Her husband, Daniil Elfimovich, was head of the counterpropaganda agency; she monitored broadcasts from Germany and refuted them in broadcasts of her own. Because of these, she was called "the Witch of the Kremlin" by Goebbels himself. Her discourse to us contained not very many pauses into which Ksenia could insert translation. In one of the pauses, returning to the subject of the revolution, I asked her if she thought it had been for the good. "Yes, it was exciting for us to have people coming to Moscow from all over the world to learn about communism," she said. "The revolution made Moscow important to the world."

She seemed eager for us to have lunch. Lena, her live-in helper, who is from Ukraine, brought out dish after dish that she had made herself—borscht, cabbage pies, mushroom pies, several different kinds of fish, salads, beef tongue, then strong Chinese tea, very large chocolates, and an immense banana torte with cream frosting. Ksenia had to concentrate to continue translating as she and I ate and Lyudmila Borisovna watched us, beaming. Afterward I received an e-mail from Alex: "I got a report from mama of your and your translator's gargantuan appetites and the amount of food you both consumed. She was proud of her feeding prowess." He added that shortage of food had been one of his mother's main worries throughout her life.

I asked Lyudmila Borisovna what she considered the single highest point of the last hundred years. "March 5, 1953," she answered, immediately. "The happiest day of my life—the day Stalin died. All the Stalin years were bad, but for us the years 1945 to 1953 were very hard. After his death the country started to become better, more free. Today life in Russia is not wonderful, but it's fairly good. People may complain, but I tell you from experience that it can get much worse than this."

At the door she helped us into our coats and bid us goodbye, with special regards to Ksenia, whom she had taken to. I'm of average height but as we stood there I realized I'm at least a head taller than she is. She smiled at us, her bluish-gray eyes vivid, but neither warm nor cold. In them I got a glimpse of the character one needs in order to live through such a time and for a hundred years.

·　　·　　·

On my first Moscow visit, the man who drove Alex and Katya and me around the city was a wry and mournful fellow named Stas. He had a serviceable, small Russian sedan, not new, that he maintained carefully. One day he couldn't drive us because the car needed repairs. When he showed up again I asked him how his car was doing now. "Is an old man ever well?" Stas replied. At Lyudmila Borisovna's, when I was having trouble dialing her phone, she corrected me. "He likes to be dialed *slowly*," she said. When people showed me examples of Moscow architecture, the buildings usually possessed a person's name indicating their particular era. Instead of saying, "That's a Khrushchev-era building," my guides said, "That's Khrushchev. That's Stalin. That's Brezhnev." When I asked what the Russian for "speed bump" is, I was told it's *lezhashchii politseiskii*, which means "lying-down policeman." When a noise thumped in an apartment we were visiting, our hosts explained to me that it was the *domovoi*, the resident spirit of the apartment. Every house or apartment has a *domovoi*.

An ancient enchantment holds Russia under its spell. Here all kinds of things and creatures are seen to be sentient and capable of odd transmigrations. In Yekaterinburg my son, while doing some babysitting for a friend, had this conversation:

Six-year-old boy: "What are you?"

Thomas: "I'm an American."

Boy: "Why are you an American?"

Thomas: "I don't know. Because I come from America."

Boy: "Can you speak English?"

Thomas: "Yes."

Boy: (after some thought): "Can you talk to wild animals?"

The question is no less than reasonable in Russia, where even the doors in the most elegant room in the Winter Palace have the feet of birds.

Russia, the country itself, inhabits a spirit as well. The visible location of this spirit's existence in the world used to be the czar.

The United States is a concept; Russia is an animate being. I think Nicholas II understood this, and it's why he believed so strongly that his countrymen needed the autocracy. Nicholas not only ruled Russia, he not only signified Russia, he *was* Russia.

The month after the murders of Nicholas and his family an assassin shot Lenin twice as he came out of an event. One of the wounds almost killed him. When, after a perilous period, he recovered, many Russians started to regard him with mystical devotion. In order to stay in power Lenin had prostrated Russia before Germany with the Treaty of Brest-Litovsk, by which Russia renounced claims on vast amounts of territory including the Baltic states, Poland, and Ukraine. When Germany lost the war and Russia got back all it had conceded, he began to look like a military-political genius, too. Before his early death, from a series of strokes, in 1924, the person of Lenin had become interchangeable with revolutionary Russia, just as the czars had been Russia before the revolution. In a way Lenin's physical death made no difference because his body could be preserved indefinitely in a glass tomb in Red Square for all citizens to see. As the words of a Communist anthem put it, *Lenin, yeshcho zhivoi!* "Lenin, living still!"

One annual celebration the country loves is Dien Pobeda, Victory Day, celebrated on May 9, the day of the German surrender in 1945. The Victory Day parade used to feature the predictable huge portraits of leaders, but for the past ten years its focus has been on the common soldiers who fought in the war. Today, on Victory Day, marchers show up in the hundreds of thousands in every major Russian city bearing portraits of their relatives who served. These portraits, typically black-and-white photographs, keep to a single size and are attached to identical wooden handles like those used for picket signs. As a group the photos are called Bezsmertnii Polk, the Deathless Regiment.

The portraits in their endless numbers evoke powerful emotions as they stream by, especially when you glimpse a young marcher who looks exactly like the young soldier in the faded photograph he or she is carrying. I attended the parade in Moscow in 2016, and as I watched the missiles and tanks that always have accompanied it, I wondered where the traditional giant portraits of The Leader had gone. As under the Soviets, Russia today is governed by what amounts to one-party rule, and again its leadership is more or less an autocracy. But inhabiting the role of Russia itself, as the czars used to do, is a demanding task. Lenin solved the problem by being dead for most of his tenure. Yeltsin made a brave start, standing on the tank, but as he admitted when he turned his power over to Putin in 1999, he got tired. And Putin seems to understand that huge images of the leader's mug look corny and old-fashioned today.

Which is not to say that Putin's mug is not everywhere. It's a common sight on our screens—today's public forum—as well as in such demotic venues as the tight T-shirts featuring his kick-ass caricature that the muscular, pale, crew-cut guys who multiply on Russian streets in summer all seem to wear. As an autocrat whose self coincides with Russia, Putin has grown into the job. Taking off his own shirt for photographers was a good move: Here is the very torso of Russia, in all its buff physicality.

But Putin also impersonates a Russia for an ironic age, letting us know he gets the joke, playing James Bond villain and real-life villain simultaneously, having his lines down pat. After being accused of ordering the murder of Alexander Litvinenko, a former FSB agent turned whistleblower who was poisoned by a radioactive substance in London, Putin denied involvement. Then he added, "The people who have done this are not God. And Mr. Litvinenko, unfortunately, is not Lazarus."

Barring major unforeseen changes, Putin will be reelected in 2018 and initiate Russia's transmogrified, resilient autocracy into its next hundred years.

.        .        .

Problems left unsolved take their own course. The river in flood cuts an oxbow, the overfull dam gives way. The Russian Revolution started as a network of cracks that suddenly broke open in a massive rush. Drastic Russian failures had been mounting—the question of how to divide the land among the people who worked it, the inadequacy of a clumsy autocracy to deal with a fast-growing industrial society, the wretched conditions of hundreds of thousands of rural-born workers who had packed into bad housing in Petrograd and other industrial cities, to name a few. But nobody predicted the shape that the cataclysm would take.

The speed and strength of the revolution that began in February of 1917 surprised even the Bolsheviks, and they hurried to batten onto its power before it ran away from them. An early sense of unexpectedness and improvisation gave the February Revolution its joyful spirit. Russians had always acted communally, perhaps because everybody had to work together to make the most of the short Russian growing season. This cultural tendency produced little soviets in the factories and barracks, which came together in a big Soviet in Petrograd; and suddenly the People, stomped-down for centuries, emerged as a living entity.

One simple lesson of the revolution might be that if a situation looks as if it can't go on, it won't. Imbalance seeks balance. By this logic, climate change will likely continue along the path it seems headed for. And a world in which the richest eight people control as much wealth as 3.6 billion of their global coinhabitants (half the human race) will probably see a readjustment. The populist movements now gaining momentum around the world, however localized or distinct, may signal a beginning of a bigger process.

When you have a few leaders to choose from you get sick of them eventually and want to throw them out. And when you have just one leader of ultimate importance in your whole field of vision—in Russia, the czar—the irritation becomes acute.

So, enough! Let's think about ordinary folks for a change: That was the message of Lenin's too-long pants, of the Bolsheviks' leather chauffeur coats and workers' caps, and of all socialist-realist paintings. But it takes a certain discipline to think about People in general. The mind craves specifics, and in time you go back to thinking about individuals. As Stalin supposedly said, "One person's death is a tragedy, but the death of a million people is a statistic." Czar Nicholas II was sainted not for being a martyr but for being an individual, suffering person you can relate to. It's remarkable that Russia cares about the Romanovs again, having once discarded them so casually. Thousands of pilgrims come to Yekaterinburg every year to pray at the sites of the royal family's murder and subsequent indignities. Dina Sorokina, the young director of the Yeltsin Museum, told me that as far as she knows they don't also visit her museum when they're in town.

The worldwide socialist revolution that the Bolsheviks predicted within months of their takeover proved a disappointment. In fact, no other country immediately followed Russia's lead. During Stalin's time the goal changed to "Building Socialism in One Country"—that is, in Russia. Other countries eventually did go through their own revolutions, and of those, China's made by far the largest addition to the number of people under communist rule. This remains the most significant long-term result of Lenin's dream of global proletarian uprising.

Fifty years after the Russian Revolution, one-third of the world's population lived under some version of communism. That number has shrunk significantly, as one formerly communist state after another converted to a market-based economy; today even Cuba welcomes capitalist enterprises from America. The supposed onward march of communism, so frightening to America in the sixties—first Vietnam, then all of Southeast Asia, then somehow my own hometown in Ohio—scares nobody nowadays.

But if Russia no longer exports international socialism, it has not stopped involving itself in other countries' internal affairs.

Which is not to suggest that other countries, including us, don't sometimes do the same. But by turning the state's secret and coercive forces actively outward, the Bolsheviks invented something new under the sun for Russia. It has found exporting mischief to be a great relief—and, evidently, a point of strategy and of pride. On the street in Yekaterinburg, an older woman, recognizing Thomas and me as Americans, cackled with great glee. "Americans!" she called out. "Trump won! We chose him!" In June, James Comey, the former director of the FBI, testifying before Congress, said, "We're talking about a foreign government that, using technical intrusion, lots of other methods, tried to shape the way we think, we vote, we act. That is a big deal." The habit of Russian intrusion that Comey is talking about began at the revolution.

Individuals change history. There would be no St. Petersburg without Peter the Great and no United States of America without George Washington. There would have been no Soviet Union without Lenin. Today he might feel discouraged to see the failure of his Marxist utopia—a failure so thorough that no country is likely to try it again soon. But his political methods may be his real legacy.

Unlike Marxism-Leninism, Lenin's tactics enjoy excellent health today. In a capitalist Russia, Putin favors his friends, holds power closely, and doesn't compromise with rivals. In America, too, we've reached a point in our politics where the strictest partisanship rules. Steve Bannon, the head of the right-wing media organization Breitbart News, who went on to be an adviser to the president, told a reporter in 2013, "I'm a Leninist . . . I want to bring everything crashing down, and destroy today's establishment." Of course he didn't mean he admired Lenin's ideology— far from it—but Lenin's methods have a powerfully modern appeal. Lenin showed the world how well not compromising can work. A response to that revolutionary innovation of his has yet to be figured out.

## New York

FINALIST—ESSAYS
AND CRITICISM

The headline is frightening enough, but it is the section titles that explain with terrifying specificity the future that awaits everyone who lives on this planet: "Heat Death," "The End of Food," "Climate Plagues," "Unbreathable Air," "Perpetual War, "Permanent Economic Collapse," "Poisoned Oceans." Within one day of its publication, "The Uninhabitable Earth" was the most-read article in the history of New York. As the Ellie judges said, "The impact of David Wallace-Wells's bleak and gripping essay spread beyond climate scientists, journalists, and activists, forcing every reader to confront the existential crisis that threatens us all." In response to critics of the story, New York also published an annotated version online. David Wallace-Wells is the deputy editor of the magazine. Widely admired for its innovativeness both in print and online, New York celebrated its fiftieth anniversary in 2017.

David Wallace-Wells

# The Uninhabitable Earth

## I. "Doomsday"

It is, I promise, worse than you think. If your anxiety about global warming is dominated by fears of sea-level rise, you are barely scratching the surface of what terrors are possible, even within the lifetime of a teenager today. And yet the swelling seas—and the cities they will drown—have so dominated the picture of global warming and so overwhelmed our capacity for climate panic that they have occluded our perception of other threats, many much closer at hand. Rising oceans are bad, in fact very bad, but fleeing the coastline will not be enough.

Indeed, absent a significant adjustment to how billions of humans conduct their lives, parts of the Earth will likely become close to uninhabitable, and other parts horrifically inhospitable, as soon as the end of this century.

Even when we train our eyes on climate change, we are unable to comprehend its scope. This past winter, a string of days sixty and seventy degrees warmer than normal baked the North Pole, melting the permafrost that encased Norway's Svalbard seed vault—a global food bank nicknamed "Doomsday," designed to ensure that our agriculture survives any catastrophe, and which appeared to have been flooded by climate change less than ten years after being built.

The Doomsday vault is fine, for now: The structure has been secured and the seeds are safe. But treating the episode as a parable of impending flooding missed the more important news. Until recently, permafrost was not a major concern of climate scientists because, as the name suggests, it was soil that stayed permanently frozen. But Arctic permafrost contains 1.8 trillion tons of carbon, more than twice as much as is currently suspended in the Earth's atmosphere. When it thaws and is released, that carbon may evaporate as methane, which is thirty-four times as powerful a greenhouse-gas warming blanket as carbon dioxide when judged on the timescale of a century; when judged on the timescale of two decades, it is eighty-six times as powerful. In other words, we have, trapped in Arctic permafrost, twice as much carbon as is currently wrecking the atmosphere of the planet, all of it scheduled to be released at a date that keeps getting moved up, partially in the form of a gas that multiplies its warming power eighty-six times over.

Maybe you know that already—there are alarming stories in the news every day, like those, last month, that seemed to suggest satellite data showed the globe warming since 1998 more than twice as fast as scientists had thought (in fact, the underlying story was considerably less alarming than the headlines). Or the news from Antarctica this past May, when a crack in an ice shelf grew eleven miles in six days then kept going; the break now has just three miles to go—by the time you read this, it may already have met the open water, where it will drop into the sea one of the biggest icebergs ever, a process known poetically as "calving."

But no matter how well informed you are, you are surely not alarmed enough. Over the past decades, our culture has gone apocalyptic with zombie movies and *Mad Max* dystopias, perhaps the collective result of displaced climate anxiety, and yet when it comes to contemplating real-world warming dangers, we suffer from an incredible failure of imagination. The reasons for that are many: the timid language of scientific probabilities, which the climatologist James Hansen once called "scientific reticence" in a paper chastising scientists for editing their own observations so conscientiously that they failed to communicate how dire the threat really was; the fact that the country is dominated by a group of technocrats who believe any problem can be solved and an opposing culture that doesn't even see warming as a problem worth addressing; the way that climate denialism has made scientists even more cautious in offering speculative warnings; the simple speed of change and, also, its slowness, such that we are only seeing effects now of warming from decades past; our uncertainty about uncertainty, which the climate writer Naomi Oreskes in particular has suggested stops us from preparing as though anything worse than a median outcome were even possible; the way we assume climate change will hit hardest elsewhere, not everywhere; the smallness (two degrees) and largeness (1.8 trillion tons) and abstractness (400 parts per million) of the numbers; the discomfort of considering a problem that is very difficult, if not impossible, to solve; the altogether incomprehensible scale of that problem, which amounts to the prospect of our own annihilation; simple fear. But aversion arising from fear is a form of denial, too.

In between scientific reticence and science fiction is science itself. This article is the result of dozens of interviews and exchanges with climatologists and researchers in related fields and reflects hundreds of scientific papers on the subject of climate change. What follows is not a series of predictions of what will happen—that will be determined in large part by the much-less-certain science of human response. Instead, it is a portrait of our best understanding of where the planet is heading absent aggressive action. It is unlikely that all of these warming scenarios will be fully realized, largely because the devastation along the way will shake our complacency. But those scenarios, and not the present climate, are the baseline. In fact, they are our schedule.

The present tense of climate change—the destruction we've already baked into our future—is horrifying enough. Most people talk as if Miami and Bangladesh still have a chance of surviving; most of the scientists I spoke with assume we'll lose them within the century, even if we stop burning fossil fuel in the next decade. Two degrees of warming used to be considered the threshold of catastrophe: tens of millions of climate refugees unleashed upon an unprepared world. Now two degrees is our goal, per the Paris climate accords, and experts give us only slim odds of hitting it. The UN Intergovernmental Panel on Climate Change issues serial reports, often called the "gold standard" of climate research; the most recent one projects us to hit four degrees of warming by the beginning of the next century, should we stay the present course. But that's just a median projection. The upper end of the probability curve runs as high as eight degrees—and the authors still haven't figured out how to deal with that permafrost melt. The IPCC reports also don't fully account for the albedo effect (less ice means less reflected and more absorbed sunlight, hence more warming); more cloud cover (which traps heat); or the dieback of forests and other flora (which extract carbon from the atmosphere). Each of these promises to accelerate warming, and the history of the planet shows that temperature can shift as much as five degrees Celsius within thirteen years. The last time the planet was even four degrees warmer, Peter Brannen points out in *The Ends of the World*, his new history of the planet's major extinction events, the oceans were hundreds of feet higher.

The Earth has experienced five mass extinctions before the one we are living through now, each so complete a slate-wiping of the evolutionary record it functioned as a resetting of the planetary clock, and many climate scientists will tell you they are the best analog for the ecological future we are diving headlong into. Unless you are a teenager, you probably read in your high-school textbooks that these extinctions were the result of asteroids. In fact, all but the one that killed the dinosaurs were caused by climate change produced by greenhouse gas. The most notorious was 252 million years ago; it began when carbon warmed the planet by five degrees, accelerated when that warming triggered the release of methane in the Arctic, and ended with 97 percent of all life on Earth dead. We are currently adding carbon to the atmosphere at a considerably faster rate; by most estimates, at least ten times faster. The rate is accelerating. This is what Stephen Hawking had in mind when he said, this spring, that the species needs to colonize other planets in the next century to survive and what drove Elon Musk, last month, to unveil his plans to build a Mars habitat in forty to one hundred years. These are nonspecialists, of course, and probably as inclined to irrational panic as you or I. But the many sober-minded scientists I interviewed over the past several months—the most credentialed and tenured in the field, few of them inclined to alarmism, and many advisers to the IPCC who nevertheless criticize its conservatism—have quietly reached an apocalyptic conclusion, too: No plausible program of emissions reductions alone can prevent climate disaster.

Over the past few decades, the term "Anthropocene" has climbed out of academic discourse and into the popular imagination—a name given to the geologic era we live in now and a way to signal that it is a new era, defined on the wall chart of deep history by human intervention. One problem with the term is that it implies a conquest of nature (and even echoes the biblical "dominion"). And however sanguine you might be about the proposition that we have already ravaged the natural world, which we surely have, it is another thing entirely to consider the possibility that we have only provoked it, engineering first in ignorance and then in denial a climate system that will now go to war with us for many centuries, perhaps until it destroys us. That is what Wallace Smith Broecker, the avuncular oceanographer who coined the term "global warming," means when he calls the planet an "angry beast." You could also go with "war machine." Each day we arm it more.

## II. Heat Death

Humans, like all mammals, are heat engines; surviving means having to continually cool off, like panting dogs. For that, the temperature needs to be low enough for the air to act as a kind of refrigerant, drawing heat off the skin so the engine can keep pumping. At seven degrees of warming, that would become impossible for large portions of the planet's equatorial band and especially the tropics, where humidity adds to the problem; in the jungles of Costa Rica, for instance, where humidity routinely tops 90 percent, simply moving around outside when it's over 105 degrees Fahrenheit would be lethal. And the effect would be fast: Within a few hours, a human body would be cooked to death from both inside and out.

Climate-change skeptics point out that the planet has warmed and cooled many times before, but the climate window that has allowed for human life is very narrow, even by the standards of planetary history. At eleven or twelve degrees of warming, more than half the world's population, as distributed today, would die of direct heat. Things almost certainly won't get that hot this century, though models of unabated emissions do bring us that far eventually. This century, and especially in the tropics, the pain points will pinch much more quickly even than an increase of seven degrees. The key factor is something called wet-bulb temperature, which is a term of measurement as home-laboratory-kit as it sounds: the heat registered on a thermometer wrapped in a damp sock as it's swung around in the air (since the moisture evaporates from a sock more quickly in dry air, this single number reflects both heat and humidity). At present, most regions reach a wet-bulb maximum of twenty-six or twenty-seven degrees Celsius; the true red line for habitability is thirty-five degrees. What is called heat stress comes much sooner.

Actually, we're about there already. Since 1980, the planet has experienced a fiftyfold increase in the number of places experiencing dangerous or extreme heat; a bigger increase is to come. The five warmest summers in Europe since 1500 have all occurred since 2002, and soon, the IPCC warns, simply being outdoors that time of year will be unhealthy for much of the globe. Even if we meet the Paris goals of two degrees warming, cities like Karachi and Kolkata will become close to uninhabitable, annually encountering deadly heat waves like those that crippled them in 2015. At four degrees, the deadly European heat wave of 2003, which killed as many as 2,000 people a day, will be a normal summer. At six, according to an assessment focused only on effects within the United States from the National Oceanic and Atmospheric Administration, summer labor of any kind would become impossible in the lower Mississippi Valley, and everybody in the country east of the Rockies would be under more heat stress than anyone, anywhere, in the world today. As Joseph Romm has put it in his authoritative primer *Climate Change: What Everyone Needs to Know*, heat stress in New York City would exceed that of present-day Bahrain, one of the planet's hottest spots, and the temperature in Bahrain "would induce hyperthermia in even sleeping humans." The high-end IPCC estimate, remember, is two degrees warmer still. By the end of the century, the World Bank has estimated, the coolest months in tropical South America, Africa, and the Pacific are likely to be warmer than the warmest months at the end of the twentieth century. Air-conditioning can help but will ultimately only add to the carbon problem; plus, the climate-controlled malls of the Arab emirates aside, it is not remotely plausible to wholesale air-condition all the hottest parts of the world, many of them also the poorest. And indeed, the crisis will be most dramatic across the Middle East and Persian Gulf, where in 2015 the heat index registered temperatures as high as 163 degrees Fahrenheit. As soon as several decades from now, the hajj will become physically impossible for the 2 million Muslims who make the pilgrimage each year.

It is not just the hajj, and it is not just Mecca; heat is already killing us. In the sugarcane region of El Salvador, as much as one-fifth of the population has chronic kidney disease, including over a quarter of the men, the presumed result of dehydration from working the fields they were able to comfortably harvest as recently as two decades ago. With dialysis, which is expensive, those with kidney failure can expect to live five years; without it, life expectancy is in the weeks. Of course, heat stress promises to pummel us in places other than our kidneys, too. As I type that sentence, in the California desert in mid-June, it is 121 degrees outside my door. It is not a record high.

## III. The End of Food

Climates differ and plants vary, but the basic rule for staple cereal crops grown at optimal temperature is that for every degree of warming, yields decline by 10 percent. Some estimates run as high as 15 or even 17 percent. Which means that if the planet is five degrees warmer at the end of the century, we may have as many as 50 percent more people to feed and 50 percent less grain to give them. And proteins are worse: It takes sixteen calories of grain to produce just a single calorie of hamburger meat, butchered from a cow that spent its life polluting the climate with methane farts.

Pollyannaish plant physiologists will point out that the cereal-crop math applies only to those regions already at peak growing temperature, and they are right—theoretically, a warmer climate will make it easier to grow corn in Greenland. But as the path-breaking work by Rosamond Naylor and David Battisti has shown, the tropics are already too hot to efficiently grow grain, and those places where grain is produced today are already at optimal growing temperature—which means even a small warming will push them down the slope of declining productivity. And you can't easily move croplands north a few hundred miles because yields in places like remote Canada and Russia are limited by the quality of soil there; it takes many centuries for the planet to produce optimally fertile dirt.

Drought might be an even bigger problem than heat, with some of the world's most arable land turning quickly to desert. Precipitation is notoriously hard to model, yet predictions for later this century are basically unanimous: unprecedented droughts nearly everywhere food is today produced. By 2080, without dramatic reductions in emissions, southern Europe will be in permanent extreme drought, much worse than the American dust bowl ever was. The same will be true in Iraq and Syria and much of the rest of the Middle East; some of the most densely populated parts of Australia, Africa, and South America; and the breadbasket regions of China. None of these places, which today supply much of the world's food, will be reliable sources of any. As for the original dust bowl: The droughts in the American plains and Southwest would not just be worse than in the 1930s, a 2015 NASA study predicted, but worse than any droughts in a thousand years—and that includes those that struck between 1100 and 1300, which "dried up all the rivers East of the Sierra Nevada mountains" and may have been responsible for the death of the Anasazi civilization.

Remember, we do not live in a world without hunger as it is. Far from it: Most estimates put the number of undernourished at 800 million globally. In case you haven't heard, this spring has already brought an unprecedented quadruple famine to Africa and the Middle East; the UN has warned that separate starvation events in Somalia, South Sudan, Nigeria, and Yemen could kill 20 million this year alone.

## IV. Climate Plagues

Rock, in the right spot, is a record of planetary history, eras as long as millions of years flattened by the forces of geological time into strata with amplitudes of just inches or just an inch or even less. Ice works that way, too, as a climate ledger, but it is also frozen history, some of which can be reanimated when unfrozen. There are now, trapped in Arctic ice, diseases that have not circulated in the air for millions of years—in some cases, since before humans were around to encounter them. Which means our immune systems would have no idea how to fight back when those prehistoric plagues emerge from the ice.

The Arctic also stores terrifying bugs from more recent times. In Alaska, already, researchers have discovered remnants of the 1918 flu that infected as many as 500 million and killed as many as 100 million—about 5 percent of the world's population and almost six times as many as had died in the world war for which the pandemic served as a kind of gruesome capstone. As the BBC reported in May, scientists suspect smallpox and the bubonic plague are trapped in Siberian ice, too—an abridged history of devastating human sickness, left out like egg salad in the Arctic sun.

Experts caution that many of these organisms won't actually survive the thaw and point to the fastidious lab conditions under which they have already reanimated several of them—the 32,000-year-old "extremophile" bacteria revived in 2005, an 8-million-year-old bug brought back to life in 2007, the 3.5-million-year-old one a Russian scientist self-injected just out of curiosity—to suggest that those are necessary conditions for the return of such ancient plagues. But already last year, a boy was killed and twenty others infected by anthrax released when retreating permafrost exposed the frozen carcass of a reindeer killed by the bacteria at least seventy-five years earlier; 2,000 present-day reindeer were infected, too, carrying and spreading the disease beyond the tundra.

What concerns epidemiologists more than ancient diseases are existing scourges relocated, rewired, or even re-evolved by warming. The first effect is geographical. Before the early-modern period, when adventuring sailboats accelerated the mixing of peoples and their bugs, human provinciality was a guard against pandemic. Today, even with globalization and the enormous intermingling of human populations, our ecosystems are mostly stable, and this functions as another limit, but global warming will scramble those ecosystems and help disease trespass those limits as surely as Cortés did. You don't worry much about dengue or malaria if you are living in Maine or France. But as the tropics creep northward and mosquitoes migrate with them, you will. You didn't much worry about Zika a couple of years ago, either.

As it happens, Zika may also be a good model of the second worrying effect—disease mutation. One reason you hadn't heard about Zika until recently is that it had been trapped in Uganda; another is that it did not, until recently, appear to cause birth defects. Scientists still don't entirely understand what happened or what they missed. But there are things we do know for sure about how climate affects some diseases: Malaria, for instance, thrives in hotter regions not just because the mosquitoes that carry it do, too, but because for every degree increase in temperature, the parasite reproduces ten times faster. Which is one reason that the World Bank estimates that by 2050, 5.2 billion people will be reckoning with it.

## V. Unbreathable Air

Our lungs need oxygen, but that is only a fraction of what we breathe. The fraction of carbon dioxide is growing: It just crossed 400 parts per million, and high-end estimates extrapolating from current trends suggest it will hit 1,000 ppm by 2100. At that concentration, compared to the air we breathe now, human cognitive ability declines by 21 percent.

Other stuff in the hotter air is even scarier, with small increases in pollution capable of shortening life spans by ten years. The warmer the planet gets, the more ozone forms, and by mid-century, Americans will likely suffer a 70 percent increase in unhealthy ozone smog, the National Center for Atmospheric Research has projected. By 2090, as many as 2 billion people globally will be breathing air above the WHO "safe" level; one paper last month showed that, among other effects, a pregnant mother's exposure to ozone raises the child's risk of autism (as much as tenfold, combined with other environmental factors). Which does make you think again about the autism epidemic in West Hollywood.

Already, more than 10,000 people die each day from the small particles emitted from fossil-fuel burning; each year, 339,000 people die from wildfire smoke, in part because climate change has extended forest-fire season (in the United States, it's increased by seventy-eight days since 1970). By 2050, according to the U.S. Forest Service, wildfires will be twice as destructive as they are today; in some places, the area burned could grow fivefold. What worries people even more is the effect that would have on emissions, especially when the fires ravage forests arising out of peat. Peatland fires in Indonesia in 1997, for instance, added to the global $CO_2$ release by up to 40 percent, and more burning only means more warming only means more burning. There is also the terrifying possibility that rain forests like the Amazon, which in 2010 suffered its second "hundred-year drought" in the space of five years, could dry out enough to become vulnerable to these kinds of devastating, rolling forest fires—which would not only expel enormous amounts of carbon into the atmosphere but also shrink the size of the forest. That is especially bad because the Amazon alone provides 20 percent of our oxygen.

Then there are the more familiar forms of pollution. In 2013, melting Arctic ice remodeled Asian weather patterns, depriving industrial China of the natural ventilation systems it had come to depend on, which blanketed much of the country's north in an unbreathable smog. Literally unbreathable. A metric called the Air Quality Index categorizes the risks and tops out at the 301-to-500 range, warning of "serious aggravation of heart or lung disease and premature mortality in persons with cardiopulmonary disease and the elderly" and, for all others, "serious risk of respiratory effects"; at that level, "everyone should avoid all outdoor exertion." The Chinese "airpocalypse" of 2013 peaked at what would have been an Air Quality Index of over 800. That year, smog was responsible for a third of all deaths in the country.

## VI. Perpetual War

Climatologists are very careful when talking about Syria. They want you to know that while climate change did produce a drought that contributed to civil war, it is not exactly fair to say that the conflict is the result of warming; next door, for instance, Lebanon suffered the same crop failures. But researchers like Marshall Burke and Solomon Hsiang have managed to quantify some of the nonobvious relationships between temperature and violence: For every half-degree of warming, they say, societies will see between a 10 and 20 percent increase in the likelihood of armed conflict. In climate science, nothing is simple, but the arithmetic is harrowing: A planet five degrees warmer would have at least half again as many wars as we do today. Overall, social conflict could more than double this century.

This is one reason that, as nearly every climate scientist I spoke to pointed out, the U.S. military is obsessed with climate change: The drowning of all American Navy bases by sea-level rise is trouble enough, but being the world's policeman is quite a bit harder when the crime rate doubles. Of course, it's not just Syria where climate has contributed to conflict. Some speculate that the elevated level of strife across the Middle East over the past generation reflects the pressures of global warming—a hypothesis all the more cruel considering that warming began accelerating when the industrialized world extracted and then burned the region's oil.

What accounts for the relationship between climate and conflict? Some of it comes down to agriculture and economics; a lot has to do with forced migration, already at a record high, with at least 65 million displaced people wandering the planet right now. But there is also the simple fact of individual irritability. Heat increases municipal crime rates and swearing on social media and the likelihood that a major-league pitcher, coming to the mound after his teammate has been hit by a pitch, will hit an opposing batter in retaliation. And the arrival of air-conditioning in the developed world, in the middle of the past century, did little to solve the problem of the summer crime wave.

## VII. Permanent Economic Collapse

The murmuring mantra of global neoliberalism, which prevailed between the end of the Cold War and the onset of the Great Recession, is that economic growth would save us from anything and everything. But in the aftermath of the 2008 crash, a growing number of historians studying what they call "fossil capitalism" have begun to suggest that the entire history of swift economic growth, which began somewhat suddenly in the eighteenth century, is not the result of innovation or trade or the dynamics of global capitalism but simply our discovery of fossil fuels and all their raw power—a onetime injection of new "value" into a system that had previously been characterized by global subsistence living. Before fossil fuels, nobody lived better than their parents or grandparents or ancestors from 500 years before, except in the immediate aftermath of a great plague like the Black Death, which allowed the lucky survivors to gobble up the resources liberated by mass graves. After we've burned all the fossil fuels, these scholars suggest, perhaps we will return to a "steady state" global economy. Of course, that onetime injection has a devastating long-term cost: climate change.

The most exciting research on the economics of warming has also come from Hsiang and his colleagues, who are not historians of fossil capitalism but who offer some very bleak analysis of their own: Every degree Celsius of warming costs, on average, 1.2 percent of GDP (an enormous number, considering we count growth in the low single digits as "strong"). This is the sterling work in the field, and their median projection is for a 23 percent loss in per capita earning globally by the end of this century (resulting from changes in agriculture, crime, storms, energy, mortality, and labor).

Tracing the shape of the probability curve is even scarier: There is a 12 percent chance that climate change will reduce global output by more than 50 percent by 2100, they say, and a 51 percent chance that it lowers per capita GDP by 20 percent or more by then, unless emissions decline. By comparison, the Great Recession lowered global GDP by about 6 percent, in a onetime shock; Hsiang and his colleagues estimate a one-in-eight chance of an ongoing and irreversible effect by the end of the century that is eight times worse.

The scale of that economic devastation is hard to comprehend, but you can start by imagining what the world would look like today with an economy half as big, which would produce only half as much value, generating only half as much to offer the workers of the world. It makes the grounding of flights out of heat-stricken Phoenix last month seem like pathetically small economic potatoes. And, among other things, it makes the idea of postponing government action on reducing emissions and relying solely on growth and technology to solve the problem an absurd business calculation.

Every round-trip ticket on flights from New York to London, keep in mind, costs the Arctic three more square meters of ice.

## VIII. Poisoned Oceans

That the sea will become a killer is a given. Barring a radical reduction of emissions, we will see at least four feet of sea-level rise and possibly ten by the end of the century. A third of the world's major cities are on the coast, not to mention its power plants, ports, navy bases, farmlands, fisheries, river deltas, marshlands, and rice-paddy empires, and even those above ten feet will flood much more easily, and much more regularly, if the water gets that high. At least 600 million people live within ten meters of sea level today.

But the drowning of those homelands is just the start. At present, more than a third of the world's carbon is sucked up by the oceans—thank God, or else we'd have that much more warming already. But the result is what's called "ocean acidification," which, on its own, may add a half a degree to warming this century. It is also already burning through the planet's water basins—you may remember these as the place where life arose in the first place. You have probably heard of "coral bleaching"—that is, coral dying— which is very bad news because reefs support as much as a quarter of all marine life and supply food for half a billion people. Ocean acidification will fry fish populations directly, too, though scientists aren't yet sure how to predict the effects on the stuff we haul out of the ocean to eat; they do know that in acid waters, oysters and mussels will struggle to grow their shells, and that when the pH of human blood drops as much as the oceans' pH has over the past generation, it induces seizures, comas, and sudden death.

That isn't all that ocean acidification can do. Carbon absorption can initiate a feedback loop in which underoxygenated waters breed different kinds of microbes that turn the water still more "anoxic," first in deep ocean "dead zones," then gradually up toward the surface. There, the small fish die out, unable to breathe, which means oxygen-eating bacteria thrive, and the feedback loop doubles back. This process, in which dead zones grow like cancers, choking off marine life and wiping out fisheries, is already quite advanced in parts of the Gulf of Mexico and just off Namibia, where hydrogen sulfide is bubbling out of the sea along a thousand-mile stretch of land known as the "Skeleton Coast." The name originally referred to the detritus of the whaling industry, but today it's more apt than ever. Hydrogen sulfide is so toxic that evolution has trained us to recognize the tiniest, safest traces of it, which is why our noses are so exquisitely skilled at registering flatulence. Hydrogen sulfide is also the thing that finally did us in that time 97 percent of all life on Earth died, once all the feedback loops had been triggered and the circulating jet streams of a warmed ocean ground to a halt—it's the planet's preferred gas for a natural holocaust. Gradually, the ocean's dead zones spread, killing off marine species that had dominated the oceans for hundreds of millions of years, and the gas the inert waters gave off into the atmosphere poisoned everything on land. Plants, too. It was millions of years before the oceans recovered.

## IX. The Great Filter

So why can't we see it? In his recent book-length essay *The Great Derangement*, the Indian novelist Amitav Ghosh wonders why global warming and natural disaster haven't become major subjects of contemporary fiction—why we don't seem able to imagine climate catastrophe, and why we haven't yet had a spate of novels in the genre he basically imagines into half-existence and names "the environmental uncanny." "Consider, for example, the stories that congeal around questions like, 'Where were you when the Berlin Wall fell?' or 'Where were you on 9/11?'" he writes. "Will it ever be possible to ask, in the same vein, 'Where were you at 400 ppm?' or 'Where were you when the Larsen B ice shelf broke up?'" His answer: probably not, because the dilemmas and dramas of climate change are simply incompatible with the kinds of stories we tell ourselves about ourselves, especially in novels, which tend to emphasize the journey of an individual conscience rather than the poisonous miasma of social fate.

Surely this blindness will not last—the world we are about to inhabit will not permit it. In a six-degree-warmer world, the Earth's ecosystem will boil with so many natural disasters that we will just start calling them "weather": a constant swarm of out-of-control typhoons and tornadoes and floods and droughts, the planet assaulted regularly with climate events that not so long ago destroyed whole civilizations. The strongest hurricanes will come more often, and we'll have to invent new categories with which to describe them; tornadoes will grow longer and wider and strike much more frequently; and hail rocks will quadruple in size. Humans used to watch the weather to prophesy the future; going forward, we will see in its wrath the vengeance of the past. Early naturalists talked often about "deep time"—the perception they had, contemplating the grandeur of this valley or that rock basin, of the profound slowness of nature. What lies in store for us is more like what the Victorian anthropologists identified as "dreamtime," or "everywhen": the semimythical experience, described by Aboriginal Australians, of encountering, in the present moment, an out-of-time past, when ancestors, heroes, and demigods crowded an epic stage. You can find it already watching footage of an iceberg collapsing into the sea—a feeling of history happening all at once.

It is. Many people perceive climate change as a sort of moral and economic debt, accumulated since the beginning of the Industrial Revolution and now come due after several centuries—a helpful perspective, in a way, since it is the carbon-burning processes that began in eighteenth-century England that lit the fuse of everything that followed. But more than half of the carbon humanity has exhaled into the atmosphere in its entire history has been emitted in just the past three decades; since the end of World War II, the figure is 85 percent. Which means that, in the length of a single generation, global warming has brought us to the brink of planetary catastrophe, and that the story of the industrial world's kamikaze mission is also the story of a single lifetime. My father's, for instance: born in 1938, among his first memories the news of Pearl Harbor and the mythic Air Force of the propaganda films that followed, films that doubled as advertisements for imperial-American industrial might; and among his last memories the coverage of the desperate signing of the Paris climate accords on cable news, ten weeks before he died of lung cancer last July. Or my mother's: born in 1945, to German Jews fleeing the smokestacks through which their relatives were incinerated, now enjoying her seventy-second year in an American commodity paradise, a paradise supported by the supply chains of an industrialized developing world. She has been smoking for fifty-seven of those years, unfiltered.

Or the scientists': Some of the men who first identified a changing climate (and given the generation, those who became famous were men) are still alive; a few are even still working. Wally Broecker is eighty-four years old and drives to work at the Lamont-Doherty Earth Observatory across the Hudson every day from the Upper West Side. Like most of those who first raised the alarm, he believes that no amount of emissions reduction alone can meaningfully help avoid disaster. Instead, he puts his faith in carbon capture—untested technology to extract carbon dioxide from the atmosphere, which Broecker estimates will cost at least several trillion dollars—and various forms of "geoengineering," the catchall name for a variety of moon-shot technologies far-fetched enough that many climate scientists prefer to regard them as dreams, or nightmares, from science fiction. He is especially focused on what's called the aerosol approach—dispersing so much sulfur dioxide into the atmosphere that when it converts to sulfuric acid, it will cloud a fifth of the horizon and reflect back 2 percent of the sun's rays, buying the planet at least a little wiggle room, heat-wise. "Of course, that would make our sunsets very red, would bleach the sky, would make more acid rain," he says.

"But you have to look at the magnitude of the problem. You got to watch that you don't say the giant problem shouldn't be solved because the solution causes some smaller problems." He won't be around to see that, he told me. "But in your lifetime . . ."

Jim Hansen is another member of this godfather generation. Born in 1941, he became a climatologist at the University of Iowa, developed the groundbreaking "Zero Model" for projecting climate change, and later became the head of climate research at NASA, only to leave under pressure when, while still a federal employee, he filed a lawsuit against the federal government charging inaction on warming (along the way he got arrested a few times for protesting, too). The lawsuit, which is brought by a collective called Our Children's Trust and is often described as "kids versus climate change," is built on an appeal to the equal-protection clause, namely, that in failing to take action on warming, the government is violating it by imposing massive costs on future generations; it is scheduled to be heard this winter in Oregon district court. Hansen has recently given up on solving the climate problem with a carbon tax alone, which had been his preferred approach, and has set about calculating the total cost of the additional measure of extracting carbon from the atmosphere.

Hansen began his career studying Venus, which was once a very Earth-like planet with plenty of life-supporting water before runaway climate change rapidly transformed it into an arid and uninhabitable sphere enveloped in an unbreathable gas; he switched to studying our planet by thirty, wondering why he should be squinting across the solar system to explore rapid environmental change when he could see it all around him on the planet he was standing on. "When we wrote our first paper on this, in 1981," he told me, "I remember saying to one of my co-authors, 'This is going to be very interesting. Sometime during our careers, we're going to see these things beginning to happen.'"

Several of the scientists I spoke with proposed global warming as the solution to Fermi's famous paradox, which asks, If the universe is so big, then why haven't we encountered any other intelligent life in it? The answer, they suggested, is that the natural life span of a civilization may be only several thousand years, and the life span of an industrial civilization perhaps only several hundred. In a universe that is many billions of years old, with star systems separated as much by time as by space, civilizations might emerge and develop and burn themselves up simply too fast to ever find one another. Peter Ward, a charismatic paleontologist among those responsible for discovering that the planet's mass extinctions were caused by greenhouse gas, calls this the "Great Filter": "Civilizations rise, but there's an environmental filter that causes them to die off again and disappear fairly quickly," he told me. "If you look at planet Earth, the filtering we've had in the past has been in these mass extinctions." The mass extinction we are now living through has only just begun; so much more dying is coming.

And yet, improbably, Ward is an optimist. So are Broecker and Hansen and many of the other scientists I spoke to. We have not developed much of a religion of meaning around climate change that might comfort us, or give us purpose, in the face of possible annihilation. But climate scientists have a strange kind of faith: We will find a way to forestall radical warming, they say, because we must.

It is not easy to know how much to be reassured by that bleak certainty, and how much to wonder whether it is another form of delusion; for global warming to work as parable, of course, someone needs to survive to tell the story. The scientists know that to even meet the Paris goals, by 2050, carbon emissions from energy and industry, which are still rising, will have to fall by half each decade; emissions from land use (deforestation, cow farts, etc.) will have to zero out; and we will need to have invented technologies to extract, annually, twice as much carbon from the atmosphere as the entire planet's plants now do. Nevertheless, by and large, the scientists have an enormous confidence in the ingenuity of humans—a confidence perhaps bolstered by their appreciation for climate change, which is, after all, a human invention, too. They point to the Apollo project, the hole in the ozone we patched in the 1980s, the passing of the fear of mutually assured destruction. Now we've found a way to engineer our own doomsday, and surely we will find a way to engineer our way out of it, one way or another. The planet is not used to being provoked like this, and climate systems designed to give feedback over centuries or millennia prevent us—even those who may be watching closely—from fully imagining the damage done already to the planet. But when we do truly see the world we've made, they say, we will also find a way to make it livable. For them, the alternative is simply unimaginable.

## The Atlantic

*This wide-ranging account of Barack Obama's eight years in office honors his achievements while insisting that the success of his presidency was coupled with failure—not Obama's but America's. "In the days after Donald Trump's victory, there would be an insistence that something as 'simple' as racism could not explain it," Coates writes. "As if enslavement had nothing to do with global economics, or as if lynchings said nothing about the idea of women as property." The Ellie judges described "My President Was Black" as "a historic achievement, elegiac yet celebratory, a rare combination of analysis and reflection." Long associated with* The Atlantic, *Coates only recently announced his departure from the magazine. His* Atlantic *essay "Fear of a Black President" won the National Magazine Award in 2013. His work for the magazine also received Ellie nominations in 2014 and 2015.*

Ta-Nehisi Coates

# My President Was Black

"They're a rotten crowd," I shouted across the lawn. "You're worth the whole damn bunch put together."

—F. Scott Fitzgerald, *The Great Gatsby*

## I. "Love Will Make You Do Wrong"

In the waning days of President Barack Obama's administration, he and his wife, Michelle, hosted a farewell party, the full import of which no one could then grasp. It was late October, Friday the 21st, and the president had spent many of the previous weeks, as he would spend the two subsequent weeks, campaigning for the Democratic presidential nominee, Hillary Clinton. Things were looking up. Polls in the crucial states of Virginia and Pennsylvania showed Clinton with solid advantages. The formidable GOP strongholds of Georgia and Texas were said to be under threat. The moment seemed to buoy Obama. He had been light on his feet in these last few weeks, cracking jokes at the expense of Republican opponents and laughing off hecklers. At a rally in Orlando on October 28, he greeted a student who would be introducing him by dancing toward her and then noting that the song playing over the loudspeakers—the Gap Band's "Outstanding"— was older than she was. "This is classic!" he said. Then he flashed the smile that had launched America's first black presidency and started dancing again. Three months still remained before Inauguration Day, but staffers had already begun to count down the days. They did this with a mix of pride and longing—like college seniors in early May. They had no sense of the world they were graduating into. None of us did.

The farewell party, presented by BET (Black Entertainment Television), was the last in a series of concerts the first couple had hosted at the White House. Guests were asked to arrive at five-thirty p.m. By six, two long lines stretched behind the Treasury Building, where the Secret Service was checking names. The people in these lines were, in the main, black, and their humor reflected it. The brisker queue was dubbed the "good-hair line" by one guest, and there was laughter at the prospect of the Secret Service subjecting us all to a "brown-paper-bag test." This did not come to pass, but security was tight. Several guests were told to stand in a makeshift pen and wait to have their backgrounds checked a second time. Dave Chappelle was there. He coolly explained the peril and promise of comedy in what was then still only a remotely potential Donald Trump presidency: "I mean, we never had a guy have his own pussygate scandal." Everyone laughed. A few weeks later, he would be roundly criticized for telling a crowd at the Cutting Room, in New York, that he had voted for Clinton but did not feel good about it. "She's going to be on a coin someday," Chappelle said. "And her behavior has not been coinworthy." But on this crisp October night, everything felt inevitable and grand. There was a slight wind. It had been in the eighties for much of that week. Now, as the sun set, the season remembered its name. Women shivered in their cocktail dresses. Gentlemen chivalrously handed over their suit coats. But when Naomi Campbell strolled past the security pen in a sleeveless number, she seemed as invulnerable as ever.

Cell phones were confiscated to prevent surreptitious recordings from leaking out. (This effort was unsuccessful. The next day, a partygoer would tweet a video of the leader of the free world

dancing to Drake's "Hotline Bling.") After withstanding the barrage of security, guests were welcomed into the East Wing of the
White House and then ushered back out into the night, where they
boarded a succession of orange-and-green trolleys. The singer and
actress Janelle Monáe, her famous and fantastic pompadour pre-
ceding her, stepped on board and joked with a companion about
the historical import of "sitting in the back of the bus." She took a
seat three rows from the front and hummed into the night. The
trolley dropped the guests on the South Lawn, in front of a giant
tent. The South Lawn's fountain was lit up with blue lights. The
White House proper loomed like a ghost in the distance. I heard
the band, inside, beginning to play Al Green's "Let's Stay Together."

"Well, you can tell what type of night this is," Obama said
from the stage, opening the event. "Not the usual ruffles and
flourishes!"

The crowd roared.

"This must be a BET event!"

The crowd roared louder still.

Obama placed the concert in the White House's musical tradition, noting that guests of the Kennedys had once done the twist
at the residence—"the twerking of their time," he said, before adding, "There will be no twerking tonight. At least not by me."

The Obamas are fervent and eclectic music fans. In the past
eight years, they have hosted performances at the White House
by everyone from Mavis Staples to Bob Dylan to Tony Bennett to
the Blind Boys of Alabama. After the rapper Common was invited
to perform in 2011, a small fracas ensued in the right-wing media.
He performed anyway—and was invited back again this glorious
fall evening and almost stole the show. The crowd sang along to
the hook for his hit ballad "The Light." And when he brought on
the gospel singer Yolanda Adams to fill in for John Legend on the
Oscar-winning song "Glory," glee turned to rapture.

De La Soul was there. The hip-hop trio had come of age as boyish B-boys with Gumby-style high-top fades. Now they moved

across the stage with a lovely mix of lethargy and grace, like your favorite uncle making his way down the *Soul Train* line, wary of throwing out a hip. I felt a sense of victory watching them rock the crowd, all while keeping it in the pocket. The victory belonged to hip-hop—an art form birthed in the burning Bronx and now standing full grown, at the White House, unbroken and unedited. Usher led the crowd in a call-and-response: "Say it loud, I'm black and I'm proud." Jill Scott showed off her operatic chops. Bell Biv DeVoe, contemporaries of De La, made history with their performance by surely becoming the first group to suggest to a presidential audience that one should "never trust a big butt and a smile."

The ties between the Obama White House and the hip-hop community are genuine. The Obamas are social with Beyoncé and Jay-Z. They hosted Chance the Rapper and Frank Ocean at a state dinner and last year invited Swizz Beatz, Busta Rhymes, and Ludacris, among others, to discuss criminal-justice reform and other initiatives. Obama once stood in the Rose Garden passing large flash cards to the *Hamilton* creator and rapper Lin-Manuel Miranda, who then freestyled using each word on the cards. "Drop the beat," Obama said, inaugurating the session. At fifty-five, Obama is younger than pioneering hip-hop artists like Afrika Bambaataa, DJ Kool Herc, and Kurtis Blow. If Obama's enormous symbolic power draws primarily from being the country's first black president, it also draws from his membership in hip-hop's foundational generation.

That night, the men were sharp in their gray or black suits and optional ties. Those who were not in suits had chosen to make a statement, like the dark-skinned young man who strolled in, sockless, with blue jeans cuffed so as to accentuate his gorgeous black-suede loafers. Everything in his ensemble seemed to say, "My fellow Americans, do not try this at home." There were women in fur jackets and high heels; others with sculpted naturals, the sides shaved close, the tops blooming into curls; others still in gold bamboo earrings and long blond dreads. When the actor Jesse Williams took the stage, seemingly awed before such black excellence, before such black opulence, assembled just feet from where slaves had once toiled, he simply said, "Look where we are. Look where we are right now."

This would not happen again, and everyone knew it. It was not just that there might never be another African American president of the United States. It was the feeling that this particular black family, the Obamas, represented the best of black people, the ultimate credit to the race, incomparable in elegance and bearing. "There are no more," the comedian Sinbad joked back in 2010. "There are no black men raised in Kansas and Hawaii. That's the last one. Y'all better treat this one right. The next one gonna be from Cleveland. He gonna wear a perm. Then you gonna see what it's really like." Throughout their residency, the Obamas had refrained from showing America "what it's really like" and had instead followed the first lady's motto, "When they go low, we go high." This was the ideal—black and graceful under fire—saluted that evening. The president was lionized as "our crown jewel." The first lady was praised as the woman "who put the *O* in *Obama.*"

Barack Obama's victories in 2008 and 2012 were dismissed by some of his critics as merely symbolic for African Americans. But there is nothing "mere" about symbols. The power embedded in the word *nigger* is also symbolic. Burning crosses do not literally raise the black poverty rate, and the Confederate flag does not directly expand the wealth gap.

Much as the unbroken ranks of forty-three white male presidents communicated that the highest office of government in the country—indeed, the most powerful political offices in the world—was off-limits to black individuals, the election of Barack Obama communicated that the prohibition had been lifted. It communicated much more. Before Obama triumphed in 2008, the most-famous depictions of black success tended to be entertainers or athletes. But Obama had shown that it was "possible to be smart and cool at the same damn time," as Jesse Williams put it at the BET party. Moreover, he had not embarrassed his people with a string of scandals. Against the specter of black pathology, against the narrow images of welfare moms and deadbeat dads, his time in the White House had been an eight-year showcase of a healthy and successful black family spanning three generations, with two dogs to boot. In short, he became a symbol of black people's everyday, extraordinary Americanness.

Whiteness in America is a different symbol—a badge of advantage. In a country of professed meritocratic competition, this badge has long ensured an unerring privilege, represented in a 220-year monopoly on the highest office in the land. For some not-insubstantial sector of the country, the elevation of Barack Obama communicated that the power of the badge had diminished. For eight long years, the badge-holders watched him. They saw footage of the president throwing bounce passes and shooting jumpers. They saw him enter a locker room, give a business-like handshake to a white staffer, and then greet Kevin Durant with something more soulful. They saw his wife dancing with Jimmy Fallon and posing, resplendent, on the covers of magazines that had, only a decade earlier, been almost exclusively, if unofficially, reserved for ladies imbued with the great power of the badge.

For the preservation of the badge, insidious rumors were concocted to denigrate the first black White House. Obama gave free cell phones to disheveled welfare recipients. Obama went to Europe and complained that "ordinary men and women are too small-minded to govern their own affairs." Obama had inscribed an Arabic saying on his wedding ring then stopped wearing the ring, in observance of Ramadan. He canceled the National Day of Prayer, refused to sign certificates for Eagle Scouts, faked his attendance at Columbia University, and used a teleprompter to address a group of elementary-school students. The badge holders fumed. They wanted their country back. And, though no one at the farewell party knew it, in a couple of weeks they would have it.

On this October night, though, the stage belonged to another America. At the end of the party, Obama looked out into the crowd, searching for Dave Chappelle. "Where's Dave?" he cried. And then, finding him, the president referenced Chappelle's legendary Brooklyn concert. "You got your block party. I got my block party." Then the band struck up Al Green's "Love and Happiness"—the evening's theme. The president danced in a line next to Ronnie DeVoe. Together they mouthed the lyrics: "Make you do right. Love will make you do wrong."

## II. He Walked on Ice but Never Fell

Last spring, I went to the White House to meet the president for lunch. I arrived slightly early and sat in the waiting area. I was introduced to a deaf woman who worked as the president's receptionist, a black woman who worked in the press office, a Muslim woman in a head scarf who worked on the National Security Council, and an Iranian American woman who worked as a personal aide to the president. This receiving party represented a healthy cross section of the people Donald Trump had been mocking, and would continue to spend his campaign mocking. At the time, the president seemed untroubled by Trump. When I told Obama that I thought Trump's candidacy was an explicit reaction to the fact of a black president, he said he could see that but then enumerated other explanations. When assessing Trump's chances, he was direct: He couldn't win.

This assessment was born out of the president's innate optimism and unwavering faith in the ultimate wisdom of the American people—the same traits that had propelled his unlikely five-year ascent from assemblyman in the Illinois state legislature to U.S. senator to leader of the free world. The speech that launched his rise, the keynote address at the 2004 Democratic National Convention, emerged right from this logic. He addressed himself to his "fellow Americans, Democrats, Republicans, independents," all of whom, he insisted, were more united than they had been led to believe. America was home to devout worshippers and Little League coaches in blue states, civil libertarians and "gay friends" in red states. The presumably white "counties around Chicago" did not want their taxes burned on welfare, but they didn't want them wasted on a bloated Pentagon budget either. Inner-city black families, no matter their perils, understood "that government alone can't teach our kids to learn . . . that children can't achieve unless we raise their expectations and turn off the television sets and eradicate the slander that says a black youth with a book is acting white."

Perceived differences were the work of "spinmasters and negative-ad peddlers who embrace the politics of 'anything goes.'" Real America had no use for such categorizations. By Obama's lights, there was no liberal America, no conservative America, no black America, no white America, no Latino America, no Asian America, only "the United States of America." All these disparate strands of the American experience were bound together by a common hope:

> It's the hope of slaves sitting around a fire singing freedom songs; the hope of immigrants setting out for distant shores; the hope of a young naval lieutenant bravely patrolling the Mekong Delta; the hope of a mill worker's son who dares to defy the odds; the hope of a skinny kid with a funny name who believes that America has a place for him, too.

This speech ran counter to the history of the people it sought to address. Some of those same immigrants had firebombed the homes of the children of those same slaves. That young naval lieutenant was an imperial agent for a failed, immoral war. American division was real. In 2004, John Kerry did not win a single southern state. But Obama appealed to a belief in innocence—in particular a white innocence—that ascribed the country's historical errors more to misunderstanding and the work of a small cabal than to any deliberate malevolence or widespread racism. America was good. America was great.

Over the next twelve years, I came to regard Obama as a skilled politician, a deeply moral human being, and one of the greatest presidents in American history. He was phenomenal—the most agile interpreter and navigator of the color line I had ever seen. He had an ability to emote a deep and sincere connection to the hearts of black people while never doubting the hearts of white people. This was the core of his 2004 keynote, and it marked his historic race speech during the 2008 campaign at Philadelphia's National Constitution Center—and blinded him to the appeal of Trump. ("As a general proposition, it's hard to run for president by telling people how terrible things are," Obama once said to me.)

But if the president's inability to cement his legacy in the form of Hillary Clinton proved the limits of his optimism, it also revealed the exceptional nature of his presidential victories. For eight years Barack Obama walked on ice and never fell. Nothing in that time suggested that straight talk on the facts of racism in American life would have given him surer footing.

.        .        .

I had met the president a few times before. In his second term, I'd written articles criticizing him for his overriding trust in color-blind policy and his embrace of "personal responsibility" rhetoric when speaking to African Americans. I saw him as playing both sides. He would invoke his identity as a president of all people to decline to advocate for black policy—and then invoke his black identity to lecture black people for continuing to "make bad choices." In response, Obama had invited me, along with other journalists, to the White House for off-the-record conversations. I attempted to press my points in these sessions. My efforts were laughable and ineffective. I was always inappropriately dressed and inappropriately calibrated in tone: In one instance, I was too deferential; in another, too bellicose. I was discombobulated by fear—not by fear of the power of his office (though that is a fearsome and impressive thing) but by fear of his obvious brilliance. It is said that Obama speaks "professorially," a fact that understates the quickness and agility of his mind. These were not like press conferences—the president would speak in depth and with great familiarity about a range of subjects. Once, I watched him effortlessly reply to queries covering everything from electoral politics to the American economy to environmental policy. And then he turned to me. I thought of George Foreman, who once booked an exhibition with multiple opponents in which he pounded five straight journeymen—and I suddenly had some idea of how it felt to be the last of them.

Last spring, we had a light lunch. We talked casually and candidly. He talked about the brilliance of LeBron James and Stephen Curry—not as basketball talents but as grounded individuals. I asked him whether he was angry at his father, who had abandoned him at a young age to move back to Kenya, and whether that motivated any of his rhetoric. He said it did not, and he credited the attitude of his mother and grandparents for this. Then it was my turn to be autobiographical. I told him that I had heard the kind of "straighten up" talk he had been giving to black youth, for instance in his 2013 Morehouse commencement address, all my life. I told him that I thought it was not sensitive to the inner turmoil that can be obscured by the hardness kids often evince. I told him I thought this because I had once been one of those kids. He seemed to concede this point, but I couldn't tell whether it mattered to him. Nonetheless, he agreed to a series of more formal conversations on this and other topics.

The improbability of a black president had once been so strong that its most vivid representations were comedic. Witness Dave Chappelle's profane Black Bush from the early 2000s ("This nigger very possibly has weapons of mass destruction! I can't sleep on that!") or Richard Pryor's black president in the 1970s promising black astronauts and black quarterbacks ("Ever since the Rams got rid of James Harris, my jaw's been uptight!"). In this model, so potent is the force of blackness that the presidency is forced to conform to it. But once the notion advanced out of comedy and into reality, the opposite proved to be true.

Obama's DNC speech is the key. It does not belong to the literature of "the struggle"; it belongs to the literature of prospective presidents—men (as it turns out) who speak not to gravity and reality but to aspirations and dreams. When Lincoln invoked the dream of a nation "conceived in liberty" and pledged to the ideal that "all men are created equal," he erased the near-extermination of one people and the enslavement of another. When Roosevelt told the country that "the only thing we have to fear is fear itself," he invoked the dream of American omnipotence and boundless capability. But black people, then living under a campaign of terror for more than half a century, had quite a bit to fear, and Roosevelt could not save them. The dream Ronald Reagan invoked in 1984—that "it's morning again in America"—meant nothing to the inner cities, besieged as they were by decades of redlining policies, not to mention crack and Saturday-night specials. Likewise, Obama's keynote address conflated the slave and the nation of immigrants who profited from him. To reinforce the majoritarian dream, the nightmare endured by the minority is erased. That is the tradition to which the "skinny kid with a funny name" who would be president belonged. It is also the only tradition in existence that could have possibly put a black person in the White House.

Obama's embrace of white innocence was demonstrably necessary as a matter of political survival. Whenever he attempted to buck this directive, he was disciplined. His mild objection to the arrest of Henry Louis Gates Jr. in 2009 contributed to his declining favorability numbers among whites—still a majority of voters. His comments after the killing of Trayvon Martin—"If I had a son, he'd look like Trayvon"—helped make that tragedy a rallying point for people who did not care about Martin's killer as much as they cared about finding ways to oppose the president. Michael Tesler, a political-science professor at UC Irvine, has studied the effect of Obama's race on the American electorate. "No other factor, in fact, came close to dividing the Democratic primary electorate as powerfully as their feelings about African Americans," he and his coauthor, David O. Sears, concluded in their book, *Obama's Race: The 2008 Election and the Dream of a Post-Racial America*. "The impact of racial attitudes on individual vote decisions . . . was so strong that it appears to have even outstripped the substantive impact of racial attitudes on Jesse Jackson's more racially charged campaign for the nomination in 1988." When Tesler looked at the 2012 campaign in his second book, *Post-Racial or Most-Racial? Race and Politics in the Obama Era*, very little had improved. Analyzing the extent to which racial attitudes affected people associated with Obama during the 2012 election, Tesler concluded that "racial attitudes spilled over from Barack Obama into mass assessments of Mitt Romney, Joe Biden, Hillary Clinton, Charlie Crist, and even the Obama family's dog Bo."

Yet despite this entrenched racial resentment, and in the face of complete resistance by congressional Republicans, overtly launched from the moment Obama arrived in the White House, the president accomplished major feats. He remade the nation's health-care system. He revitalized a Justice Department that vigorously investigated police brutality and discrimination, and he began dismantling the private-prison system for federal inmates.

Obama nominated the first Latina justice to the Supreme Court, gave presidential support to marriage equality, and ended the U.S. military's Don't Ask, Don't Tell policy, thus honoring the civil-rights tradition that had inspired him. And if his very existence inflamed America's racist conscience, it also expanded the country's antiracist imagination. Millions of young people now know their only president to have been an African American. Writing for *The New Yorker*, Jelani Cobb once noted that "until there was a black Presidency it was impossible to conceive of the limitations of one." This is just as true of the possibilities. In 2014, the Obama administration committed itself to reversing the War on Drugs through the power of presidential commutation. The administration said that it could commute the sentences of as many as 10,000 prisoners. As of November, the president had commuted only 944 sentences. By any measure, Obama's effort fell woefully short, except for this small one: the measure of almost every other modern president who preceded him. Obama's 944 commutations are the most in nearly a century—and more than the past eleven presidents' combined.

Obama was born into a country where laws barring his very conception—let alone his ascendancy to the presidency—had long stood in force. A black president would always be a contradiction for a government that, throughout most of its history, had oppressed black people. The attempt to resolve this contradiction through Obama—a black man with deep roots in the white world—was remarkable. The price it exacted, incredible. The world it gave way to, unthinkable.

## III. "I Decided to Become Part of That World"

When Barack Obama was ten, his father gave him a basketball, a gift that connected the two directly. Obama was born in 1961 in Hawaii and raised by his mother, Ann Dunham, who was white, and her parents, Stanley and Madelyn. They loved him ferociously, supported him emotionally, and encouraged him intellectually. They also told him he was black. Ann gave him books to read about famous black people. When Obama's mother had begun dating his father, the news had not been greeted with the threat of lynching (as it might have been in various parts of the continental United States), and Obama's grandparents always spoke positively of his father. This biography makes Obama nearly unique among black people of his era.

In the president's memoir, *Dreams from My Father*, he says he was not an especially talented basketball player, but he played with a consuming passion. That passion was directed at something more than just the mastering of the pick-and-roll or the perfecting of his jump shot. Obama came of age during the time of the University of Hawaii basketball team's "Fabulous Five"—a name given to its all-black starting five, two decades before it would be resurrected at the University of Michigan by the likes of Chris Webber and Jalen Rose. In his memoir, Obama writes that he would watch the University of Hawaii players laughing at "some inside joke," winking "at the girls on the sidelines," or "casually flipping lay-ups." What Obama saw in the Fabulous Five was not just game, but a culture he found attractive:

> By the time I reached high school, I was playing on Punahou's teams, and could take my game to the university courts, where a handful of black men, mostly gym rats and has-beens, would teach me an attitude that didn't just have to do with the sport. That respect came from what you did and not who your daddy was. That you could talk stuff to rattle an opponent, but that you should shut the hell up if you couldn't back it up. That you didn't let anyone sneak up behind you to see emotions—like hurt or fear—you didn't want them to see.

These are lessons, particularly the last one, that for black people apply as much on the street as they do on the court. Basketball was a link for Obama, a medium for downloading black culture from the mainland that birthed the Fabulous Five. Assessing his own thought process at the time, Obama writes, "I decided to become part of that world." This is one of the most incredible sentences ever written in the long, decorated history of black memoir, if only because very few black people have ever enjoyed enough power to write it.

Historically, in black autobiography, to be remanded into the black race has meant exposure to a myriad of traumas, often commencing in childhood. Frederick Douglass is separated from his grandmother. The enslaved Harriet Ann Jacobs must constantly cope with the threat of rape before she escapes. After telling his teacher he wants to be a lawyer, Malcolm X is told that the job isn't for "niggers." Black culture often serves as the balm for such traumas, or even the means to resist them. Douglass finds the courage to face the "slave-breaker" Edward Covey after being given an allegedly enchanted root by "a genuine African" possessing powers from "the eastern nations." Malcolm X's dancing connects him to his "long-suppressed African instincts." If black racial identity speaks to all the things done to people of recent African ancestry, black cultural identity was created in response to them. The division is not neat; the two are linked, and it is incredibly hard to be a full participant in the world of cultural identity without experiencing the trauma of racial identity.

Obama is somewhat different. He writes of bloodying the nose of a white kid who called him a "coon" and of chafing at racist remarks from a tennis coach and of feeling offended after a white woman in his apartment building told the manager that he was following her. But the kinds of traumas that marked African Americans of his generation—beatings at the hands of racist police, being herded into poor schools, grinding out a life in a tenement building—were mostly abstract for him. Moreover, the kind of spatial restriction that most black people feel at an early age—having rocks thrown at you for being on the wrong side of the tracks, for instance—was largely absent from his life. In its place, Obama was gifted with a well-stamped passport and admittance to elite private schools—all of which spoke of other identities, other lives, and other worlds where the color line was neither determinative nor especially relevant. Obama could have grown into a raceless cosmopolitan. Surely he would have lived in a world of problems, but problems not embodied by him.

Instead, he decided to enter this world.

"I always felt as if being black was cool," Obama told me while traveling to a campaign event. He was sitting on *Air Force One*, his tie loosened, his shirtsleeves rolled up. "[Being black] was not something to run away from but something to embrace. Why that is, I think, is complicated. Part of it is I think that my mother thought black folks were cool, and if your mother loves you and is praising you—and says you look good, are smart—as you are, then you don't kind of think in terms of *How can I avoid this?* You feel pretty good about it."

As a child, Obama's embrace of blackness was facilitated, not impeded, by white people. Obama's mother pointed him toward the history and culture of African Americans. Stanley, his grandfather, who came originally from Kansas, took him to basketball games at the University of Hawaii, as well as to black bars. Stanley introduced him to the black writer Frank Marshall Davis. The facilitation was as much indirect as direct. Obama recalls watching his grandfather at those black bars and understanding that "most of the people in the bar weren't there out of choice" and that "our presence there felt forced." From his mother's life of extensive travel, he learned to value the significance of having a home.

That suspicion of rootlessness extends throughout *Dreams from My Father.* He describes integration as a "one-way street" on which black people are asked to abandon themselves to fully experience America's benefits. Confronted with a woman named Joyce, a mixed-race, green-eyed college classmate who insists that she is not "black" but "multiracial," Obama is scornful. "That was the problem with people like Joyce," he writes. "They talked about the richness of their multicultural heritage and it sounded real good, until you noticed that they avoided black people." Later in the memoir, Obama tells the story of falling in love with a white woman. During a visit to her family's country house, he found himself in the library, which was filled with pictures of the woman's illustrious relations. But instead of being in awe, Obama realized that he and the woman lived in different worlds. "And I knew that if we stayed together, I'd eventually live in hers," he writes. "Between the two of us, I was the one who knew how to live as an outsider."

After college, Obama found a home, as well as a sense of himself, working on the South Side of Chicago as a community organizer. "When I started doing that work, my story merges with a larger story. That happens naturally for a John Lewis," he told me, referring to the civil-rights hero and Democratic congressman. "That happens more naturally for you. It was less obvious to me. *How do I pull all these different strains together: Kenya and Hawaii and Kansas, and white and black and Asian— how does that fit?* And through action, through work, I suddenly see myself as part of the bigger process for, yes, delivering justice for the [African American community] and specifically the South Side community, the low-income people—justice on behalf of the African American community. But also thereby promoting my ideas of justice and equality and empathy that my mother taught me were universal. So I'm in a position to understand those essential parts of me not as separate and apart from any particular community but connected to every community. And I can fit the African American struggle for freedom and justice in the context of the universal aspiration for freedom and justice."

Throughout Obama's 2008 campaign and into his presidency, this attitude proved key to his deep support in the black community. African Americans, weary of high achievers who distanced themselves from their black roots, understood that Obama had paid a price for checking "black" on his census form and for living black, for hosting Common, for brushing dirt off his shoulder during the primaries, for marrying a woman who looked like Michelle Obama. If women, as a gender, must suffer the constant evaluations and denigrations of men, black women must suffer that, plus a broad dismissal from the realm of what American society deems to be beautiful. But Michelle Obama is beautiful in the way that black people know themselves to be. Her prominence as first lady directly attacks a poison that diminishes black girls from the moment they are capable of opening a magazine or turning on a television.

The South Side of Chicago, where Obama began his political career, is home to arguably the most prominent and storied black political establishment in the country. In addition to Oscar Stanton De Priest, the first African American elected to Congress in the twentieth century, the South Side produced the city's first black mayor, Harold Washington; Jesse Jackson, who twice ran for president; and Carol Moseley Braun, the first African American woman to win a Senate race. These victories helped give rise to Obama's own. Harold Washington served as an inspiration to Obama and looms heavily over the Chicago section of *Dreams from My Father*.

Washington forged the kind of broad coalition that Obama would later assemble nationally. But Washington did this in the mid-1980s in segregated Chicago, and he had not had the luxury, as Obama did, of becoming black with minimal trauma. "There was an edge to Harold that frightened some white voters," David Axelrod, who worked for both Washington and Obama, told me recently. Axelrod recalled sitting around a conference table with Washington after he had won the Democratic primary for his reelection in 1987, just as the mayor was about to hold a press conference. Washington asked what percentage of Chicago's white vote he'd received. "And someone said, 'Well, you got 21 percent. And that's really good because last time'"—in his successful 1983 mayoral campaign—"'you only got 8,'" Axelrod recalled. "And he kind of smiled, sadly, and said, 'You know, I probably spent 70 percent of my time in those white neighborhoods, and I think I've been a good mayor for everybody, and I got 21 percent of the white vote and we think it's good.' And he just kind of shook his head and said, 'Ain't it a bitch to be a black man in the land of the free and the home of the brave?'

"That was Harold. He felt those things. He had fought in an all-black unit in World War II. He had come up in times—and that and the sort of indignities of what you had to do to come up through the machine really seared him." During his 1983 mayoral campaign, Washington was loudly booed outside a church in northwest Chicago by middle-class Poles, Italians, and Irish, who feared blacks would uproot them. "It was as vicious and ugly as anything you would have seen in the old South," Axelrod said.

Obama's ties to the South Side tradition that Washington represented were complicated. Like Washington, Obama attempted to forge a coalition between black South Siders and the broader community. But Obama, despite his adherence to black cultural mores, was, with his roots in Kansas and Hawaii, his Ivy League pedigree, and his ties to the University of Chicago, still an exotic out-of-towner. "They were a bit skeptical of him," says Salim Muwakkil, a journalist who has covered Obama since before his days in the Illinois state Senate. "Chicago is a very insular community, and he came from nowhere, seemingly."

Obama compounded people's suspicions by refusing to humble himself and go along with the political currents of the South Side. "A lot of the politicians, especially the black ones, were just leery of him," Kaye Wilson, the godmother to Obama's children and one of the president's earliest political supporters, told me recently.

But even as many in the black political community were skeptical of Obama, others encouraged him—sometimes when they voted against him. When Obama lost the 2000 Democratic-primary race against Bobby Rush, the African American incumbent congressman representing Illinois's First Congressional District, the then-still-obscure future president experienced the defeat as having to do more with his age than his exoticism. "I'd go meet people and I'd knock on doors and stuff, and some of the grandmothers who were the folks I'd been organizing and working with doing community stuff, they weren't parroting back some notion of 'You're too Harvard' or 'You're too Hyde Park' or what have you," Obama told me. "They'd say, 'You're a wonderful young man, you're going to do great things. You just have to be patient.' So I didn't feel the loss as a rejection by black people. I felt the loss as 'politics anywhere is tough.' Politics in Chicago is especially tough. And being able to break through in the African American community is difficult because of the enormous loyalty that people feel towards anybody who has been around awhile."

There was no one around to compete for loyalty when Obama ran for Senate in 2004, or for president in 2008. He was no longer competing against other African Americans; he was representing them. "He had that hybridity which told the 'do-gooders'—in Chicago they call the reformers the do-gooders—that he was acceptable," Muwakkil told me.

Obama ran for the Senate two decades after the death of Harold Washington. Axelrod checked in on the precinct where Washington had been so loudly booed by white Chicagoans. "Obama carried, against seven candidates for the Senate, almost the entire northwest side and that precinct," he said. "And I told him, 'Harold's smiling down on us tonight.'"

Obama believes that his statewide victory for the Illinois Senate seat held particular portent for the events of 2008. "Illinois is the most demographically representative state in the country," he told me. "If you took all the percentages of black, white, Latino; rural, urban; agricultural, manufacturing—[if] you took that cross section across the country and you shrank it, it would be Illinois."

Illinois effectively allowed Obama to play a scrimmage before the big national game in 2008. "When I ran for the Senate I had to go into southern Illinois, downstate Illinois, farming communities—some with very tough racial histories, some areas where there just were no African Americans of any number," Obama told me. "And when we won that race, not just an African American from Chicago, but an African American with an exotic history and [the] name Barack Hussein Obama, [it showed that I] could connect with and appeal to a much broader audience."

The mix of Obama's "hybridity" and the changing times allowed him to extend his appeal beyond the white ethnic corners of Chicago, past the downstate portions of Illinois, and out into the country at large. "Ben Nelson, one of the most conservative Democrats in the Senate, from Nebraska, would only bring in one national Democrat to campaign for him," Obama recalls. "And it was me. And so part of the reason I was willing to run [for president in 2008] was that I had had two years in which we were generating enormous crowds all across the country—and the majority of those crowds were not African American; and they were in pretty remote places, or unlikely places. They weren't just big cities or they weren't just liberal enclaves. So what that told me was, it was possible."

What those crowds saw was a black candidate unlike any other before him. To simply point to Obama's white mother or to his African father or even to his rearing in Hawaii is to miss the point. For most African Americans, white people exist either as a direct or an indirect force for bad in their lives. Biraciality is no shield against this; often it just intensifies the problem. What proved key for Barack Obama was not that he was born to a black man and a white woman but that his white family approved of the union and approved of the child who came from it. They did this in 1961—a time when sex between black men and white women, in large swaths of the country, was not just illegal but fraught with mortal danger. But that danger is not part of Obama's story. The first white people he ever knew, the ones who raised him, were decent in a way that very few black people of that era experienced.

I asked Obama what he made of his grandparents' impressively civilized reception of his father. "It wasn't Harry Belafonte," Obama said laughingly of his father. "This was like an *African* African. And he was like a blue-black brother. Nilotic. And so, yeah, I will always give my grandparents credit for that. I'm not saying they were happy about it. I'm not saying that they were not, after the guy leaves, looking at each other like, 'What the heck?' But whatever misgivings they had, they never expressed to me, never spilled over into how they interacted with me.

"Now, part of it, as I say in my book, was we were in this unique environment in Hawaii where I think it was much easier. I don't know if it would have been as easy for them if they were living in Chicago at the time, because the lines just weren't as sharply drawn in Hawaii as they were on the mainland."

Obama's early positive interactions with his white family members gave him a fundamentally different outlook toward the wider world than most blacks of the 1960s had. Obama told me he rarely had "the working assumption of discrimination, the working assumption that white people would not treat me right or give me an opportunity or judge me [other than] on the basis of merit." He continued, "The kind of working assumption" that white people would discriminate against him or treat him poorly "is less embedded in my psyche than it is, say, with Michelle."

In this, the first lady is more representative of black America than her husband is. African Americans typically raise their children to protect themselves against a presumed hostility from white teachers, white police officers, white supervisors, and white coworkers. The need for that defense is, more often than not, reinforced either directly by actual encounters or indirectly by observing the vast differences between one's own experience and those across the color line. Marty Nesbitt, the president's longtime best friend, who, like Obama, had positive interactions with whites at a relatively early age, told me that when he and his wife went to buy their first car, she was insistent on buying from a black salesperson. "I'm like, 'We've got to find a salesman,'" Nesbitt said. "She's like, 'No, no, no. We're waiting for the brother.' And I'm like, 'He's with a customer.' They were filling out documents and she was like, 'We're going to stay around.' And a white guy came up to us. 'Can I help you?' 'Nope.'" Nesbitt was not out to condemn anyone with this story. He was asserting that "the willingness of African Americans [in Chicago] to help lift each other up is powerful."

But that willingness to help is also a defense, produced by decades of discrimination. Obama sees race through a different lens, Kaye Wilson told me. "It's just very different from ours," she explained. "He's got buddies that are white, and they're his buddies, and they love him. And I don't think they love him just because he's the president. They love him because they're his friends from Hawaii, some from college and all.

"So I think he's got that, whereas I think growing up in the racist United States, we enter this thing with, you know, 'I'm looking at you. I'm not trusting you to be one hundred with me.' And I think he grew up in a way that he had to trust [white people]—how can you live under the roof with people and think that they don't love you? He needs that frame of reference. He needs that lens. If he didn't have it, it would be . . . a Jesse Jackson, you know? Or Al Sharpton. Different lens."

That lens, born of literally relating to whites, allowed Obama to imagine that he could be the country's first black president. "If I walked into a room and it's a bunch of white farmers, trade unionists, middle age—I'm not walking in thinking, *Man, I've got to show them that I'm normal,"* Obama explained. "I walk in there, I think, with a set of assumptions: like, these people look just like my grandparents. And I see the same Jell-O mold that my grand-mother served, and they've got the same, you know, little stuff on their mantelpieces. And so I am maybe disarming them by just assuming that we're okay."

What Obama was able to offer white America is something very few African Americans could—trust. The vast majority of us are, necessarily, too crippled by our defenses to ever consider such a proposition. But Obama, through a mixture of ancestral connections and distance from the poisons of Jim Crow, can cred-ibly and sincerely trust the majority population of this country. That trust is reinforced, not contradicted, by his blackness. Obama isn't shuffling before white power (Herman Cain's "shucky ducky" act) or flattering white ego (O. J. Simpson's listing not being seen as black as a great accomplishment). That, too, is defensive, and deep down, I suspect, white people know it. He stands firm in his own cultural traditions and says to the country something virtually no black person can but every president must: "I believe you."

## IV. "You Still Gotta Go Back to the Hood"

Just after Columbus Day, I accompanied the president and his for-midable entourage on a visit to North Carolina A&T State Uni-versity, in Greensboro. Four days earlier, the *Washington Post* had published an old audio clip that featured Donald Trump lament-ing a failed sexual conquest and exhorting the virtues of sexual assault. The next day, Trump claimed that this was "locker room" talk. As we flew to North Carolina, the president was in a state of bemused disbelief. He plopped down in a chair in the staff cabin of *Air Force One* and said, "I've been in a lot of locker rooms. I don't think I've ever heard that one before." He was casual and relaxed. A feeling of cautious inevitability emanated from his staff, and why not? Every day seemed to bring a new, more shocking revelation or piece of evidence showing Trump to be unfit for the presidency: He had lost nearly $1 billion in a single year. He had likely not paid taxes in eighteen years. He was running a "university," for which he was under formal legal investigation. He had trampled on his own campaign's messaging by engaging in a Twitter crusade against a former beauty-pageant contestant. He had been denounced by leadership in his own party, and the trickle of prominent Republicans—both in and out of office—who had publicly repudiated him threatened to become a geyser. At this moment, the idea that a campaign so saturated in open bigotry, misogyny, chaos, and possible corruption could win a national election was ludicrous. This was America.

The president was going to North Carolina to keynote a campaign rally for Clinton, but first he was scheduled for a conversation about My Brother's Keeper, his initiative on behalf of disadvantaged youth. Announcing My Brother's Keeper—or MBK, as it's come to be called—in 2014, the president had sought to avoid giving the program a partisan valence, noting that it was "not some big new government program." Instead, it would involve the government in concert with the nonprofit and business sectors to intervene in the lives of young men of color who were "at risk." MBK serves as a kind of network for those elements of federal, state, and local government that might already have a presence in the lives of these young men. It is a quintessentially Obama program—conservative in scope, with impacts that are measurable.

"It comes right out of his own life," Broderick Johnson, the cabinet secretary and an assistant to the president, who heads MBK, told me recently. "I have heard him say, 'I don't want us to have a bunch of forums on race.' He reminds people, 'Yeah, we can talk about this. But what are we going to *do*?'" On this afternoon in North Carolina, what Obama did was sit with a group of young men who'd turned their lives around in part because of MBK.

They told stories of being in the street, of choosing quick money over school, of their homes being shot up, and—through the help of mentoring or job programs brokered by MBK—transitioning into college or a job. Obama listened solemnly and empathetically to each of them. "It doesn't take that much," he told them. "It just takes someone laying hands on you and saying, 'Hey, man, you count.'"

When he asked the young men whether they had a message he should take back to policy makers in Washington, D.C., one observed that despite their best individual efforts, they still had to go back to the very same deprived neighborhoods that had been the sources of trouble for them. "It's your environment," the young man said. "You can do what you want, but you still gotta go back to the hood."

He was correct. The ghettos of America are the direct result of decades of public-policy decisions: the redlining of real-estate zoning maps, the expanded authority given to prosecutors, the increased funding given to prisons. And all of this was done on the backs of people still reeling from the 250-year legacy of slavery. The results of this negative investment are clear—African Americans rank at the bottom of nearly every major socioeconomic measure in the country.

Obama's formula for closing this chasm between black and white America, like that of many progressive politicians today, proceeded from policy designed for all of America. Blacks disproportionately benefit from this effort, since they are disproportionately in need. The Affordable Care Act, which cut the uninsured rate in the black community by at least a third, was Obama's most prominent example. Its full benefit has yet to be felt by African Americans because several states in the South have declined to expand Medicaid. But when the president and I were meeting, the ACA's advocates believed that pressure on state budgets would force expansion, and there was evidence to support this: Louisiana had expanded Medicaid earlier in 2016, and advocates were gearing up for wars to be waged in Georgia and Virginia.

Obama also emphasized the need for a strong Justice Department with a deep commitment to nondiscrimination. When Obama moved into the White House in 2009, the Justice Department's Civil Rights Division "was in shambles," former attorney general Eric Holder told me recently. "I mean, I had been there for twelve years as a line guy. I started out in '76, so I served under Republicans and Democrats. And what the [George W.] Bush administration, what the Bush DOJ did, was unlike anything that had ever happened before in terms of politicized hiring." The career civil servants below the political appointees, Holder said, were not even invited to the meetings in which the key hiring and policy decisions were made. After Obama's inauguration, Holder told me, "I remember going to tell all the folks at the Civil Rights Division, 'The Civil Rights Division is open for business again.' The president gave me additional funds to hire people."

The political press developed a narrative that because Obama felt he had to modulate his rhetoric on race, Holder was the administration's true, and thus blacker, conscience. Holder is certainly blunter, and this worried some of the White House staff. Early in Obama's first term, Holder gave a speech on race in which he said the United States had been a "nation of cowards" on the subject. But positioning the two men as opposites elides an important fact: Holder was appointed by the president and went only as far as the president allowed. I asked Holder whether he had toned down his rhetoric after that controversial speech. "Nope," he said. Reflecting on his relationship with the president, Holder said, "We were also kind of different people, you know? He is the Zen guy. And I'm kind of the hot-blooded West Indian. And I thought we made a good team, but there's nothing that I ever did or said that I don't think he would have said, 'I support him 100 percent.'

"Now, the 'nation of cowards' speech, the president might have used a different phrase—maybe, probably. But he and I share a worldview, you know? And when I hear people say, 'Well, you are blacker than him' or something like that, I think, *What are you all talking about?*"

For much of his presidency, a standard portion of Obama's speeches about race riffed on black people's need to turn off the television, stop eating junk food, and stop blaming white people for their problems. Obama would deliver this lecture to any black audience, regardless of context. It was bizarre, for instance, to see the president warning young men who'd just graduated from Morehouse College, one of the most storied black colleges in the country, about making "excuses" and blaming whites.

This part of the Obama formula is the most troubling and least thought-out. This judgment emerges from my own biography. I am the product of black parents who encouraged me to read, of black teachers who felt my work ethic did not match my potential, of black college professors who taught me intellectual rigor. And they did this in a world that every day insulted their humanity. It was not so much that the black layabouts and dead-beats Obama invoked in his speeches were unrecognizable. I had seen those people too. But I'd also seen the same among white people. If black men were overrepresented among drug dealers and absentee dads of the world, it was directly related to their being underrepresented among the Bernie Madoffs and Kenneth Lays of the world. Power was what mattered, and what characterized the differences between black and white America was not a difference in work ethic, but a system engineered to place one on top of the other.

The mark of that system is visible at every level of American society, regardless of the quality of one's choices. For instance, the unemployment rate among black college graduates (4.1 percent) is almost the same as the unemployment rate among white high-school graduates (4.6 percent). But that college degree is generally purchased at a higher price by blacks than by whites. According to research by the Brookings Institution, African Americans tend to carry more student debt four years after graduation ($53,000 versus $28,000) and suffer from a higher default rate on their loans (7.6 percent versus 2.4 percent) than white Americans. This is both the result and the perpetuator of a sprawling wealth gap between the races. White households, on average, hold seven times as much wealth as black households—a difference so large as to make comparing the "black middle class" and "white middle class" meaningless; they're simply not comparable. According to Patrick Sharkey, a sociologist at New York University who studies economic mobility, black families making $100,000 a year or more live in more-disadvantaged neighborhoods than white families making less than $30,000. This gap didn't just appear by magic; it's the result of the government's effort over many decades to create a pigmentocracy—one that will continue without explicit intervention.

Obama had been on the record as opposing reparations. But now, late in his presidency, he seemed more open to the idea—in theory, at least, if not in practice.

"Theoretically, you can make obviously a powerful argument that centuries of slavery, Jim Crow, discrimination are the primary cause for all those gaps," Obama said, referencing the gulf in education, wealth, and employment that separates black and white America. "That those were wrongs to the black community as a whole, and black families specifically, and that in order to close that gap, a society has a moral obligation to make a large, aggressive investment, even if it's not in the form of individual reparations checks but in the form of a Marshall Plan."

The political problems with turning the argument for reparations into reality are manifold, Obama said. "If you look at countries like South Africa, where you had a black majority, there have been efforts to tax and help that black majority, but it hasn't come in the form of a formal reparations program. You have countries like India that have tried to help untouchables, with essentially affirmative-action programs, but it hasn't fundamentally changed the structure of their societies. So the bottom line is that it's hard to find a model in which you can practically administer and sustain political support for those kinds of efforts."

Obama went on to say that it would be better, and more realistic, to get the country to rally behind a robust liberal agenda and build on the enormous progress that's been made toward getting white Americans to accept nondiscrimination as a basic operating premise. But the progress toward nondiscrimination did not appear overnight. It was achieved by people willing to make an unpopular argument and live on the frontier of public opinion. I asked him whether it wasn't—despite the practical obstacles—worth arguing that the state has a collective responsibility not only for its achievements but for its sins.

"I want my children—I want Malia and Sasha—to understand that they've got responsibilities beyond just what they themselves have done," Obama said. "That they have a responsibility to the larger community and the larger nation, that they should be sensitive to and extra thoughtful about the plight of people who have been oppressed in the past, are oppressed currently. So that's a wisdom that I want to transmit to my kids . . . But I would say that's a high level of enlightenment that you're looking to have from a majority of the society. And it may be something that future generations are more open to, but I am pretty confident that for the foreseeable future, using the argument of nondiscrimination, and 'Let's get it right for the kids who are here right now,' and giving them the best chance possible, is going to be a more persuasive argument."

Obama is unfailingly optimistic about the empathy and capabilities of the American people. His job necessitates this: "At some level what the people want to feel is that the person leading them sees the best in them," he told me. But I found it interesting that that optimism does not extend to the possibility of the public's accepting wisdoms—such as the moral logic of reparations—that the president, by his own account, has accepted for himself and is willing to teach his children. Obama says he always tells his staff that "better is good." The notion that a president would attempt to achieve change within the boundaries of the accepted consensus is appropriate. But Obama is almost constitutionally skeptical of those who seek to achieve change outside that consensus.

.        .        .

Early in 2016, Obama invited a group of African American leaders to meet with him at the White House. When some of the activists affiliated with Black Lives Matter refused to attend, Obama began calling them out in speeches. "You can't refuse to meet because that might compromise the purity of your position," he said. "The value of social movements and activism is to get you at the table, get you in the room, and then start trying to figure out how is this problem going to be solved. You then have a responsibility to prepare an agenda that is achievable—that can institutionalize the changes you seek—and to engage the other side."

Opal Tometi, a Nigerian American community activist who is one of the three founders of Black Lives Matter, explained to me that the group has a more diffuse structure than most civil-rights organizations. One reason for this is to avoid the cult of personality that has plagued black organizations in the past. So the founders asked its membership in Chicago, the president's hometown, whether they should meet with Obama. "They felt—and I think many of our members felt—there wouldn't be the depth of discussion that they wanted to have," Tometi told me. "And if there wasn't that space to have a real heart-to-heart, and if it was just surface level, that it would be more of a disservice to the movement."

Tometi noted that some other activists allied with Black Lives Matter had been planning to attend the meeting, so they felt their views would be represented. Nevertheless, Black Lives Matter sees itself as engaged in a protest against the treatment of black people by the American state, and so Tometi and much of the group's leadership, concerned about being used for a photo op by the very body they were protesting, opted not to go.

When I asked Obama about this perspective, he fluctuated between understanding where the activists were coming from and being hurt by such brush-offs. "I think that where I've gotten frustrated during the course of my presidency has never been because I was getting pushed too hard by activists to see the justness of a cause or the essence of an issue," he said. "I think where I got frustrated at times was the belief that the president can do anything if he just decides he wants to do it. And that sort of lack of awareness on the part of an activist about the constraints of our political system and the constraints on this office, I think, sometimes would leave me to mutter under my breath. Very rarely did I lose it publicly. Usually I'd just smile."

He laughed, then continued, "The reason I say that is because those are the times where sometimes you feel actually a little bit hurt. Because you feel like saying to these folks, '[Don't] you think if I could do it, I [would] have just done it? Do you think that the only problem is that I don't care enough about the plight of poor people, or gay people?'"

I asked Obama whether he thought that perhaps protesters' distrust of the powers that be could ultimately be healthy. "Yes," he said. "Which is why I don't get too hurt. I mean, I think there is a benefit to wanting to hold power's feet to the fire until you actually see the goods. I get that. And I think it is important. And frankly, sometimes it's useful for activists just to be out there to keep you mindful and not get complacent, even if ultimately you think some of their criticism is misguided."

Obama himself was an activist and a community organizer, albeit for only two years—but he is not, by temperament, a protester. He is a consensus builder; consensus, he believes, ultimately drives what gets done. He understands the emotional power of protest, the need to vent before authority—but that kind of approach does not come naturally to him. Regarding reparations, he said, "Sometimes I wonder how much of these debates have to do with the desire, the legitimate desire, for that history to be recognized. Because there is a psychic power to the recognition that is not satisfied with a universal program; it's not satisfied by the Affordable Care Act, or an expansion of Pell Grants, or an expansion of the earned-income tax credit." These kinds of programs, effective and disproportionately beneficial to black people though they may be, don't "speak to the hurt, and the sense of injustice, and the self-doubt that arises out of the fact that [African Americans] are behind now, and it makes us sometimes feel as if there must be something wrong with us—unless you're able to see the history and say, 'It's amazing we got this far given what we went through.'

"So in part, I think the argument sometimes that I've had with folks who are much more interested in sort of race-specific programs is less an argument about what is practically achievable and sometimes maybe more an argument of 'We want society to see what's happened and internalize it and answer it in demonstrable ways.' And those impulses I very much understand—but my hope would be that as we're moving through the world right now, we're able to get that psychological or emotional peace by seeing very concretely our kids doing better and being more hopeful and having greater opportunities."

Obama saw—at least at that moment, before the election of Donald Trump—a straight path to that world. "Just play this out as a thought experiment," he said. "Imagine if you had genuine, high-quality early-childhood education for every child, and suddenly every black child in America—but also every poor white child or Latino [child], but just stick with every black child in America—is getting a really good education. And they're graduating from high school at the same rates that whites are, and they are going to college at the same rates that whites are, and they are able to afford college at the same rates because the government has universal programs that say that you're not going to be barred from school just because of how much money your parents have.

"So now they're all graduating. And let's also say that the Justice Department and the courts are making sure, as I've said in a speech before, that when Jamal sends his résumé in, he's getting treated the same as when Johnny sends his résumé in. Now, are we going to have suddenly the same number of CEOs, billionaires, etc., as the white community? In ten years? Probably not, maybe not even in twenty years.

"But I guarantee you that we would be thriving, we would be succeeding. We wouldn't have huge numbers of young African American men in jail. We'd have more family formation as college-graduated girls are meeting boys who are their peers, which then in turn means the next generation of kids are growing up that much better. And suddenly you've got a whole generation that's in a position to start using the incredible creativity that we see in music and sports and frankly even on the streets, channeled into starting all kinds of businesses. I feel pretty good about our odds in that situation."

The thought experiment doesn't hold up. The programs Obama favored would advance white America too—and without a specific commitment to equality, there is no guarantee that the programs would eschew discrimination. Obama's solution relies on a goodwill that his own personal history tells him exists in the larger country. My own history tells me something different. The large numbers of black men in jail, for instance, are not just the result of poor policy but of not seeing those men as human.

When President Obama and I had this conversation, the target he was aiming to reach seemed to me to be many generations away, and now—as President-Elect Trump prepares for office—seems even many more generations off. Obama's accomplishments were real: a $1 billion settlement on behalf of black farmers, a Justice Department that exposed Ferguson's municipal plunder, the increased availability of Pell Grants (and their availability to some prisoners), and the slashing of the crack/cocaine disparity in sentencing guidelines, to name just a few. Obama was also the first sitting president to visit a federal prison. There was a feeling that he'd erected a foundation upon which further progressive policy could be built. It's tempting to say that foundation is now endangered. The truth is, it was never safe.

## V. "They Rode the Tiger"

Obama's greatest misstep was born directly out of his greatest insight. Only Obama, a black man who emerged from the best of white America, and thus could sincerely trust white America, could be so certain that he could achieve broad national appeal. And yet only a black man with that same biography could underestimate his opposition's resolve to destroy him. In some sense an Obama presidency could never have succeeded along the normal presidential lines; he needed a partner, or partners, in Congress who could put governance above party. But he struggled to win over even some of his own allies. Ben Nelson, the Democratic senator from Nebraska whom Obama helped elect, became an obstacle to health-care reform. Joe Lieberman, whom Obama saved from retribution at the hands of Senate Democrats after Lieberman campaigned for Obama's 2008 opponent, John McCain, similarly obstructed Obamacare. Among Republicans, senators who had seemed amenable to Obama's agenda—Chuck Grassley, Susan Collins, Richard Lugar, Olympia Snowe—rebuffed him repeatedly.

The obstruction grew out of narrow political incentives. "If Republicans didn't cooperate," Obama told me, "and there was not a portrait of bipartisan cooperation and a functional federal government, then the party in power would pay the price and they could win back the Senate and/or the House. That wasn't an inaccurate political calculation."

Obama is not sure of the degree to which individual racism played into this calculation. "I do remember watching Bill Clinton get impeached and Hillary Clinton being accused of killing Vince Foster," he said. "And if you ask them, I'm sure they would say, 'No, actually what you're experiencing is not because you're black, it's because you're a Democrat.'"

But personal animus is just one manifestation of racism; arguably, the more profound animosity occurs at the level of interests. The most recent Congress boasted 138 members from the states that constituted the old Confederacy. Of the 101 Republicans in that group, 96 are white and 1 is black. Of the 37 Democrats, 18 are black and 15 are white. There are no white congressional Democrats in the Deep South. Exit polls in Mississippi in 2008 found that 96 percent of voters who described themselves as Republicans were white. The Republican Party is not simply the party of whites, but the preferred party of whites who identify their interest as defending the historical privileges of whiteness. The researchers Josh Pasek, Jon A. Krosnick, and Trevor Tompson found that in 2012, 32 percent of Democrats held antiblack views, while 79 percent of Republicans did. These attitudes could even spill over to white Democratic politicians because they are seen as representing the party of blacks. Studying the 2016 election, the political scientist Philip Klinkner found that the most predictive question for understanding whether a voter favored Hillary Clinton or Donald Trump was "Is Barack Obama a Muslim?"

In our conversations, Obama said he didn't doubt that there was a sincerely nonracist states'-rights contingent of the GOP. And yet he suspected that there might be more to it. "A rudimentary knowledge of American history tells you that the relationship between the federal government and the states was very much mixed up with attitudes towards slavery, attitudes towards Jim

Crow, attitudes towards antipoverty programs and who benefited and who didn't," he said.

"And so I'm careful not to attribute any particular resistance or slight or opposition to race. But what I do believe is that if somebody didn't have a problem with their daddy being employed by the federal government, and didn't have a problem with the Tennessee Valley Authority electrifying certain communities, and didn't have a problem with the interstate highway system being built, and didn't have a problem with the GI Bill, and didn't have a problem with the [Federal Housing Administration] subsidizing the suburbanization of America, and that all helped you build wealth and create a middle class—and then suddenly as soon as African Americans or Latinos are interested in availing themselves of those same mechanisms as ladders into the middle class, you now have a violent opposition to them—then I think you at least have to ask yourself the question of how consistent you are, and what's different, and what's changed."

Racism greeted Obama in both his primary and general-election campaigns in 2008. Photos were circulated of him in Somali garb. Rush Limbaugh dubbed him "Barack the Magic Negro." Roger Stone, who would go on to advise the Trump campaign, claimed that Michelle Obama could be heard on tape yelling "Whitey." Detractors circulated e-mails claiming that the future first lady had written a racist senior thesis while at Princeton. A fifth of all West Virginia Democratic-primary voters in 2008 openly admitted that race had influenced their vote. Hillary Clinton trounced him 67 to 26 percent.

After Obama won the presidency in defiance of these racial headwinds, traffic to the white-supremacist website Stormfront increased sixfold. Before the election, in August, just before the Democratic National Convention, the FBI uncovered an assassination plot hatched by white supremacists in Denver. Mainstream conservative publications floated the notion that Obama's memoir was too "stylish and penetrating" to have been written by the candidate, and found a plausible ghostwriter in the radical (and white) former Weatherman Bill Ayers. A Republican women's club in California dispensed "Obama Bucks" featuring slices of watermelon, ribs, and fried chicken. At the Values Voter Summit that year, conventioneers hawked "Obama Waffles," a waffle mix whose box featured a bug-eyed caricature of the candidate. Fake hip-hop lyrics were scrawled on the side ("Barry's Bling Bling Waffle Ring"), and on the top, the same caricature was granted a turban and tagged with the instructions "Point box toward Mecca for tastier waffles." The display was denounced by the summit's sponsor, the Family Research Council. One would be forgiven for meeting this denunciation with guffaws: The council's president, Tony Perkins, had once addressed the white-supremacist Council of Conservative Citizens with a Confederate flag draped behind him. By 2015, Perkins had deemed the debate over Obama's birth certificate "legitimate" and was saying that it "makes sense" to conclude that Obama was actually a Muslim.

By then, birtherism—inflamed in large part by a real-estate mogul and reality-TV star named Donald Trump—had overtaken the Republican rank and file. In 2015, one poll found that 54 percent of GOP voters thought Obama was a Muslim. Only 29 percent believed he'd been born in America.

Still, in 2008, Obama had been elected. His supporters rejoiced. As Jay-Z commemorated the occasion:

My president is black, in fact he's half-white,
So even in a racist mind, he's half-right.

Not quite. A month after Obama entered the White House, a CNBC personality named Rick Santelli took to the trading floor of the Chicago Mercantile Exchange and denounced the president's efforts to help homeowners endangered by the housing crisis. "How many of you people want to pay for your neighbor's mortgage that has an extra bathroom and can't pay their bills?" Santelli asked the assembled traders. He asserted that Obama should "reward people that could carry the water" as opposed to those who "drink the water" and denounced those in danger of foreclosure as "losers." Race was implicit in Santelli's harangue— the housing crisis and predatory lending had devastated black communities and expanded the wealth gap—and it culminated with a call for a "Tea Party" to resist the Obama presidency. In fact, right-wing ideologues had been planning just such a resistance for decades. They would eagerly answer Santelli's call.

•     •     •

One of the intellectual forerunners of the Tea Party is said to be Ron Paul, the heterodox two-time Republican presidential candidate, who opposed the war in Iraq and championed civil liberties. On other matters, Paul was more traditional. Throughout the nineties, he published a series of racist newsletters that referred to New York City as "Welfaria," called Martin Luther King Jr. Day "Hate Whitey Day," and asserted that 95 percent of black males in Washington, D.C., were either "semi-criminal or entirely criminal." Paul's apologists have claimed that he had no real connection to the newsletters, even though virtually all of them were published in his name ("The Ron Paul Survival Report," "Ron Paul Political Report," "Dr. Ron Paul's Freedom Report") and written in his voice. Either way, the views of the newsletters have found their expression in his ideological comrades. Throughout Obama's first term, Tea Party activists voiced their complaints in racist terms. Activists brandished signs warning that Obama would implement "white slavery," waved the Confederate flag, depicted Obama as a witch doctor, and issued calls for him to "go back to Kenya." Tea Party supporters wrote "satirical" letters in the name of "We Colored People" and stoked the flames of birtherism. One of the Tea Party's most prominent sympathizers, the radio host Laura Ingraham, wrote a racist tract depicting Michelle Obama gorging herself on ribs while Glenn Beck said the president was a "racist" with a "deep-seated hatred for white people." The Tea Party's leading exponent, Andrew Breitbart, engineered the smearing of Shirley Sherrod, the U.S. Department of Agriculture's director of rural development for Georgia, publishing egregiously misleading videos that wrongly made her appear to be engaging in antiwhite racist invective, which led to her dismissal. (In a rare act of cowardice, the Obama administration cravenly submitted to this effort.)

In those rare moments when Obama made any sort of comment attacking racism, firestorms threatened to consume his governing agenda. When, in July 2009, the president objected to the arrest of the eminent Harvard professor Henry Louis Gates Jr. while he was trying to get into his own house, pointing out that the officer had "acted stupidly," a third of whites said the remark made them feel less favorably toward the president, and nearly two-thirds claimed that Obama had "acted stupidly" by commenting. A chastened Obama then determined to make sure his public statements on race were no longer mere riffs but designed to have an achievable effect. This was smart, but still the invective came. During Obama's 2009 address on health care before a joint session of Congress, Joe Wilson, a Republican congressman from South Carolina, incredibly, and in defiance of precedent and decorum, disrupted the proceedings by crying out "You lie!" A Missouri congressman equated Obama with a monkey. A California GOP official took up the theme and e-mailed her friends an image depicting Obama as a chimp, with the accompanying text explaining, "Now you know why [there's] no birth certificate!" Former vice-presidential candidate Sarah Palin assessed the president's foreign policy as a "shuck and jive shtick." Newt Gingrich dubbed him the "food-stamp president." The rhetorical attacks on Obama were matched by a very real attack on his political base—in 2011 and 2012, nineteen states enacted voting restrictions that made it harder for African Americans to vote.

Yet in 2012, as in 2008, Obama won anyway. Prior to the election, Obama, ever the optimist, had claimed that intransigent Republicans would decide to work with him to advance the country. No such collaboration was in the offing. Instead, legislation ground to a halt and familiar themes resurfaced. An Idaho GOP official posted a photo on Facebook depicting a trap waiting for Obama. The bait was a slice of watermelon. The caption read, "Breaking: The secret service just uncovered a plot to kidnap the president. More details as we get them . . ." In 2014, conservatives assembled in support of Cliven Bundy's armed protest against federal grazing fees. As reporters descended on the Bundy ranch in Nevada, Bundy offered his opinions on "the Negro." "They abort their young children, they put their young men in jail, because they never learned how to pick cotton," Bundy explained. "And I've often wondered, are they better off as slaves, picking cotton and having a family life and doing things, or are they better off under government subsidy? They didn't get no more freedom. They got less freedom."

That same year, in the wake of Michael Brown's death, the Justice Department opened an investigation into the police department in Ferguson, Missouri. It found a city that, through racial profiling, arbitrary fines, and wanton harassment, had exploited law enforcement for the purposes of municipal plunder. The plunder was sanctified by racist humor dispensed via internal e-mails among the police that later came to light. The president of the United States, who during his first year in office had reportedly received three times the number of death threats of any of his predecessors, was a repeat target.

Much ink has been spilled in an attempt to understand the Tea Party protests, and the 2016 presidential candidacy of Donald Trump, which ultimately emerged out of them. One theory

popular among (primarily) white intellectuals of varying political persuasions held that this response was largely the discon-
tented rumblings of a white working class threatened by the
menace of globalization and crony capitalism. Dismissing these
rumblings as racism was said to condescend to this proletariat,
which had long suffered the slings and arrows of coastal elites,
heartless technocrats, and reformist snobs. Racism was not
something to be coolly and empirically assessed but a slander
upon the working man. Deindustrialization, globalization, and
broad income inequality are real. And they have landed with at
least as great a force upon black and Latino people in our country as upon white people. And yet these groups were strangely
unrepresented in this new populism.

Christopher S. Parker and Matt A. Barreto, political scientists
at the University of Washington and UCLA, respectively, have
found a relatively strong relationship between racism and Tea
Party membership. "Whites are less likely to be drawn to the Tea
Party for material reasons, suggesting that, relative to other
groups, it's really more about social prestige," they say. The notion
that the Tea Party represented the righteous, if unfocused, anger
of an aggrieved class allowed everyone from leftists to neoliber-
als to white nationalists to avoid a horrifying and simple reality:
A significant swath of this country did not like the fact that their
president was black, and that swath was not composed of those
most damaged by an unquestioned faith in the markets. Far better to imagine the grievance put upon the president as the ghost
of shambling factories and defunct union halls, as opposed to
what it really was—a movement inaugurated by ardent and frightened white capitalists, raging from the commodities-trading
floor of one of the great financial centers of the world.

That movement came into full bloom in the summer of 2015,
with the candidacy of Donald Trump, a man who'd risen to political prominence by peddling the racist myth that the president
was not American. It was birtherism—not trade, not jobs, not

isolationism—that launched Trump's foray into electoral politics. Having risen unexpectedly on this basis into the stratosphere of Republican politics, Trump spent the campaign freely and liberally trafficking in misogyny, Islamophobia, and xenophobia. And on November 8, 2016, he won election to the presidency. Historians will spend the next century analyzing how a country with such allegedly grand democratic traditions was, so swiftly and so easily, brought to the brink of fascism. But one needn't stretch too far to conclude that an eight-year campaign of consistent and open racism aimed at the leader of the free world helped clear the way.

"They rode the tiger. And now the tiger is eating them," David Axelrod, speaking of the Republican Party, told me. That was in October. His words proved too optimistic. The tiger would devour us all.

## VI. "When You Left, You Took All of Me with You"

One Saturday morning last May, I joined the presidential motorcade as it slipped out of the southern gate of the White House. A mostly white crowd had assembled. As the motorcade drove by, people cheered, held up their smartphones to record the procession, and waved American flags. To be within feet of the president seemed like the thrill of their lives. I was astounded. An old euphoria, which I could not immediately place, gathered up in me. And then I remembered, it was what I felt through much of 2008, as I watched Barack Obama's star shoot across the political sky. I had never seen so many white people cheer on a black man who was neither an athlete nor an entertainer. And it seemed that they loved him for this, and I thought in those days, which now feel so long ago, that they might then love me, too, and love my wife and love my child and love us all in the manner that the God they so fervently cited had commanded. I had been raised amid a people who wanted badly to believe in the possibility of a

Barack Obama, even as their very lives argued against that possibility. So they would praise Martin Luther King Jr. in one breath and curse the white man, "the Great Deceiver," in the next. Then came Obama and the Obama family, and they were black and beautiful in all the ways we aspired to be, and all that love was showered upon them. But as Obama's motorcade approached its destination—Howard University, where he would give the commencement address—the complexion of the crowd darkened, and I understood that the love was specific, that even if it allowed Barack Obama, even if it allowed the luckiest of us, to defy the boundaries, then the masses of us, in cities like this one, would still enjoy no such feat.

These were our fitful, spasmodic years.

We were launched into the Obama era with no notion of what to expect, if only because a black presidency had seemed such a dubious proposition. There was no preparation because it would have meant preparing for the impossible. There were few assessments of its potential import because such assessments were regarded as speculative fiction. In retrospect it all makes sense, and one can see a jagged but real political lineage running through black Chicago. It originates in Oscar Stanton De Priest; continues through Congressman William Dawson, who, under Roosevelt, switched from the Republican to the Democratic Party; crescendos with the legendary Harold Washington; rises still with Jesse Jackson's 1988 victory in Michigan's Democratic caucuses; rises again with Carol Moseley Braun's triumph; and reaches its recent apex with the election of Barack Obama. If the lineage is apparent in hindsight, so are the limits of presidential power. For a century after emancipation, quasi slavery haunted the South. And more than half a century after *Brown v. Board of Education*, schools throughout much of this country remain segregated.

There are no clean victories for black people nor, perhaps, for any people. The presidency of Barack Obama is no different. One can now say that an African American individual can rise to the same level as a white individual and yet also say that the number of black individuals who actually qualify for that status will be small. One thinks of Serena Williams, whose dominance and stunning achievements can't, in and of themselves, ensure equal access to tennis facilities for young black girls. The gate is open and yet so very far away.

I felt a mix of pride and amazement walking onto Howard's campus that day. Howard alumni, of which I am one, are an obnoxious fraternity, known for yelling the school chant across city blocks, sneering at other historically black colleges and universities, and condescending to black graduates of predominantly white institutions. I like to think I am more reserved, but I felt an immense satisfaction in being in the library where I had once found my history and now found myself with the first black president of the United States. It seemed providential that he would give the commencement address here in his last year. The same pride I felt radiated out across the Yard, the large green patch in the main area of the campus where the ceremony would take place. When Obama walked out, the audience exploded, and when the time came for the color guard to present arms, a chant arose: "O-Ba-Ma! O-Ba-Ma! O-Ba-Ma!"

He gave a good speech that day, paying heed to Howard's rituals, calling out its famous alumni, shouting out the university's various dormitories, and urging young people to vote. (His usual riff on respectability politics was missing.) But I think he could have stood before that crowd, smiled, and said "Good luck," and they would have loved him anyway. He was their champion, and this was evident in the smallest of things. The national anthem was played first, but then came the black national anthem, "Lift Every Voice and Sing." As the lyrics rang out over the crowd, the students held up the black-power fist—a symbol of defiance before power. And yet here, in the face of a black man in his last year in power, it scanned not as a protest, but as a salute.

Six months later the awful price of a black presidency would be known to those students, even as the country seemed determined not to acknowledge it. In the days after Donald Trump's victory, there would be an insistence that something as "simple" as racism could not explain it. As if enslavement had nothing to do with global economics or as if lynchings said nothing about the idea of women as property. As though the past 400 years could be reduced to the irrational resentment of full lips. No. Racism is never simple. And there was nothing simple about what was coming or about Obama, the man who had unwittingly summoned this future into being.

It was said that the Americans who'd supported Trump were victims of liberal condescension. The word *racist* would be dismissed as a profane slur put upon the common man, as opposed to an accurate description of actual men. "We simply don't yet know how much racism or misogyny motivated Trump voters," David Brooks would write in the *New York Times*. "If you were stuck in a jobless town, watching your friends OD on opiates, scrambling every month to pay the electric bill, and then along came a guy who seemed able to fix your problems and hear your voice, maybe you would stomach some ugliness, too." This strikes me as perfectly logical. Indeed, it could apply just as well to Louis Farrakhan's appeal to the black poor and working class. But whereas the followers of an Islamophobic white nationalist enjoy the sympathy that must always greet the salt of the earth, the followers of an anti-Semitic black nationalist endure the scorn that must ever greet the children of the enslaved.

Much would be made of blue-collar voters in Wisconsin, Pennsylvania, and Michigan who'd pulled the lever for Obama in 2008 and 2012 and then for Trump in 2016. Surely these voters disproved racism as an explanatory force. It's still not clear how many individual voters actually flipped. But the underlying presumption—that Hillary Clinton and Barack Obama could be swapped in for each other—exhibited a problem. Clinton was a candidate who'd won one competitive political race in her life, whose political instincts were questioned by her own advisers, who took more than half a million dollars in speaking fees from an investment bank because it was "what they offered," who proposed to bring back to the White House a former president dogged by allegations of rape and sexual harassment. Obama was a candidate who'd become only the third black senator in the modern era; who'd twice been elected president, each time flipping red and purple states; who'd run one of the most scandal-free administrations in recent memory. Imagine an African American facsimile of Hillary Clinton: She would never be the nominee of a major political party and likely would not be in national politics at all.

Pointing to citizens who voted for both Obama and Trump does not disprove racism; it evinces it. To secure the White House, Obama needed to be a Harvard-trained lawyer with a decade of political experience and an incredible gift for speaking to cross sections of the country; Donald Trump needed only money and white bluster.

In the week after the election, I was a mess. I had not seen my wife in two weeks. I was on deadline for this article. My son was struggling in school. The house was in disarray. I played Marvin Gaye endlessly—"When you left, you took all of me with you." Friends began to darkly recall the ghosts of post-Reconstruction. The election of Donald Trump confirmed everything I knew of my country and none of what I could accept. The idea that America would follow its first black president with Donald Trump accorded with its history. I was shocked at my own shock. I had wanted Obama to be right.

I still want Obama to be right. I still would like to fold myself into the dream. This will not be possible.

By some cosmic coincidence, a week after the election I received a portion of my father's FBI file. (I was made aware of the FBI file by the diligent work of researchers from the show

*Finding Your Roots.* I was taping an episode on my family the day of my last interview with the president.) My father had grown up poor in Philadelphia. His father was struck dead on the street. His grandfather was crushed to death in a meatpacking plant. He'd served his country in Vietnam, gotten radicalized there, and joined the Black Panther Party, which brought him to the attention of J. Edgar Hoover. A memo written to the FBI director was "submitted aimed at discrediting WILLIAM PAUL COATES, Acting Captain of the BPP, Baltimore." The memo proposed that a fake letter be sent to the Panthers' cofounder Huey P. Newton. The fake letter accused my father of being an informant and concluded, "I want somethin done with this bootlikin facist pig nigger and I want it done now." The words *somethin done* need little interpretation. The Panthers were eventually consumed by an internecine war instigated by the FBI, one in which being labeled a police informant was a death sentence.

A few hours after I saw this file, I had my last conversation with the president. I asked him how his optimism was holding up, given Trump's victory. He confessed to being surprised at the outcome but said that it was tough to "draw a grand theory from it, because there were some very unusual circumstances." He pointed to both candidates' high negatives, the media coverage, and a "dispirited" electorate. But he said that his general optimism about the shape of American history remained unchanged. "To be optimistic about the long-term trends of the United States doesn't mean that everything is going to go in a smooth, direct, straight line," he said. "It goes forward sometimes, sometimes it goes back, sometimes it goes sideways, sometimes it zigs and zags."

I thought of Hoover's FBI, which harassed three generations of black activists, from Marcus Garvey's black nationalists to Martin Luther King Jr.'s integrationists to Huey Newton's Black Panthers, including my father. And I thought of the enormous power accrued to the presidency in the post-9/11 era—the power to obtain American citizens' phone records en masse, to access their e-mails, to detain them indefinitely. I asked the president whether it was all worth it. Whether this generation of black activists and their allies should be afraid.

"Keep in mind that the capacity of the NSA, or other surveillance tools, are specifically prohibited from being applied to U.S. citizens or U.S. persons without specific evidence of links to terrorist activity or, you know, other foreign-related activity," he said. "So, you know, I think this whole story line that somehow Big Brother has massively expanded and now that a new president is in place it's this loaded gun ready to be used on domestic dissent is just not accurate."

He counseled vigilance, "because the possibility of abuse by government officials always exists. The issue is not going to be that there are new tools available; the issue is making sure that the incoming administration, like my administration, takes the constraints on how we deal with U.S. citizens and persons seriously." This answer did not fill me with confidence. The next day, President-Elect Trump offered Lieutenant General Michael Flynn the post of national-security adviser and picked Senator Jeff Sessions of Alabama as his nominee for attorney general. Last February, Flynn tweeted, "Fear of Muslims is RATIONAL" and linked to a YouTube video that declared followers of Islam want "80 percent of humanity enslaved or exterminated." Sessions had once been accused of calling a black lawyer "boy," claiming that a white lawyer who represented black clients was a disgrace to his race, and joking that he thought the Ku Klux Klan "was okay until I found out they smoked pot." I felt then that I knew what was coming—more Freddie Grays, more Rekia Boyds, more informants and undercover officers sent to infiltrate mosques.

And I also knew that the man who could not countenance such a thing in his America had been responsible for the only time in my life when I felt, as the first lady had once said, proud of my country, and I knew that it was his very lack of countenance, his incredible faith, his improbable trust in his countrymen that had made that feeling possible. The feeling was that little black boy touching the president's hair. It was watching Obama on the campaign trail, always expecting the worst and amazed that the worst never happened. It was how I'd felt seeing Barack and Michelle during the inauguration, the car slow-dragging down Pennsylvania Avenue, the crowd cheering, and then the two of them rising up out of the limo, rising up from fear, smiling, waving, defying despair, defying history, defying gravity.

## ESPN the Magazine

FINALIST—REPORTING

*For those who look forward to Sunday as an opportunity to shed their worries, the most recent NFL season was as disappointing as the performance of a 1–15 team. Instead of commentary on screen passes and nickel defenses, we were treated to angry tweets about politics and race. Fortunately, we had a frequent Ellie winner—ESPN the Magazine—to help us understand what was going on. As the Ellie judges wrote: "The NFL is a fortress. Getting inside is all but impossible. But in this gripping ESPN series, Don Van Natta Jr. and Seth Wickersham offered a groundbreaking, inside-the-room view of the power brokers behind America's most popular sport. From a minute-by-minute account of the confrontation between owners and players to a revealing look at the Dallas Cowboys' Jerry Jones, this impressively reported series showed football fans how the NFL really works."*

Seth Wickersham and
Don Van Natta Jr.

# Standing Down *and* Roger Goodell Has a Jerry Jones Problem

## Standing Down

Nobody knew where to sit. Side by side or across from one another?

It was the final question raised by a group of eleven NFL team owners as they mingled inside the sixth-floor conference room at the league's Park Avenue headquarters in New York City, minutes before they were to meet with a group of twelve players, one former player, and three union leaders on the morning of Tuesday, October 17. The day already had been stressful, and the meeting hadn't even started. League executives had spent that morning as they had the previous four weeks: grappling with a series of events the league and owners could not control, unleashed by President Donald Trump's harsh criticism of the decision by a handful of players to kneel during the national anthem.

Morale was bad inside the league office, and the pressure was not letting up. There was the looming notion that sponsors would leave the NFL—not just because of the protests but because of an array of challenges confronting the league, including the continuing decline in TV ratings. Nearly all of the league's longtime sponsors, from Papa John's to USAA, were rattled, and fissures within the league offices and teams, to say nothing of the players, were starting to expand.

Among many league and team executives, the games had become, improbably, an afterthought. These two days of New York meetings held the potential to provide a measure of hope—a way for owners to formulate a plan with players that would satisfy disenchanted fans and advertisers. It was no secret that commissioner Roger Goodell and the owners wanted the players to stop kneeling during the anthem immediately. A week earlier, Goodell said that he hoped owners and players could "move past" the anthem issue at the meetings. If and how that could be accomplished was unclear. After Goodell's statement, Jerry Jones, the Dallas Cowboys owner, threatened to bench any player who knelt, the only owner to issue such an ultimatum, one that won praise in Texas and across much of America's heartland. Spurred on by Jones's stance, some hard-line owners looked at the meetings as the opportunity to vote on a mandate that would force all players to stand for the anthem.

For weeks, Goodell had tried to get in front of the issue. One owner had complained that NBA commissioner Adam Silver got away with ordering players to stand because, unlike Goodell, he has a good relationship with the union. Another owner had remarked to a colleague that Trump would like nothing more than for players to strike over the protests, maybe forcing a suspension of the season.

As owners filed into the large conference room featuring a massive, football-shaped table, everyone feared the discussion could get ugly. NFL executive Troy Vincent, who cared deeply about the players' concerns but had little patience for the protests, called San Francisco 49ers GM John Lynch the Saturday before the meeting. He told him that if safety Eric Reid, one of the most ardent protesters, knelt the next day, he shouldn't "bother to show up" at the players-owners meeting because nobody would take him seriously, according to people briefed on the call. Reid knelt anyway. And he intended to show up.

Just before Reid and the other players and union leadership arrived, talk among the owners turned to a final issue, small but symbolic: the seating arrangement. In collective bargaining negotiations, the owners sat opposite players and union representatives. But Goodell told the owners their job that morning was to listen; the session was not a negotiation or anything that could be resolved by a quid pro quo. The owners decided the meeting would have to start with the tiniest of gestures:

*We'll sit side by side with the players.*

.        .        .

The night before that meeting, Jerry Jones stood in a suite at Yankee Stadium, watching the Yankees play the Houston Astros in the ALCS but also, perhaps, catching a terrifying glimpse into his future. The Cowboys are what the Yankees once were: America's most iconic team in America's most iconic—and patriotic—sport. Jones was a man at the pinnacle of his profession that chilly night, the Hall of Fame owner whose power among his peers is drawn from a relentless skill at growing the NFL's total revenues and the guile to outmuscle everyone. But those who have spoken with him sense a dull panic, as if so much of what the NFL has built—what he has built since buying the Cowboys in 1989—is eroding. Jones and his fellow owners had arrived in New York that day like heads of state, setting up shop at the Four Seasons and in their own apartments with a clear agenda: *Stop Trump from attacking our business. Find a way to persuade players to stop kneeling. Get the focus back to football.*

But the owners had far different ideas about how to accomplish such difficult goals, according to nearly two dozen interviews Outside the Lines conducted with owners, league and team executives, players, and lawyers briefed on the two days of closed-door meetings. For one thing, this was not the usual scandal or crisis the league could fight in the court system or the court of public opinion and then march away from. The game itself had come under a month-long attack by the president of the United States, with no letting up. It was also a prickly regional problem. The players' protests and the president's criticism played far differently in New England and California than they did in Texas, where Jones and Houston Texans owner Bob McNair were fielding an avalanche of complaints from outraged fans. This time, Goodell didn't have to simply manage owners' bruised egos and simmering feuds; this was a national political crisis threatening the league's business and its brand, seen through a different lens by each owner depending on his or her own political leanings and each team's fan base. It would require leadership, diplomacy and, most likely, a little luck.

Yet in many ways, the meetings would be a referendum on the same argument owners have been holding in private meetings for years: What is the NFL's identity? Is it a strict entertainment company that Jones and others envision, controlling the behavior of its players in service of its financial bottom line? Or should it attempt to transform itself into a more socially conscious league that would strive, through the forging of a rare and fragile owners-players partnership in this moment, to use its mammoth platform to try to change society for the good, even if the cost of that process, slow and complicated, would likely be measured in short-term declining popularity and lower revenues?

Some owners left the Yankees game early, seeking a good night's sleep before the meeting with the players the next morning. Jones could afford to stay out late. Goodell had personally decided which owners would attend, and he had not invited Jones. The commissioner, sources say, wanted to prevent the players-owners meeting from devolving into an argument about whether a player should be benched if he kneels—an argument that was more likely to break out if Jones attended. For his part, Jones, who declined comment for this story, didn't seem bothered. He beamed in the Yankee Stadium suite alongside his oldest son, Stephen, masking worries over what was now at stake for the NFL in 2017.

Polls show that the protest issue has resonated with millions of fans who insist all players should stand for the national anthem; some are calling for an NFL boycott and vowing to never watch another NFL game. Owners are alarmed at how rapidly fans' outrage is eroding many of the league's key business metrics, and executives at some broadcast partners have complained to owners about how the NFL lurches from crisis to crisis. A recent Morning Consult poll revealed that the NFL's net favorability has dropped to 11 percent from a high of 56 percent in May. Jones was furious that local TV ratings in Dallas were down, especially a 19 percent drop for this year's game against Green Bay, compared with last year's. "There is no question the league is suffering negative effects from these protests," he would tell reporters after the Cowboys routed the 49ers. "All times, I want to do the right thing by [NFL sponsors] and their customers. I have a great responsibility to the people who support us. . . . We all get great benefits from having a lot of us watching our games. All of us do."

Jones arrived in New York to have a good time—and to deliver a reckoning. The only question was whether his billionaire partners and Goodell would heed that reckoning.

•　　•　　•

As the historic players-owners meeting began, the players, led by retired wide receiver Anquan Boldin and Philadelphia Eagles safety Malcolm Jenkins, entered the conference room and shook the owners' hands, an uncommon occurrence at prior tension-filled joint meetings. The players took seats side by side with the owners. Goodell wanted to put the players at ease by allowing every one of their voices to be heard. The players said that they felt the owners—as a collective more than the small group in the room—were being duplicitous; they were empathetic to their concerns behind closed doors but not publicly. Fans needed to hear from owners that players who knelt or raised fists were good men who loved their country, they argued. Messages of support couldn't be delivered only inside the locker rooms. Finally, New York Jets linebacker Demario Davis stood up in the center of the room and told owners: "I'm going to break it down for you guys. You guys aren't supporting us, and until you do, there's going to be an issue."

Davis's message, and passion, seemed to relieve the tension. Atlanta Falcons owner Arthur Blank later told Davis that he'd "missed his calling" as a great public speaker. A few owners tried to separate their deep dislike of unemployed quarterback Colin Kaepernick, who started the protests a little more than a year ago, from the players' broader message: This wasn't an "anthem protest" but rather an "inequality in America" protest. Knowing that their motives and message had largely been lost in the political chaos, the players told stories of their personal connections to the military and showed a good grasp of the business problems suddenly confronting the league. Left unsaid was the warning issued on October 11 by Buccaneers defensive tackle Gerald McCoy about forcing players to stand: "I think it's gonna be an uproar if that is to happen, because you're basically taking away a constitutional right to freedom of speech."

League executives tried to show they understood the players' concerns. Several league staff members presented a three-pronged action plan: expand the My Cause, My Cleats initiative; help convene more meetings with lawmakers to ramp up lobbying for players' causes on Capitol Hill and, through the clubs, in statehouses across the country; and use the NFL's platform to promote it all. The league had scrapped a staff idea to extend an olive branch to Kaepernick—who in October filed a collusion claim against the owners—by inviting him to visit the league headquarters.

The action plan had met harsh criticism when it was first introduced inside the league office the Thursday before the owners' meetings. Anna Isaacson, the NFL's vice president of social responsibility, chief marketing officer Dawn Hudson, and others had presented the plan to Goodell and top executives, including public relations chief Joe Lockhart, chief operating officer Tod Leiweke, chief media and business officer Brian Rolapp, and general counsel Jeff Pash. Isaacson characterized the plan as a chance to seize the social moment and make an impact beyond football. There was also a request for a huge marketing budget. The league's business executives ripped it, accusing Isaacson—who had joined the NFL after working in merchandising and community relations for baseball's Brooklyn Cyclones—and Hudson of losing sight of the goal, which was to persuade all the players to stand for the anthem. The plan was "too political," they said, and would likely invite further attacks by Trump. "How could you possibly present this to owners?" one executive asked. As the proposal was discussed, Goodell remained mostly quiet but seethed because he felt the plan was uninspired.

Neither Goodell nor the business executives liked the action plan at that moment, but what worried the business executives was that Goodell was not focused on what they deemed the priority: the very real financial problems facing the NFL. Fact was, they were right. Goodell believed that all players should stand, but he and Vincent had been working with them for more than a year on their concerns, calling them individually and holding meetings, and the commissioner deeply cared about their cause.

Now, in the meeting with players, Goodell, despite his initial reservations about Isaacson's plan, supported it "full bore," an owner says. Not only that, the commissioner moved around the room to guide the conversation about its pluses. Many times he told the owners they weren't hearing the players' core arguments. "We're all in this together," Goodell told them. The players and the union executives, who have been at odds with Goodell for years, were impressed. "It was the proudest I've ever been in the NFL," one owner said later. This was Goodell leading in a manner they'd rarely seen: He was not playing a zero-sum game, he was not risk averse, and his compassion clearly lay with the players in the face of severe pressure from hard-line owners and business executives. "He did a great job because he didn't say much," Blank says. "I don't mean that in a negative way."

The players had arrived at NFL headquarters wanting to be their own voice rather than have the union speak for them. DeMaurice Smith, the players' association chief, was uncharacteristically quiet during the session, having found a way to move forward on this issue with Goodell after a private meeting at Dulles International Airport on October 3. In a similar sort of way, the players concluded that Goodell seemed to be speaking for himself more than for many owners and even the league—something that stunned them because, after all, some players privately view the commissioner as the puppet of ruthless billionaire owners. "There was sincerity on both sides," 49ers CEO Jed York says.

The meeting was going so well that even the unintentionally awkward moments were forgiven. At one point, Buffalo Bills co-owner Terry Pegula, moved by Anquan Boldin's story about his cousin being shot and killed by a police officer, complimented him on how impressive he was but kept calling him "Antwan." Then Pegula suggested that Boldin would be the perfect NFL spokesman on social issues not only because he had walked away from the game to pursue causes but because, the owner said, it couldn't be a "white owner but needs to be someone who's black."

Some people quickly glanced at one another; others looked down, cringing. But the discussion resumed, and soon the session was running so long—by ninety minutes—that nobody knew how to end it. At one point, Robert Kraft mumbled to the two Jets players seated on either side of him, "Can we just shut the f— up and end this?" Everyone on that side of the table laughed, and the optics of the Patriots owner laughing with two players from his team's rival seemed to have accomplished the mission.

But it was hard to tell if it was just optics. Shortly after one p.m., Goodell and Smith stepped out of the session to tell Lockhart and union spokesman George Atallah to craft a joint NFL-NFLPA statement, a symbol of rare cooperation.

Players were still skeptical that the owners and league executives beyond Goodell were motivated to act—a week later, Chargers tackle Russell Okung would label the league's lack of urgency "disappointing" and said the players-owners meeting appeared "unproductive at best and disingenuous at worst."

Before everyone left the room that afternoon, Davis made one last point: how important it had been that acting Jets owner Chris Johnson, the brother of Woody Johnson, now Trump's ambassador to the United Kingdom, had visited with every player in the locker room to hear their concerns.

"Guys will stand up if you hear them," Davis told the owners.

.        .        .

Two hours later, those eleven owners joined their counterparts and league executives in a third-floor conference room at the Conrad Hotel in lower Manhattan. It was uncertain and tense. Most pro-stand owners, like Dan Snyder of the Washington Redskins, had been purposefully excluded from the players' meeting.

Inside the conference room, Goodell kicked off the session by asking each of the eleven owners to give his account of the players' meeting. Nearly all offered slight variations on the same theme: *It was a very good session; the players were passionate and very impressive; we've got a lot of work to do to address their concerns and to use the NFL platform to address these difficult social, racial, and justice issues.* The mandate to stand wasn't mentioned. Goodell didn't interrupt anyone, and he summed it up by saying that the two sides were "on a good path to a partnership."

Goodell then opened the floor to discussion, and something surprising happened: Nobody debated. Jones asked a pair of benign questions about the process for Isaacson's proposal, a far different occurrence than in the committee meetings three weeks earlier when, according to an owner, he had "hijacked" the protest discussion. Owners were stunned. "OK," Goodell said, "let's move on and we'll come back to this." The meeting broke around five p.m., and many of the owners left for the night believing that the ones who hated the protests most had relented. But Goodell had purposefully tabled the discussion out of deference to Jones, giving him the evening to speak to owners and gauge the support for a league-wide mandate to stand.

·        ·        ·

At the Conrad on Wednesday, day 2 of the meetings began with most owners and team executives back inside the third-floor conference room. While league staffers reviewed mundane legal matters and pored over a PowerPoint presentation showcasing this season's declining TV ratings, a strange suspense lingered over the session, given that the anthem issue remained unresolved: What would Jerry Jones say?

By late morning, Goodell finally moved the discussion to the protests. It was a "special privileged session," with only owners plus one adviser allowed. Snyder spoke first. He said that there were real business issues at stake, and he mentioned that in his market, the defense industry and other sponsors were angry about the protests. He didn't put any dollars on it. To many in the room, Snyder's speech felt like an opening act for the headlining band.

After Snyder sat down, Jones stood and left no question that it was his floor. "I'm the ranking owner here," he said.

At first, some in the room admired Jones's pure bravado, the mix of folksy politician and visionary salesman he has perfected.

But he was angry. He said the owners had to take the business impact seriously, as the league was threatened by a polarizing issue it couldn't contain or control. To some in the room, it was clear Jones was trying to build momentum for an anthem-mandate resolution, and in the words of one owner, "he brought up a lot of fair points." Jones believed he was one of the few showing any urgency on the matter and seemed to be more frustrated that not everybody was listening than he was passionate about the mandate.

As Jones spoke, Snyder mumbled out loud, "See, Jones gets it—96 percent of Americans are for guys standing," a claim some dismissed as a grand overstatement. McNair, a multi-million-dollar Trump campaign contributor, spoke next, echoing many of the same business concerns. "We can't have the inmates running the prison," McNair said.

That statement stunned some in the room. Then Kraft, who is close friends with Trump, politely rebuked the hardliners, saying that he supported the league's marketing proposal and predicted the issue would work itself out over time. This argument seemed to find a receptive audience in the room. An unofficial count had only nine owners in favor of a mandate, though the reasons for the opposition varied: Some owners had tired of Jones always commandeering such meetings; some were jealous of his power and eager to see him go down; some saw the players-must-stand mandate as bad policy to invoke in the middle of the season; some owners were angry with Jones's hard-line public stance on kneeling, feeling that it had backed them all into a corner. "The majority of owners understand this is important to the players and want to be supportive, even if they don't exactly know how to be supportive," one owner says.

Now, suddenly, Jones found himself in an unfamiliar position: He wasn't getting his way. He knew it, and everyone knew it. Like the numerous reasons behind the protests, the business concerns were nuanced—one major sponsor had threatened to pull out if the NFL were to issue a mandate to stand. York spoke next. Though Jones and Snyder were angry with him—they felt that if he had forced Kaepernick to stand a year ago, this crisis could have been averted—York and Jeffrey Lurie of the Eagles had emerged as thoughtful leaders. Knowing that many of the players who were still kneeling were on his 49ers, York emphasized that he understood the business concerns and that each market was different and that he had been talking to his players for a long time and would continue to do so. Lurie had spoken up during the meeting, supporting the players' right to kneel.

After the owners finished, Troy Vincent stood up. He was offended by McNair's characterization of the players as "inmates." Vincent said that in all his years of playing in the NFL—during which, he said, he had been called every name in the book, including the N-word—he never felt like an "inmate."

It was starting to get nasty. Vincent and Jones had a sharp but quick back-and-forth, with Jones finally reminding the room that rather than league office vice presidents, it was he and fellow owners who had helped build the NFL's $15 billion-a-year business, and they would ultimately decide what to do. McNair later pulled Vincent aside and apologized, saying that he felt horrible and that his words weren't meant to be taken literally, which Vincent appreciated. The meetings were already running long and were ending on a raw note—and there were more agenda items to hit. For the second time in a month, a few frustrated owners grumbled about Lockhart, angry that the league was, as usual, appearing to be reactive in a public-relations sense in the face of a crippling crisis. League executives worried that during upcoming events—Veterans Day and the NFL's Salute to Service—pro-military groups might stage protests.

Goodell left the meeting room to be ushered to a news conference. The final topic of a long morning was the most salient one: the commissioner's next contract. Jones is not technically on the six-person committee that determines Goodell's compensation, but he has willed himself onto it. And so, before everyone could leave, he spoke for twenty minutes, delving into all of the league's problems that everyone knew by heart. He wanted Goodell's contract to be more incentive-based than it is. "This is the most one-sided contract ever," he said. This speech, like the one earlier in the day by him, was not vintage Jones: His usual annoying but endearing Jerryisms were replaced by a palpable urgency; it seemed to a few owners as if only Jones could see that an opportunity to regain control of the league was slipping away.

As Jones spoke, a few owners wondered what exactly had been accomplished during the week in New York. Had Goodell won? Had the players won? Had Jones lost? For most, it was enough that the owners and players had come together and that perhaps the promise of their newly formed partnership would bury the desire of some players to take a knee or raise their fists again. As a top league executive remarked when it was over, it took a president's attacks to get everyone to come together—or at least agree to keep talking, as they intend to do at the next owners-players summit, scheduled for October 31, a meeting that the players have invited Kaepernick to attend.

Just after two p.m., the New York meetings adjourned, two hours late. Owners filed out to meet in the lobby with reporters, explaining the league's baby steps toward turning "protest into progress." All of the reporters waited for Jones. A day earlier, he had tried to duck underneath a staircase at the hotel to avoid them, but about two-dozen reporters swarmed, ready to assume their common position of being his rapt audience. But Jones didn't stop walking. He searched for a way out of the hotel and hit a dead end before turning back and going down an escalator. Jones likes to talk the most when he's selling. For now, at least, he had nothing to sell. But there was a very real sense that he wasn't done fighting, not on the anthem, not on Goodell's contract, and not on his worries about the NFL's future. As he left the meeting room, Jerry Jones was silent. And then he was gone, slipping out a hotel side door and out of New York, where so much had been discussed and so little had been decided.

# Roger Goodell Has a Jerry Jones Problem

There was a pause. It was August 9, inside Roger Goodell's sixth-floor office at the NFL's Park Avenue headquarters in New York City—down the hall, past the executives' offices and his assistant's desk, and through a large, thick wooden door that is both imposing and usually left open to serve as a welcome. Goodell huddled over a speakerphone with general counsel Jeff Pash. On the other end was Jerry Jones. Adhering to the protocol of giving owners a forty-eight-hour heads-up before a major disciplinary issue involving their team is announced, Goodell and Pash informed Jones that after a thirteen-month domestic violence inquiry, the Dallas Cowboys star running back, Ezekiel Elliott, would face punishment—a six-game suspension.

The line went quiet. Seconds passed. Goodell's decision was an unconscionable violation of trust, Jones later told associates, because he believed that the commissioner had assured him this past spring that there would be no suspension. Jones saw in Elliott a genuine opportunity, a player so good that he had made Jones believe that this year he just might win a Super Bowl for the first time since 1996. His anger was palpable. Finally, according to sources with direct knowledge of the call, Jones broke the silence. He aimed his words not only at Goodell's decision but also at his role as judge, jury, and executioner in the case.

"I'm gonna come after you with everything I have," Jones said. Then he mentioned Deflategate. "If you think Bob Kraft came after you hard, Bob Kraft is a p——y compared to what I'm going to do."

Nobody knows what Jones is going to do. But at the age of fifty-eight, Goodell is fighting to keep his job. In public, he looks fresh and energetic, and he is more resolute than ever to leave with a legacy of having come close to fixing football's long-standing issues. Up close, though, his face has changed due to relentless stress; it is now sallow and lined and tired. Roger Goodell is in a battle few saw coming, with the league's membership teetering on an all-out, unprecedented civil war.

.        .        .

A little less than a week before that contentious conference call, Goodell and Jones seemed as close as ever at Glenmoor Country Club in Canton, Ohio, even as friction burned beneath the surface. Goodell was among the guests at Jones's multi-million-dollar Hall of Fame celebration inside a white tent big enough to accommodate a pair of Boeing 767 jets. Goodell knew that Elliott would be suspended, but he held off on the league announcement of it so that Jones could enjoy his moment. Goodell hugged Jones and offered his hearty congratulations as Justin Timberlake delivered a two-hour set, telling the crowd: "The greatest owner in the history of sports is being honored tonight!"

For years, America's most powerful sports owner has heaped praise on America's most powerful commissioner for being a visionary, a "grow-the-pie thinker." Jones, now seventy-five, uses a cost-benefit analysis to measure the value of many relationships, and as the NFL grew from a $6 billion-a-year to a $14 billion-a-year enterprise under Goodell, their relationship seemed strong. But then Goodell suspended Elliott, and it's only gotten nastier since, with that decision clarifying Jones's long-standing worries about Goodell's leadership, his current total annual compensation of $42 million, and the approval process for a contract extension expected to pay even more, according to documents and nearly two dozen interviews by Outside the Lines with owners, league and team executives and lawyers, and union leaders. Trust among owners and among senior executives inside the league office has all but evaporated. In early November, when Jones threatened to sue his fellow owners and the league to stop progress on Goodell's next contract, Falcons owner and compensation committee chairman Arthur Blank told Jones, "This is not how we do things in the NFL."

As the league's TV ratings and favorability polls have drifted downward this autumn, a growing number of owners have expressed their dissatisfaction with Goodell's stewardship: He has not held many executives accountable despite a long line of mishandled crises; even with tens of millions of dollars invested in new executives and consultants, Goodell still has not managed to resolve high-profile cases of player discipline without embarrassing legal battles; behind closed doors, even perfunctory policy decisions, like the posting of game highlights on Twitter, have become bitter showdowns among owners and executives. At the same time, the league has been exposed to unprecedented pressure over player protests during the national anthem that have polarized fans and players while angering sponsors and TV network partners. Even more, throughout the past few months, the war for the future of the NFL has played out uncomfortably and publicly, often through competing leaks between owners, all of which has distracted fans from the actual games.

It is a turmoil that seems new but actually began years ago in a shadow war waged inside the cloistered world of NFL offices, owners' suites, private meetings, and conference calls, rooted in very different visions, mostly by Jerry Jones and Roger Goodell, about what the NFL's future should be.

·　　·　　·

Before envisioning an NFL without Goodell, Jones needed him in it. More than a decade ago in a league meeting, Jones stood before his fellow owners and, in the words of an executive in the room, "all but begged" for a loan. The price tag had skyrocketed on his $1.3 billion AT&T Stadium, and he needed more cash from the league's G3 loan program. Jones also knew that many owners were angry with him; years earlier, he had disposed of thousands of seats at Texas Stadium and replaced them with club suites, trading revenue shareable with visiting teams' owners for money that went straight into his own pocket. So on this day, he told owners that he realized what he had done was unfair—but that he was building a stadium that would be a great showplace for the NFL and needed tens of millions in additional loans.

Goodell was silent during the meeting. Back then, he was the NFL's chief operating officer, commissioner Paul Tagliabue's number two, and the favorite of a clique of powerful owners to succeed Tagliabue. But after Jones's speech, owners approved the loan, in no small part because Goodell helped muscle the proposal through in private conversations with owners, selling them on Jones's vision of a football palace. In August 2006, Jones returned the favor. Goodell was elected commissioner, aided in part by Jones, who, along with others, twisted arms to put Goodell over his closest challenger, league attorney Gregg Levy. After Goodell won, the owners were deeply divided. Owners of the smaller-market clubs who had supported Levy worried that Goodell would leave them behind. Goodell had to find concepts that everyone could support, setting up the fight playing out today:

To fulfill the vision of Jones and others, Goodell promised to increase revenue.

To fulfill his own vision, Goodell promised to defend the brand, in his words "to protect the shield."

•　　　•　　　•

At the time, nobody saw those two agendas at odds. But almost as soon as Goodell took over, the NFL plunged into crisis, from

Michael Vick's dogfighting scandal to Spygate and Bountygate. The league's flat-footed, obfuscating response to head injuries lingered over it all. Many called for Goodell to step down, but Jones was among the owners who always publicly backed Goodell— even when he was upset with him. Jones threatened to sue the league in 2012 after being penalized $10 million in salary cap room for manipulating a contract. But in 2014, Jones publicly supported Goodell after the Ray Rice domestic violence mismanagement, Goodell's low point as commissioner. "He's acknowledged that he's mishandled this," Jones said on his Dallas radio show at the time, "and he said that he'll do better in the future."

What troubled Jones more than the crises was the way Goodell had responded. In most cases, Goodell expanded the power of the league office and broadened its scope, adding executives, many of whom are paid seven-figure salaries and given generous operating budgets. Among others, Goodell named former lobbyist Jeff Miller to oversee the league's health and safety policy in response to head injuries; former Manhattan prosecutor Lisa Friel to investigate criminal allegations in the wake of Rice; longtime sports executive Tod Leiweke in 2015 as chief operating officer to manage the new cabinet; and, in 2016, former White House spokesman and league consultant Joe Lockhart to run public relations and attempt to rehabilitate Goodell's image. Some owners, most notably Jones, quietly questioned the wisdom of such moves—especially the hiring of Friel. Before her position was established, Jones argued to owners in a closed-door meeting that creating its own law-enforcement arm might not solve the problems of the NFL and would, more likely, create a new set of them. As Steelers owner Art Rooney II says, "We've expanded staff in areas that ten or twenty years ago I probably would have never dreamt."

"Roger was trying to solve two things," former NFL attorney Jodi Balsam says. "One, cosmetic: Get people in there with the right credentials and diversity with experience to show that we are serious. It was also deeply substantive. The league needed to refresh its talent in some areas."

Jones, though, was conditioned in the spirit of Raiders owner and mentor Al Davis to never allow the league office to amass too much power. And in recent years, Jones felt that owners were being relegated to the role of mere "suggesters." One of the first times his anger over that power shift spilled out into plain view came during a league meeting in October 2015 in Manhattan. The owners were frustrated. The movie *Concussion* was about to be released, and they conceded that years of inaction and denials about football-related brain injuries had damaged the league. But more recently, owners had approved rule changes that they believed made the game safer. Some owners complained, "Why aren't we perceived as being part of the solution?"

In his deep Arkansas drawl, Jones argued that everyone was overreacting, both about the film and the fallout over head injuries.

"This is a pimple on a baby's ass," Jones said, drawing an awkward silence from the room.

The frustration of Jones and other owners continued over issues big and small. Last year, TV ratings declined, and anxiety mounted. Many owners concluded that former Pepsi executive Dawn Hudson, whom Goodell hired as the league's chief marketing officer, was providing analysis that was too optimistic. At an October 2016 league meeting in Houston, Hudson and Lockhart presented a slide that showed different variables measuring the popularity of the major sports leagues. At the top was the NFL. Various others, including Major League Soccer, were labeled "up-and-coming." At the bottom, under the category of "eroding," was the NBA, which had just signed a $24 billion TV deal with ESPN and TNT and was coming off its most watched Finals since 1998.

"Do you buy this bulls—t?" one owner said to another.

Owners wanted to hear an insider's state of the union, as the league's future depended on whether the slide reflected a temporary blip or the beginning of an alarming long-term trend. Instead, they felt they were being spun. Jones, in particular, seemed eager for a fight. And the next day, an argument erupted between Jones and other owners and league executives over the league's in-game video and social-media policy. At the time, the league tightly controlled the posting of video highlights on social media and team sites. Jones blasted the policy.

"Why are you restricting this?" Jones asked. "We're best suited to handle our content."

Patriots president Jonathan Kraft, who cochairs the digital-media committee, walked to the front of the room and defended the policy, then returned to his seat. Jones dug in again, saying, "If the league can post highlights, we should be able to post highlights."

Kraft stood up again to explain the policy. Several owners concluded that Jones didn't understand the policy's details, but it didn't matter. He was hot. Kraft left the room. Jones turned to Brian Rolapp, now the NFL's chief media and business officer, and said, "I don't know why it has to be that difficult, Brian."

The committee eventually amended the policy. But Jones now had league executives in his crosshairs, and, as he would tell associates, such matters ultimately reflected poorly on Goodell. Jones wasn't alone. Bob Kraft told associates that the league office had become "bloated." Says another owner: "Nobody knows what to expect from the league office. Who's really making decisions?"

Suspicions ran high. League officials who visited teams used to be given the red-carpet treatment; now they often were left to wait in team lobbies and quickly ushered in and out of meetings. That tension flowed into the league's Park Avenue headquarters. Despite Leiweke's efforts to play peacemaker, many of the top executives didn't and don't trust one another. They felt they were in an impossible position, taking bullets for owners, who would turn around and complain about their performances and salaries. But owners also feel that Goodell hasn't been served well, especially by Miller on player health, Lockhart on the league's overall image, and Pash on player discipline. Sensing that many of his executives are afraid of him and seem unwilling to offer objective counsel on vital issues, Goodell has become exhausted and distrusting—yet more determined to succeed. Owners grumble that, as a result, Goodell has marginalized many executive vice presidents, including Leiweke—and that they have even marginalized themselves, often leaving Goodell unsupported.

"The executives want to protect themselves by isolating Roger," one owner says. "They don't care if they burn the league down to keep their jobs."

Another owner, though, pointed out that for as sincere as Goodell seemed in his 2006 speech to owners pitching himself for commissioner—that he would "hire a great team" and "make people accountable"—he has been too loyal to most top executives, no matter how badly an issue has been handled. "His strengths and his weaknesses are kind of the same," Rooney says of Goodell. "He can be very firm in his positions, and at times that frustrates people who want to have somebody with more of an open mind."

And so Jones and other owners began to quietly ask: Are we getting the right people for what we're paying?

At the October 2016 meetings in Houston, the league was, as usual, enduring crisis. The NFL had recently suspended Giants kicker Josh Brown for only one game after domestic assault allegations, which made it appear that Goodell had not learned the hard lessons from the Ray Rice debacle. The *New York Daily News* had obtained incriminating evidence from Washington-state law-enforcement authorities that Friel, with her multi-million-dollar budget, had failed to gather. It all came to a head at the meetings. (The NFL would retroactively suspend Brown for six games the following season; the entire public relations mess was exactly what Jones and other owners and executives feared and predicted could occur from the beginning.)

On the first night of the meetings, Jones and a few other executives walked into the hotel bar shortly before midnight. Friel was there. In February and July 2016, Elliott's former girlfriend had claimed that he assaulted her on six separate days in Ohio and Florida; he had been neither arrested nor charged with any wrongdoing by the authorities in both states. Jones believed there was no case. At the bar, Friel explained to Jones that the Elliott investigation was open and would be indefinitely as she finished her job.

Jones's eyes widened, his brow furrowed. He raised his finger and wagged it in her face. "I'm saying this as an owner!" he yelled. "Your bread and butter is going to get both of us thrown out on the street!"

The bar got quiet. Everyone stared. After a minute or so, a Cowboys executive ushered Jones up to his room.

•       •       •

Several months later, at the Arizona Biltmore, during the owners' winter meetings this past March, Jones looked cocky, carrying a cocktail in the lobby—and for good reason. His power and influence were never greater. He had just helped engineer the second team relocation in fourteen months, first the Rams to Los Angeles and now the Raiders to Las Vegas—two months after being elected to the Pro Football Hall of Fame. "He's the shadow commissioner—or Roger is a puppet one," an owner said at the hotel bar.

During one meeting, Jones reminded Goodell of his impatience with the ongoing Elliott inquiry. Behind closed doors, Jones repeated to other owners that the NFL shouldn't be in the "investigative business." Jones knew many owners agreed; Bob Kraft, for example, has complained for years that the league "wastes" money on seemingly endless player-discipline investigations, including a reported $22.5 million on Deflategate. Jones also challenged Goodell's practice of punishing players who are not charged with crimes, let alone convicted.

Jones didn't mention Elliott by name, but he didn't need to.

During an executive session, Goodell left the conference room, and the topic turned to his contract, which expires in March 2019. An extension seemed like a formality; even owners who weren't pleased with Goodell's performance wanted him to lead negotiations against the union when the collective bargaining agreement expires in 2021. Jones, though, complained to fellow owners about the power vested in the six-member compensation committee that would negotiate the terms of Goodell's contract with him. Jones, who was not a committee member, said that for Goodell's next contract, all thirty-two owners should be kept apprised of all the negotiations' key developments and be given the opportunity to approve the contract's final terms.

The unspoken issue, again, was Elliott.

When Goodell returned to New York from the Biltmore, he told his deputies that he wanted the Elliott case closed by June to avoid having yet another disciplinary case against one of the NFL's stars hanging over the start of the season. Elliott's accuser and ex-girlfriend was interviewed by Kia Roberts, the NFL's newly hired director of investigations, a total of six times—twice in person and four more times on the phone. By the spring, Roberts had concluded that the accuser was not a credible witness, an opinion she conveyed to Friel.

In May, Jones asked Goodell by phone for a status update on the Elliott investigation. Jones later told several people that he came away from their conversation with an assurance that there would be no suspension for Elliott and that Goodell felt the running back should enter counseling and perhaps issue a statement showing contrition for his behavior. Jones replied that Elliott wouldn't be contrite about domestic violence because he hadn't committed it. "[Jones] told me, 'Roger told me there was nothing to worry about—the evidence just isn't there,'" says a high-level source briefed on the call. "Jerry . . . was damn sure that Zeke was free and clear."

Lockhart, the NFL spokesman, disputes that account: "Absolutely no assurances were given to Jerry by the commissioner that there would be no discipline, at any point in the process."

Later that month, the owners were set to vote on granting the six-member compensation committee, led by Arthur Blank, authority to begin negotiating Goodell's extension. To get the requisite twenty-one votes to move forward, Blank felt he needed the powerful Jones behind him. "I want you on the committee," Blank said.

"I won't go on the committee," Jones replied. "I want to be an ombudsman. I want to literally represent the owners who are not on the committee."

That position was approved. At the NFL's spring meetings in Chicago, owners—including Jones—voted unanimously to extend Goodell's contract, giving Blank, and Goodell, enormous leverage. Jones railed later that he and owners didn't spend a single minute reviewing Goodell's job performance.

Back at the league office, the Elliott investigation dragged on despite Goodell's directive to have the case wrapped up by June. Friel's 160-page report, listing Roberts as a coauthor, was dated June 6. In a highly unusual move, Friel did not include a punishment recommendation for Goodell. The NFL's chief investigator always concludes an investigative report with a recommendation for the commissioner.

It left some league executives and others close to the case baffled; some agreed with Roberts's conclusion that there were credibility questions around the accuser while others wondered whether Friel and other league executives sought a makeup call for the mishandled Josh Brown case.

.    .    .

After the report was written, Goodell met with Friel, Pash, and several other league executives. Roberts, however, did not attend. At Friel's recommendation, Goodell convened a four-person panel of advisers to consider the evidence collected in the Elliott matter, hear from Elliott himself, and make recommendations—proof, a league source says, that Goodell never had assured Jones that Elliott was in the clear. And so, on June 26 in the NFL offices, the advisory group reviewed witness statements, medical records, and text messages exchanged by Elliott, his accuser, and others. The panel questioned Friel, but again, Roberts was not invited and didn't have a chance to express her opinion. Friel later testified that she did not know whose decision it was not to invite Roberts. "I've never seen a situation when a league office takes an official position in federal court that they are willfully blind to key facts in their own process and owners tolerate it," says Jeffrey Kessler, the attorney for the players. "Everybody now knows that they suppressed the findings of their own investigation—and kept their chief investigator on the sidelines—to get the result that they wanted."

During the session, former U.S. attorney Mary Jo White asked Friel what she had concluded about the credibility of Elliott's accuser. Friel said she found the accuser not credible on one occasion but credible overall; however, Friel did not bring up the credibility concerns raised by her investigator, Roberts. Under questioning by Kessler, Friel described Roberts's concerns about the accuser's credibility.

For her part, Friel has privately told colleagues that despite the resources at her disposal—the Elliott case has cost an estimated $2 million and counting—she was hamstrung without subpoena power. Her worst fears, and Jones's, were coming true. Still, Goodell gave considerable weight to the opinions of the panelists, who unanimously concluded that Elliott deserved to be punished.

Jones didn't know that Goodell was changing his mind. And he didn't know that Goodell was facing pressure both from a handful of league executives who felt Elliott should be suspended and from owners wanting Jones to be humbled. Kraft had called Goodell in the summer and, referring to the Elliott case, told the commissioner, "My guy got four games for footballs and there's still nothing on this?"

Just before the Cowboys training camp opened in Oxnard, California, Jones told reporters on July 23 there was "absolutely nothing" to the domestic violence accusations against Elliott, a refrain he repeated several days later during Hall of Fame activities. And on August 9, Blank's compensation committee convened a dinner meeting in Manhattan to discuss Goodell's contract; Jones attended via phone. During the session, Jones did not raise any concerns about Goodell's contract extension, sources say.

The next day, Blank called Goodell, telling the commissioner that Jones had participated in the meeting. That's when Goodell told Blank, "He's not going to be too happy with me tomorrow," explaining that Elliott's suspension was coming.

On August 11, Goodell announced the six-game suspension of Elliott. Jones saw it as a "complete betrayal," a source now says. "An overcorrection" by Goodell, Jones later called it publicly. Privately, Jones seethed to confidants that Goodell hadn't studied the case's many details, and he considered suing the NFL to get the suspension overturned. "Roger blew off his own investigator's conclusion—it's just patently unfair," Jones told a confidant, a charge that a league source denies. Jones had turned on Goodell, perhaps for good. An ESPN report in mid-September detailed that Jones was impeding progress on Goodell's contract extension. And then, at league meetings a month later, Jones took over a meeting about Goodell's contract, irritating his colleagues by calling himself, more than once, the "ranking owner" and adding, "I'm going to be a pain in the ass" to committee members.

Lockhart has insisted that Roberts's recommendation that she did not believe Elliott should be suspended had been communicated to Goodell. But on October 30, at another hearing over Elliott's suspension before U.S. District Judge Katherine Polk Failla, NFL lawyer Paul Clement suggested that it didn't matter because of the broad authority Goodell has over player discipline. Failla asked, "Would it not have assisted [Goodell] in determining whether punishment were appropriate to hear from the very person that had been tasked with interviewing this very key witness?"

"I don't know that it would," Clement replied.

To Jones and to Elliott's lawyers, Clement's position was proof that Goodell had failed to obtain a critical fact before handing down punishment—permissible under the CBA but fundamentally unfair to Elliott. It didn't matter: On November 9, Elliott's six-game suspension was upheld by a federal appeals court, sending him to the sideline, after more than two months of appeals, and escalating the anger and determination of the league's most powerful owner.

·      ·      ·

A long-held assumption has been that Goodell wants another long-term deal. Those who have discussed the contract situation with him have described him as "furious" and "emboldened" at the notion of accepting a deep pay cut after making the owners a lot of money over the years, watching their teams' valuations skyrocket, and taking many bullets for them. ESPN has reported that he asked in August for a compensation package of about $49 million a year, if every incentive is met, plus use of a private jet for life and health care for life for his family. But most owners expect him to land in the range of $40 million a year. If owners decide to squeeze him too hard, he might walk away. He knows that there's no clear successor, which is both a failing on his part and a source of leverage.

The owners, though, have considered other successors. A confidant of one owner reached out to gauge whether Adam Silver, the NBA commissioner, would be interested in running the NFL, to which Silver immediately said no. Owners have also considered looking to the International Olympic Committee for someone with global experience to grow the game—or even installing the seventy-six-year-old Tagliabue for a year while a committee searched for the ideal successor. Jones has told confidants that he has his own candidate in mind, which Jones has publicly denied. Few owners are interested in allowing Jones to essentially handpick the next commissioner. Even so, Jones has vowed, sources say, to make Goodell's life miserable. "Jerry's message to Roger was 'I run this league. You better get with it,'" a senior league executive says. "This is about power and control, not the contract. That's all white noise."

That's why, no matter how often some team executives say not to underestimate Jones, and no matter how frustrated many owners are with the state of the league, the support to remove Goodell doesn't seem to be there. Jones has the Redskins' Dan Snyder and a handful of other owners on his side; there are a dozen or so owners who just want to extend Goodell and get the story out of the headlines; and the rest don't approve of Goodell's performance not because they agree with Jones but because they believe Goodell has empowered him to a fault, especially given the ugly situation with two relocated franchises drawing small crowds in Los Angeles. "Switching commissioners is like switching from an iPhone to a Samsung," one ownership source says. "Do my pictures transfer? Do my contacts? Does my music? In the end, why take the risk?"

It's Goodell who now seems more willing to take risks, as if he realizes he has less to lose than before. He defied many owners, including Jones, and many league business executives by refusing to back a mandate that all players stand for the national anthem. His relationship with the union and some players has improved this fall; he is not merely serving as the puppet of the owners, as players have long suspected. A day after Outside the Lines reported that, in an owners-only meeting in New York, Texans owner Bob McNair said, "We can't have the inmates running the prison," McNair released a statement insisting that he was referring to league executives as inmates, not the players, drawing skepticism. According to sources, McNair asked Goodell to publicly back him up. Goodell refused.

If Goodell does re-sign, nobody knows exactly how long he will serve. "There's always a risk that people stay too long, and I don't want to be in that category," he said at a Bloomberg conference in early November. Some of the tension, sources say, has been over a severance package that could approach $100 million—should either Goodell or the owners choose to end the contract early. Few owners want a new commissioner before the expiration of the CBA in 2021; any replacement would have to repair the damaged relationship with the players' union by giving away concessions that the owners prize. Goodell is already beginning to duplicate his most valuable contribution to the 2011 CBA deal: unifying the owners en masse against the union. Pash has advised the owners in meetings to prepare for a bloody and bitter battle in four years—a fitting possible capstone to the tumultuous Goodell era. "I'm here for you through that," Goodell has told some owners. "After that, you guys should start having a conversation."

•     •     •

On a Sunday afternoon in mid-November, three days after Elliott began serving his suspension, Jerry Jones walked onto the field at Mercedes-Benz Stadium in Atlanta for a game between his Cowboys and Arthur Blank's Falcons. Blank stood about twenty yards from Jones. The anger and suspicion were unmistakable. It had been only a few days since Blank effectively fired Jones as compensation committee ombudsman, after Jones, through an attorney, accused him of misleading owners about the details of Goodell's extension, a charge Blank denied. After he was removed, Jones told Blank, "You're making a big mistake."

Nothing more needed to be said on game day. It is customary for the owner of the home team to greet the owner of the visiting team, but as this fall has revealed, this is not a season for tradition. The two men never spoke, opting instead in the coming days for power plays on letterhead: Blank's compensation committee accused Jones of "conduct detrimental to the league's best interests"; Jones asked for a special owners-only meeting to discuss Goodell's new deal.

A few hours after the 27–7 Falcons rout, Jones emerged from the Cowboys locker room, looking drained but sounding defiant. Even some of his closest advisers aren't on board with the war he is raging. In a black suit and black cowboy boots, Jones found himself in the middle of a mob of cameras and reporters. He spoke quietly, saying that he wanted to "do everything I can" to help the league improve and that "this is one of those times" when "you need to adjust." He was asked, point-blank, whether he thought Goodell should continue as commissioner.

"I'm not going to discuss that right now," Jones said.

A few minutes later, he moved down a long hallway at the bottom of the stadium, surrounded by four security guards. He walked with a slight limp. He said nothing. Everyone cleared out of his way, and when he exited the stadium into a cold and stiff wind, a crowd of Cowboys fans lining a fence cheered. Jones stopped, and for a moment he seemed unsure of where to go: right toward the fans or left toward the limo? Jones stood, a man alone in so many ways. He turned left, away from the fans. The cheering ceased. The idling limo pulled away. A gate was raised, opening a route out of the stadium. A police escort flared its siren, and Jones was off, with nobody knowing exactly how far he'll go.

## BuzzFeed News

*In these columns for* BuzzFeed
News, *Bim Adewunmi explores the
intersection of race and culture.
Whether addressing the ideology
of white supremacy ("Even where
it does not actively kill, it commits
smaller, more insidious crimes, too.
It belittles and dismisses humanity
and accomplishment, and it does
so by using words that appear to
be innocent of illogical animus,"
she writes in "Maria Sharapova's
Rivalry with Serena Williams Is in
Her Head)" or celebrating Oprah
Winfrey's career as an actor
("Oprah appears to revel in
highlighting the overlooked stories
of black women. . . . Her oeuvre is
an exploration of the many facets
of that identity, and over the last
thirty years, she has crafted a
surprisingly strong body of work"),
Adewunmi's work is, as the
Ellie judges said, "engaging,
informative, and steeped in
history." A self-described
"Londoner in NY," Adewunmi
writes for the* Guardian *as well as*
BuzzFeed.

Bim Adewunmi

# How the Oscar Flub Demonstrates the Limits of Black Graciousness *and* How Oprah Got Her Acting Groove Back *and* Maria Sharapova's Rivalry With Serena Williams Is in Her Head

## How the Oscar Flub Demonstrates the Limits of Black Graciousness

Grace, we are told—specifically God's grace—comes free of charge. It is available to all, with only a few entirely reasonable terms and conditions. This kind of grace elevates us and allows us to go about our days being productive members of the human family. And we get to extend that grace to the next person we meet, by being gracious in turn.

But grace and graciousness can also be a burden.

On Sunday night at the Academy Awards ceremony, an envelope flub created one of the most memorable fuckups in Oscars history, in which the Best Picture award was wrongly announced as belonging to *La La Land*, before being given to its rightful owner, *Moonlight*. Barry Jenkins, *Moonlight*'s director, came up to that stage with the rest of his *Moonlight* family and delivered a speech from his gut—a reaction to an absurd turn of events, a moment that if not stolen was slightly marred (a win's a win even if your face is streaked in mud and your muscles ache, but wouldn't it have been nice to arrive at the finish line drenched in nothing but honest sweat?). Jenkins had prepared a speech, but on live television, he said: "Very clearly, even in my dreams this could not be true. But to hell with dreams!" Later, tweets and editorial copy declared producer Jordan Horowitz a heroic "truth teller" because he did the correct thing and ended *La La Land*'s borrowed time on the stage, and thus the story centered on his perceived grace, rather than *Moonlight*'s historic win.

There is almost nothing pedestrian we will not assign as a superhuman sacrifice if it is embodied by a white person.

And *Variety*'s post-Oscars issue, traditionally with a cover star from the night's big winner (over the last few years directors and a cinematographer have been the chosen ones), featured Best Director winner Damien Chazelle alongside Barry Jenkins, the director of the year's Best Picture. Seeing the cover line—"Amazing Grace"—I wonder to whom it is referring: Jenkins or Chazelle? Its purpose was seemingly to convey a narrative of solidarity, in an industry in which that value seems like a rare commodity, but who is the default beneficiary of that solidarity? Co–editor in chief Claudia Eller's letter introducing the issue says the shared cover idea came from Chazelle's camp "in the eleventh hour." Her letter went on to note "the humility and humanity displayed by the film's producers" after the envelope mix-up was revealed.

On Tuesday, after the cover image was released, Jenkins replied to an exasperated tweet from MTV News writer Ira Madison III, saying that he was "the guest" here, and while I would never presume to speak for him regarding his thought process in writing that tweet, I can't help but consider what the word "guest" means in general, and also in this specific context, and how gracious Barry Jenkins is being. Many of us are unfailingly gracious, all the time, and to be fair, this is sometimes unsolicited (but somehow still expected). In thinking about all of this, I feel a little tired. It's nice to be nice. But it is also a burden, this grace and graciousness. And some days it weighs heavier than others.

Michelle Obama's incredibly succinct and quotable election-season sound bite "when they go low, we go high" is something of a double-edged sword. On the one hand, we have that grace, the kind that elevates us to a relatively higher plane of existence, where transgressions are borne and shaken off so we can continue to glide through life. But in reality, the most apt retort to that well-meaning and almost superhuman exhortation came from writer Kashana Cauley: "When they go low, we lower the bar."

Which is not to say that *La La Land* was somehow "going low" as a side effect of its mere existence. The narrative around mediocrity and white supremacy in the larger culture was sometimes clumsily foisted upon the film, in the same way *Moonlight*'s explicit blackness and queerness placed it in a specific location within the viewing public's minds. The two films duked it out during awards season, picking up various accolades—the American Film Institute, Critics Choice Awards, the Golden Globes, the London Film Critics' Circle Awards, and so on—and in doing so, took on far more symbolism than either needed to carry.

I loved both films. Their accomplishments, both in the actual delivery of movie magic and prowess in hoovering up awards, has only made me love them more. But they were placed into an oddly pat narrative, in which to love one was to despise the other. It was a burden added to the already weighty load atop *Moonlight*'s shoulders: In addition to being a story about a black boy and his coming of age and sexuality, *Moonlight* became a needed underdog in a new cultural narrative. It's a good thing it's a stunning, genuinely beautiful film in its own right, otherwise it would've completely disappeared under the various new mantles it was suddenly forced to bear.

The destinies of *Moonlight* and *La La Land* will forever be intertwined; expect every lazy trivia quizmaster to chuck this twosome into pub quizzes until the end of parlor games. And because history's first pressing happens directly in the moments after the event, many of us will see a graciousness where we should have seen a clear case of honest responsibility.

Calling a halt to the celebratory speeches the producers of *La La Land* had begun making and ceding the floor to the *Moonlight* cast and crew was simply *the right thing to do*. No more, no less. It required very little beyond an understanding of right and wrong, a lesson many of us learn very early on in life. There was no need to hand out rewards for grace, celestial or earthbound. And none were *required* from those involved with *Moonlight*.

Facts matter. On Oscar night, *Moonlight* was judged to be the better film. Barry Jenkins is a brilliant director who made a masterpiece. His place on the cover of *Variety* in any context is earned for sure, and never just as a "guest." Graciousness is appreciated (it is a "want," not a "need"), but it was not necessary. That the incredible win for *Moonlight*—a film about black gay love, black masculinity, blackness in microcosm and writ large, cowritten and directed by a black man—will forever be linked to *La La Land* and misplaced graciousness is a damn shame.

# How Oprah Got Her Acting Groove Back

Oprah Winfrey is like space, which is to say she is all around us: familiar enough that we can rattle off her greatest hits with ease (talk show! book club! a whole network!), yet for all that familiarity, she remains vastly unknowable. Being beamed directly into our homes via her eponymous show for twenty-five years means she should be quotidian, but seeing her onscreen as an actor uncurls a mild thrill in the belly. That's because there's still something exotic about Oprah Winfrey the actor. Every role she takes on—choices that reflect both her personal power and the very specific identity of black American womanhood—reveals a new layer and adds to our understanding of her as a person, a performer, and a cultural icon.

Never mind actual acting talent, Oprah's greatest gift has been the ability to sniff out the most interesting enterprises that are simultaneously the best possible exhibition of her own skills. Both as a behind-the-scenes producer and in her onscreen performances, there is a stunningly clear throughline in her projects, and what we know of her suggests this is by design rather than mere serendipity. One thing is for certain: Oprah appears to revel in highlighting the overlooked stories of black women. When viewed as a grand mosaic, her oeuvre is an exploration of the many facets of that identity, and over the last thirty years, she has crafted a surprisingly strong body of work: culturally important, critically acclaimed, and often hugely profitable. Perhaps cutting through the hundreds of projects that have been waved under her nose over three decades of sustained bankability has honed her focus into something laserlike. And given the power she wields as a producer, the temptation to cast herself in vanity projects must be huge, but her choices have largely been unimpeachable.

As a TV host, Oprah's job was a peculiar one. For many white Americans, she was a sort of remote "interesting black friend"—they could look to her to talk about weight loss; discuss the regular, petty (or serious) dramas of families; or have an impromptu book club meeting about the latest nationwide best-seller. Oprah was one of the cultural forces that introduced and helped normalize the language of therapy in the everyday lives of Americans in the 1990s: Her plush couch may as well have been situated in a posh therapist's office, her show your weekly appointment. Perhaps inevitably over the years, she morphed into something more than just a "friend" and became something more akin to a caretaker. A desexualisation, not uncommon for black women who are older, had occurred.

But to be clear, in the public's imagination, Oprah was almost never *fully* a mammy, rather, she was just a tad . . . magical. Her first few screen acting roles—most notably *The Color Purple* and *The Women of Brewster Place*—were specifically of wives and mothers for whom life was a slog, under the thumb of toxic patriarchy in some form or another. A viewer might find it hard to see beyond the pain of these women (whose survival was sometimes only barely eked out) in her early roles.

By contrast, starting with the 1998 adaptation of Toni Morrison's Pulitzer Prize–winning *Beloved*, Oprah's latter choices have been strikingly complex, a master class in leaning the fuck in to ever more knotty, often corrective iterations of black womanhood. In this period, Oprah may play downtrodden or troubled or angry. But the characters she has chosen to portray, on both big and small screen, are crucially fully rendered—acutely drawn and compassionately written human beings allowed to feel the full gamut of emotional life. Whether as an animated mother (*The Princess and the Frog*), a black-sheep truth teller (*Greenleaf*), or a civil rights activist (*Selma*), Oprah has been quietly carving out a stellar acting career. And as she takes on the role of Deborah Lacks in a new HBO film based on Rebecca Skloot's *The*

*Immortal Life of Henrietta Lacks*, she's making a point: Oprah Winfrey's second-wind acting career, like much of her work over the last three decades, is a quiet revolution.

•        •        •

Oprah's acting career started with a bang. Her first big screen role at age thirty-two was uncommonly successful, as Sofia in the 1985 Steven Spielberg adaptation of Alice Walker's Pulitzer- and National Book Award–winning masterpiece *The Color Purple*. Oprah's first appearance onscreen was iconic: "All my life I had to fight," she tells Celie (Whoopi Goldberg) in a still-powerful scene in a film full of them, resisting the violence her husband visits on her. All the way through the movie, Sofia's broken spirit is manifested in her blank expression, Oprah's performance indelible. She was nominated for both a Golden Globe and an Academy Award for best supporting actress for this debut (she was not the only one snubbed; the film didn't win a single one of its eleven nominations).

That adaptation of Walker's novel would be the start of a fruitful relationship between Oprah and icons of African American literature. In 1986, with an Oscar nomination already secured for her last role, Oprah took on the role of Bigger Thomas's mother in an adaptation of Richard Wright's (now much-maligned) novel *Native Son*. Despite some plaudits for her performance, the film got a mixed critical response. (Roger Ebert's review quoted a 1961 foreword to the book, written by Richard Sullivan, that essentially described it as "unbearable" and added: "So it was, so it remains.") Only a couple of months before the release of the film, in September 1986, *The Oprah Winfrey Show* had gone national. It would go on to become the highest-rated talk show in the history of American television—a feat that would be a distraction from a solid acting career, no matter how great the desire to pursue one.

Three years later, in 1989, Oprah made her first foray into producing a literary adaptation. Harpo Productions chose the 1983 National Book Award winner *The Women of Brewster Place*, by Gloria Naylor. She starred as Mattie in both the original miniseries and a spinoff sequel, the rapidly cancelled *Brewster Place*—two overwhelmingly black casts, and noticeably female with it, telling black stories without much of an inherent white gaze to pervert their course. Oprah followed up *Brewster Place* with voice acting, playing formerly enslaved woman Elizabeth Keckley, a confidante to Mary Todd Lincoln, in *Lincoln* (1992), before another book adaptation, this time about an inner-city black family living in Chicago's West Side, *There Are No Children Here*. Costarring alongside Maya Angelou (who played her mother) and Keith David, Oprah was praised for her performance, with the *LA Times* TV critic Ray Loynd describing it as "her most serious role since *The Color Purple*." But her acting career stalled at this point, a consequence, perhaps, of the astonishing growth and global reach of *The Oprah Winfrey Show* in the nineties. "I love the idea of acting [and] have always wanted to be an actress but got diverted with a little day job of a talk show," as she told Charlie Rose in 1998.

By the time we saw her play Ellen Degeneres's therapist on *Ellen*'s iconic "The Puppy Episode" in 1997, the Oprah we were seeing was the one we'd come to know by that point: a talk-show host with a pseudo-therapist facade. The *Ellen* producers could not have cast the role better. A supporting role in a TV movie, *Before Women Had Wings* (1997), followed the *Ellen* guest spot, before Oprah's movie role in 1998 marked a stark turning point in the kind of project that would define her ongoing acting career. *Beloved*, her most ambitious project, was based yet again on an era-defining work by an African American author.

·   ·   ·

Oprah's second wind as an actor actually started more than a decade before it began. Even before Morrison was awarded the Pulitzer Prize for *Beloved* in 1987, Oprah had the foresight to purchase the rights. "I had no idea how you make a movie," she told Rose in the same 1998 interview, "but I felt that it should be a movie." The film adaptation, which was directed by Academy Award winner Jonathan Demme, was a coproduction of Harpo Films, a subsidiary of her Harpo Productions; no one can lock a property down quite like Oprah can. Her self-belief was unshakeable, even with her relative inexperience. In the same Rose interview, she said: "I didn't question what Jonathan (Demme) questioned, and what Toni (Morrison) questioned—whether I could lose the persona of 'Oprah Winfrey.'"

The story of Sethe, a formerly enslaved woman who literally slits her child's throat to spare her a life of enslavement, is Morrison's masterwork. In telling Sethe's story, the film did a rare thing, centering the narrative of a black American woman and following her life through its various fault lines. Surrounded by a cast of veterans, including her previous costar Danny Glover and Thandie Newton along with newcomer Kimberly Elise, Oprah's Sethe was a quietly moving character, fierce and deeply human. While reviews were largely positive, the film underperformed at the box office, as she told Al Roker in a 2013 interview: "*Beloved* was not a successful box office hit—I went into a depression afterwards."

In *The Princess and the Frog* (2009), she played Eudora, a mother of a different sort of intensity, selling a version of the American Dream to Princess Tiana (Anika Noni Rose). It is somewhat easy to dismiss it as yet another "wife or mum" role but in a movie like *Frog*, with its focus on a black female character, the presence of a black mother—however fleeting—is worth noting. And when considered in the context of the Disneyverse, with its weird and enduring motherlessness, Oprah's small role in the film is something close to revolutionary.

Away from her voice work (she also played Coretta Scott King in *Our Friend, Martin* in 1999, which again falls into that therapeutic zone of warm and familiar), Oprah's gift is her look. She has a malleable face (you can see it showcased in the many reaction GIF memes she features in), and the feeling is that she has played women who seem far older than she herself is. Part of this is the physicality required of the roles she has taken on: If you're playing an exhausted mother of young children or an assertive woman who, over the course of a life, is ultimately defeated by life's cruelties, then the movie *is going to make sure your very mien matches that*. But it's also worth noting audiences' propensity to perceive black womanhood (in real life and onscreen) through a splintered lens—associating older, plus-size, and desexualised "caring" roles with black women.

At sixty-three, it is instructive to view Oprah's most recent choices alongside other Hollywood actors in the same age bracket. A consideration of the traditional trajectory of female actors of a certain age hardly reveals a post-sixties boom time—unless you're Meryl Streep or Jessica Lange, who are very much outliers. By the time you add in the fact that black Hollywood actresses are hit even worse than their white counterparts when it comes to their industry's sexism and ageism, it all makes a weird sort of sense.

In Ava DuVernay's *Selma* (2014), the role of Annie Lee Cooper, the civil rights activist who famously punched back after being goaded by Alabama sheriff Jim Clark, was an obvious slam dunk for Oprah. Her decision to play Cooper is not hard to decipher—in choosing to tell her story, DuVernay reinserts the missing and overlooked women of the movement, and it aligns perfectly with Oprah's own unofficial interests, namely highlighting storied African American history and playing a character of substantial cultural heft while doing so. Her portrayal is a fine one—Oprah's Cooper comes across as a woman forced to bow to inhumane policy until she can no longer do so: exactly as Oprah intended. Unsurprisingly, she coproduced the film.

Oprah played another woman with a front seat to the unfolding of history in Lee Daniels's *The Butler* just the year before. Gloria Gaines is a rare Oprah performance, in that she finally gets to play sexy—her nails tapered and painted red, her brows sharply drawn, her lashes thick with falsies—and sexual: When we first see Gloria, she is enabling the shooing away of her son so she can kiss up on her husband Cecil (Forest Whitaker), and it is implied throughout that the fires burned all the way to the line. Gloria's hair and fashions change, as the movie moves over the decades—a sleek bob becomes a beehive, which turns into an afro before morphing into the big waves of the eighties. Inevitably, all that buoyancy is later weighed down by family discord, sharp fragments of American life, and drink, and Oprah delivers a fluent performance. In a role that requires a lot of heavy lifting, she bends at the knees admirably, earning herself supporting actress nominations at both the BAFTAs and SAG Awards.

Her role in the Oprah Winfrey Network drama *Greenleaf,* about an African American Southern church-rooted family and its many secrets, could be a sort of parallel existence to Gloria's. As Mavis McCready, a bar owner and relative wild child compared to her sister, bishop's wife Lady Mae, she is worldly in a way that sits well on Oprah. She is tough, soft, and warm as required and, in appearing alongside fellow *Brewster Place* alum Lynn Whitfield (also aged sixty-three, Whitfield's career offers a useful companion comparison to her costar's), provides a thrilling retort to the pat narrative of the "revolution" in women's roles on television—when was the last time you saw two black women over sixty share screen time?

The inherent glamour and wealth of Mavis and the Greenleaf family is totally absent in HBO's upcoming *The Immortal Life of Henrietta Lacks,* the true story of an African American woman whose cancer cells were taken during a biopsy at Johns Hopkins Hospital in 1951 and have been at the forefront of medical breakthroughs ever since. As Deborah, the youngest daughter of

Henrietta, Oprah gives a nervy, often emotive performance as she is forced to reckon with her (justified) paranoia while trying to let go just enough to learn the truth about her family. With a cane to assist her walking, an ever-present "WWJD" lanyard, and a "Ghana Must Go" bag stuffed with her mother's closely guarded medical records, Oprah's Deborah is a regular African American woman, forced to take a losing role in a symbolic narrative wider and far older than she is. At one point, Deborah cheekily encourages reporter Rebecca Skloot, who is getting answers where she herself had previously stumbled. "Go 'head on, girl. Keep on being white," she says with a knowing smile, and you smile back at her, aware of the historical significance behind her joke.

It's uncanny how a literal billionaire can so easily embody "one of us" but Oprah does it again and again; she's playing only slightly younger than her years this time (Deborah Lacks was sixty when she died suddenly, of a heart attack), and her hair and makeup is reflective of a life Oprah has not had to live in decades.

·　　　·　　　·

Here is the considered, cold oatmeal take: Oprah Winfrey is a *good* actor. The intention in that statement is not to damn with faint praise but to highlight a fact that is sometimes too easy forget, given her outsize influence and image in the popular consciousness. Her acting debut at thirty-two was *Oscar-nominated*, and she has been turning in solid work, on and off, for literally decades. Oprah herself is straight on her ability, as she told Rose: "I know inside myself I'm an actor. I always wanted to be an actress and I know that I can do that."

She appears refreshingly without vanity, and the very thing that made her famous—that empathy, that ability to tap into the universal human frequency—is also what makes her so effective as an actor. That you feel compelled to watch her when she's onscreen may have to do with the ease of familiarity. But it's also more than that. Her face, already interesting in its composition, has become something more at this stage of life—more open, capable of telling entire stories in a few muscle movements. She engaged the services of an acting coach (who'd previously worked with Tom Cruise, Diddy, and Nicole Kidman) at the suggestion of Lee Daniels, her *Butler* director—"It's an instrument," he told her, "and you haven't picked up the instrument in what, seventeen years?"

But even before this, she has been using her body like her pro, yet another tool to tell stories, and it is the body of a middle-aged black woman, a body that viewers are perhaps not used to seeing all that often. So you look, and you keep looking.

That Oprah is buttressed by institutional power is a welcome plus and arguably *necessary*, even in 2017. She takes full advantage of the behind-the-scenes power in her Harpo Films and OWN-running hands—power that just isn't the norm in Hollywood, where even bankable actors are sometimes treated like barely sentient props. *The Immortal Life* is a Harpo Films coproduction, and there was evidence of Oprah's own personal hiring power on *Greenleaf*: On a first-season episode, I was thrilled to note the name of director Donna Deitch in the opening credits, thirty years after she and Oprah worked together on *The Women of Brewster Place*. In an industry where women are still playing catch-up, it really does help to have a producer with institutional memory on your side.

But while it may be difficult to divorce her acting career from her other interests, the core of Oprah Winfrey: Actor is not just about her producing power. In Sofia and Sethe and Gloria and Annie and Mavis and now Deborah, Oprah is telling specific stories, over and over. These are people we rarely get to see onscreen, and so they do not feel like arbitrary choices. More than ever, Oprah appears to be settling fully into her acting career.

The second stage of her career is calculated and precise, and at least from the outside, seems to represent a woman keen to break free of the still-too-narrow strictures placed on black women in and out of Hollywood. She is no longer *just* America's therapist—instead she is (almost) just another citizen, only one with uncommon power and reach, as well as a good deal of cultural discernment. In this half of her acting career, these roles—in *Selma*, in *Greenleaf*, in her turns in the upcoming *A Wrinkle in Time* adaptation and Daniels's *Terms of Endearment* remake— seem less about appeasing mainstream America and far more about a performer flexing her wings and seeing what she can do to claim cultural and ideological space for herself but also, by extension, for black women in America and beyond.

# Maria Sharapova's Rivalry with Serena Williams Is in Her Head

The language of racism has long been a slippery thing. It maneuvers like a greased pig, sliding out of the grasp of those who would like to hold it up as egregious, and runs along merrily, dodging responsibility all the while. It is how we got to calling for "law and order" and how we get away with calling for the annihilation of "thugs" in political speeches on both sides of the aisle. It is how a section of us gets to say with a straight face, "I'm not racist" and truly believe it. "Where was the N-word?" people will ask, obtusely. At this point, it doesn't need to be present to make itself felt.

The ideology of white supremacy ends lives, as the evidence of hundreds of years attests. But even where it does not actively kill, it commits smaller, more insidious crimes, too. It belittles and dismisses humanity and accomplishment, and it does so by using words that appear to be innocent of illogical animus.

In reading excerpts from Russian tennis player Maria Sharapova's new memoir, *Unstoppable*, it would be reasonable to see the reality of her situation: an athlete humiliated and angered by a far superior opponent over the years. But there is also an inescapable undercurrent of bitterness that relies on something more sinister when it comes to discussing the number-one player in women's tennis, Serena Williams.

"First of all," Sharapova writes, "[Williams's] physical presence is much stronger and bigger than you realize watching TV. She has thick arms and thick legs and is so intimidating and strong." Focusing on people's bodies is par for the course in sports—there are inescapable requirements to do what athletes do. And the fact of the matter is that Serena Williams *is* strong. You have to be, to be perhaps the best athlete in the world, pound for pound. But Sharapova's description has nothing to do with Serena's world-straddling skill and ability. It is about setting her up as "other," as superhuman (but in the detrimental way that curls into itself and reemerges as subhuman) and therefore unfair and unworthy to be in that space, on that court.

Thick arms and thick legs (coded as masculine) in addition to being intimidating ("I felt threatened, officer") and strong (read: *too* strong, ergo masculine)? Well, that's too much. *How could I, a slender blonde, be expected to play against this, and win?* Never mind that at six-feet-two-inches, Maria Sharapova stands a clean five inches above Serena Williams's five-feet-nine-inch frame. Sharapova painted a shorthand cultural picture we have come to understand very well, in which a dainty white lady is menaced by a hulking black specter. It's fake news. Misogynoir both coded and explicit. But the facts are meaningless here because this narrative is too compelling.

The Williams sisters, and Serena especially, are no strangers to having their bodies and ability discussed in othering ways over the years. In 2012, Danish tennis player Caroline Wozniacki "impersonated" Serena at an exhibition match in Brazil by stuffing the front of her top and the back of her skirt with towels. (Novak Djokovic's done similar, as has Andy Roddick.) Serena's response to her friend Caroline's action was to say she doubted there was anything racist about the actions (various publications lined up to tell concerned readers emphatically that it was not racist), but, in an e-mail to *USA Today*, she added, "I must add if people feel this way she should take reason and do something different next time."

Both Williams sisters have been likened to men for the absolute power of their serves, and due to that style of play, they are rarely afforded credit for playing with nuance or strategic tactics. In 2014, the president of the Russian tennis federation, Shamil Tarpischev, called the sisters "the Williams brothers" and "scary." A year earlier, after losing to Serena at the French Open finals, Sharapova had stated it baldly. "[Serena] has no pressure going in and serving and being up a break at 5–4, and serving harder than David Ferrer when he gets to the final of Roland Garros," Sharapova said in the after-match press conference. "I mean, I think if I was built like Serena I hope I'd be able to hit a big serve like that, too."

Remember: There are five inches of air between Sharapova and Williams, and the latter is five years older, in a sport where age is a liability and precocious wunderkinder are fetishized. (Sharapova was one; she ascended into international stardom at the age of seventeen, when she beat Serena at the Wimbledon final in 2004, one of only two times this has happened.) Lastly, I urge you to remember that between Williams and Sharapova, only one has been the recipient of a two-year ban for using the banned substance meldonium. That was Sharapova. In an interview with *Net-A-Porter* magazine, Sharapova brings up her decision to include the ban in her memoir. "I talk about it with a lot of vulnerability and rawness. How it made me feel; how I felt like the world looked at me; how I felt so small. For a woman who's tall and powerful—an athlete—it was a very distant feeling."

The dog whistle was deafening. *I am playing by the rules, and she is not.* Except Serena is. She always has. She's simply *better*.

.   .   .

The narrative of the alleged Williams-Sharapova rivalry was orchestrated by fate, in which a young upstart unseats the more established incumbent, as Sharapova did to Williams at Wimbledon in 2004. But what happened after that match failed to truly live up to that setup. A true rivalry would suggest a more balanced stats board than their match history *actually* gives us. Look at McEnroe and Borg (7–7), or Evert and Navratilova (37–43). Hell, even S. Williams and V. Williams (17–11) offers up something more equal. No one is denying the competitiveness. But a 19–2 W-L ratio is not a paragraph, and it is not even a chapter, let alone a whole book. It's a sentence.

What needed to be proven has been, convincingly and repeatedly. But because we need certain lies—a world in which the willowy tall blonde wins at life, for example—we have allowed a narrative to form in which the two are evenly matched. Or at the very least, we have maintained conditions that have allowed Sharapova to profit from this line of thought. If they ever were truly equal in terms of sporting ability, that window was fleeting, and the evidence bears this out.

Sharapova posits a theory in *Unstoppable* as to the root of Serena's apparent problem with her. She refers to that first time she beat her, when Serena had been the tournament favorite. She overheard Serena crying over the loss, says Sharapova, and "I don't think she's ever forgiven me" for witnessing this "low and vulnerable moment." She expands on this by writing, "I think Serena hated me for being the *skinny* [*emphasis mine*] kid who beat her, against all odds, at Wimbledon. I think she hated me for taking something that she believed belonged to her. I think she hated me for seeing her at her lowest moment. But mostly

I think she hated me for hearing her cry. She's never forgiven me for it."

It's ironic that Sharapova says Serena believed that win "belonged" to her. Because history's quite clear on who has traditionally gotten to advance in the sport of tennis. The Williams sisters broke into a lily-white field when they went pro back in 1994 and 1995 and were subjected to their share of racist abuse. Their emergence as champions (and specifically Serena's absolute dominance in latter years) was not the norm, and some tennis fans as well as establishment figures have made that clear to them every step of the way. When Sharapova writes, "This is a story about sacrifice, what you have to give up. But it's also just the story of a girl and her father and their crazy adventure," you could say the exact same thing about Serena Williams. But that's not the narrative she's allowed to inhabit, is it?

The projection here is also worth noting. Sharapova reminds one of the 2014 essay by Jen Caron, in which the writer got caught up in the imagined inner thoughts of a co-yogi, a "heavyset black woman" and wondering what she could do to "help her." And it also brings to mind the white women mentioned in "White Women Drive Me Crazy," Aisha Mirza's 2017 essay, who mask jealousy with faux concern, because their discomfort makes them feel powerless. She writes, "They say, 'Are you okay?' instead of 'I feel uncomfortable,' because they are not used to feeling uncomfortable and they are happy for us to be the problem instead."

In *Unstoppable*, Sharapova writes of Serena, "Even now, she can make me feel like a little girl," and one has to ask, *Is that a Serena problem or a* you *problem?* Consider that what you are feeling is your own personal lack. Sharapova's feelings of fear and shame and disappointment are natural and very real. But that may muffle the very real dog whistle her words conjure. And while it's probably unconscious that she reaches for those specific terms and words when it comes to detailing her own inadequacies, that doesn't mean it's OK.

In the meantime, the jig is up. The US Open final this weekend will feature two American women; one black (Sloane Stephens, who beat thirty-seven-year-old Venus Williams to get there) and one biracial (Madison Keys, who does not call herself black). Serena's on maternity leave, but the future of American tennis (at least) is irrevocably in black women's hands.

Let *that* be what scares you and makes you better.

## ESPN the Magazine

Injustice, plain and simple, is the subject of these columns by Howard Bryant. In "The Williams Movement," Bryant examines the unthinking disdain so many apparently feel for the accomplishments of Venus and Serena Williams; in "Power Play," the unequal treatment of women athletes; in "How Is This Still a Debate?," the unconcealed racism of team mascots (think Chief Wahoo and the Redskins). Sports fans don't like to think about these things, even when they sit in the Oval Office. "As Colin Kaepernick can attest," writes Bryant, "the mainstream public and media too often place more emphasis on the reaction to injustice than on the injustice itself." But Bryant isn't willing to let it drop—any of it. Nor were the Ellie judges. "His columns linger in your mind and leave you wanting more," they wrote. Bryant joined ESPN in 2007; his work was also nominated for the National Magazine Award in 2016.

Howard Bryant

# The Williams Movement *and* Power Play *and* How Is This Still a Debate?

## The Williams Movement

You watch the protests. You hear them outside your window in your small town and watch them on TV, millions marching across the globe on January 21.

You talk with a man you've known since the eleventh grade—white, respectable, of unremarkable wealth or accomplishment yet carrying a learned smugness, completely secure in the legitimacy of his status—who you discover is offended more by the vulgarity of the protest signs than the vulgarity that created them. Fortified by the protections and perks of maleness in perpetuity, he speaks of the women as a minor inconvenience, a moth on his tweed.

"It was a moment, not a movement," he tells you. "It changed nothing."

You know this comment, after a lifetime of diminishment, should carry no value, and yet it remains inside you, eats at you. During this same conversation, he tells you of his "loss of respect" for civil rights icon John Lewis, and you know then that this person you've known for decades is not only talking about the women marching. He's talking about you too.

You watch the Australian Open championship final between Venus and Serena Williams with this tumult in mind, and when Venus's ball lands in the doubles alley and Serena becomes a champion again, *"It was a moment, not a movement"* rises up like bile, and you wonder if the day will ever come when the presence of Venus and Serena will *not* feel like defiance. But you know better. It will not.

You see the hug at the net and the tears of the fans. The humanity of it all. You want to trust that this breathtaking show of respect for these two champions is part of the natural ritual of sports—swords falling as the twilight nears, ceremonial respect for the athlete's journey becoming a final, unifying act—but you cannot shake the slights. The latest occurred during her second-round match against Stefanie Voegele, with the way ESPN commentator Doug Adler described Venus's strategy in attacking the second serve. Adler said he was referring to the word "guerrilla" when talking about how she moved to the net, but after all the years when Venus and Serena have had their looks and sexuality questioned, the clarification is unconvincing. Gorillas charge, guerrillas sneak attack.

You watch the final, and if you have eyes and a heart, you see just how different and difficult and brilliant these matches really are. You see Serena turn her back to her sister after a point to show her emotion; against any other opponent, that emotion would not be so cloaked. She will scream "COME ON!" at Victoria Azarenka, but she will not embarrass her sister. You see Venus, overmatched but knowing she is playing at a championship level against any other opponent but her sister, flashing the resolve of a legend but resigned to grace in defeat—partially. During her runner-up speech, she reminds the audience of her pride of family. "Serena Williams, that's my little sister, guys," Venus says. She receives compliments for being gracious and elegant; she is both elegant and protective. Even in their finals, it was never one against the other, but two against everyone.

You see the enormous pressure the sisters put on each other with their serves because they know a weak serve will be a pummeled one. As you watch the twenty-four-shot second-set rally, you realize the legacy of Venus and Serena cannot be located in either of their trophy cases or in the tired, confining narratives of mentioning their influence only when a new young black girl hits the scene. Their legacy is in six-foot-two, all-legs-and-power Maria Sharapova; six-foot, all-legs-and-power Garbine Muguruza; in the devastating cross-court forehand of six-one CoCo Vandeweghe. Their legacy stands in all of the athletic big hitters who now define the women's game. The Williams sisters are the measure of the women's game, and if you can't hit with them, you can't play. Venus and Serena, somewhat sadly, have forever diminished the championship hopes of the waifish and the crafty, the Agnieszka Radwanskas and Carla Suarez Navarros, who before the arrival of the sisters might very well have held up multiple Grand Slam trophies. There will be youngsters weeded out of the game earlier because they lack the power unnecessary in 1987 but critical in 2017. You see a sport revolutionized; you see not just generations of black girls but the wealth of Eastern Europeans who now inhabit the sport. You see legacy in action.

You also see the patriarchy step on the Williamses even when it wants to share the sunshine. Even when it blows them kisses. Serena, in victory, thanked the crowd for its fervor, the tournament for its professionalism, her sister for their blood, and her team for their commitment—but not her new fiancé, Reddit cofounder Alexis Ohanian, an omission that was mentioned often by broadcasters. In your mind, you flip through the victory speeches you've heard and try to remember a moment when Roger Federer or Rafael Nadal or Andy Murray was chastised for not mentioning his spouse or girlfriend by name. You can find none.

Throughout the fortnight, as the prospect of an all-Williams final creeps toward reality, you hear only one person, the legend Chris Evert, give credit to Richard Williams, the father who had a vision for his daughters that was ridiculed for the overwhelming majority of their story. Richard was the lens through which the sisters were viewed inside and out of the game, the head of the family that didn't belong, until the championship trophies and gold medals were piled so high the critics finally had to surrender.

You remember the first time you really spoke to Richard Williams, in June 2012, at Wimbledon, when he smoked those skinny cigarettes, when it was just the two of you on the deck between the players area and media center, when he told you players should spend less time on the court and more time learning geometry because tennis really is a game of angles, as every opponent of Serena's has discovered the hard way. He talked about his daughters and about the family not being wanted by the blue bloods of tennis, and you knew by the way his eyes drew sharper, fixed on you—older black man to younger one in the United Kingdom—that he was really talking about the American blueprint for anyone who isn't white, how you don't get to be smug because you're not protected by perks in perpetuity, that you never get to be so secure in the legitimacy of your status that you can determine for other people what is a movement and what is a moment.

"There was only one way: Win," Richard Williams said, and when the sisters are standing on the podium in Melbourne, you see their excellence triumph once again, their blood vindicated, as a family. "Win and make them deal with us. Win and they have to give you a seat at the table, even if they don't want you there."

# Power Play

Before the Women's Tennis Association was formed in 1973, its founder, Billie Jean King, had to pry many players from their conviction not to fight for its creation. In an interview with former pro and current broadcaster Mary Carillo, King recalled the moment that became the turning point.

"If we do this," one of the players said, "we'll *lose* everything."

"Don't you understand?" King responded. "You *have nothing*. You literally have nothing to lose. Can't you see that? What worse can happen that isn't happening now?"

King's response, Carillo told me, won the room and, later, history—a history not lost on the U.S. women's national hockey team, which more than forty years later resolved to fight too. The women, earning $6,000 every four years with no hefty NHL salary to supplement them, flying coach when the men fly better, were unable to convince their federation that they deserved an equal seat at the table—a grievance similar to that of the underappreciated women's national soccer team, which finally ratified a collective bargaining agreement after a contentious negotiation with its own federation. And so the hockey players threatened to boycott the women's world championship in what was a basic and remarkable act: They bet on themselves.

On the historical scale of labor negotiations, the players' demands were modest: a raise in pay plus travel and insurance arrangements equal to the men. In response, USA Hockey showed the little regard in which it held the women by its willingness to have America serve as host of the world championship without its two-time defending champions. The federation, likely banking on public sentiment that in so many cases sides with employers, scoured the college and junior ranks, ready to field a team of replacement players to represent the United States. The women, out of insults to take and damns to give, did not wilt and by fighting found allies from the Senate and the players' associations of the NHL, NBA, NFL, and MLB.

The experience of going on strike also served as a reminder to the players that they are part of a historical continuum of conflict between labor and management, of the power of men versus the value of women. The conflict has been heightened by the current wave of athlete activism and the harsh response—in this case USA Hockey's draconian reaction—to any resistance to authority. Team USA confronted what America is today: antilabor, antiprotest, antiaction, each under heavy assault by law and by custom. As Colin Kaepernick can attest, the mainstream public and media too often place more emphasis on the reaction to injustice than on the injustice itself. While the women received some support for their stance, just as Kaepernick had allies in many quarters, there were those who justified USA Hockey's position because the women's game is less popular and less lucrative. Ultimately, though, the thought of strike breakers was too great of an overstep, an unnecessary instigation.

USA Hockey counted on public antipathy toward mobilized labor—especially sports labor—that has defined the country since the 1980s. For once, that stance backfired. The federation and the players reached a deal three days before the world championship opener.

So often the people who have everything to lose become the conscience of a dulled, overindulged nation. So often that conscience is women. The big names—LeBron James, Carmelo Anthony, Chris Paul—received attention for pleading for police and public confrontations to end, but the players negotiated with the NBA about when and how they would express themselves this season. Asking for guidance on how to protest is no protest. The NBA has twenty-one players earning over $20 million this season, but they responded to the obvious racism of Donald Sterling in 2014 not with a wildcat strike but by reaching out to commissioner Adam Silver. They trusted the power to protect them. Meanwhile, the WNBA players, most of whom don't earn $100,000 and actually had something to lose, were far more defiant in their solidarity against police brutality than their multimillionaire male counterparts, even in the face of league fines.

The U.S. women's hockey team, now part of King's legacy, stood unified too. The Americans beat nemesis Canada 2–0 to start the world championship and went on to beat Russia 7–0, Finland 5–3, and Germany 11–0. But the real victory was being on the ice on their terms, a message sent to the next generation of women whose bosses tell them to shut up and play.

# How Is This Still a Debate?

Thirteen months ago, before game 2 of the World Series, baseball commissioner Rob Manfred shared a podium with Hall of Famer Henry Aaron and retiring Red Sox titan David Ortiz. Manfred was asked how, with the world watching baseball's marquee event, the league could still abide the Indians' using Chief Wahoo as a mascot. Manfred fidgeted, annoyed by the presence of a fastball where there were supposed to be only softballs. He insisted there was no place for racism in baseball and, attempting to douse the issue, said he and Cleveland Indians owner Paul Dolan would revisit the issue in the offseason.

A year later, Manfred suspended Astros first baseman Yuli Gurriel for making a racist gesture at Yu Darvish during the World Series—yet has left intact the smiling stereotype of Chief Wahoo. Players are so much easier to punish.

While plates and bellies are loaded with turkey and stuffing this year, the Washington Redskins will, for the first time and quite controversially, host a game on Thanksgiving. Some eyes will roll at the suggestion that sports is humiliating a people, but neither fatigue nor cynicism can undo a central fact: There is plenty of room for racism in American sports. All the eye rolls in the world won't change that.

Instead of debating racism, it is more appropriate to wonder why Native Americans are spared the dignity of progress, why the sports industry continues to insult them today as society commonly did one hundred years ago. To many fans, perhaps nothing feels more American than logos like those of the Indians, Blackhawks, and Redskins, but that feeling requires ignoring the history. Native Americans were excluded from being American—from the Fourteenth Amendment of 1868, which granted equal protection and naturalization of all citizens born on United States soil, to the Fifteenth, which granted African American men the right to vote, in 1870. Native Americans were not granted American citizenship until 1924 and did not receive full nationwide voting rights until 1957. By that time, each of the team names, as racist then as they are today, was well fixed within the sports culture. America has chosen logos over people.

The customer is always right, but only if you're the seller. If you're not, it is obvious that the fan acts from selfishness. This is their entertainment, and the racist logos and offensive names are a nostalgic part of their memories and experience, and they aren't willing to give them up. Washington owner Daniel Snyder knows this, which is why he has spent his time and money bankrolling studies and Native American leaders who agree with him, to use them as cover instead of using common sense.

"You cannot have capitalism without racism," Malcolm X once said. His statement was directed toward the class warfare that lies at the root of capitalism, and it applies even to the blankets, foam fingers, jerseys, caps, and T-shirts the sports teams sell, even on a day ostensibly dedicated to a giving of thanks and peace between settlers and natives. The hypocrisy is disgusting.

Once more, there is a difference between *difficult* and *complicated*. For the leagues, it might be *difficult* to once and for all treat Native Americans with humanity by having the courage to risk the money and start a new history with new names and better attitudes. But there is precedent. When spoken and written, people now commonly use "the N-word" to replace its more offensive antecedent; the patronizing, sexualized connotations of "stewardess" long ago gave way to "flight attendant." Society did not come unmoored.

It might be difficult for sports leagues to appear to capitulate to the protest behind a word's usage, even if that capitulation is out of simple decency. It might be difficult for teams and the public to admit their casual racism. It is not, however, *complicated* to understand that these logos must go. It is not complicated to know a relic from the first decades of the twentieth century, routinely regarded by historians as the most racist period since the antebellum era, is inappropriate today. In classic misdirection, the Boston Celtics are often used as a false equivalent in this ersatz debate—a team name harmlessly based on an ethnicity. But people freely use the word "Celtic" in common speech without offense. Consider this while passing the cranberry sauce: Outside of discussing the Washington football team, who in mixed company comfortably and routinely uses the word "Redskins"?

Enough. We all know better.

## The Atlantic

WINNER—ESSAYS
AND CRITICISM

"She was eighteen years old when my grandfather gave her to my mother as a gift, and when my family moved to the United States, we brought her with us," wrote Alex Tizon of the woman he knew as Lola. "No other word but 'slave' encompassed the life she lived." Tizon died before this story was published, but it is as much his story as it is hers—as the Ellie judges put it, "a personal confession that explores issues of race, colonialism, immigration and, ultimately, human freedom." After Tizon's death, Jeffrey Goldberg, the editor in chief of The Atlantic, said: "Alex Tizon built an exemplary career by listening to certain types of people—forgotten people, people on the margins, people who had never before been asked for their stories. . . . The eradication of all forms of slavery remains an unfinished goal of civilization, and of this magazine, and stories like Alex's help us understand slavery's awful persistence."

Alex Tizon

# Lola's Story

The ashes filled a black plastic box about the size of a toaster. It weighed three and a half pounds. I put it in a canvas tote bag and packed it in my suitcase this past July for the transpacific flight to Manila. From there I would travel by car to a rural village. When I arrived, I would hand over all that was left of the woman who had spent fifty-six years as a slave in my family's household.

Her name was Eudocia Tomas Pulido. We called her Lola. She was four-foot-eleven, with mocha-brown skin and almond eyes that I can still see looking into mine—my first memory. She was eighteen years old when my grandfather gave her to my mother as a gift, and when my family moved to the United States, we brought her with us. No other word but *slave* encompassed the life she lived. Her days began before everyone else woke and ended after we went to bed. She prepared three meals a day, cleaned the house, waited on my parents, and took care of my four siblings and me. My parents never paid her, and they scolded her constantly. She wasn't kept in leg irons, but she might as well have been. So many nights, on my way to the bathroom, I'd spot her sleeping in a corner, slumped against a mound of laundry, her fingers clutching a garment she was in the middle of folding.

.   .   .

At baggage claim in Manila, I unzipped my suitcase to make sure Lola's ashes were still there. Outside, I inhaled the familiar smell: a thick blend of exhaust and waste, of ocean and sweet fruit and sweat.

Early the next morning I found a driver, an affable middle-aged man who went by the nickname "Doods," and we hit the road in his truck, weaving through traffic. The scene always stunned me. The sheer number of cars and motorcycles and jeepneys. The people weaving between them and moving on the sidewalks in great brown rivers. The street vendors in bare feet trotting alongside cars, hawking cigarettes and cough drops and sacks of boiled peanuts. The child beggars pressing their faces against the windows.

Doods and I were headed to the place where Lola's story began, up north in the central plains: Tarlac province. Rice country. The home of a cigar-chomping army lieutenant named Tomas Asuncion, my grandfather. The family stories paint Lieutenant Tom as a formidable man given to eccentricity and dark moods, who had lots of land but little money and kept mistresses in separate houses on his property. His wife died giving birth to their only child, my mother. She was raised by a series of *utusans*, or "people who take commands."

Slavery has a long history on the islands. Before the Spanish came, islanders enslaved other islanders, usually war captives, criminals, or debtors. Slaves came in different varieties, from warriors who could earn their freedom through valor to household servants who were regarded as property and could be bought and sold or traded. High-status slaves could own low-status slaves, and the low could own the lowliest. Some chose to enter servitude simply to survive: In exchange for their labor, they might be given food, shelter, and protection.

When the Spanish arrived, in the 1500s, they enslaved islanders and later brought African and Indian slaves. The Spanish crown eventually began phasing out slavery at home and in its colonies, but parts of the Philippines were so far-flung that authorities couldn't keep a close eye. Traditions persisted under different guises, even after the United States took control of the islands in 1898. Today even the poor can have *utusans* or *katulongs* ("helpers") or *kasambahays* ("domestics"), as long as there are people even poorer. The pool is deep.

Lieutenant Tom had as many as three families of *utusans* living on his property. In the spring of 1943, with the islands under Japanese occupation, he brought home a girl from a village down the road. She was a cousin from a marginal side of the family, rice farmers. The lieutenant was shrewd—he saw that this girl was penniless, unschooled, and likely to be malleable. Her parents wanted her to marry a pig farmer twice her age, and she was desperately unhappy but had nowhere to go. Tom approached her with an offer: She could have food and shelter if she would commit to taking care of his daughter, who had just turned twelve.

Lola agreed, not grasping that the deal was for life.

"She is my gift to you," Lieutenant Tom told my mother.

"I don't want her," my mother said, knowing she had no choice.

Lieutenant Tom went off to fight the Japanese, leaving Mom behind with Lola in his creaky house in the provinces. Lola fed, groomed, and dressed my mother. When they walked to the market, Lola held an umbrella to shield her from the sun. At night, when Lola's other tasks were done—feeding the dogs, sweeping the floors, folding the laundry that she had washed by hand in the Camiling River—she sat at the edge of my mother's bed and fanned her to sleep.

One day during the war Lieutenant Tom came home and caught my mother in a lie—something to do with a boy she wasn't supposed to talk to. Tom, furious, ordered her to "stand at the table." Mom cowered with Lola in a corner. Then, in a quivering voice, she told her father that Lola would take her punishment. Lola looked at Mom pleadingly, then without a word walked to the dining table and held on to the edge. Tom raised the belt and delivered twelve lashes, punctuating each one with a word. *You. Do. Not. Lie. To. Me. You. Do. Not. Lie. To. Me.* Lola made no sound.

My mother, in recounting this story late in her life, delighted in the outrageousness of it, her tone seeming to say, *Can you believe I did that?* When I brought it up with Lola, she asked to hear Mom's version. She listened intently, eyes lowered, and afterward she looked at me with sadness and said simply, "Yes. It was like that."

Seven years later, in 1950, Mom married my father and moved to Manila, bringing Lola along. Lieutenant Tom had long been haunted by demons, and in 1951 he silenced them with a .32-caliber slug to his temple. Mom almost never talked about it. She had his temperament—moody, imperial, secretly fragile— and she took his lessons to heart, among them the proper way to be a provincial *matrona*: You must embrace your role as the giver of commands. You must keep those beneath you in their place at all times, for their own good and the good of the household. They might cry and complain, but their souls will thank you. They will love you for helping them be what God intended.

My brother Arthur was born in 1951. I came next, followed by three more siblings in rapid succession. My parents expected Lola to be as devoted to us kids as she was to them. While she looked after us, my parents went to school and earned advanced degrees, joining the ranks of so many others with fancy diplomas but no jobs. Then the big break: Dad was offered a job in foreign affairs as a commercial analyst. The salary would be meager, but the position was in America—a place he and Mom had grown up dreaming of, where everything they hoped for could come true.

Dad was allowed to bring his family and one domestic. Figuring they would both have to work, my parents needed Lola to care for the kids and the house. My mother informed Lola, and to her great irritation, Lola didn't immediately acquiesce. Years later

Lola told me she was terrified. "It was too far," she said. "Maybe your Mom and Dad won't let me go home."

In the end what convinced Lola was my father's promise that things would be different in America. He told her that as soon as he and Mom got on their feet, they'd give her an "allowance." Lola could send money to her parents, to all her relations in the village. Her parents lived in a hut with a dirt floor. Lola could build them a concrete house, could change their lives forever. *Imagine.*

We landed in Los Angeles on May 12, 1964, all our belongings in cardboard boxes tied with rope. Lola had been with my mother for twenty-one years by then. In many ways she was more of a parent to me than either my mother or my father. Hers was the first face I saw in the morning and the last one I saw at night. As a baby, I uttered Lola's name (which I first pronounced "Oh-ah") long before I learned to say "Mom" or "Dad." As a toddler, I refused to go to sleep unless Lola was holding me, or at least nearby.

I was four years old when we arrived in the United States—too young to question Lola's place in our family. But as my siblings and I grew up on this other shore, we came to see the world differently. The leap across the ocean brought about a leap in consciousness that Mom and Dad couldn't, or wouldn't, make.

·　　·　　·

Lola never got that allowance. She asked my parents about it in a roundabout way a couple of years into our life in America. Her mother had fallen ill (with what I would later learn was dysentery), and her family couldn't afford the medicine she needed. "*Pwede ba?*" she said to my parents. *Is it possible?* Mom let out a sigh. "How could you even ask?" Dad responded in Tagalog. "You see how hard up we are. Don't you have any shame?"

My parents had borrowed money for the move to the United States and then borrowed more in order to stay. My father was transferred from the consulate general in L.A. to the Philippine consulate in Seattle. He was paid $5,600 a year. He took a second job cleaning trailers and a third as a debt collector. Mom got work as a technician in a couple of medical labs. We barely saw them, and when we did they were often exhausted and snappish.

Mom would come home and upbraid Lola for not cleaning the house well enough or for forgetting to bring in the mail. "Didn't I tell you I want the letters here when I come home?" she would say in Tagalog, her voice venomous. "It's not hard *naman*! An idiot could remember." Then my father would arrive and take his turn. When Dad raised his voice, everyone in the house shrank. Sometimes my parents would team up until Lola broke down crying, almost as though that was their goal.

It confused me: My parents were good to my siblings and me, and we loved them. But they'd be affectionate to us kids one moment and vile to Lola the next. I was eleven or twelve when I began to see Lola's situation clearly. By then Arthur, eight years my senior, had been seething for a long time. He was the one who introduced the word *slave* into my understanding of what Lola was. Before he said it I'd thought of her as just an unfortunate member of the household. I hated when my parents yelled at her, but it hadn't occurred to me that they—and the whole arrangement—could be immoral.

"Do you know anybody treated the way she's treated?" Arthur said. "Who lives the way she lives?" He summed up Lola's reality: Wasn't paid. Toiled every day. Was tongue-lashed for sitting too long or falling asleep too early. Was struck for talking back. Wore hand-me-downs. Ate scraps and leftovers by herself in the kitchen. Rarely left the house. Had no friends or hobbies outside the family. Had no private quarters. (Her designated place to sleep in each house we lived in was always whatever was left—a couch or storage area or corner in my sisters' bedroom. She often slept among piles of laundry.)

We couldn't identify a parallel anywhere except in slave characters on TV and in the movies. I remember watching a Western called *The Man Who Shot Liberty Valance*. John Wayne plays Tom Doniphon, a gunslinging rancher who barks orders at his servant, Pompey, whom he calls his "boy." *Pick him up, Pompey. Pompey, go find the doctor. Get on back to work, Pompey!* Docile and obedient, Pompey calls his master "Mistah Tom." They have a complex relationship. Tom forbids Pompey from attending school but opens the way for Pompey to drink in a whites-only saloon. Near the end, Pompey saves his master from a fire. It's clear Pompey both fears and loves Tom, and he mourns when Tom dies. All of this is peripheral to the main story of Tom's showdown with bad guy Liberty Valance, but I couldn't take my eyes off Pompey. I remember thinking: *Lola is Pompey, Pompey is Lola.*

One night when Dad found out that my sister Ling, who was then nine, had missed dinner, he barked at Lola for being lazy. "I tried to feed her," Lola said, as Dad stood over her and glared. Her feeble defense only made him angrier, and he punched her just below the shoulder. Lola ran out of the room and I could hear her wailing, an animal cry.

"Ling said she wasn't hungry," I said.

My parents turned to look at me. They seemed startled. I felt the twitching in my face that usually preceded tears, but I wouldn't cry this time. In Mom's eyes was a shadow of something I hadn't seen before. Jealousy?

"Are you defending your Lola?" Dad said. "Is that what you're doing?"

"Ling said she wasn't hungry," I said again, almost in a whisper.

I was thirteen. It was my first attempt to stick up for the woman who spent her days watching over me. The woman who used to hum Tagalog melodies as she rocked me to sleep and when I got older would dress and feed me and walk me to school in the mornings and pick me up in the afternoons. Once, when I was sick for a long time and too weak to eat, she chewed my food for me and put the small pieces in my mouth to swallow. One summer when I had plaster casts on both legs (I had problem joints), she bathed me with a washcloth, brought medicine in the middle of the night, and helped me through months of rehabilitation. I was cranky through it all. She didn't complain or lose patience, ever.

To now hear her wailing made me crazy.

·        ·        ·

In the old country, my parents felt no need to hide their treatment of Lola. In America, they treated her worse but took pains to conceal it. When guests came over, my parents would either ignore her or, if questioned, lie and quickly change the subject. For five years in North Seattle, we lived across the street from the Misslers, a rambunctious family of eight who introduced us to things like mustard, salmon fishing, and mowing the lawn. Football on TV. Yelling during football. Lola would come out to serve food and drinks during games, and my parents would smile and thank her before she quickly disappeared. "Who's that little lady you keep in the kitchen?" Big Jim, the Missler patriarch, once asked. A relative from back home, Dad said. Very shy.

Billy Missler, my best friend, didn't buy it. He spent enough time at our house, whole weekends sometimes, to catch glimpses of my family's secret. He once overheard my mother yelling in the kitchen and when he barged in to investigate found Mom red-faced and glaring at Lola, who was quaking in a corner. I came in a few seconds later. The look on Billy's face was a mix of embarrassment and perplexity. *What was that?* I waved it off and told him to forget it.

I think Billy felt sorry for Lola. He'd rave about her cooking and make her laugh like I'd never seen. During sleepovers, she'd make his favorite Filipino dish, beef *tapa* over white rice. Cooking was Lola's only eloquence. I could tell by what she served whether she was merely feeding us or saying she loved us.

When I once referred to Lola as a distant aunt, Billy reminded me that when we'd first met I'd said she was my grandmother.

"Well, she's kind of both," I said mysteriously.

"Why is she always working?"

"She likes to work," I said.

"Your dad and mom—why do they yell at her?"

"Her hearing isn't so good . . ."

Admitting the truth would have meant exposing us all. We spent our first decade in the country learning the ways of the new land and trying to fit in. Having a slave did not fit. Having a slave gave me grave doubts about what kind of people we were, what kind of place we came from. Whether we deserved to be accepted. I was ashamed of it all, including my complicity. Didn't I eat the food she cooked and wear the clothes she washed and ironed and hung in the closet? But losing her would have been devastating.

There was another reason for secrecy: Lola's travel papers had expired in 1969, five years after we arrived in the United States. She'd come on a special passport linked to my father's job. After a series of fallings-out with his superiors, Dad quit the consulate and declared his intent to stay in the United States. He arranged for permanent-resident status for his family, but Lola wasn't eligible. He was supposed to send her back.

Lola's mother, Fermina, died in 1973; her father, Hilario, in 1979. Both times she wanted desperately to go home. Both times my parents said "Sorry." No money, no time. The kids needed her. My parents also feared for themselves, they admitted to me later. If the authorities had found out about Lola, as they surely would have if she'd tried to leave, my parents could have gotten into trouble, possibly even been deported. They couldn't risk it. Lola's legal status became what Filipinos call *tago nang tago*, or TNT—"on the run." She stayed TNT for almost twenty years.

After each of her parents died, Lola was sullen and silent for months. She barely responded when my parents badgered her. But the badgering never let up. Lola kept her head down and did her work.

·　　　·　　　·

My father's resignation started a turbulent period. Money got tighter, and my parents turned on each other. They uprooted the family again and again—Seattle to Honolulu back to Seattle to the southeast Bronx and finally to the truck-stop town of Umatilla, Oregon, population 750. During all this moving around, Mom often worked twenty-four-hour shifts, first as a medical intern and then as a resident, and Dad would disappear for days, working odd jobs but also (we'd later learn) womanizing and who knows what else. Once, he came home and told us that he'd lost our new station wagon playing blackjack.

For days in a row Lola would be the only adult in the house. She got to know the details of our lives in a way that my parents never had the mental space for. We brought friends home, and she'd listen to us talk about school and girls and boys and whatever else was on our minds. Just from conversations she overheard, she could list the first name of every girl I had a crush on from sixth grade through high school.

When I was fifteen, Dad left the family for good. I didn't want to believe it at the time, but the fact was that he deserted us kids and abandoned Mom after twenty-five years of marriage. She wouldn't become a licensed physician for another year, and her specialty—internal medicine—wasn't especially lucrative. Dad didn't pay child support, so money was always a struggle.

My mom kept herself together enough to go to work, but at night she'd crumble in self-pity and despair. Her main source of comfort during this time: Lola. As Mom snapped at her over small things, Lola attended to her even more—cooking Mom's favorite meals, cleaning her bedroom with extra care. I'd find the two of them late at night at the kitchen counter, griping and telling stories about Dad, sometimes laughing wickedly, other times working themselves into a fury over his transgressions. They barely noticed us kids flitting in and out.

One night I heard Mom weeping and ran into the living room to find her slumped in Lola's arms. Lola was talking softly to her, the way she used to with my siblings and me when we were young. I lingered, then went back to my room, scared for my mom and awed by Lola.

$\bullet$      $\bullet$      $\bullet$

Doods was humming. I'd dozed for what felt like a minute and awoke to his happy melody. "Two hours more," he said. I checked the plastic box in the tote bag by my side—still there—and looked up to see open road. The MacArthur Highway. I glanced at the time. "Hey, you said 'two hours' two hours ago," I said. Doods just hummed.

His not knowing anything about the purpose of my journey was a relief. I had enough interior dialogue going on. *I was no better than my parents. I could have done more to free Lola. To make her life better. Why didn't I?* I could have turned in my parents, I suppose. It would have blown up my family in an instant. Instead, my siblings and I kept everything to ourselves, and rather than blowing up in an instant, my family broke apart slowly.

Doods and I passed through beautiful country. Not travel-brochure beautiful but real and alive and, compared with the city, elegantly spare. Mountains ran parallel to the highway on each side, the Zambales Mountains to the west, the Sierra Madre Range to the east. From ridge to ridge, west to east, I could see every shade of green all the way to almost black.

Doods pointed to a shadowy outline in the distance. Mount Pinatubo. I'd come here in 1991 to report on the aftermath of its eruption, the second-largest of the twentieth century. Volcanic mudflows called *lahars* continued for more than a decade, burying ancient villages, filling in rivers and valleys, and wiping out entire ecosystems. The *lahars* reached deep into the foothills of Tarlac province, where Lola's parents had spent their entire lives and where she and my mother had once lived together. So much of our family record had been lost in wars and floods, and now parts were buried under twenty feet of mud.

Life here is routinely visited by cataclysm. Killer typhoons that strike several times a year. Bandit insurgencies that never end. Somnolent mountains that one day decide to wake up. The Philippines isn't like China or Brazil, whose mass might absorb the trauma. This is a nation of scattered rocks in the sea. When disaster hits, the place goes under for a while. Then it resurfaces and life proceeds, and you can behold a scene like the one Doods and I were driving through, and the simple fact that it's still there makes it beautiful.

·        ·        ·

A couple of years after my parents split, my mother remarried and demanded Lola's fealty to her new husband, a Croatian immigrant named Ivan, whom she had met through a friend. Ivan had never finished high school. He'd been married four times and was an inveterate gambler who enjoyed being supported by my mother and attended to by Lola.

Ivan brought out a side of Lola I'd never seen. His marriage to my mother was volatile from the start, and money—especially his use of her money—was the main issue. Once, during an argument in which Mom was crying and Ivan was yelling, Lola walked over and stood between them. She turned to Ivan and firmly said his name. He looked at Lola, blinked, and sat down.

My sister Inday and I were floored. Ivan was about 250 pounds, and his baritone could shake the walls. Lola put him in his place with a single word. I saw this happen a few other times, but for the most part Lola served Ivan unquestioningly, just as Mom wanted her to. I had a hard time watching Lola vassalize herself to another person, especially someone like Ivan. But what set the stage for my blowup with Mom was something more mundane.

She used to get angry whenever Lola felt ill. She didn't want to deal with the disruption and the expense and would accuse Lola of faking or failing to take care of herself. Mom chose the second tack when, in the late 1970s, Lola's teeth started falling out. She'd been saying for months that her mouth hurt.

"That's what happens when you don't brush properly," Mom told her.

I said that Lola needed to see a dentist. She was in her fifties and had never been to one. I was attending college an hour away, and I brought it up again and again on my frequent trips home. A year went by, then two. Lola took aspirin every day for the pain, and her teeth looked like a crumbling Stonehenge. One night, after watching her chew bread on the side of her mouth that still had a few good molars, I lost it.

Mom and I argued into the night, each of us sobbing at different points. She said she was tired of working her fingers to the bone supporting everybody, and sick of her children always taking Lola's side, and why didn't we just take our goddamn Lola, she'd never wanted her in the first place, and she wished to God she hadn't given birth to an arrogant, sanctimonious phony like me.

I let her words sink in. Then I came back at her, saying she would know all about being a phony, her whole life was a masquerade, and if she stopped feeling sorry for herself for one minute she'd see that Lola could barely eat because her goddamn teeth were rotting out of her goddamn head, and couldn't she think of her just this once as a real person instead of a slave kept alive to serve her?

"A slave," Mom said, weighing the word. "A *slave*?"

The night ended when she declared that I would never understand her relationship with Lola. *Never.* Her voice was so guttural and pained that thinking of it even now, so many years later, feels like a punch to the stomach. It's a terrible thing to hate your own mother, and that night I did. The look in her eyes made clear that she felt the same way about me.

The fight only fed Mom's fear that Lola had stolen the kids from her, and she made Lola pay for it. Mom drove her harder. Tormented her by saying, "I hope you're happy now that your kids hate me." When we helped Lola with housework, Mom would fume. "You'd better go to sleep now, Lola," she'd say sarcastically. "You've been working too hard. Your kids are worried about you." Later she'd take Lola into a bedroom for a talk, and Lola would walk out with puffy eyes.

Lola finally begged us to stop trying to help her.

Why do you stay? we asked.

"Who will cook?" she said, which I took to mean, *Who would do everything?* Who would take care of us? Of Mom? Another time she said, "Where will I go?" This struck me as closer to a real answer. Coming to America had been a mad dash, and before we caught a breath a decade had gone by. We turned around, and a second decade was closing out. Lola's hair had turned gray. She'd heard that relatives back home who hadn't received the promised support were wondering what had happened to her. She was ashamed to return.

She had no contacts in America and no facility for getting around. Phones puzzled her. Mechanical things—ATMs, intercoms, vending machines, anything with a keyboard—made her panic. Fast-talking people left her speechless, and her own broken English did the same to them. She couldn't make an appointment, arrange a trip, fill out a form, or order a meal without help.

I got Lola an ATM card linked to my bank account and taught her how to use it. She succeeded once, but the second time she got flustered, and she never tried again. She kept the card because she considered it a gift from me.

I also tried to teach her to drive. She dismissed the idea with a wave of her hand, but I picked her up and carried her to the car and planted her in the driver's seat, both of us laughing. I spent twenty minutes going over the controls and gauges. Her eyes went from mirthful to terrified. When I turned on the ignition and the dashboard lit up, she was out of the car and in the house before I could say another word. I tried a couple more times.

I thought driving could change her life. She could go places. And if things ever got unbearable with Mom, she could drive away forever.

·          ·          ·

Four lanes became two, pavement turned to gravel. Tricycle drivers wove between cars and water buffalo pulling loads of bamboo. An occasional dog or goat sprinted across the road in front of our truck, almost grazing the bumper. Doods never eased up. Whatever didn't make it across would be stew today instead of tomorrow—the rule of the road in the provinces.

I took out a map and traced the route to the village of Mayantoc, our destination. Out the window, in the distance, tiny figures folded at the waist like so many bent nails. People harvesting rice, the same way they had for thousands of years. We were getting close.

I tapped the cheap plastic box and regretted not buying a real urn, made of porcelain or rosewood. What would Lola's people think? Not that many were left. Only one sibling remained in the area, Gregoria, ninety-eight years old, and I was told her memory was failing. Relatives said that whenever she heard Lola's name, she'd burst out crying and then quickly forget why.

I'd been in touch with one of Lola's nieces. She had the day planned: When I arrived, a low-key memorial, then a prayer, followed by the lowering of the ashes into a plot at the Mayantoc Eternal Bliss Memorial Park. It had been five years since Lola died, but I hadn't yet said the final goodbye that I knew was about to happen. All day I had been feeling intense grief and resisting the urge to let it out, not wanting to wail in front of Doods. More than the shame I felt for the way my family had treated Lola, more than my anxiety about how her relatives in Mayantoc would treat me, I felt the terrible heaviness of losing her, as if she had died only the day before.

Doods veered northwest on the Romulo Highway then took a sharp left at Camiling, the town Mom and Lieutenant Tom came from. Two lanes became one, then gravel turned to dirt. The path ran along the Camiling River, clusters of bamboo houses off to the side, green hills ahead. The homestretch.

·        ·        ·

I gave the eulogy at Mom's funeral, and everything I said was true. That she was brave and spirited. That she'd drawn some short straws but had done the best she could. That she was radiant when she was happy. That she adored her children and gave us a real home—in Salem, Oregon—that through the eighties and nineties became the permanent base we'd never had before. That I wished we could thank her one more time. That we all loved her.

I didn't talk about Lola. Just as I had selectively blocked Lola out of my mind when I was with Mom during her last years. Loving my mother required that kind of mental surgery. It was the only way we could be mother and son—which I wanted, especially after her health started to decline, in the mid-nineties. Diabetes. Breast cancer. Acute myelogenous leukemia, a fast-growing cancer of the blood and bone marrow. She went from robust to frail seemingly overnight.

After the big fight, I mostly avoided going home, and at age twenty-three I moved to Seattle. When I did visit I saw a change. Mom was still Mom, but not as relentlessly. She got Lola a fine set of dentures and let her have her own bedroom. She cooperated when my siblings and I set out to change Lola's TNT status. Ronald Reagan's landmark immigration bill of 1986 made millions of illegal immigrants eligible for amnesty. It was a long process, but Lola became a citizen in October 1998, four months after my mother was diagnosed with leukemia. Mom lived another year.

During that time, she and Ivan took trips to Lincoln City, on the Oregon coast, and sometimes brought Lola along. Lola loved the ocean. On the other side were the islands she dreamed of returning to. And Lola was never happier than when Mom relaxed around her. An afternoon at the coast or just fifteen minutes in the kitchen reminiscing about the old days in the province, and Lola would seem to forget years of torment.

I couldn't forget so easily. But I did come to see Mom in a different light. Before she died, she gave me her journals, two steamer trunks' full. Leafing through them as she slept a few feet away, I glimpsed slices of her life that I'd refused to see for years. She'd gone to medical school when not many women did. She'd come to America and fought for respect as both a woman and an immigrant physician. She'd worked for two decades at Fairview Training Center, in Salem, a state institution for the developmentally disabled. The irony: She tended to underdogs most of her professional life. They worshipped her. Female colleagues became close friends. They did silly, girly things together—shoe shopping, throwing dress-up parties at one another's homes, exchanging gag gifts like penis-shaped soaps and calendars of half-naked men, all while laughing hysterically. Looking through their party pictures reminded me that Mom had a life and an identity apart from the family and Lola. Of course.

Mom wrote in great detail about each of her kids and how she felt about us on a given day—proud or loving or resentful. And she devoted volumes to her husbands, trying to grasp them as complex characters in her story. We were all persons of consequence. Lola was incidental. When she was mentioned at all, she was a bit character in someone else's story. "Lola walked my beloved Alex to his new school this morning. I hope he makes new friends quickly so he doesn't feel so sad about moving again . . ." There might be two more pages about me, and no other mention of Lola.

The day before Mom died, a Catholic priest came to the house to perform last rites. Lola sat next to my mother's bed, holding a cup with a straw, poised to raise it to Mom's mouth. She had become extra attentive to my mother, and extra kind. She could have taken advantage of Mom in her feebleness, even exacted revenge, but she did the opposite.

The priest asked Mom whether there was anything she wanted to forgive or be forgiven for. She scanned the room with heavy-lidded eyes, said nothing. Then, without looking at Lola, she reached over and placed an open hand on her head. She didn't say a word.

.        .        .

Lola was seventy-five when she came to stay with me. I was married with two young daughters, living in a cozy house on a wooded lot. From the second story, we could see Puget Sound. We gave Lola a bedroom and license to do whatever she wanted: sleep in, watch soaps, do nothing all day. She could relax—and be free— for the first time in her life. I should have known it wouldn't be that simple.

I'd forgotten about all the things Lola did that drove me a little crazy. She was always telling me to put on a sweater so I wouldn't catch a cold (I was in my forties). She groused incessantly about Dad and Ivan: My father was lazy, Ivan was a leech. I learned to tune her out. Harder to ignore was her fanatical thriftiness. She threw nothing out. And she used to go through the trash to make sure that the rest of us hadn't thrown out anything useful. She washed and reused paper towels again and again until they disintegrated in her hands. (No one else would go near them.) The kitchen became glutted with grocery bags, yogurt containers, and pickle jars, and parts of our house turned into storage for—there's no other word for it—garbage.

She cooked breakfast even though none of us ate more than a banana or a granola bar in the morning, usually while we were running out the door. She made our beds and did our laundry. She cleaned the house. I found myself saying to her, nicely at first, "Lola, you don't have to do that." "Lola, we'll do it ourselves." "Lola, that's the girls' job." Okay, she'd say, but keep right on doing it.

It irritated me to catch her eating meals standing in the kitchen or see her tense up and start cleaning when I walked into the room. One day, after several months, I sat her down.

"I'm not Dad. You're not a slave here," I said, and went through a long list of slavelike things she'd been doing. When I realized she was startled, I took a deep breath and cupped her face, that elfin face now looking at me searchingly. I kissed her forehead. "This is *your* house now," I said. "You're not here to serve us. You can relax, okay?"

"Okay," she said. And went back to cleaning.

She didn't know any other way to be. I realized I had to take my own advice and relax. If she wanted to make dinner, let her. Thank her and do the dishes. I had to remind myself constantly: *Let her be.*

One night I came home to find her sitting on the couch doing a word puzzle, her feet up, the TV on. Next to her, a cup of tea. She glanced at me, smiled sheepishly with those perfect white dentures, and went back to the puzzle. *Progress*, I thought.

She planted a garden in the backyard—roses and tulips and every kind of orchid—and spent whole afternoons tending it. She took walks around the neighborhood. At about eighty, her arthritis got bad and she began walking with a cane. In the kitchen she went from being a fry cook to a kind of artisanal chef who created only when the spirit moved her. She made lavish meals and grinned with pleasure as we devoured them.

Passing the door of Lola's bedroom, I'd often hear her listening to a cassette of Filipino folk songs. The same tape over and over. I knew she'd been sending almost all her money—my wife and I gave her $200 a week—to relatives back home. One afternoon, I found her sitting on the back deck gazing at a snapshot someone had sent of her village.

"You want to go home, Lola?"

She turned the photograph over and traced her finger across the inscription then flipped it back and seemed to study a single detail.

"Yes," she said.

Just after her eighty-third birthday, I paid her airfare to go home. I'd follow a month later to bring her back to the United States—if she wanted to return. The unspoken purpose of her trip was to see whether the place she had spent so many years longing for could still feel like home.

She found her answer.

"Everything was not the same," she told me as we walked around Mayantoc. The old farms were gone. Her house was gone. Her parents and most of her siblings were gone. Childhood friends, the ones still alive, were like strangers. It was nice to see them, but . . . everything was not the same. She'd still like to spend her last years here, she said, but she wasn't ready yet.

"You're ready to go back to your garden," I said.

"Yes. Let's go home."

·      ·      ·

Lola was as devoted to my daughters as she'd been to my siblings and me when we were young. After school, she'd listen to their stories and make them something to eat. And unlike my wife and me (especially me), Lola enjoyed every minute of every school event and performance. She couldn't get enough of them. She sat up front, kept the programs as mementos.

It was so easy to make Lola happy. We took her on family vacations, but she was as excited to go to the farmer's market down the hill. She became a wide-eyed kid on a field trip: "Look at those zucchinis!" The first thing she did every morning was open all the blinds in the house, and at each window she'd pause to look outside.

And she taught herself to read. It was remarkable. Over the years, she'd somehow learned to sound out letters. She did those puzzles where you find and circle words within a block of letters. Her room had stacks of word-puzzle booklets, thousands of words circled in pencil. Every day she watched the news and listened for words she recognized. She triangulated them with words in the newspaper and figured out the meanings. She came to read the paper every day, front to back. Dad used to say she was simple. I wondered what she could have been if, instead of working the rice fields at age eight, she had learned to read and write.

During the twelve years she lived in our house, I asked her questions about herself, trying to piece together her life story, a habit she found curious. To my inquiries she would often respond first with "Why?" Why did I want to know about her childhood? About how she met Lieutenant Tom?

I tried to get my sister Ling to ask Lola about her love life, thinking Lola would be more comfortable with her. Ling cackled, which was her way of saying I was on my own. One day, while Lola and I were putting away groceries, I just blurted it out: "Lola, have you ever been romantic with anyone?" She smiled, and then she told me the story of the only time she'd come close. She was about fifteen, and there was a handsome boy named Pedro from a nearby farm. For several months they harvested rice together side by side. One time, she dropped her *bolo*—a cutting implement—and he quickly picked it up and handed it back to her. "I liked him," she said.

Silence.

"And?"

"Then he moved away," she said.

"And?"

"That's all."

"Lola, have you ever had sex?" I heard myself saying.

"No," she said.

She wasn't accustomed to being asked personal questions. "*Katulong lang ako*," she'd say. *I'm only a servant.* She often gave one- or two-word answers, and teasing out even the simplest story was a game of twenty questions that could last days or weeks.

Some of what I learned: She was mad at Mom for being so cruel all those years, but she nevertheless missed her. Sometimes, when Lola was young, she'd felt so lonely that all she could do was cry. I knew there were years when she'd dreamed of being with a man. I saw it in the way she wrapped herself around one large pillow at night. But what she told me in her old age was that living with Mom's husbands made her think being alone wasn't so bad. She didn't miss those two at all. Maybe her life would have been better if she'd stayed in Mayantoc, gotten married, and had a family like her siblings. But maybe it would have been worse. Two younger sisters, Francisca and Zepriana, got sick and died. A brother, Claudio, was killed. What's the point of wondering about it now? she asked. *Bahala na* was her guiding principle. *Come what may.* What came her way was another kind of family. In that family, she had eight children: Mom, my four siblings and me, and now my two daughters. The eight of us, she said, made her life worth living.

None of us was prepared for her to die so suddenly.

Her heart attack started in the kitchen while she was making dinner and I was running an errand. When I returned she was in the middle of it. A couple of hours later at the hospital, before

I could grasp what was happening, she was gone—10:56 p.m. All the kids and grandkids noted, but were unsure how to take, that she died on November 7, the same day as Mom. Twelve years apart.

Lola made it to eighty-six. I can still see her on the gurney. I remember looking at the medics standing above this brown woman no bigger than a child and thinking that they had no idea of the life she had lived. She'd had none of the self-serving ambition that drives most of us, and her willingness to give up everything for the people around her won her our love and utter loyalty. She's become a hallowed figure in my extended family.

Going through her boxes in the attic took me months. I found recipes she had cut out of magazines in the 1970s for when she would someday learn to read. Photo albums with pictures of my mom. Awards my siblings and I had won from grade school on, most of which we had thrown away and she had "saved." I almost lost it one night when at the bottom of a box I found a stack of yellowed newspaper articles I'd written and long ago forgotten about. She couldn't read back then, but she'd kept them anyway.

·　　·　　·

Doods's truck pulled up to a small concrete house in the middle of a cluster of homes mostly made of bamboo and plank wood. Surrounding the pod of houses: rice fields, green and seemingly endless. Before I even got out of the truck, people started coming outside.

Doods reclined his seat to take a nap. I hung my tote bag on my shoulder, took a breath, and opened the door.

"This way," a soft voice said, and I was led up a short walkway to the concrete house. Following close behind was a line of about twenty people, young and old, but mostly old. Once we were all inside, they sat down on chairs and benches arranged along the walls, leaving the middle of the room empty except for me.

I remained standing, waiting to meet my host. It was a small room, and dark. People glanced at me expectantly.

"Where is Lola?" A voice from another room. The next moment, a middle-aged woman in a housedress sauntered in with a smile. Ebia, Lola's niece. This was her house. She gave me a hug and said again, "Where is Lola?"

I slid the tote bag from my shoulder and handed it to her. She looked into my face, still smiling, gently grasped the bag, and walked over to a wooden bench and sat down. She reached inside and pulled out the box and looked at every side. "Where is Lola?" she said softly. People in these parts don't often get their loved ones cremated. I don't think she knew what to expect. She set the box on her lap and bent over so her forehead rested on top of it, and at first I thought she was laughing (out of joy) but I quickly realized she was crying. Her shoulders began to heave, and then she was wailing—a deep, mournful, animal howl, like I once heard coming from Lola.

I hadn't come sooner to deliver Lola's ashes in part because I wasn't sure anyone here cared that much about her. I hadn't expected this kind of grief. Before I could comfort Ebia, a woman walked in from the kitchen and wrapped her arms around her, and then she began wailing. The next thing I knew, the room erupted with sound. The old people—one of them blind, several with no teeth—were all crying and not holding anything back. It lasted about ten minutes. I was so fascinated that I barely noticed the tears running down my own face. The sobs died down, and then it was quiet again.

Ebia sniffled and said it was time to eat. Everybody started filing into the kitchen, puffy-eyed but suddenly lighter and ready to tell stories. I glanced at the empty tote bag on the bench, and knew it was right to bring Lola back to the place where she'd been born.

## *Wired* with *Epic Magazine*

FINALIST—FEATURE
WRITING

In "Love in the Time of Robots," Alex Mar profiles Hiroshi Ishiguro, fifty-four, "a distinguished professor at one of the country's top universities, with two labs, partnerships with a dozen private companies throughout Japan, a recent $16 million grant from the government (one of its most generous in science and engineering, he says), and seven secretaries to manage it all." Or in the words of the Ellie judges, "an eccentric visionary who has spent a lifetime building androids, each more complex and human-like than its predecessor." This beautifully written story addresses the moral quandaries posed by artificial intelligence. "A meditation on human intimacy and loneliness in the twenty-first century," continued the judges, "it is both unnerving and unforgettable." Alex Mar's first book, Witches in America, explored the occult. Now at work on her second book, she also directed the documentary American Mystic.

Alex Mar

# Love in the Time of Robots

I t is summer 2002, midmorning in a university research lab on the edge of Osaka, Japan. Two girls—both dressed in pale yellow, with child-puffy cheeks, black shoulder-length hair, and bangs—stand opposite each other under fluorescent lights. More precisely: One is a girl, five years old; the other is her copy, her android replica. They are the same size, one modeled on the other, and they are meeting for the first time.

The girl stares hard into the eyes of her counterpart; its expression is stern and stiff. It seems to return her gaze.

A man is videotaping the pair—he is the father of one, creator of the other—and from off-camera he asks, "Would you like to say something?"

The girl turns to him, disoriented. She turns back to the android.

"Talk to her!" he says. "Hello."

The girl repeats the word, quietly, to her robot-self. It nods.

Her father feeds her another line: "Let's play."

The android wiggles its head. Her father chuckles behind the camera. But the girl does not budge. She simply stares at her double, the look on her face one of focus and perhaps concern.

Each member of this pair continues making the barely there gestures that serve, through reflex or ruse, as signs of life: Each blinks at regular intervals; each tilts her head from side to side.

One is processing, in the raw, sensory-overload manner of a human child; the other is performing a series of simple movements made possible by the servomotors installed inside the silicone casing that is its skin.

"Is it difficult to play with her?" the father asks. His daughter looks to him, then back at the android. Its mouth begins to open and close slightly, like a dying fish. He laughs. "Is she eating something?"

The girl does not respond. She is patient and obedient and listens closely. But something inside is telling her to resist.

"Do you feel strange?" her father asks. Even he must admit that the robot is not entirely believable.

Eventually, after a few long minutes, the girl's breathing grows heavier, and she announces, "I am so tired." Then she bursts into tears.

That night, in a house in the suburbs, her father uploads the footage to his laptop for posterity. His name is Hiroshi Ishiguro, and he believes this is the first record of a modern-day android.

.  .  .

In the fifteen years since, Ishiguro has produced some thirty androids, most of them female. They have included replicas of a newscaster, an actress, and a fashion model. These androids have made numerous public appearances—in cafés and department stores, singing in malls, performing in a play. Mostly, though, Ishiguro's brood of pretty "women" is used for his academic experiments, many of which are conducted at two locations in Japan: the Advanced Telecommunications Research Institute International in Nara and the Intelligent Robotics Laboratory on the campus of Osaka University.

The lab, known as IRL, is embedded within a maze of austere, gray university buildings. In one of these industrial boxes, about thirty students and assistant professors work in a series of near-silent computer pods and observation rooms. Teams of young men shuffle down the long, linoleum-lined hallways in sweatshirts, pace the research rooms in their socks, or hover over laptops in rows, heads down, subsisting mostly on Red Bull, crackers, and Pocky Sticks. (Women do not seem like a natural fit here. As if to underline this fact, a sign by the restrooms reads, "Watch out for male strangers in the ladies toilet.")

Presiding over this disheveled scene is Ishiguro-sensei. He is immediately recognizable, looking just as he does in promotional photos from recent years: perfectly mod in slim-fitting black with matching leather backpack and fanny pack. He wears tinted hexagonal glasses and styles his jet-black hair into a mop top that swoops across his forehead. This is his department: Ishiguro, fifty-four, is a distinguished professor at one of the country's top universities, with two labs, partnerships with a dozen private companies throughout Japan, a recent $16 million grant from the government (one of its most generous in science and engineering, he says), and seven secretaries to manage it all.

Today, the technical ability to produce a robot that truly looks and moves and speaks like a human remains well beyond our reach. Even further beyond our grasp is the capacity to imbue such a machine with humanness—that ineffable presence the Japanese call *sonzai-kan*. Because to re-create human presence we need to know more about ourselves than we do—about the accumulation of cues and micromovements that trigger our empathy, put us at ease, and earn our trust. Someday we may crack the problem of creating artificial general intelligence—a machine brain that can intuitively perform any human intellectual task—but why would we choose to interact with it?

Ishiguro believes that since we're hardwired to interact with and place our faith in humans, the more humanlike we can make a robot appear, the more open we'll be to sharing our lives with it. Toward this end, his teams are pioneering a young field of research called human-robot interaction.

HRI is a hybrid discipline: part engineering, part AI, part social psychology and cognitive science. The aim is to analyze and cultivate our evolving relationship with robots. HRI seeks to understand why and when we're willing to interact with and maybe even feel affection for a machine. And with each android he produces, Ishiguro believes he is moving closer to building that trust.

In a secluded room at IRL, a collection of androids is stored and maintained: his hardest workers. Arranged in this space today, with its blackout curtains, thin corporate carpeting, and shelves cluttered with cables and monitors and an array of wigs, is a pair of his replicas of grown women. They are models of the Geminoid F series. The name is a play off *geminus* (Latin for "twin"), a reminder that their human counterparts exist some-where in the world.

At any given time, students and staff may be testing, measur-ing, and recording the responses of dozens of volunteers to the androids at their disposal. What about its behavior or appearance, its specific facial expressions and minute body movements, do they find alienating? What draws them closer? These androids are used to find answers to an ever-growing list of research questions: How important is nonverbal communication to establishing trust between humans (and, therefore, between human and android)? Under what circumstances might we treat an android like a human? In this way, Ishiguro's collective of labs is dedicated to the engineering of human intimacy.

.  .  .

Over the several months we are in contact, Ishiguro will share information that strikes me as deeply personal: He has contem-plated suicide twice in his life; though he has a family, he considers himself a lonely man. I will hear him use that word to describe himself—*lonely*—about half a dozen times.

As for me, when I first visit Ishiguro, my situation is this:

I am twenty-three months away from what had seemed like the start of a serious relationship but was not. I am fifteen months away from a rebound relationship that lingered too long. I am thirteen months into a period of spending long stints in a small town in upstate New York for the sake of productive quiet. I'm readying a book to go to the printers—work that, for me, is all-consuming and necessary. And lately, when I step back from the manuscript for an afternoon or at night, I feel it: isolation. This isolation is not complete—I have my close friends, a wider circle of less-close friends, my family—but it is the absence of intimacy. Nothing romantic, no sexual life.

This absence has been, in part, a choice; certain men have always been curious about me. But what I miss more than sex is the feeling of closeness with another person, something I've never believed could be conjured up. And though the sensory deprivation has become a little extreme, most of the time—can I put a percentage on it? Is it as high as 80 percent?—I do not think about it. I am semiradically independent and some kind of artist and in many ways an unconventional liberal woman. However alienating, for me this is a time of deep creativity. It's that additional 20 percent of the time—that's when I feel dizzy.

This is where I'm at when I fly seventeen hours to meet Ishiguro. And as a result, if I am honest with myself, my time abroad feels particularly fraught. The very concept of "human connection" has never felt so enigmatic to me. It makes sense that someone would be trying to measure it, to weigh it, to calculate its dimensions. To be able to replicate the sensation of human intimacy would be to control the very thing that confuses us most and eludes so many.

·　　·　　·

This is how Ishiguro remembers his childhood:

IIis family lives in the town of Adogawa, on the western shore of Lake Biwa, from which a river flows through Kyoto into Osaka Bay. At school, in a classroom of disciplined children, Hiroshi doesn't listen to the instructor. It's as if he doesn't notice she is speaking at all. He spends the day making drawings that have nothing to do with the lesson. His mother worries that there may be something wrong with him.

Hiroshi rarely sees his mother or father—as schoolteachers they are as consumed by their work as their son will one day become. Instead, his grandparents are raising him. His mother's father is a farmer, a devout Buddhist with fixed, traditional ideas about "how to behave like a Japanese man." He shows the boy the proper way to use chopsticks, to pray, to prepare the house for the New Year's celebration. Unlike at school, Hiroshi has the patience for these lessons: His grandfather is not telling him how he should think; he is teaching him to aspire to perfection.

They live at the foot of the Hira Mountains, and Hiroshi likes to comb the mountainside for snakes and insects. Maybe a stag beetle, glossy black and segmented, nearly three inches long, with a pair of antler-shaped mandibles emerging straight from its head. He fixes new parts to its body: razor blades, found pieces of metal. It is an improvement. The insect may continue living like this, if the glue doesn't kill it. These are his earliest cyborgs.

One of Hiroshi's close friends is a boy who lives in a poorer community, down by the water, and his parents collect and prepare the bodies of the recently dead for burial. Hiroshi does not yet understand that these people are considered to be lesser than his family because they have a job that, according to local prejudice, is tainted. For this reason, when Hiroshi's mother discovers the friendship, she asks that her son break it off. He will remember this moment for the next forty years.

Hiroshi is a delicate child. He has suffered from extreme skin allergies from the time he was born; his back and chest and arms are covered in itchy, ugly rashes. His only comfort comes from constant touch: Every night, his grandparents take turns sitting beside him and scratching his back until he is able to nod off. Every week his doctor gives him three painful injections to try to cure the condition—to no effect. (When he is about twelve, steroids will finally help, requiring him to keep the drug on hand to this day.) His own body will always be alien to him.

·        ·        ·

When it comes time for Ishiguro to go to college, he chooses a school using three criteria: It will accept an eccentric, sometimes indifferent student like himself; it's somewhere he can pursue his drawing and painting; and it's not very close to home. In the fall of 1981, he lands at the University of Yamanashi, near Mount Fuji.

Once there, Ishiguro continues his careless approach to his studies, finding more pleasure in the string of odd jobs he takes to pay the bills—he works as a cook, the supervisor of a children's after-school program, a door-to-door textbook salesman (that one lasts a week), and, most lucrative of all, a professional pachinko player. He finds himself on the fringes of student life, rejecting any semblance of mainstream Japanese ambition.

At the same time, he is fashioning himself into that most romantic of outsiders: an artist. Always in a black leather jacket, he skips classes, packs his pads and pencils, and rides his Yamaha chopper into the nearby countryside to sketch the landscape. This is his focus: the strange, organic shapes of the trees, the peach blossoms that appear in the springtime. He produces drawings and oil paintings and manages to sell a few.

But in his third year, Ishiguro abruptly gives up painting. Unless he can become a great artist and a tremendous public success, he sees no point in it. (He blames, in part, his color blindness: He is drawn to landscapes, but the entire spectrum of green eludes him.) He has lost what little direction he had. On his darker days, when he takes his motorcycle on a steep and winding road, Ishiguro imagines giving in to the impulse to not make the turn. To drive straight ahead, fly right off the edge—what would that feel like?

Then a path presents itself. Yamanashi offers courses in the new field of computer science, and Ishiguro begins to wonder what relationship computer graphics and computer vision might have to the visual arts. These are the early days of the PC, and programming seems wildly creative. Feeling he has little to lose, he switches majors.

Almost immediately, certain elements in his brain click into place: Ishiguro realizes he can continue to think like a painter in this unpoliced field but with different tools. He falls in love with the new vocabulary: Assembler, Pascal. The students are relegated to working in a single room kept bitterly cold, loud with the hum of the huge computers—conditions designed for the comfort of machines, not humans. He works alone, on software development, but he is learning to communicate with a system—a system that responds to his commands. They have entered into a dialogue.

Ishiguro soon gives up his rides through the country for entire days spent in the lab. And as he becomes more fluent in this new language, more immersed in a conversation with the large machines, a fantasy takes shape: Could there be a way to make this language more humanlike, so that someday computers might understand us intuitively, on our own terms? So that this dialogue might become a relationship?

This relationship becomes his singular pursuit, his dream.

●    ●    ●

In 2000, Ishiguro, as an associate professor at Kyoto University, produces his first humanoid robot: a mechanical-looking contraption that moves on a wheeled platform, waving its jointed steel arms. But he has started to think that a relatable, human-like appearance is essential if people are going to form real attachments to robots.

It's about a decade into his marriage (to a pianist he met through a university friend), and he asks his wife if he can make videotapes of her—sitting, breathing, responding to random stimuli. He is trying to determine the nuances of human behavior, to isolate the physical signs that read to us, consciously or unconsciously, as "human." One minor revelation: Humans never truly sit still.

Ishiguro is aware of resistance to the concept of an android—at least in the West, from which many Japanese researchers take their cue. Some are worried that consumer revulsion to a human-like robot (the so-called uncanny valley effect) would be too great to overcome and that a failed android project could undercut public support of robotics. Ishiguro, too, is worried that pushing ahead with an untraditional approach might cost him his academic career. But he can't resist. And so when the company he has partnered with on a new robot insists on hiring a respected designer that makes it look, in Ishiguro's opinion, "like an insect," he loses his patience. With his next project, he decides to go rogue. He will create an android "to convince them."

Ishiguro believes that his first android should be the same height as the insect (about three-and-a-half feet tall), for purposes of comparison. In other words, it will have to be modeled after a human child. And given the painstaking production process—a model must spend hours encased in plaster to cast an accurate replica—there is only one child he can possibly get permission to use: his own.

A few years earlier, Ishiguro became a father to a daughter, named Risa, and he now turns to his wife to explain his plan. She agrees—she is in charge of raising the girl, and the experiment would be difficult without her help. And so, in early 2002, the entire family, along with makeup and special effects artists, gathers in his lab on campus and begins the two-day process of creating a replica of Risa.

.        .        .

In the lab, Risa's mother helps her to undress. She takes off the girl's clothes and stands her up on a small wooden platform. Together her father and an artist smooth a layer of pale-green paste over her torso and upper thighs; over that, they apply wide swatches of fabric dipped in plaster, asking her to hold very still as it dries. Then the five-year-old girl, wrapped in a pink towel, her scalp covered in a rubber cap and her ears plugged with cotton, is laid down on a tabletop, her head fenced in with Styrofoam and packing tape. An artist lifts a plastic bucket and pours the paste in until it rises to cover her ears, as father and mother try to reassure her: "Don't worry!" and "You're fine!" At last they prepare the girl for the final part of the process: her face.

Through a video camera's viewfinder, Ishiguro watches the rigid expression on his small daughter's face as her mother and an artist slowly cover it in thick paste. "Once we're done," her father says, "you can eat anything you like!" They slather it across her forehead, around her chin, and down the front of her neck; they apply it thickly on her cheeks and across her nose, then subsume her entire mouth, her mother laughing, keeping the mood light. "Keep your eyes closed. Like you're going to bed . . . Good night!" The whole time, remarkable for a child her age, she does not move or make a sound. And then the paste closes in on her as they smooth it over her eyelids, and within moments her face is layered in the creamy stuff, which has already begun to harden. Her entire face is under—save her nostrils: a single hole left clear for breathing.

"You're OK," the artist says. "Just a little bit longer . . ."

Then Ishiguro, from behind the camera: "Risa, you're totally fine . . . If you're feeling sleepy, if your head feels heavy, you can just lean back. Just like sleeping . . ."

They press a square of plaster-soaked fabric over her face (again, a hole for breathing) and it begins to stiffen. And perhaps the professor is now concerned because he loses the shot, tilting the camera up to point at the wall. "Risa, if you can breathe properly through your nose, please squeeze my hand . . ."

"Risa," her mother says, "make sure you don't cry, because it'll block your nose. Anyway, there's no need to cry! Be patient . . . It's OK to sleep. Go to sleep . . ."

When, months later, the package arrives at the lab, Ishiguro and his team open the crate to reveal the full-body silicone-skin casing of his daughter: Risa, bald, naked, made of rubber. They stretch the skin around foam-padded machinery and prop it up in the lab. His wife has donated one of their daughter's sundresses so it has something to wear. Ishiguro names it Repliee R1—*R* for Risa.

The results of the experiment are mixed. Ishiguro has to admit that the low-budget android, with its limited, stuttering movements, is more zombie than human. And though he shows the project only to a trusted inner circle, word of the "daughter android" spreads, becoming a weird legend. (In describing it, one roboticist I speak with uses the word "crazy," another "strange" and "a little bit scary.") But Repliee R1 gives Ishiguro the confidence to move forward.

As for his daughter, Ishiguro rewards her with several Hello Kitty dolls. "But still," he says, "she cried." To this day, they've never spoken about the incident.

.        •        •

Three years later, in 2005, Ishiguro unveils Repliee Q1 Expo to the public. Modeled on a grown woman (a popular Tokyo newscaster) and produced with better funding, this version can move its upper body fluidly and lip-synch to recorded speech. Ishiguro's lab conducts several studies with it; the results are featured in a major Japanese robotics journal; the lab is filmed for television; he hears about a copycat android in South Korea. As a growing audience is drawn to Ishiguro's simulated human, his instincts are validated.

But he now wants something more. Twice he has witnessed others have the opportunity, however confusing, to encounter their robot self, and he covets that experience. Besides, his daughter was too young, and the newscaster, though an adult, was, in his words, merely an "ordinary" person: Neither was able to analyze their android encounter like a trained scientist. A true researcher should have his own double. Flashing back to his previous life as a painter, Ishiguro thinks: This will be another form of self-portrait. He gives the project his initials: Geminoid HI. His mechanical twin.

Ishiguro has hundreds of photos of the Geminoid's assembly. Here is his assistant wrapping the facsimile of his then-forty-three-year-old face around the machine head and zipping it up the back, its bald scalp studded with sensors. Here is the Geminoid seated upright, a padded vest in place of its torso, its mechanical biceps visible, its arms only "flesh" below the elbows, as if it were wearing elegant gloves. The hands have veins and sunspots and the faint wrinkles that gather around the wrists; the nails have cuticles, pale and precise. Here it is dressed, in a fitted black shirt identical to Ishiguro's. His assistant raises its arms, one by one, to tug down the sleeves, as if dressing a complicated child.

It also wears fitted black slacks, like Ishiguro's, and black sneakers stuffed with prosthetic feet in matching socks; a black wig, styled like the hair of its maker, is fastened onto the android's scalp with snaps. Here is the machine that pumps air into its chest—a series of cables runs from its tailbone into a metal box—as the professor's double sits at attention and speaks for the first time.

This android is a step forward, but it still falls well short of verisimilitude. Its hands, at rest on its lap, are rubbery to the touch; its eyes have a surprising intensity, not unlike Ishiguro's, but they are clearly made of a hard, bright plastic. Lean in close and you can hear the soft hum of a hidden motor; a gentle click is audible each time it blinks. At times, its overall effect, and that of its sisters, is of a human-sized puppet—like the animatronics in a Disney World display. But the Geminoid is also unsettling. Because, somehow, all these elements work in concert to simulate a sympathetic interaction with a human. The viewer cannot help but assign an entire range of emotions to its face: melancholic (mouth downturned), upset (eyes squinted shut), skeptical (a sideways glance), pensive (the tilt of its head to the left). When its eyes meet yours, motion sensors detecting your position, just for a moment you feel that it—this "he," this "Ishiguro"—is aware of you.

This replica, Geminoid HI, brings Ishiguro the recognition he has longed for. Using his double, he and his team publish dozens of studies, analyzing the participants' range of reactions to him and his doppelganger. (The studies involve operating the android remotely and wirelessly: teleoperation.) Side by side, he and his Geminoid make appearances on TV shows across Asia and Europe. Ishiguro also begins giving lectures around the world without leaving his lab in Osaka, teleoperating and speaking through the android, which is carefully transported abroad by an assistant. (Its legs and torso are checked with the luggage; its head is carry-on.) Ishiguro-sensei becomes a source of fascination; he is transformed from a researcher to the man who made his copy. Invitations for conferences and festivals stream in.

The success of this particular android is due, in part, to how it seems to operate on several levels. It is, like its predecessors, a circus trick: *Look at the human, look at his copy! Try to tell them apart!* It is also Ishiguro's bid at solving an existential dilemma—a striking attempt by the maker to master himself, to make of himself something more enduring.

At the same time, it has created a new predicament. Ishiguro has discovered unexpected consequences of living alongside his own replica. He's been dressing in black since his grad-school years, and now this has become both his and the HI's official uniform; he was thrilled to realize this clearer vision of himself. But now he must keep his (naturally shifting, aging) human body corralled within the android's static limits. He finds himself accommodating his android, measuring himself against it, being defined by it, his worth determined by it. In this way, his android makes him both painfully conscious of his aging body and more physically confident than he's ever been.

Ishiguro is multiple myths simultaneously. With his female androids, he is Pygmalion, bringing his Galatea to life. But with his own replica, he is Narcissus, staring into his reflection for hours. Unlike Narcissus, of course, Ishiguro is conscious of the situation he has created, but he's set an unexpected trap for himself through his image. He poses beside his android, in press photos and TV appearances, in ways that accommodate the Geminoid, setting his face to mirror its expression. (At one point at the research institute, Ishiguro notices me photographing him in front of his android and reflexively drops his smile to match the robot at rest.)

Soon his students begin comparing him to the Geminoid—"Oh, professor, you are getting old," they tease—and Ishiguro finds little humor in it. A few years later, at forty-six, he has another cast of his face made, to reflect his aging, producing a second version of HI. But to repeat this process every few years would be costly and hard on his vanity. Instead, Ishiguro embraces the logical alternative: to alter his human form to match that of his copy. He opts for a range of cosmetic procedures—laser treatments and the injection of his own blood cells into his face. He also begins watching his diet and lifting weights; he loses about twenty pounds. "I decided not to get old anymore," says Ishiguro, whose English is excellent but syntactically imperfect. "Always I am getting younger."

Remaining twinned with his creation has become a compulsion. "Android has my identity," he says. "I need to be identical with my android, otherwise I'm going to lose my identity." I think back to another photo of his first double's construction: Its robot skull, exposed, is a sickly yellow plastic shell with openings for glassy teeth and eyeballs. When I ask what he was thinking as he watched this replica of his own head being assembled, Ishiguro says, perhaps only half-joking, "I thought I might have this kind of skull if I removed my face."

Now he points at me. "Why are you coming here? Because I have created my copy. The work is important; android is important. But you are not interested in myself."

.       .       .

On a winter day in 2012, a crowd clusters around a large glass case in Tokyo's Takashimaya department store. Perched inside is a Geminoid F in an elegant silk day dress, long brown bangs parted like curtains around its face. Valentine's Day is coming soon, and "she" sits, as if waiting for someone, before a backdrop of gift boxes wrapped in rose-patterned paper and large red bows.

She spends her days staring at her smartphone and mostly ignoring the thousands of visitors who press close to the glass. All the while, she goes through a range of facial expressions, a spectrum of subtle emotions, as if reacting to some text she has just received. It's a clever ploy: By not interacting much with her onlookers, the simulation maintains the appearance of a human likeness—after all, real people spend a lot of time willfully ignoring their surroundings. But occasionally, when you approach, she looks up at you and smiles, and for a moment this feels like an encounter with a pretty stranger.

Some days, Ishiguro stands across the aisle, by the main entrance, and watches the people who stop in front of her. He likes to imagine what they believe she is thinking.

As complex as we assume ourselves to be, our bonds with one another are often built on very little. Given all the time we now spend living through technology, not many of us would notice, at least at first, if the friend we were messaging were replaced by a bot. And humans do not require much to stir up feelings of empathy with another person or creature—even an object. In 2011 a University of Calgary test found that subjects were quick to assign emotions and intentions to a piece of balsa wood operated with a joystick. In other words, we are so hardwired for empathy that our brains are willing to make the leap to humanizing a piece of wood. It's a level of animal instinct that's slapstick-hilarious and a degree of vulnerability that's terrifying.

But as the object of our attention moves closer in appearance to human, our expectations of them grow far more complex. The uncanny valley effect kicks in—a huge drop-off in the graph of our empathy as we sense we're encountering something both familiar and not quite right. The same year as the Calgary test, having recently developed his first-generation Geminoid F, Ishiguro and the University of California at San Diego published a study of neurons associated with empathy. The team used an fMRI machine to scan the brains of twenty people in their twenties and thirties as they watched separate videos of one of Ishiguro's female androids, the same android with its machinery revealed, and the living human that the android was modeled after.

· · ·

The subjects saw each in turn wave its hand, nod, pick up a piece of paper, wipe a table with a cloth. Of the three videos, it was while watching the humanlike android's motions that the parietal cortex of the subjects' brains would light up most—in particular, the areas that connect our detection of bodily movement with our so-called empathy neurons. The researchers believe this revealed that the smallest gestures can create perceptual contradictions in the brain, sparking the uncanny valley effect. Ishiguro returned to the lab and redoubled his focus on the android's most minute movements: the precise tilt of the chin, the rotation of the head, the restraint of the smile.

Around the same time as the department store display, Ishiguro managed to use the Geminoid F to generate a bond between two humans. Tettchan, then a game designer based in Tokyo, was recently divorced when he met Ishiguro in 2012, and he mentioned that he was curious about the possibility of a romance with a longtime friend named Miki. Ishiguro invited them both to his research institute in Nara, where he'd asked his students to have a female android ready for teleoperation. He placed Tettchan at the teleoperation desk and closed the door; he took Miki into the other room to meet the Geminoid F. Then he invited Tettchan (who was listening in) to talk to him and Miki through the robot. As Tettchan spoke, his voice computer-altered to sound female, the android's lips moved in sync with his words, the tilt of her head and her long human hair in rhythm with his own movements. "It's like a real female," Ishiguro told Miki, enjoying himself. "This is not Tettchan, this is a new woman, really cute and beautiful."

And so they "played," making small talk, Tettchan trying out his new female incarnation. He made Miki and Ishiguro laugh, and watching Miki's face through the monitor, he could see a change. That was when Ishiguro, knowing Tettchan's complicated feelings for Miki, said to her, "OK, you should kiss her." And Miki, looking hesitant, leaned in toward the android—the android inhabited by Tettchan—and kissed it on the cheek. The feeling, Tettchan said, was "like thunder." Any boundary between them suddenly vanished.

Not long afterward, Tettchan and Miki decided to live together. Tettchan is still not exactly sure how Ishiguro's machine worked on them, but he remains convinced that it made them into a couple.

.        .        .

Over dinner with Hiroshi:

He has spent a lot of time talking to himself through his androids, testing them, imagining their effect on other people. Hiroshi (who by now has asked me to call him by his first name) tells me he'd like to record himself saying "I love you" and then program an android to repeat it back to him in a female voice. He is kidding when he says this—but maybe it's another of his half jokes. At the very least, he believes the need for such an exchange exists. It would be, he says, "a real conversation." A conversation with himself.

"A conversation is a kind of illusion," he says. "I don't know what is going on in your brain. All I can know is what I'm thinking. Always I am asking questions to myself, but through conversations." Over the years of operating his androids, communicating through them or with them, he has found that he isn't really concerned about the other person's thoughts. "Always I am thinking of myself. I need to understand your intention, but it is not priority. Before that, I want to make clear something in my brain. Otherwise, what is the motivation to talk?"

In other words, he can only imagine using conversation with others as a means to better understand himself—and nothing is more pressing than that. He turns to the conversation the two of us are having. "We don't know how much information we are sharing," he tells me. "I am always guessing, and you are always guessing, and through our conversation patterns we can believe that we exchange information. But I cannot access your brain directly.

"What is 'connection'?" he asks. "Other person is just a mirror."

On some fundamental level, we understand each other's immediate intentions and desires—of course, we do; how else would we function? But Hiroshi's view, though stark, seems sadly right: There are entire planets of intimate information, our most interior level of consciousness, that we will never fully be able to share. Our longing to connect, to bridge this divide, is a driving human desire—one that Hiroshi believes will someday be satisfied through humanlike machines. He is convinced that human emotions, whether empathy or romantic love, are nothing more than responses to stimuli, subject to manipulation. Through the fluid interplay of its pneumatic joints, the arch of its mechanical brow, the tilt of its plastic skull, the many subtle movements achieved through years of research studying the human template, the android becomes more able to span that gap, to form a perfectly engineered bond with us. An elaborate metaphysical trick, perhaps—but what does that matter, if it fills a need? If it feels real?

I think of the gentle look on the face of Geminoid F as she glances down at a smartphone that she cannot read. He wants us to imagine her reading notes we have sent her, to imagine her loneliness, to love her. Every time we project our own feelings onto her—imagine a shared experience, a connection—his work inches forward.

·　　·　　·

Hiroshi says little about his personal life, but, with his constant travel and self-imposed sixteen-hour workdays, I understand that he and his wife lead fairly independent lives. "We have some simple rules. She never asks about my job, I never ask about her hobbies."

Quickly, he brightens up—he has found a way to return, in his mind, to the work. "I want to know the meaning of 'love.' Do you know the real meaning? What is 'love'?"

I think for a moment. "It changes all the time in my mind."

"That's good!" he says, surprised. "You are like a scientist. I am always changing too. I am having different hypotheses every year. Before I pass away, I want to have a better understanding about love."

Hiroshi now tells me of the two times he has seriously considered suicide: first at thirty-six, when one of his top students bested him at a computer-programming challenge (his focus at the time), and again ten years later, when another student proved to be a sharper, more prolific writer of technical papers (something Hiroshi took great pride in). Both times, he swerved out of the depression by finding a new angle on his work. But those instances heightened his dread that he might not be able to prevent the slow, natural deterioration of his mind. He is already certain that his concentration is not what it once was. Developing dementia as he ages is his worst fear. Without being able to generate new ideas, "probably I cannot find any reason to survive in this world. I don't like to imagine that."

We are quiet for a moment—then he leans in again.

"Do you know what is the soul?" he asks. "Soul is not so personal. In Japan, when we pass away, our soul goes back to the same place, back to the mountain. So now we are living individually, like this"—he motions to the two of us sitting on mats. "We have our own souls. But when we pass away, we're going to share something. Soul is going back to the place where souls are coming together.

"Soul is not lonely," he says. "Soul is not alone."

●   ●   ●

On a Saturday night, I meet up with Hiroshi and Rosario Sorbello, a robotics professor from the University of Palermo who makes a couple of pilgrimages to Hiroshi's lab each year. He often sends his students to study there, and he arranged for Hiroshi's android play to be performed in Sicily. For a tall man in a well-tailored suit and fine leather shoes, Sorbello is boyish, and he clearly relishes his access to Hiroshi—he reminds me, twice, that Hiroshi is "a very important person."

We meet in Minami, one of Osaka's hectic shopping districts, and have an evening of street food: huge bowls of ramen and batter-fried balls of octopus. (Hiroshi used to come here a lot in his days as a poor grad student.) After red-bean dessert soup, served by a woman in a ruffled apron, Hiroshi makes a decision: Rather than head to a bar, he says we should go to "the bar in my office." En route, we stop at a fluorescent-lit, twenty-four-hour convenience store to pick up drinking food—wasabi peas, octopus jerky, chocolate Pocky Sticks—before boarding the train back to the university.

As Hiroshi scrolls through his phone, Sorbello talks about the desire for intimacy with androids—something he's clearly thought a lot about. "Can you imagine what it would be like," he asks, "to want to kiss a robot? To want to kiss that rubber, not-human flesh? There are people who have those kinds of desires. Imagine if you could run heat through its skin so that it feels not like cold rubber but warm to the touch? There are people who want to try things with that." Human sexual and romantic relationships are unavoidably messy, he says, and many people would like to keep their lives simple—in which case a relationship with an android might be a solution. "I think this is the future," he says.

Sex is arguably the ultimate physical act of human connection—but it can also be merely that: an act, a simulation of intimacy. Sex can be thought of as something that transcends the purely physical, but in reality it is often an experience that's *mostly* physical, not as intimate as we pretend it can or should be. Looked at in this light, a whole range of sexual experience, at least in theory, could be replicated with an android.

On Sorbello's recommendation, I later read *Love and Sex with Robots*, a 2007 book by AI expert David Levy. In it he proposes that we are not far from a time (he suggests roughly the year 2050) when humans will desire robots as friends, sexual partners, even spouses—a premise he seems unnervingly OK with. It all comes down to our willingness to believe in the robot's emotional life and desires. Designed with the physical proportions that its human owner prefers, the preferred voice timbre and eye color and personality type, and the ability to recall and riff on its owner's personal stories and little jokes, android will captivate human.

Levy takes Alan Turing's famous claim that the convincing appearance of intelligence (in AI) is proof of intelligence, and he expands that into the emotional realm: "If a robot behaves as though it has feelings, can we reasonably argue that it does not? If a robot's artificial emotions prompt it to say things such as 'I love you,' surely we should be willing to accept these statements at face value . . . Why, if a robot that we know to be emotionally intelligent, says, 'I love you' or 'I want to make love to you,' should we doubt it?" Human emotions, he argues, are no less "programmed" than those of an intelligent machine: "We have hormones, we have neurons, and we are 'wired' in a way that creates our emotions."

In other words, Levy argues, our inner lives are essentially algorithmic, much like an AI's. A few decades from now, he writes, the differences between human and android may be "no greater than the cultural differences between peoples from different countries or even from different parts of the same country." As for the actual sex, Levy believes that it will become not only a recourse for the socially isolated but also an accepted outlet for the sexually adventurous or for someone whose partner is sick or traveling.

·          ·          ·

These are pretty radical ideas about human nature and intimacy, and yet I recognize the desire some might have to turn to an android for closeness, for companionship—for comfort when you're far from home, maybe on the other side of the planet, on assignment for weeks at a time. And if someone provides you with a salve, why not take it? Most of us already allow technology to mediate what was once simple, direct human interaction—what really is the difference? And is that difference so essential to the experience of being human that it must be preserved?

Back on campus, we pass the few students who are still sequestered in the lab, working late, and hide out in Hiroshi's office. There he slides back his whiteboard to reveal a hidden liquor cabinet. He pours us some excellent local whiskey, and we sit back and listen to his collection of music, everything from Japanese pop ballads to Simon and Garfunkel. We've all had a few. Hiroshi tells us about how, from the moment he started exposing people to his androids, a shift took place: The androids, he says, seemed to unmask the humans around them, to reveal a desire they'd carefully been hiding—for connection, for touch. There was the expected: Men who leered at the female androids during industry showcases, men who had to be watched closely, for fear they'd try to kiss and grope the robots. But something more complicated was also taking place.

Shortly after the android of his daughter was completed in 2002, Hiroshi had his students at Kyoto University use it to test the differences in human response to a mechanical-looking robot and one that was humanlike. When not in use, the android was left in the middle of the lab, and soon a few students complained that they were having trouble working in front of it. They felt it looking at them. (From then on, they made a habit of placing it with its face to the wall.)

Things were further complicated when Hiroshi was informed that one of the students had become attached to his daughter's replica. During the day, this student would run the experiments, but late at night, when he thought he was alone in the lab, he would serenade the android with his flute and then chat with it, asking what it thought of his playing. It was as if he felt he could only reach out for companionship this way, in secret.

This incident made Hiroshi realize that these androids could have unexpected emotional impact. "That was the first android," Hiroshi says. "We did not know what would happen." He moved the android to Osaka University and assigned another student to oversee the work. He also laid some ground rules for how it could be used: not late at night and not alone.

When he then created the first replica of a grown woman, he was a little wary of what his students might do with it in the lab. Would they want to sleep holding her in their arms? Hiroshi witnessed how one staff member, who'd been closely involved in the Geminoid's production, became visibly flustered in front of "her." Hiroshi's theory is that a friendly human woman will always be merely a "real person," never as "elegant" as her android counterpart. "We want to have some ideal partner, and the android can be a very strong mirror to reflect your own idea." In this way, a relationship with an android is like having a partner who is, literally, an extension of yourself.

The response of so many men to Hiroshi's female androids unsettles him. But it's also one he's been cultivating. In 2014, he embarked on a new project that marries his personal perfectionism with his ideas about female beauty: During my visit, he and his robotics team are at work on what he refers to as "the most beautiful woman." His not-entirely-empirical approach to its appearance has included speaking with a popular cosmetic surgeon in Osaka (his own), analyzing images of Miss Universe pageant finalists, and, in the end, trusting his gut. (He has reminded me a few times that he thinks more like an "artist" than other roboticists.) Hiroshi worked for two twelve-hour sessions with a technician to create the android's 3-D rendering. He was thrilled to discover that the slightest change to its eyes or nose transformed the rendering into a completely different person. "It feels like—how can I say?—not my daughter, but a special person for me," he says.

Now, when I ask Hiroshi why he puts such emphasis on good-looking mechanical women, he reminds me that the larger goal of his field is to have people accept robots into their lives. "And which is more acceptable to many people," he asks, "beautiful woman or ugly woman?" In a corporate lecture I later hear him give, he sums it up like this: "A beautiful woman you don't picture going to the restroom or getting tired. So I think beauty is better represented by android."

At this point, Hiroshi stands up from his ergonomic chair, as if inspiration has struck. He turns his back to me and Sorbello, rummages through his drawers, and produces a black zipper bag. From inside, he pulls out two hand-size foam mock-ups of a humanoid figure and offers me one as a gift. He picks up the other and holds it out to me.

"Let's make an experiment," he says. "We bring them together and we make them kiss."

I'm unsure of where this is going. "OK."

I bring the face of my tiny figure to meet the face of his, and their motionless mouths touch.

"It feels funny, right?" he asks. And it does. It feels just a little like crossing a line.

.        .        .

I return to Tokyo for a few days to meet more of Hiroshi's colleagues. And in the midst of this back-and-forth from Osaka, something is starting to happen: I am falling for someone I met on the second night of my trip.

I was introduced to Ethan over e-mail by my literary agent, who knew I'd been searching for helpful contacts in Japan. He's an American (also in his thirties) who moved to Tokyo for graphic-design work a decade ago and is fluent in Japanese. Ethan (a pseudonym) e-mailed me the names of fixers and translators and boutique hotels and agreed to join me for dinner before I took the Shinkansen bullet train west to Osaka. When I found him that evening, at our meeting spot in front of a Shibuya-ku Metro station, his eyes reflected back to me the thought just then crossing my mind: This will be a very good night.

I've never been particularly drawn to men who are handsome in a conventional way. But Ethan's looks are so classically handsome, it seems impossible that he walks around with such a face and such a strong jawline and such a finely shaped head. (Have I ever before thought about the shape of a man's head?) There is also the small hollow at the back of his neck and the width of his shoulders (something about their proportion gives me a startled feeling in my chest) and the smell of his skin and the timbre of his voice (deep and musical).

He becomes my guide in an unfamiliar city. I am led around and am much happier for it. We drink in a white bar with sliding paper screens; a jazz bar in which no one is allowed to laugh out loud; a space with eight seats, covered in Wim Wenders film posters; a hotel lounge with a piano singer and fifty-second-floor views of the city. We talk about books; we talk about our families; we talk about the people we've thought we loved. We walk down the streets at night with our arms lightly touching; we sit with our knees lightly touching; I lay my palm on that hollow at the back of his neck. And in private, we lie down in his bedroom, on a thin mattress on the floor, and remove all our clothes. It has been ages since either of us was drawn to someone in this way, an attraction that feels like a planetary pull, seemingly outside the realm of reason and predictability—the very thing we spend so much time trying to conjure up but over which we have no control.

It is thrilling. And for me right now, immersed in the world of android design—a heavily mediated world in which soft silicone shells stand in for human skin, in which we search for signs of human kindness or sadness or pity in a mechanical face—it is also a relief that something so simple can still happen. It is a relief because it means that we are animals, not ideas; that our chemistry is not as cool as a set of programmed responses—there's an immediate magic to it. To know that that instinct is not broken in me, and to be able to answer it, makes me feel like a person again.

·　　　·　　　·

When Hiroshi first considered building an android, he began a search for the right silicone. He turned to Orient Industry, a company that specializes in high-end "love dolls," sex dolls that can cost thousands of dollars. They collaborated on a trial model—but Hiroshi soon severed the relationship. As his reputation grew, he worried about how such a collaboration might look. The government does not want its money associated with love dolls.

The sex industry, however, does not need government approval to thrive. Back when they briefly worked together, Orient Industry operated out of a single room; now, almost two decades later, it occupies an entire building—and it sells nothing more advanced than poseable dolls. Human-robot sex, Hiroshi believes, will definitely be part of our future, it's merely a question of when. He knows that his research would be very helpful in that arena, but as a respected academic he would require a noncommercial, for-the-betterment-of-society reason to pursue that line of inquiry. Perhaps for people with disabilities, he suggests. "Once we create a pretty good sex doll, you know, definitely other people want to use it," he says. "It's a basic desire."

We're heading back to Osaka from Nara as he says this, speeding down the highway in his slim black Mazda—Hiroshi drives the way he walks: irrationally fast—and eventually our talk turns to the 1982 film *Blade Runner*. He's stuck on the lead female replicant, whose name he can't remember. "She looks like you!"

Hiroshi pauses for a moment, and when he speaks again, it's in a thoughtful voice. "Someday I want to have my own replicant," he says. "Probably everybody want to have one, right? Don't you think?"

"Their own attractive robot?"

"Yeah. I think so." In what must be another of his one-sided conversations, he's agreeing with himself. "It is not just robot—it's almost human. It's ideal."

"An ideal woman?"

"Probably. No idea." He laughs. "That is one of the projects"—the "most beautiful" android.

We drive on in silence, then he asks a surprising question: What would people think if he made *my* copy?

For whatever reason, the possibility—even in the abstract—has never occurred to me, and the idea is unexpectedly intimate.

I try to imagine how this would play out. They would encase my body in plaster, and then my various parts would be molded and manufactured and bolted together. And a silicone replica of my face, a bald and half-smiling not-me, would be stretched around its mechanical skull. And then my parts would be delivered to one of Hiroshi's labs and unpacked and assembled and dressed in a skirt and blouse and a long black wig; maybe a student would take a pair of heels (patent leather, slipped off an older model) and place them on my feet. Eyes that are not my own, but of a convincing shine and color, would appear to stare back at the gathering of researchers.

Let's say I'm not used in the lab at first but put out into the world, on display: destined for a new stage play or an android opera. An assistant professor and I will travel together from venue to venue; at the end of each international stop, back at the hotel, maybe he will crack open the valise that holds my head and talk to me about his frustrations. And eventually, when this android theater comes to the end of its run, I will be retired to an observation room, stacked against the wall with my clothes and hair stripped off and my head bowed. And the students will sometimes entertain themselves late at night by making my replica sing karaoke while they drink beer. And for the rest of time—or until my silicone is no longer considered worth replacing—this facsimile of myself will be made to do things, to say things, that are beyond my control, always borrowing my appearance, my face, my expressions, the memory of the living woman who was her model.

I'm not prepared to give away my likeness.

$$\bullet \qquad \bullet \qquad \bullet$$

I compared Hiroshi to Pygmalion, but that comparison is only partly right. His desire to create, that personal obsession, is driven less by romance and more by ego. In all my time with him, I never get the sense that Hiroshi—unlike some of his robots' fans and perhaps some of his colleagues—fetishizes his female androids. What excites him is the power of his role as Creator, the notion that he may one day crack the code of our emotional bonds. And he doesn't care what shape that solution takes. If he could reduce the human form to its barest, most minimal structure, he would. What if so many of these physical details—the precise silicone mold, the perfect eyelashes and cuticles—were a distraction from the true nature of *sonzai-kan*? One way to know would be to strip the android down to something more essential.

He has done just that. The shape came to him in a dream. When he awoke, he sculpted a model out of clay. The Telenoid is about one-and-a-half feet tall and ghost-white, a toddler with an alien-smooth face. It has stunted arms and, instead of legs, a bulbous stump—as if, in place of genitalia, the halves of the ass had continued all the way around to form two spheres. A stretch of silky white spandex serves as the lower neck, bridging the head and the body, but it is otherwise a continuous, jointless piece of supple plastic, as smooth as a naked child.

In repose, the expression on its face is serene enough to be unsettling—perhaps because of its deep-set black eyes; its thin, pursed lips, ever so slightly upturned at the corners; and its gentle, barely perceptible brow. Its delicate, thin features sometimes appear feminine, sometimes like those of a small boy—but altogether too knowing, too serene, for someone so young.

In a research room at Hiroshi's institute, his team shows a group of Danish visitors the latest model. Propped up on a tripod, low to the floor, the Telenoid squirms to life once activated. It looks up at us and begins to make a play for our attention, glancing around, wiggling its short arms. Its little movements are completely fluid and easy, giving it a sweet demeanor. It starts speaking to us in Japanese in a feminine voice, drawing a grad student named Miriam into an animated conversation. For now the Telenoid is teleoperated, but Hiroshi hopes to make it autonomous within the next few years. Its face conveys a calm authority that a human toddler would not possess, but its body and small gestures transmit the vulnerability and neediness of a child.

Miriam lifts the toddler-thing to cradle its stump in the crooks of her arms, and the two continue chatting in cooing, affectionate tones. And at this point, after a few minutes of observation, the words that come to mind are no longer *repulsive* and *nightmare* but *small* and *dear* and *friend*. It becomes easy to feel protective of the little alien.

As it turns out, the visitors at the lab when I visited were there because Hiroshi was hoping to partner with a venture-capital firm to install Telenoids in senior care facilities throughout Denmark. For a couple of years, he had been traveling there every few months. Hiroshi's team and their Danish partners were in the final stage of their field tests; they hoped to have a viable business plan in place soon. Everyone was optimistic: Test subjects have been quick to connect with the strange humanoid. Media events for the Telenoid in Denmark were attended by Japanese ambassadors and the Danish crown prince, who embraced the humanoid on-camera. He said the experience reminded him of holding his own child.

And the video footage—of elderly people in nursing homes, each supposedly with some degree of dementia—is compelling. In one, an older woman in a colorful turtleneck sits on a sofa in a facility in Kyoto with a Telenoid on her lap. Though her caretakers have explained that she rarely speaks with them, she is shown here in excited conversation with the humanoid (which she may or may not understand is being teleoperated by a volunteer in Osaka). In another clip, a far frailer-looking woman, more than one hundred years old, sits slumped at a desk, her arms wrapped around herself. "She's depressed and does not talk with others," one of Hiroshi's researchers says. When a caretaker sits beside her and hands her a Telenoid, however, she lights up, grinning and laughing. Out of sheer pleasure, she begins making short, clipped babylike sounds: "Ah-ah-ah-ah!" She grips the mechanical toddler to her chest, a blissful expression on her face, and starts to rock it slowly back and forth.

This clip is powerful evidence that a machine can conjure up an emotional connection—but a connection to what? Is it a look of recognition that flashes in this century-old woman's face, the resurrecting of some long-ago happiness? "We don't know yet, exactly," the researcher says. "But those who love Telenoid tend to be someone who used to have a baby." It takes a moment for the horror of this statement to sink in—that someone would be left alone in their advanced age to relive the joy of having a child through the cradling of a robot with stunted limbs.

More than a dozen years of progress have brought Hiroshi full circle: from his young daughter's android to another child robot—one that is blank, one that can be anyone's small child. A humanlike robot that is both terrifying in appearance on the most primal, gut level and undeniably effective: Once it's in operation, you are drawn to it, in sync with it, cannot help but feel empathy with it. The countless ways in which we judge someone based on their appearance all evaporate in the face of this "neutral appearance," as Hiroshi calls the Telenoid's blank, abstract body. And what is left in its place is that ineffable thing he has been trying to define: a distinctly human presence, free of the uncanny. It is an outsider, like its maker—but one who manages to trigger our affection. While holding the android, it hardly matters that this humanness is emitting from something that barely resembles a human at all.

.        .        .

Today, Hiroshi's daughter-android stands on a white platform, sealed inside a glass display in one of his labs. Even draped in a pale-yellow sundress, it is an unnerving sight. Its arms are too long, almost simian, its hands dangling far too low, one posed awkwardly over the crotch, as if to shield it. The face, with its grimly downturned mouth, is imprinted with tension. It appears to wear the look of its inception fifteen years ago—the very human discomfort of the little girl who was its prototype.

Risa is now studying in her father's department at the university, one of only a handful of women. The family is pleased—though Hiroshi is a little confounded: They had never discussed his work. "But this is positive, right?" he asks me with a note of vindication. "I'm not sure if making her android was positive or negative effect for her. And finally, she come to my lab," he says. "I can have some excuse for people now." This makes him laugh.

For Hiroshi, Risa seems to exist in opposition to his "most beautiful" female archetype: smart and impatient, not girlish, a free thinker. She seems to surprise him. He sees her as a mix of "typical female characteristics and some strong character like me." She's talented at math and physics, and he has the impression that she's competitive—particularly with the boys. "She is very tough sometimes," he says.

Meeting her for the first time in a small conference room down the hall from her father's office, I am immediately struck by Risa's calm intelligence. With the same round face and high-set eyes, Risa is undeniably the girl from the video clips, now in a fitted blouse, eyeglasses, and wearing a crystal pendant, her hair pulled back in a low-hanging ponytail. This is the girl who as a toddler was already playing with her father's early robots, blissed out, trying to make them chase her around the lab. (He still uses this footage in his PowerPoint presentations.) She has never seen him lecture and only recently read his books for the first time. On the subject of her replica, Risa is as pragmatic as her father. "I was the closest example that he was able to find on which to model an android—I haven't really thought about it more deeply than that." (Risa and I spoke through a translator.)

Students sometimes ask Risa about her last name. "Because, I guess, my father is famous," she says. But just as there remains a clear distinction between Hiroshi and his rubber-and-steel look-alike, Risa sees "Professor Ishiguro" and her father as two very different (if look-alike) entities. At the university, surrounded by students and faculty, he's charismatic, a "role model," drawing others into his work; at home he becomes himself again, a researcher focused on satisfying his own curiosities. A true researcher, Risa says, "is someone who is trying to find out what's interesting for himself."

Though Risa has not yet declared a major, she knows she's not interested in android science. Her level of ambition, however, is familial: "Whatever comes after the internet," she says, "the next major innovation—whatever that is, that's what I'd like to be a part of." She believes that being roped into her father's work at such a young age—an experience she won't call positive or negative—has made her bolder than she might otherwise have been. "I was sort of forced to become part of my father's project. And because I had this experience that others had never had before, I had a sense that anything could be done. And since then, when other people say 'No, that's not possible, we can't do that,' I think maybe I can do it. My father can do what other people can't do, and I am his daughter."

As far as I can tell, Hiroshi has no idea that she talks this way.

Risa was nine when he created his own replica, and she made a visit to the university then, to interact with the Geminoid, while Hiroshi teleoperated it. "I didn't focus as much on the android as I did on my father's voice," she says. What she remembers best from that day was the presence of her father—not at her side, but in another room, beyond the wall, just out of sight.

.  .  .

One night after a long dinner at a traditional restaurant in Osaka, Hiroshi takes me to a karaoke bar. Maybe it's the particular weekday or the late hour, but the place appears empty when we arrive. Hiroshi pays the bored young attendant, who leads us to the last in a long chain of rooms and shuts the door.

The surfaces are black formica and fake leather. In the blue light of the flatscreen, Hiroshi queues up ballad after ballad in Japanese. Seated on the banquette, I watch as he takes up the mic and sings, each song more saccharine than the one before. With the same look on his face that I've seen in the lab, Hiroshi takes his performance—to me, to the empty room—very seriously.

Another number begins, and this time he extends his hand to me; I stand to take it. With the microphone in one hand as he croons (in a small, artless voice) and the other hand on my waist, Hiroshi leads me through a slow dance. We dance awkwardly, like two kids in junior high—barely touching, glancing away, focusing on our steps. The time I've spent with Hiroshi—months of correspondence and Skype calls, weeks of unbroken hours with him, poring over what he values most (his work)—has been yet another strain of choreographed intimacy: journalist and subject. The version of me that Hiroshi knows is a woman completely fascinated with him, a mirror that reflects his image, an echo chamber for his ideas, a conversation with himself; the version of Hiroshi that I know is an eccentric in black, the man who made his double, a valuable subject for my work. These models of ourselves are the ones now dancing together in a small black room. What connects them is a narrow fascination that serves a narrow purpose.

What sort of connection do we need most? How much is enough—enough to sustain us, to alleviate the feeling of being alone? Would you trade four months in a bad relationship for an hour of karaoke and a slow dance with a roboticist in Osaka, Japan? Would you trade a few weeks of meaningless sex for the physical comfort of a Telenoid? Would you trade a couple of unsatisfying dates for an affectionate phone conversation with a woman you may never realize is a chatbot? Is the feeling of your hands on someone's waist while dancing equal to the touch of your fingertips on the most perfect silicone "skin" of the future? Does a dance with me have the same value as a dance with a Geminoid?

When the track finishes, it's time to leave. Outside, the shopping plaza is dark and dead-quiet. Hiroshi and I part ways.

·　　·　　·

My time with Hiroshi is over. I leave Japan.

My time with Ethan may also be over. Neither of us knows what's to come. What we do know is that there are now 7,000 miles between us.

And so we do what comes instinctively. As a substitute for physical closeness, we use our voices. We insist on the link between us through language: carefully scheduled phone calls, bursts of text messages. I listen closely to his voice (deep and musical); I picture him seated in that corner room surrounded by tall windows. I tell him the stories that I save for the people I like best; he tells me his. We send each other music and movie titles; we trade photographs, so we can imagine each other better. I picture him tilting his head into his phone, and that small hollow at the back of his neck.

We barely know each other, but something between us has been synchronized. Each of us carries a piece of the other's presence, built up through touch and then the remembrance of touch. A small collection of sensory memories. In the week since I left, he tells me, he's twice gotten up in the middle of the night, half-asleep, to make me more comfortable—turned up the heater, pulled an extra pillow from the closet—some part of him convinced I was still in his bed. I am echoing through his home, even though I am no longer there.

For a brief period of time, this feels just like falling in love.

## The New Yorker

FINALIST—ASME AWARD
FOR FICTION

*One of the most widely read short stories of the year, certainly the most discussed, "Cat Person" is about—what? Text messaging? A bad date? Unwanted sex between a younger woman and an older man? In a conversation with the* New Yorker *fiction editor, Deborah Treisman, Kristen Roupenian offered her own explanation: "The story was inspired by a small but nasty encounter I had with a person I met online. . . . The incident got me thinking about the strange and flimsy evidence we use to judge the contextless people we meet outside our existing social networks." But that, as the online reaction showed, was only the beginning. Roupenian's first collection of short stories,* You Know You Want This, *is scheduled for publication in 2019. As for* The New Yorker, *the award judges said the publication of "Cat Person" placed the magazine "on the cutting edge of storytelling."*

Kristen Roupenian

# Cat Person

Margot met Robert on a Wednesday night toward the end of her fall semester. She was working behind the concession stand at the artsy movie theater downtown when he came in and bought a large popcorn and a box of Red Vines.

"That's an . . . unusual choice," she said. "I don't think I've ever actually sold a box of Red Vines before."

Flirting with her customers was a habit she'd picked up back when she worked as a barista, and it helped with tips. She didn't earn tips at the movie theater, but the job was boring otherwise, and she did think that Robert was cute. Not so cute that she would have, say, gone up to him at a party, but cute enough that she could have drummed up an imaginary crush on him if he'd sat across from her during a dull class—though she was pretty sure that he was out of college, in his mid-twenties at least. He was tall, which she liked, and she could see the edge of a tattoo peeking out from beneath the rolled-up sleeve of his shirt. But he was on the heavy side, his beard was a little too long, and his shoulders slumped forward slightly, as though he were protecting something.

Robert did not pick up on her flirtation. Or, if he did, he showed it only by stepping back, as though to make her lean toward him, try a little harder. "Well," he said. "OK, then." He pocketed his change.

But the next week he came into the movie theatre again, and bought another box of Red Vines. "You're getting better at your job," he told her. "You managed not to insult me this time."

She shrugged. "I'm up for a promotion, so," she said.

After the movie, he came back to her. "Concession-stand girl, give me your phone number," he said, and, surprising herself, she did.

.  .  .

From that small exchange about Red Vines, over the next several weeks they built up an elaborate scaffolding of jokes via text, riffs that unfolded and shifted so quickly that she sometimes had a hard time keeping up. He was very clever, and she found that she had to work to impress him. Soon she noticed that when she texted him he usually texted her back right away, but if she took more than a few hours to respond his next message would always be short and wouldn't include a question, so it was up to her to reinitiate the conversation, which she always did. A few times, she got distracted for a day or so and wondered if the exchange would die out altogether, but then she'd think of something funny to tell him or she'd see a picture on the Internet that was relevant to their conversation, and they'd start up again. She still didn't know much about him, because they never talked about anything personal, but when they landed two or three good jokes in a row there was a kind of exhilaration to it, as if they were dancing.

Then, one night during reading period, she was complaining about how all the dining halls were closed and there was no food in her room because her roommate had raided her care package, and he offered to buy her some Red Vines to sustain her. At first, she deflected this with another joke, because she really did have to study, but he said, "No, I'm serious, stop fooling around and come now," so she put a jacket over her pajamas and met him at the 7-Eleven.

It was about eleven o'clock. He greeted her without ceremony, as though he saw her every day, and took her inside to choose some snacks. The store didn't have Red Vines, so he bought her a Cherry Coke Slurpee and a bag of Doritos and a novelty lighter shaped like a frog with a cigarette in its mouth.

"Thank you for my presents," she said, when they were back outside. Robert was wearing a rabbit-fur hat that came down over his ears and a thick, old-fashioned down jacket. She thought it was a good look for him, if a little dorky; the hat heightened his lumberjack aura, and the heavy coat hid his belly and the slightly sad slump of his shoulders.

"You're welcome, concession-stand girl," he said, though of course he knew her name by then. She thought he was going to go in for a kiss and prepared to duck and offer him her cheek, but instead of kissing her on the mouth he took her by the arm and kissed her gently on the forehead, as though she were something precious. "Study hard, sweetheart," he said. "I will see you soon."

On the walk back to her dorm, she was filled with a sparkly lightness that she recognized as the sign of an incipient crush.

While she was home over break, they texted nearly nonstop, not only jokes but little updates about their days. They started saying good morning and good night, and when she asked him a question and he didn't respond right away she felt a jab of anxious yearning. She learned that Robert had two cats, named Mu and Yan, and together they invented a complicated scenario in which her childhood cat, Pita, would send flirtatious texts to Yan, but whenever Pita talked to Mu she was formal and cold, because she was jealous of Mu's relationship with Yan.

"Why are you texting all the time?" Margot's stepdad asked her at dinner. "Are you having an affair with someone?"

"Yes," Margot said. "His name is Robert, and I met him at the movie theater. We're in love, and we're probably going to get married."

"Hmm," her stepdad said. "Tell him we have some questions for him."

"My parents are asking about u," Margot texted, and Robert sent her back a smiley-face emoji whose eyes were hearts.

•     •     •

When Margot returned to campus, she was eager to see Robert again, but he turned out to be surprisingly hard to pin down. "Sorry, busy week at work," he replied. "I promise I will c u soon." Margot didn't like this; it felt as if the dynamic had shifted out of her favor, and when eventually he did ask her to go to a movie she agreed right away.

The movie he wanted to see was playing at the theater where she worked, but she suggested that they see it at the big multiplex just outside town instead; students didn't go there very often, because you needed to drive. Robert came to pick her up in a muddy white Civic with candy wrappers spilling out of the cup holders. On the drive, he was quieter than she'd expected, and he didn't look at her very much. Before five minutes had gone by, she became wildly uncomfortable, and, as they got on the highway, it occurred to her that he could take her someplace and rape and murder her; she hardly knew anything about him, after all.

Just as she thought this, he said, "Don't worry, I'm not going to murder you," and she wondered if the discomfort in the car was her fault, because she was acting jumpy and nervous, like the kind of girl who thought she was going to get murdered every time she went on a date.

"It's OK—you can murder me if you want," she said, and he laughed and patted her knee. But he was still disconcertingly quiet, and all her bubbling attempts at making conversation bounced right off him. At the theater, he made a joke to the cashier at the concession stand about Red Vines, which fell flat in a way that embarrassed everyone involved, but Margot most of all.

During the movie, he didn't hold her hand or put his arm around her, so by the time they were back in the parking lot she was pretty sure that he had changed his mind about liking her. She was wearing leggings and a sweatshirt, and that might have been the problem. When she got into the car, he'd said, "Glad to see you dressed up for me," which she'd assumed was a joke, but maybe she actually had offended him by not seeming to take the date seriously enough, or something. He was wearing khakis and a button-down shirt.

"So, do you want to go get a drink?" he asked when they got back to the car, as if being polite were an obligation that had been imposed on him. It seemed obvious to Margot that he was expecting her to say no and that, when she did, they wouldn't talk again. That made her sad, not so much because she wanted to continue spending time with him as because she'd had such high expectations for him over break, and it didn't seem fair that things had fallen apart so quickly.

"We could go get a drink, I guess?" she said.

"If you want," he said.

"If you want" was such an unpleasant response that she sat silently in the car until he poked her leg and said, "What are you sulking about?"

"I'm not sulking," she said. "I'm just a little tired."

"I can take you home."

"No, I could use a drink, after that movie." Even though it had been playing at the mainstream theater, the film he'd chosen was a very depressing drama about the Holocaust, so inappropriate for a first date that when he suggested it she said, "Lol r u serious," and he made some joke about how he was sorry that he'd misjudged her taste and he could take her to a romantic comedy instead.

But now, when she said that about the movie, he winced a little, and a totally different interpretation of the night's events occurred to her. She wondered if perhaps he'd been trying to impress her by suggesting the Holocaust movie, because he didn't understand that a Holocaust movie was the wrong kind of "serious" movie with which to impress the type of person who worked at an artsy movie theater, the type of person he probably assumed she was. Maybe, she thought, her texting "lol r u serious" had hurt him, had intimidated him and made him feel uncomfortable around her. The thought of this possible vulnerability touched her, and she felt kinder toward him than she had all night.

When he asked her where she wanted to go for a drink, she named the place where she usually hung out, but he made a face and said that it was in the student ghetto and he'd take her somewhere better. They went to a bar she'd never been to, an underground speakeasy type of place, with no sign announcing its presence. There was a line to get inside, and, as they waited, she grew fidgety trying to figure out how to tell him what she needed to tell him, but she couldn't, so when the bouncer asked to see her ID she just handed it to him. The bouncer hardly even looked at it; he just smirked and said, "Yeah, no," and waved her to the side, as he gestured toward the next group of people in line.

Robert had gone ahead of her, not noticing what was playing out behind him. "Robert," she said quietly. But he didn't turn around. Finally, someone in line who'd been paying attention tapped him on the shoulder and pointed to her, marooned on the sidewalk.

She stood, abashed, as he came back over to her. "Sorry!" she said. "This is so embarrassing."

"How old *are* you?" he demanded.

"I'm twenty," she said.

"Oh," he said. "I thought you said you were older."

"I told you I was a sophomore!" she said. Standing outside the bar, having been rejected in front of everyone, was humiliating enough, and now Robert was looking at her as if she'd done something wrong.

"But you did that—what do you call it? That gap year," he objected, as though this were an argument he could win.

"I don't know what to tell you," she said helplessly. "I'm twenty." And then, absurdly, she started to feel tears stinging her eyes, because somehow everything had been ruined and she couldn't understand why this was all so hard.

But, when Robert saw her face crumpling, a kind of magic happened. All the tension drained out of his posture; he stood up straight and wrapped his bearlike arms around her. "Oh, sweetheart," he said. "Oh, honey, it's OK, it's all right. Please don't feel bad." She let herself be folded against him, and she was flooded with the same feeling she'd had outside the 7-Eleven—that she was a delicate, precious thing he was afraid he might break. He kissed the top of her head, and she laughed and wiped her tears away.

"I can't believe I'm crying because I didn't get into a bar," she said. "You must think I'm such an idiot." But she knew he didn't think that, from the way he was gazing at her; in his eyes, she could see how pretty she looked, smiling through her tears in the chalky glow of the streetlight, with a few flakes of snow coming down.

He kissed her then, on the lips, for real; he came for her in a kind of lunging motion and practically poured his tongue down her throat. It was a terrible kiss, shockingly bad; Margot had trouble believing that a grown man could possibly be so bad at kissing. It seemed awful, yet somehow it also gave her that tender feeling toward him again, the sense that even though he was older than her, she knew something he didn't.

When he was done kissing her, he took her hand firmly and led her to a different bar, where there were pool tables and pinball machines and sawdust on the floor and no one checking IDs at the door. In one of the booths, she saw the grad student who'd been her English TA her freshman year.

"Should I get you a vodka soda?" Robert asked, which she thought was maybe supposed to be a joke about the kind of drink college girls liked, though she'd never had a vodka soda. She actually was a little anxious about what to order; at the places she went to, they only carded people at the bar, so the kids who were twenty-one or had good fake IDs usually brought pitchers of PBR or Bud Light back to share with the others. She wasn't sure if those brands were ones that Robert would make fun of, so, instead of specifying, she said, "I'll just have a beer."

With the drinks in front of him and the kiss behind him, and also maybe because she had cried, Robert became much more relaxed, more like the witty person she knew through his texts. As they talked, she became increasingly sure that what she'd interpreted as anger or dissatisfaction with her had, in fact, been nervousness, a fear that she wasn't having a good time. He kept coming back to her initial dismissal of the movie, making jokes that glanced off it, and watching her closely to see how she responded. He teased her about her highbrow taste, and said how hard it was to impress her because of all the film classes she'd taken, even though he knew she'd taken only one summer class in film. He joked about how she and the other employees at the artsy theater probably sat around and made fun of the people who went to the mainstream theater, where they didn't even serve wine, and some of the movies were in IMAX 3-D.

Margot laughed along with the jokes he was making at the expense of this imaginary film-snob version of her, though nothing he said seemed quite fair, since she was the one who'd actually suggested that they see the movie at the Quality 16. Although now, she realized, maybe that had hurt Robert's feelings, too. She'd thought it was clear that she just didn't want to go on a date where she worked, but maybe he'd taken it more personally than that; maybe he'd suspected that she was ashamed to be seen with him. She was starting to think that she understood him—how sensitive he was, how easily he could be wounded—and that made her feel closer to him, and also powerful, because once she knew how to hurt him she also knew how he could be soothed. She asked him lots of questions about the movies he liked, and she spoke self-deprecatingly about the movies at the artsy theater that she found boring or incomprehensible; she told him about how much her older coworkers intimidated her, and how she sometimes worried that she wasn't smart enough to form her own opinions on anything. The effect of this on him was palpable and immediate, and she felt as if she were petting a large, skittish animal, like a horse or a bear, skillfully coaxing it to eat from her hand.

By her third beer, she was thinking about what it would be like to have sex with Robert. Probably it would be like that bad kiss, clumsy and excessive, but imagining how excited he would be, how hungry and eager to impress her, she felt a twinge of desire pluck at her belly, as distinct and painful as the snap of an elastic band against her skin.

When they'd finished that round of drinks, she said, boldly, "Should we get out of here, then?" and he seemed briefly hurt, as if he thought she was cutting the date short, but she took his hand and pulled him up, and the look on his face when he realized what she was saying, and the obedient way he trailed her out of the bar, gave her that elastic-band snap again, as did, oddly, the fact that his palm was slick beneath hers.

Outside, she presented herself to him again for kissing, but, to her surprise, he only pecked her on the mouth. "You're drunk," he said, accusingly.

"No, I'm not," she said, though she was. She pushed her body against his, feeling tiny beside him, and he let out a great shuddering sigh, as if she were something too bright and painful to look at, and that was sexy, too, being made to feel like a kind of irresistible temptation.

"I'm taking you home, lightweight," he said, shepherding her to the car. Once they were inside it, though, she leaned into him again, and after a little while, by lightly pulling back when he pushed his tongue too far down her throat, she was able to get him to kiss her in the softer way that she liked, and soon after that she was straddling him, and she could feel the small log of his erection straining against his pants. Whenever it rolled beneath her weight, he let out these fluttery, high-pitched moans that she couldn't help feeling were a little melodramatic, and then suddenly he pushed her off him and turned the key in the ignition.

"Making out in the front seat like a teenager," he said, in mock disgust. Then he added, "I'd have thought you'd be too old for that, now that you're *twenty*."

She stuck her tongue out at him. "Where do you want to go, then?"

"Your place?"

"Um, that won't really work. Because of my roommate?"

"Oh, right. You live in the dorms," he said, as though that were something she should apologize for.

"Where do you live?" she asked.

"I live in a house."

"Can I . . . come over?"

"You can."

·　　　·　　　·

The house was in a pretty, wooded neighborhood not too far from campus and had a string of cheerful white fairy lights across the doorway. Before he got out of the car, he said, darkly, like a warning, "Just so you know, I have cats."

"I know," she said. "We texted about them, remember?"

At the front door, he fumbled with his keys for what seemed a ridiculously long time and swore under his breath. She rubbed his back to try to keep the mood going, but that seemed to fluster him even more, so she stopped.

"Well. This is my house," he said flatly, pushing the door open.

The room they were in was dimly lit and full of objects, all of which, as her eyes adjusted, resolved into familiarity. He had two large, full bookcases, a shelf of vinyl records, a collection of board games, and a lot of art—or, at least, posters that had been hung in frames, instead of being tacked or taped to the wall.

"I like it," she said, truthfully, and, as she did, she identified the emotion she was feeling as relief. It occurred to her that she'd never gone to someone's house to have sex before; because she'd dated only guys her age, there had always been some element of sneaking around, to avoid roommates. It was new, and a little frightening, to be so completely on someone else's turf, and the fact that Robert's house gave evidence of his having interests that she shared, if only in their broadest categories—art, games, books, music—struck her as a reassuring endorsement of her choice.

As she thought this, she saw that Robert was watching her closely, observing the impression the room had made. And, as though fear weren't quite ready to release its hold on her, she had the brief wild idea that maybe this was not a room at all but a trap meant to lure her into the false belief that Robert was a normal person, a person like her, when in fact all the other rooms in the house were empty, or full of horrors: corpses or kidnap victims or chains. But then he was kissing her, throwing her bag and their coats on the couch and ushering her into the bedroom, groping her ass and pawing at her chest, with the avid clumsiness of that first kiss.

The bedroom wasn't empty, though it was emptier than the living room; he didn't have a bed frame, just a mattress and a box spring on the floor. There was a bottle of whiskey on his dresser, and he took a swig from it, then handed it to her and kneeled down and opened his laptop, an action that confused her, until she understood that he was putting on music.

Margot sat on the bed while Robert took off his shirt and unbuckled his pants, pulling them down to his ankles before realizing that he was still wearing his shoes and bending over to untie them. Looking at him like that, so awkwardly bent, his belly thick and soft and covered with hair, Margot recoiled. But the thought of what it would take to stop what she had set in motion was overwhelming; it would require an amount of tact and gentleness that she felt was impossible to summon. It wasn't that she was scared he would try to force her to do something against her will but that insisting that they stop now, after everything she'd done to push this forward, would make her seem spoiled and capricious, as if she'd ordered something at a restaurant and then, once the food arrived, had changed her mind and sent it back.

She tried to bludgeon her resistance into submission by taking a sip of the whiskey, but when he fell on top of her with those huge, sloppy kisses, his hand moving mechanically across her breasts and down to her crotch, as if he were making some perverse sign of the cross, she began to have trouble breathing and to feel that she really might not be able to go through with it after all.

Wriggling out from under the weight of him and straddling him helped, as did closing her eyes and remembering him kissing her forehead at the 7-Eleven. Encouraged by her progress, she pulled her shirt up over her head. Robert reached up and scooped her breast out of her bra, so that it jutted half in and half out of the cup, and rolled her nipple between his thumb and forefinger. This was uncomfortable, so she leaned forward, pushing herself into his hand. He got the hint and tried to undo her bra, but he couldn't work the clasp, his evident frustration reminiscent of his struggle with the keys, until at last he said, bossily, "Take that thing off," and she complied.

The way he looked at her then was like an exaggerated version of the expression she'd seen on the faces of all the guys she'd been naked with, not that there were that many—six in total, Robert made seven. He looked stunned and stupid with pleasure, like a milk-drunk baby, and she thought that maybe this was what she loved most about sex—a guy revealed like that. Robert showed her more open need than any of the others, even though he was older, and must have seen more breasts, more bodies, than they had—but maybe that was part of it for him, the fact that he was older, and she was young.

As they kissed, she found herself carried away by a fantasy of such pure ego that she could hardly admit even to herself that she was having it. Look at this beautiful girl, she imagined him thinking. She's so perfect, her body is perfect, everything about her is perfect, she's only twenty years old, her skin is flawless, I want her so badly, I want her more than I've ever wanted anyone else, I want her so bad I might die.

The more she imagined his arousal, the more turned-on she got, and soon they were rocking against each other, getting into a rhythm, and she reached into his underwear and took his penis in her hand and felt the pearled droplet of moisture on its tip. He made that sound again, that high-pitched feminine whine, and she wished there were a way she could ask him not to do that, but she couldn't think of any. Then his hand was inside her underwear, and when he felt that she was wet he visibly relaxed. He fingered her a little, very softly, and she bit her lip and put on a show for him, but then he poked her too hard and she flinched, and he jerked his hand away. "Sorry!" he said.

And then he asked, urgently, "Wait. Have you ever done this before?"

The night did, indeed, feel so odd and unprecedented that her first impulse was to say no, but then she realized what he meant and she laughed out loud.

She didn't mean to laugh; she knew well enough already that, while Robert might enjoy being the subject of gentle, flirtatious teasing, he was not a person who would enjoy being laughed at, not at all. But she couldn't help it. Losing her virginity had been a long, drawn-out affair preceded by several months' worth of intense discussion with her boyfriend of two years, plus a visit to the gynecologist and a horrifically embarrassing but ultimately incredibly meaningful conversation with her mom, who, in the end, had not only reserved her a room at a bed-and-breakfast but, after the event, written her a card. The idea that, instead of that whole involved, emotional process, she might have watched a pretentious Holocaust movie, drunk three beers, and then gone to some random house to lose her virginity to a guy she'd met at a movie theater was so funny that suddenly she couldn't stop laughing, though the laughter had a slightly hysterical edge.

"I'm sorry," Robert said coldly. "I didn't know."

Abruptly, she stopped giggling.

"No, it was . . . nice of you to check," she said. "I've had sex before, though. I'm sorry I laughed."

"You don't need to apologize," he said, but she could tell by his face, as well as by the fact that he was going soft beneath her, that she did.

"I'm sorry," she said again, reflexively, and then, in a burst of inspiration, "I guess I'm just nervous, or something?"

He narrowed his eyes at her, as though suspicious of this claim, but it seemed to placate him. "You don't have to be nervous," he said. "We'll take it slow."

Yeah, right, she thought, and then he was on top of her again, kissing her and weighing her down, and she knew that her last chance of enjoying this encounter had disappeared, but that she would carry through with it until it was over. When Robert was naked, rolling a condom onto a dick that was only half visible beneath the hairy shelf of his belly, she felt a wave of revulsion that she thought might actually break through her sense of pinned stasis, but then he shoved his finger in her again, not at all gently this time, and she imagined herself from above, naked and spread-eagled with this fat old man's finger inside her, and her revulsion turned to self-disgust and a humiliation that was a kind of perverse cousin to arousal.

During sex, he moved her through a series of positions with brusque efficiency, flipping her over, pushing her around, and she felt like a doll again, as she had outside the 7-Eleven, though not a precious one now—a doll made of rubber, flexible and resilient, a prop for the movie that was playing in his head. When she was on top, he slapped her thigh and said, "Yeah, yeah, you like that," with an intonation that made it impossible to tell whether he meant it as a question, an observation, or an order, and when he turned her over he growled in her ear, "I always wanted to fuck a girl with nice tits," and she had to smother her face in the pillow to keep from laughing again. At the end, when he was on top of her in missionary, he kept losing his erection, and every time he did he would say, aggressively, "You make my dick so hard," as though lying about it could make it true. At last, after a frantic rabbity burst, he shuddered, came, and collapsed on her like a tree falling, and, crushed beneath him, she thought, brightly, This is the worst life decision I have ever made! And she marveled at herself for a while, at the mystery of this person who'd just done this bizarre, inexplicable thing.

After a short while, Robert got up and hurried to the bathroom in a bow-legged waddle, clutching the condom to keep it from falling off. Margot lay on the bed and stared at the ceiling, noticing for the first time that there were stickers on it, those little stars and moons that were supposed to glow in the dark.

Robert returned from the bathroom and stood silhouetted in the doorway. "What do you want to do now?" he asked her.

"We should probably just kill ourselves," she imagined saying, and then she imagined that somewhere, out there in the universe, there was a boy who would think that this moment was just as awful yet hilarious as she did, and that sometime, far in the future, she would tell the boy this story. She'd say, "And then he said, 'You make my dick so hard,'" and the boy would shriek in agony and grab her leg, saying, "Oh, my God, stop, please, no, I can't take it anymore," and the two of them would collapse into each other's arms and laugh and laugh—but of course there was no such future, because no such boy existed, and never would.

So instead she shrugged, and Robert said, "We could watch a movie," and he went to the computer and downloaded something; she didn't pay attention to what. For some reason, he'd chosen a movie with subtitles, and she kept closing her eyes, so she had no idea what was going on. The whole time, he was stroking her hair and trailing light kisses down her shoulder, as if he'd forgotten that ten minutes ago he'd thrown her around as if they were in a porno and growled, "I always wanted to fuck a girl with nice tits" in her ear.

Then, out of nowhere, he started talking about his feelings for her. He talked about how hard it had been for him when she went away for break, not knowing if she had an old high-school boyfriend she might reconnect with back home. During those two weeks, it turned out, an entire secret drama had played out in his head, one in which she'd left campus committed to him, to Robert, but at home had been drawn back to the high-school guy, who, in Robert's mind, was some kind of brutish, handsome jock, not worthy of her but nonetheless seductive by virtue of his position at the top of the hierarchy back home in Saline. "I was so worried you might, like, make a bad decision and things would be different between us when you got back," he said. "But I should have trusted you." My high-school boyfriend is gay, Margot imagined telling him. We were pretty sure of it in high school, but after a year of sleeping around at college he's definitely figured it out. In fact, he's not even a hundred percent positive that he identifies as a man anymore; we spent a lot of time over break talking about what it would mean for him to come out as nonbinary, so sex with him wasn't going to happen, and you could have asked me about that if you were worried; you could have asked me about a lot of things. But she didn't say any of that; she just lay silently, emanating a black, hateful aura, until finally Robert trailed off. "Are you still awake?" he asked, and she said yes, and he said, "Is everything OK?"

"How old are you, exactly?" she asked him.

"I'm thirty-four," he said. "Is that a problem?"

She could sense him in the dark beside her vibrating with fear. "No," she said. "It's fine."

"Good," he said. "It was something I wanted to bring up with you, but I didn't know how you'd take it." He rolled over and kissed her forehead, and she felt like a slug he'd poured salt on, disintegrating under that kiss.

She looked at the clock; it was nearly three in the morning. "I should go home, probably," she said.

"Really?" he said. "But I thought you'd stay over. I make great scrambled eggs!"

"Thanks," she said, sliding into her leggings. "But I can't. My roommate would be worried. So."

"Gotta get back to the dorm room," he said, voice dripping with sarcasm.

"Yep," she said. "Since that's where I live."

The drive was endless. The snow had turned to rain. They didn't talk. Eventually, Robert switched the radio to late-night NPR. Margot recalled how, when they first got on the highway to go to the movie, she'd imagined that Robert might murder her, and she thought, Maybe he'll murder me now.

He didn't murder her. He drove her to her dorm. "I had a really nice time tonight," he said, unbuckling his seat belt.

"Thanks," she said. She clutched her bag in her hands. "Me, too."

"I'm so glad we finally got to go on a date," he said.

"A *date*," she said to her imaginary boyfriend. "He called that a *date*." And they both laughed and laughed.

"You're welcome," she said. She reached for the door handle. "Thanks for the movie and stuff."

"Wait," he said, and grabbed her arm. "Come here." He dragged her back, wrapped his arms around her, and pushed his tongue down her throat one last time. "Oh, my God, when will it end?" she asked the imaginary boyfriend, but the imaginary boyfriend didn't answer her.

"Good night," she said, and then she opened the door and escaped. By the time she got to her room, she already had a text from him: no words, just hearts and faces with heart eyes and, for some reason, a dolphin.

·        ·        ·

She slept for twelve hours, and when she woke up she ate waffles in the dining hall and binge-watched detective shows on Netflix and tried to envision the hopeful possibility that he would disappear without her having to do anything, that somehow she could just wish him away. When the next message from him did arrive, just after dinner, it was a harmless joke about Red Vines, but she deleted it immediately, overwhelmed with a skin-crawling loathing that felt vastly disproportionate to anything he had actually done. She told herself that she owed him at least some kind of breakup message, that to ghost on him would be inappropriate, childish, and cruel. And, if she did try to ghost, who knew how long it would take him to get the hint? Maybe the messages would keep coming and coming; maybe they would never end.

She began drafting a message—*Thank you for the nice time but I'm not interested in a relationship right now*—but she kept hedging and apologizing, attempting to close loopholes that she imagined him trying to slip through ("*It's OK, I'm not interested in a relationship either, something casual is fine!*"), so that the message got longer and longer and even more impossible to send. Meanwhile, his texts kept arriving, none of them saying anything of consequence, each one more earnest than the last. She imagined him lying on his bed that was just a mattress, carefully crafting each one. She remembered that he'd talked a lot about his cats and yet she hadn't seen any cats in the house, and she wondered if he'd made them up.

Every so often, over the next day or so, she would find herself in a gray, daydreamy mood, missing something, and she'd realize that it was Robert she missed, not the real Robert but the Robert she'd imagined on the other end of all those text messages during break.

"Hey, so it seems like you're really busy, huh?" Robert finally wrote, three days after they'd fucked, and she knew that this was the perfect opportunity to send her half-completed breakup text, but instead she wrote back, "Haha sorry yeah" and "I'll text you soon," and then she thought, Why did I do that? And she truly didn't know.

"Just tell him you're not interested!" Margot's roommate, Tamara, screamed in frustration after Margot had spent an hour on her bed, dithering about what to say to Robert.

"I have to say more than that. We had *sex*," Margot said.

"*Do* you?" Tamara said. "I mean, really?"

"He's a nice guy, sort of," Margot said, and she wondered how true that was. Then, abruptly, Tamara lunged, snatching the phone out of Margot's hand and holding it far away from her as her thumbs flew across the screen. Tamara flung the phone onto the bed and Margot scrambled for it, and there it was, what Tamara had written: "Hi im not interested in you stop textng me."

"Oh, my God," Margot said, finding it suddenly hard to breathe.

"What?" Tamara said boldly. "What's the big deal? It's true."

But they both knew that it was a big deal, and Margot had a knot of fear in her stomach so solid that she thought she might retch. She imagined Robert picking up his phone, reading that message, turning to glass, and shattering to pieces.

"Calm down. Let's go get a drink," Tamara said, and they went to a bar and shared a pitcher, and all the while Margot's phone sat between them on the table, and though they tried to ignore it, when it chimed with an incoming message they screamed and clutched each other's arms.

"I can't do it—you read it," Margot said. She pushed the phone toward Tamara. "You did this. It's your fault."

But all the message said was "OK, Margot, I am sorry to hear that. I hope I did not do anything to upset you. You are a sweet girl and I really enjoyed the time we spent together. Please let me know if you change your mind."

Margot collapsed on the table, laying her head in her hands. She felt as though a leech, grown heavy and swollen with her blood, had at last popped off her skin, leaving a tender, bruised spot behind. But why should she feel that way? Perhaps she was being unfair to Robert, who really had done nothing wrong, except like her, and be bad in bed, and maybe lie about having cats, although probably they had just been in another room.

But then, a month later, she saw him in the bar—her bar, the one in the student ghetto, where, on their date, she'd suggested they go. He was alone, at a table in the back, and he wasn't reading or looking at his phone; he was just sitting there silently, hunched over a beer.

She grabbed the friend she was with, a guy named Albert. "Oh, my God, that's him," she whispered. "The guy from the movie theater!" By then, Albert had heard a version of the story, though not quite the true one; nearly all her friends had. Albert stepped in front of her, shielding her from Robert's view, as they rushed back to the table where their friends were. When Margot announced that Robert was there, everyone erupted in astonishment, and then they surrounded her and hustled her out of the bar as if she were the president and they were the Secret Service. It was all so over-the-top that she wondered if she was acting like a mean girl, but, at the same time, she truly did feel sick and scared.

Curled up on her bed with Tamara that night, the glow of the phone like a campfire illuminating their faces, Margot read the messages as they arrived:

"Hi Margot, I saw you out at the bar tonight. I know you said not to text you but I just wanted to say you looked really pretty. I hope you're doing well!"

"I know I shouldnt say this but I really miss you"

"Hey maybe I don't have the right to ask but I just wish youd tell me what it is I did wrog"

"*wrong"

"I felt like we had a real connection did you not feel that way or . . ."

"Maybe I was too old for u or maybe you liked someone else"

"Is that guy you were with tonight your boyfriend"

"???"

"Or is he just some guy you are fucking"

"Sorry"

"When u laguehd when I asked if you were a virgin was it because youd fucked so many guys"

"Are you fucking that guy right now"

"Are you"

"Are you"

"Are you"

"Answer me"

"Whore."

# Permissions

# Contributors

**BIM ADEWUNMI** is a Nigerian British journalist, playwright and podcast host. Her work has appeared in the *Guardian*, *Vogue*, *Monocle*, *Vogue*, and *BuzzFeed News*, where she is a senior culture writer. She lives in New York.

**HOWARD BRYANT** has been a senior writer for ESPN.com and *ESPN the Magazine* since 2007. He has been the sports correspondent for NPR's *Weekend Edition Saturday* since 2006 and is the author of eight books, *Shut Out: A Story of Race and Baseball in Boston* (2002); *Juicing the Game: Drugs, Power and the Fight for the Soul of Major League Baseball* (2005); *The Last Hero: A Life of Henry Aaron* (2010); *Legends* (2014–present), a three-book sports series for middle-grade readers; *Sisters and Champions: The True Story of Venus and Serena Williams* (2018); and *The Heritage: Black Athletes, a Divided America, and the Politics of Patriotism* (2018). He is also a two-time finalist for the National Magazine Award for Columns and Commentary, in 2016 and 2018.

**TA-NEHISI COATES** is a national correspondent for *The Atlantic*. He is the author of *The Beautiful Struggle*, *Between the World and Me*, and *We Were Eight Years in Power*.

**RONAN FARROW** is an investigative journalist who writes for *The New Yorker* and makes documentaries for HBO. He is the author of the bestselling *War on Peace: The End of Diplomacy and the Decline of American Influence* and is at work on a new book, *Catch and Kill*, that will explore the sexual misconduct of powerful men and the systems in place to keep victims quiet. Farrow has been an anchor and reporter at MSNBC and NBC News, and his writing has appeared in publications including the *Wall Street Journal* and the *Washington Post*. He is a winner of the George Polk Award, the National Magazine Award, and the

Pulitzer Prize, among other commendations, and has been named one of *Time*'s One Hundred Most Influential People. He is also an attorney and former State Department official. He lives in New York City.

**IAN FRAZIER** is the author of twelve books, including *Great Plains*, *On the Rez*, and *Travels in Siberia*. His work appears often in *The New Yorker*, as well as in *The New York Review of Books*, *Outside*, and other magazines.

**AZMAT KHAN** is an investigative journalist and a Future of War fellow at New America and Arizona State University. For an investigation into the civilian death toll of the U.S.-led war against ISIS, published in the *New York Times Magazine* as "The Uncounted," she teamed with **ANAND GOPAL**, an assistant research professor at Arizona State and the author of *No Good Men Among the Living*.

**ALEX MAR** is a writer based in her hometown of New York City. Her first book, *Witches of America* (Farrar, Straus & Giroux), was a *New York Times* Notable Book of 2015 in nonfiction, a *New York Times* Editors' Pick, a *Marie Claire* "Top Book-Club Pick," and one of *The Believer*'s "Favorite Books," *Huffington Post* Books' "Most Notable" and *The Millions*' "Most Anticipated Books." Some of her recent work has appeared in *The Believer*, *Elle*, the *Guardian*, *New York*, the *New York Times Book Review*, *Tin House*, *The Virginia Quarterly Review*, *Wired*, and *The Oxford American*, where she is a contributing editor. She was nominated for a 2018 National Magazine Award for Feature Writing, and her essays were included in both *Longreads* and *BuzzFeed* "Best of 2016" year-end lists. She is also the director of the 2010 feature-length documentary *American Mystic*, now streaming on Amazon. Mar is currently at work on her second nonfiction book, for Penguin Press.

**NINA MARTIN** covers sex and gender issues for *ProPublica*. She joined the staff in September 2013 after spending much of the last decade at *San Francisco* as articles editor (since 2007) and executive editor (from 2003 to 2005). Martin has been a reporter and editor specializing in women's legal and health issues for more than thirty years. Her early career included stints at the *Baltimore Sun*, the *Washington Post*, and the *International Herald Tribune*. Her work has appeared in many magazines, including *Elle*, *Health*, *Mother Jones*, and *The Nation*. Martin is based in Berkeley, California.

**RENEE MONTAGNE** is a special correspondent at NPR. Montagne cohosted NPR's *Morning Edition*—the most widely heard radio news program in the United States—from 2004 to 2016, broadcasting from NPR West in Culver City, California, with cohosts Steve Inskeep and David Greene at NPR's Washington, D.C., headquarters. She hosted *All Things Considered* with Robert Siegel for two years in the late 1980s and previously worked for NPR's Science, National, and Foreign desks. In 1994, she and a team of NPR reporters won a prestigious Alfred I. duPont–Columbia University Award for coverage of South Africa's historic presidential and parliamentary elections. Through most of the 1980s, Montagne was based in New York, working as an independent producer and reporter for both NPR and the Canadian Broadcasting Corporation. Before that, she worked as a reporter and editor for Pacific News Service in San Francisco. She began her career as news director of the city's community radio station, KPOO, while still at university. Montagne graduated from the University of California, Berkeley, as a Phi Beta Kappa. Her career includes serving as a fellow at the University of Southern California with the National Arts Journalism Program and teaching broadcast writing at New York University's Graduate Department of Journalism. In addition to the DuPont-Columbia Award, Montagne has been honored by the Overseas

Press Club for her coverage of Afghanistan and by the National Association of Black Journalists for a series on black musicians going to war in the twentieth century.

**LAURIE PENNY** is an award-winning journalist, essayist, public speaker, writer, activist, internet nanocelebrity, and author of six books. Her most recent book, *Bitch Doctrine*, was published by Bloomsbury in 2017.

**KRISTEN ROUPENIAN** a writer living in Michigan. She holds an MFA in fiction from the Helen Zell Writers' Program at the University of Michigan and a Ph.D. in English from Harvard University. Her fiction has appeared in the *Colorado Review* and *The New Yorker*.

**GINGER THOMPSON** is a senior reporter at *ProPublica*. A Pulitzer Prize winner, she previously spent fifteen years at the *New York Times*, including time as a Washington correspondent and as an investigative reporter whose stories revealed Washington's secret role in Mexico's fight against drug traffickers. Thompson served as the Mexico City Bureau chief for both the *Times* and the *Baltimore Sun*. While at the *Times*, she covered Mexico's transformation from a one-party state to a fledgling multiparty democracy and parachuted into breaking news events across the region, including Cuba, Haiti, and Venezuela. For her work in the region, she was a finalist for the Pulitzer's Gold Medal for Public Service. She won the Maria Moors Cabot Prize, the Selden Ring Award for investigative reporting, an InterAmerican Press Association Award, and an Overseas Press Club Award. Thompson was also part of a team of national reporters at the *Times* that was awarded a 2000 Pulitzer Prize for the series "How Race Is Lived in America." Thompson graduated from Purdue University, where she was managing editor of the campus newspaper, the *Exponent*. She earned a master of public policy from George Washington University, with a focus on human rights law.

**ALEX TIZON** was a Pulitzer Prize–winning journalist and the author of *Big Little Man: In Search of My Asian Self.*

**REBECCA TRAISTER** is writer at large at *New York*. She writes a regular column for the *Cut*, as well as features and columns for the print magazine, covering women in politics, media, and culture. Traister was previously a senior editor at *The New Republic* and, before that, spent ten years at *Salon*. She is a contributor to *Elle* and has also written for *Glamour, Marie Claire, The Nation*, the *New York Times Magazine*, the *Washington Post*, and other publications. Traister was awarded the 2016 Hillman Prize for Opinion and Analysis Journalism and has won several Front Page Awards from the Newswomen's Club of New York, as well as the 2012 Mirror Award for Best Commentary, Digital Media, from Syracuse University's Newhouse School. She is the author of *All the Single Ladies* (Simon & Schuster), a *New York Times* best-seller and Notable Book of 2016, which was also named one of the best books of 2016 by the *Boston Globe, Entertainment Weekly, Library Journal*, and NPR. Her first book, *Big Girls Don't Cry*, about women in the 2008 election, was a *New York Times* Notable Book of 2010 and the winner of the Ernesta Drinker Ballard Book Prize. Her third book, *Good and Mad*, about women's anger as a political catalyst, will be published by Simon & Schuster in the fall of 2018.

**DON VAN NATTA JR.** is a senior writer for *ESPN the Magazine* and a contributor to ESPN's Emmy Award–winning show *Outside the Lines*. Before joining ESPN in 2012, Van Natta worked for sixteen years as an investigative correspondent for the *New York Times*, where he was a member of two reporting teams to win the Pulitzer Prize. Van Natta is the *New York Times*-best-selling author of three books, *First Off the Tee*, *Her Way*, and *Wonder Girl*. For four consecutive years, Van Natta's writing for ESPN was anthologized in the Best American Sports Writing series. He lives in Miami with his wife, the journalist Lizette Alvarez, and their two daughters.

**DAVID WALLACE-WELLS** is deputy editor at New York magazine, where he also writes about science and the near future, including his recent cover story on worst-case scenarios for climate change (which was the most-read *New York* magazine story ever); his recurring "Tomorrow" column, on the future of science and technology; and his 2015 cover story about the epidemic of honey-bee deaths (the first magazine story to put the blame on neonicitinoid pesticides, which is now accepted science). He joined the magazine as literary editor in 2011, became features director in 2016, and has overseen the magazine's family of podcasts in addition to his writing and editing. Wallace-Wells has appeared on WNBC's *News 4 New York*, KCRW's *To the Point*, WNYC's *Brian Lehrer Show*, BBC World Service, and more. Before joining *New York* magazine, Wallace-Wells was deputy editor at *The Paris Review*, where he edited and published writers such as Ann Beattie, Jonathan Franzen, Werner Herzog, and Janet Malcolm, among others, and interviewed William Gibson as part of the magazine's "Writers at Work" series. He previously served as the *New York Sun*'s books editor. Wallace-Wells graduated from Brown University with a degree in history. He is currently working on a book about the meaning of climate change.

**SETH WICKERSHAM** is a senior writer for *ESPN the Magazine* and a contributor to ESPN's Emmy Award–winning platform *Outside the Lines*. A native of Anchorage, Alaska, Wickersham was hired by ESPN after graduation from the Missouri School of Journalism. He has profiled the likes of Tom Brady, Bill Belichick, John

Elway, Peyton Manning and Y. A. Tittle and, with Don Van Natta, has written investigations into the NFL's handling of the Spygate cheating controversy and the inside accounts of the Rams and Raiders franchise relocations. Together, they are writing an NFL book, titled *Powerball*. Wickersham has won many awards and has been anthologized by in Best American Sports Writing series several times, and he is part of a staff that has three times won the National Magazine Award for General Excellence. He lives in Connecticut with his wife and two children. He is credited as playing himself in the 2014 movie *Draft Day*, though the scene was cut before it was shot.